# Business Cor

Second edition

Effective communication in business and commercial organisations is critical, as organisations have to become more competitive and effective to sustain commercial success.

This thoroughly revamped new edition distils the principles of effective communication and applies them to organisations operating in the digital world. Techniques and processes detailed in the book include planning and preparing written communication, effective structures in documents, diverse writing styles, managing face-to-face interactions, using visual aids, delivering presentations and organising effective meetings. In every case the authors consider the potential of new technology to improve and support communication.

With helpful pedagogical features designed to aid international students, this new edition of a popular text will continue to aid business and management students for years to come.

**Peter Hartley** is an independent consultant and visiting professor at Edge Hill University, UK.

**Peter Chatterton** is an independent consultant and academic who works with universities, government departments/agencies and businesses on programmes of innovation and change.

A range of further resources for this book is available at www.routledge.com/cw/9780415640282

Much more than a book, this is an interactive guide to allow you not only to enhance your practice as a communicator in the digital age, it also enables you to assess the impact that new communication technologies, such as videoconferencing and texting, can have on your organisation and its culture. As such, it opens up a whole set of new possibilities for all leaders to update and improve their effectiveness in an increasingly crucial area.

*Phil Radcliff, Associate Fellow,*
*Henley Business School, UK*

The authors successfully provide practical ideas and advice on improving business communications, emphasising the importance of context in an environment of rapid technological change. Its structure and content reflect a deep understanding of communications and of the potential of 'new' technologies. It will be of great benefit to multiple audiences seeking to develop their careers.

*Peter Bullen, Emeritus Professor,*
*University of Hertfordshire, UK*

I am responsible at the institution I work at for internal communications. Our staff and students say they receive too much communication but then say they don't know about anything. Fundamentally different approaches to getting key information across are needed and this book provides much food for thought that I believe will help in developing practical solutions to making communication in the business context more effective.

*Gunter Saunders, Professor,*
*The University of Westminster, UK*

# Business Communication

## Rethinking your professional practice for the post-digital age

Second edition

**Peter Hartley and Peter Chatterton**

LONDON AND NEW YORK

First published 2001
by Routledge
2 Park Square, Milton Park, Abingdon, Oxon OX14 4RN

Second edition published 2015

Simultaneously published in the USA and Canada
by Routledge
711 Third Avenue, New York, NY 10017

*Routledge is an imprint of the Taylor & Francis Group, an informa business*



*British Library Cataloguing in Publication Data*
A catalogue record for this book is available from the British Library

*Library of Congress Cataloging-in-Publication Data*
Business communication: rethinking your professional practice for the post-digital age/Peter Hartley and Peter Chatterton. – 2nd Edition.
pages cm
Includes bibliographical references and index.
1. Business communication. I. Chatterton, Peter. II. Title.
HF5718.H2915 2015
658.4′5 – dc23
2014029430

ISBN: 978-0-415-64027-5 (hbk)
ISBN: 978-0-415-64028-2 (pbk)
ISBN: 978-0-203-08284-3 (ebk)

Typeset in Perpetua and Bell Gothic
by Florence Production Ltd, Stoodleigh, Devon, UK

Printed and bound by CPI Group (UK) Ltd, Croydon, CR0 4YY

*This book is dedicated to
the memory of Clive Bruckmann
who co-authored the first edition
of this book.*

# Contents

# Figures

# Tables

# Boxes

# Acknowledgements

## FROM PETER HARTLEY

To Jasmine, Jenson and Jackson; to Alexander and Gregor; and to Phoebe – the next generation of communicators. Hopefully, they will all do it better than I ever could.

## FROM PETER CHATTERTON

To Tim Berners-Lee for creating the World Wide Web that has given us so many new opportunities to support open communications – long may he succeed in his mission to keep the Internet open and neutral.

## FROM BOTH OF US

We would like to thank *all* our former and current colleagues and students, too numerous to mention individually, who have inspired our thinking.

We thank the staff at Routledge for their considerable patience and unqualified support.

# Introduction

Our book is designed to help you to reflect on and improve the way you communicate in modern business and professional settings.

We are confident it will help you if you can tick at least one of the following boxes:

- undergraduate or postgraduate student aiming for a career in business or a professional context;
- undergraduate or postgraduate student with ambitions to work for yourself and/or assemble a portfolio career;
- working in an organisation in the early stages of your career;
- have been working in organisations for some years and wanting to refresh your ideas on 'good communication';
- managing a team in an organisation;
- wondering how new technology is reshaping business communication and thinking about how you need to respond.

We have also developed a website to give you:

- updated comments and suggestions on the use of specific technologies for communication;
- further comments, links and sources for each chapter, organised under the same subheadings as this printed text;
- the opportunity to engage directly with us and with other readers.

Technology is changing so fast that no book can guarantee to be completely up to date. So make sure you check the website if you are following up specific ideas from the book.

## DO WE NEED ANOTHER BOOK ON BUSINESS COMMUNICATION?

Yes, for five reasons:

1 *The increasing pace of change*. Although the bookshelves in many libraries are already groaning with the weight of existing texts, so much has changed in the last five years

that we do need fresh approaches *and* we need to make sure that established principles still apply. In terms of the ways we work as individuals, the most important changes have been in the social and economic climate and in the ways we use computer technology. Analysing the economic changes in detail is beyond the scope of this book but we will pay attention to the economic and social context in which organisations operate as this obviously influences their communication.

2 *The impact of new computer technology*. We will emphasise the potential of new technology – e.g. mobile devices such as smartphones and tablets – devices which now contain more processing power and memory than the desktop PCs which we used in our younger days. And these devices are enabling significant changes in our social and economic behaviour. But there are also significant differences in different parts of the world. For example, which country is widely acknowledged as the 'world leader in high-tech mobile money'? Our answer is on the website.

3 *The need to review and revise basic principles.* There are some fundamental principles of communication which you will find in virtually every textbook on communication, but do these need refining or updating in the light of new technology? For example, we emphasise the notion of 'audience'. This used to be easier to define – nowadays we need to consider that *anything* you say in public or at a meeting could be on the Internet in a matter of minutes thanks to Twitter. You *always* have to operate on the basis that you are talking to multiple audiences, as there will be particular subgroups in any audience, but now you also have to consider that some of these will not be in the room. As a speaker or workshop leader, this gives you both challenges and new opportunities. A number of organisations (and educational institutions) are now capitalising on this by using what is called the 'back-channel' to increase the dialogue between speakers and audience. This can be done using specialised systems such as the 'clickers' that are now used by many colleges and higher education institutions, but you can also use Internet systems such as Poll Everywhere, which allows anyone in the audience to contribute with a suitable laptop, tablet or mobile phone. Or you can take advantage of the fact that most if not all of your audience in the room will have access to Twitter or other chat media.

4 *Information and communication overload*.The notion of information overload is not new but the growth of new communication channels has made this problem much more serious.

5 *Online media are not the 'answer to everything'*. The marketing and retailing of books has changed significantly over the last few years and all publishers are having to review their online presence and activity. We did consider moving this text to online media. In the end, we decided on a combination of book plus online support. This combination still offers some advantages in terms of flexibility and access, although we may not be able to say that with quite the same conviction in a few years' time. Experts and forecasters agree that ebooks will expand significantly but differ on how much and/or the different rates of expansion across the globe.

## OUR AIMS

We will offer you suggestions and techniques to improve the way you communicate.

Communication is complex and always affected by the social context so we *cannot* offer you a definitive approach which will always work (beware any books or courses which do offer this!). We can offer you approaches and techniques which will increase your chances of success.

We will analyse how people communicate within business and professional organisations, and how this communication is changing. We focus on commercial organisations but the main ideas and principles also apply to non-commercial and voluntary sectors, and to small, medium and large enterprises (SMEs).

We focus on communication by individuals and groups within and across the organisation and do not say much about external communication (advertising, public relations, etc.). However, all the principles we discuss can be applied to both internal and external communication. For example, we emphasise the importance of understanding how different audiences may have very different perspectives on the same message; we emphasise the importance of clear language; and we emphasise the importance of careful planning and a clear strategy in formal communication.

## WHY 'RETHINKING' BUSINESS COMMUNICATION?

The business world has changed dramatically since we wrote the first version of this book, back in 2000. Apart from the global economic crisis, advances in technology have brought fundamental change in the ways we live and work. Consider the following headlines which we paraphrased from radio and news broadcasts over a couple of days in spring 2014 – none of these headlines would have made sense to early readers of our first edition and most would have probably created confusion only five years ago:

- Man turns experience in social tweeting into professional career.
- Crowd-sourced maps save lives in crisis situations.
- Google offers 'right to forget' form.
- Are 3D printed houses the future?
- How WhatsApp beat Facebook.

All of these stories have important implications for business and professional communication and activity. How many did you recognise? See the website for further details of these stories and their background.

Among the most important trends are the following.

### The growth of mobile computing

Industrial experts in 2012 forecasted that Internet traffic would 'grow four-fold over the next four years' with this dramatic expansion fuelled by the growth of mobile computing. Many people in business can and do now work virtually anywhere, given a laptop and an

Internet connection. This means that they can also be contacted through email or text at any time, day or night. And this is having significant impact on office structures and facilities, leading to the claim that younger generations of business workers do not attach the same status or importance to individual office spaces as previous generations.

## The rise of social media

Many business organisations are now taking social media like Facebook and Twitter very seriously as they recognise opportunities for new relationships with their customers and their staff. An indication of this change is recent trends in television advertising, especially around major holidays – the focus is not to sell products directly as in previous years but to persuade the audience to go to the relevant website where the 'real' promotion of the product is located. The growing sales of televisions with built-in Internet connections is likely to force further changes in approaches to advertising. This is an example of what has been called the 'Internet of things' where Internet connections are built into devices to enable data communications and new facilities.

The growth of social media has also seen a corresponding growth in people's willingness to share much of their lives online. Does this mean that we have to modify our approach to personal relationships?

## But not everything has changed

While we have experienced dramatic change, we must also consider important principles which have not changed. To start the debate on this, we will revisit two examples which we used in 2000:

- In a business speech, Gerald Ratner described some of his company's cheaper jewellery products as 'crap' and suggested that others would not last as long as a supermarket sandwich. He did not anticipate reports in the national press the following day. Although the immediate effect on sales was actually positive – customers went looking for cheap bargains – the publicity had created an image which the company could not counteract when the economy dipped – people did not want to buy gifts from a store which now had a reputation for 'cheap rubbish'. Within months, the sales had slumped and the company never recovered. The irony was that Ratner had used these remarks before in speeches and had been quoted in the financial press, but this time the comments made the front pages in the popular papers. As he later reflected: 'Because of one ill-judged joke, 25,000 people lost their jobs' (quoted in *Tibballs*, 1999, p. 192).

  In the next few years, the phrase 'doing a Ratner' became a popular description of a chief executive or senior manager making an ill-judged comment with damaging consequences, and other examples were publicised. Ratner did manage to 'rise again' through a new company and you will find him on YouTube commenting on his experience and publicising his book on the subject. Needless to say, he now has a website and Facebook page.

- The British railway company claimed that many trains were having trouble in winter with the 'type of snow' falling at the time (1991). This was technically true – the weather conditions were very unusual. This became a newspaper headline – 'British Rail blames the wrong type of snow' – and this phrase stuck in the media and public consciousness. The company should have realised that this sort of explanation would not be taken seriously by a public already critical of the railways' poor punctuality and reliability.

  Moving on to the present day – this phrase is still used and recognised in the UK as the classic example of a lame excuse.

These examples show the importance of communication and its long-lasting impact. They both show the impact of a careless analogy on public perceptions of image and reputation. They still work as examples of important communication problems and they illustrate important principles of communication, which are independent of technological change, for example:

- If your message can be captured or summarised in a memorable phrase, then this may 'stick' with your audience for a long time.
- Messages tend to be simplified and generalised as they are passed on – Ratner made his 'crap' comment about only one of his brands but his other brands also suffered the same fate by association in the following years.
- Messages are always interpreted in context, as illustrated by the changing reactions to Ratner's description and the general dismissal of the 'wrong snow' explanation.

If these events had happened today rather than over 15 years ago, we argue that the overall impact and damage to reputation would be similarly memorable. However, it would happen much quicker and initially it would happen through new media. Ratner's quotes and messages would be on the Internet thanks to Twitter and blogging while he was talking, never mind the next day. And he would not have had the luxury to repeat his remarks and go unnoticed. The same would have happened with the railway example and we would doubtless be able to enjoy YouTube videos of both Ratner and the railway spokesperson as they unwittingly put foot to mouth.

Recent examples which illustrate the power and speed of the new media include:

- The 'business communicator of the year' who agreed to return her award after some rather ill-tempered emails she had written were posted online by disgruntled receivers and went viral.
- The university tutor who included a political comment in an email to her class about the postponement of a class and found herself featured on national media and her career under threat. One of the students took offence and used social media to publicise her complaint.
- The New York Police Department set up a Twitter hashtag to 'communicate effectively with the community' and invited the public to post photos and examples. This attempt to highlight good practice rebounded when hundreds of examples of police brutality were posted and received national/international publicity.

We said in 2000 that the boundaries between internal and external communication are sometimes difficult to draw and they are obviously related. This is even more complex today. For example, we have both taught in higher education institutions for many years. Thanks to examples such as the bullet points above, we are now very conscious that *anything* we say and do in the classroom could be available for pubic inspection at any time, thanks to the capability of the modern student's mobile phone and their fluency on text/Twitter, etc. There are some recent cases of serious misuse of these media, as in some examples of staff being bullied online by certain students. While the new media have offered major advantages, they have also offered new opportunities for negative and abusive behaviour.

We also said in 2000 that the most important external communicators in any company are the employees, as they determine the company image in their interactions with customers. This is still true. We focus on these communicators as they work *within and across* their organisation.

So we are not concentrating on what has become known as 'corporate communication', where the main responsibilities for managers include strategic planning, managing company identity and public relations. This perspective tends to concentrate on communications management. We shall obviously refer to these issues but we are concentrating on communication as a process, which *all* employees of an organisation participate in.

## COMMUNICATION WORKING WELL?

If good communication is important and can offer tangible benefits, why can we find so many examples where it does not seem to work effectively? Why do so many organisations seem to ignore the research into the practice of leading companies which have a reputation for effective communication?

When we wrote in 2000, we suggested that research consistently highlights factors listed below (based on research summarised by Tourish, 1997, and by Robbins, 1998, pp. 325 ff.).

### Management commitment

Senior management must be committed to the importance of communication and must act accordingly. Robbins regarded this as *the* most significant factor: if the senior executive is able and willing to communicate their vision of the organisation and regularly communicates face-to-face with employees, then this will set the expected standard for other managers. Of course, these other levels of management must also share this commitment. Managers must also act in ways which *confirm* their communication and those who proclaim an 'open door' policy to their staff need to make themselves available on a regular basis. This commitment by management must also extend to training. Communication training is given a high priority and is well supported.

### Two-way communication

There must be an effective balance between downward and upward communication. Tourish highlighted the importance of regular surveys of employee opinion, which must then lead to action plans and visible results.

### Face-to-face communication

Wherever possible, communication is delivered face-to-face. This obviously allows for immediate feedback and discussion.

### Messages are well-structured to meet the audience's needs

Management recognise what information their employees need to know and make sure that they receive it in the most appropriate form.

### New technology is used to speed up communication

Many companies have made an enormous investment in new technology, which enables them to spread messages very quickly across dispersed sites and offices.

#### *Are these factors still the key ones?*

More recent research comes up with similar recipes but would highlight the significance of new technology to both enable and influence the impact of communication. And there is a key development in terms of the degree of interactivity available. Above, we gave a survey as an example of two-way communication, but this has strict boundaries (not least that you can't see other people's responses). Social media allows a much greater degree of two-way/ multiple-way communication and this presents challenges to organisations.

Throughout this book we invite you to apply our ideas to your own situation. An obvious exercise arising here is to consider how many of the principles above apply to your organisation, and to what extent. For example, what evidence do you have that your senior management are committed to fostering communication? If not, then what effect does this have on the rest of the organisation?

Organisations may ignore communication because it is time-consuming and sometimes difficult, especially when the organisation is going through a bad time. Again, an example we used in 2000 is still depressingly topical. One of the major British retail chains was responding to a significant drop in profits by dramatic cost-cutting and management redundancies. Staff were quoted as 'furious' at the 'insensitive manner' in which this was done and the process was described by one as 'barbaric'. Assuming that this press coverage was fair comment, what effect would this have on the long-term development of relationships and communication in that company? What if the press coverage was not representative of general staff feelings? Does the company have effective internal communication which could counteract the public criticism?

Although communication is important, we must always recognise that it is not a universal cure. We cannot turn a message about redundancy into good news by changing the words or tone. However, organisations *should* respect their employees and treat them fairly and honestly – communication can either support or destroy these obligations. We shall explore these issues on several occasions.

## IMPROVING COMMUNICATION – USING EVIDENCE AND RESEARCH

In this book, we try to show how communication can 'work', not just by analysing what happens when people communicate within organisations but also by suggesting techniques and strategies which can make communication more effective. This does make two important assumptions:

- that we know enough about what happens in different types of organisations;
- that techniques and strategies which work in one situation can be applied equally well in others.

Both of these assumptions can be questioned. We have tried wherever possible to back up our claims with research evidence, but there is not enough research on everyday events in organisations. Some important processes do seem to be under-researched. For example, it has been suggested that 'the research literature does not adequately explore the shaping role of political behaviour in organizational change' (Buchanan and Badham, 2008, p. xviii) and this is still true. This has important implications for communication – the success or failure of a proposal at a business meeting may depend more on political manoeuvring than on how clearly the proposal is expressed.

There are also problems with the balance of research in some areas. For example, Steve Duck (2007) suggests that researchers have been less willing to look at the negative side of (personal) relationships and that we need to know much more about the impact of events such as deception, hurtful messages, gossip, boring communication, and so on. On a broader scale, we can find much more research on large organisations in Western cultures than on, say, small businesses in Asian cultures. These imbalances make it difficult to generalise. The problem of generalisation also applies to techniques and strategies.

Because of these limitations, you should approach all the recommendations in this book as *hypotheses* – as generalisations to be *tested* and not as absolute or binding truths. Even findings which are based on fairly substantial evidence are *never* 100 per cent reliable. For example, John Kirkman researched the reactions of scientists to papers which were rewritten using the plain language principles, and which we summarise and review later in this book. The scientists clearly preferred the rewritten examples, feeling that they were 'more interesting' and also that the author had a 'better organised mind'. Although this positive reaction was strong, it was not universal – nearly 70 per cent agreed that the rewritten examples were better and 75 per cent agreed that the author was better organised (Turk and Kirkman, 1989, pp. 17ff.). In other words, a small but significant minority did *not* agree with the changes. To the best of our knowledge, this specific study has not been repeated, so we do not know how far these percentages may have changed.

So deciding what is appropriate language is not just a simple technical problem – all sorts of social issues and pressures may be relevant. We know one consultant who produced a beautifully written plain language report for a major national organisation. He was asked to revise it to make it look 'more complicated' and 'academic' so that it would 'impress' the government department who had commissioned it. These issues of context and audience will recur regularly as we look at different types and levels of communication.

This means that you should consider your context and situation carefully before you apply techniques or concepts from this (or from any other) text on business communication. You should also try to check the most recent research – many of the topics we cover in this book are both controversial and subject to social change. For example, suppose you have been invited to a business lunch and one of your colleagues takes out their smartphone to respond to a text. Do you regard this as appropriate behaviour in this context? A recent survey of American business professionals found very different reactions to this, depending on age and gender. Men were much more likely to judge it as 'OK' than women; older professionals were more likely to see this behaviour as 'rude' or 'unprofessional'. Again, we suspect that these reactions will change over time.

Apart from changes in expectations and behaviour over time (which we can expect to become more frequent), there is a final very good reason for treating all our statements and suggestions as hypotheses to be tested in your context: 'the world of business isn't always what it pretends to be. Things aren't as rational, well-organised and well-oiled as we're told they are' (Vermeulen, 2010, pp. 216–217). You can say the same for other organisational sectors – education, government etc. We may assume that others are behaving openly, sensibly, fairly and honestly, but these are assumptions that we need to check. Discrimination of various sorts can easily be found in many workplaces. For example, Buchanan and Badham cite evidence that 'sex-role stereotyping, the systematic underestimation of women, and the resultant hostility' are 'widespread' behaviour in organisations (Buchanan and Badham, 2008, p. 151). Sheryl Sandberg, Chief Operating Officer (COO) of Facebook, observes that when she asks the audience at one of her talks whether they have been called too aggressive at work: 'I've never seen more than 5 per cent of men raise their hands. Every woman I know, particularly the senior ones, has been called aggressive at work' (quote from an interview in the *Guardian Weekend*, 5 April 2014). Sandberg's bestselling book, *Lean In*, offered suggestions to women on how to overcome such structural biases in the workplace (Sandberg, 2013). There is now a graduate edition (2014) and campaigning website – http://leanin.org.

There is evidence of positive change but we cannot afford to be complacent about this (as in the recent debates in the UK over 'everyday sexism' (Bates, 2014) or any other area of social discrimination (as in the recent book by the former Chief Executive Officer (CEO) of BP, John Browne, reflecting on his experiences as a gay man in a senior management position (Browne, 2014)).

## WHAT DOES COMMUNICATION INVOLVE?

As we shall see in Chapter 1, communication can be defined in rather different ways. For example, we can define it as: 'shared meaning created among two or more people through verbal and non-verbal transaction' (Daniels and Spiker, 1994, p. 27). This emphasises the sharing of ideas and/or information. Ideally, at the end of the process all parties involved share the same ideas and information. What are the important factors which will either assist or detract from achieving this goal? We emphasise some important factors which are often neglected in practice, including the following, for example.

## Purpose and strategy

The 'art' of communication is finding the most effective means of sharing ideas and information. We need to study how people choose and develop the strategies and tactics of sharing ideas and information. Implicit in this is the idea of a communicative purpose or objective, such as informing or persuading. Many problems in communication arise from unclear or inappropriate purposes or strategies.

We also need to consider how these purposes are expressed. For example, business objectives may be set out in the organisation's mission statement. But is a mission statement the best way of expressing objectives in a way that the employees will accept and understand? Some organisations explicitly reject mission statements. One British vice-chancellor suggested that 'although universities should be run in a business-like way . . . there are some business techniques that we should tear up into shreds. Mission statements, for instance, are an abject waste of time. We were just as effective before we had one' (*Times Higher*, 24 July 1998). Eden and Ackermann (2013) have found similar concerns with mission/vision statements in the business world:

> the last two decades have seen managers being bombarded with vision statements and mission statements and the requirement for vision and mission statements, with many of these statements being regarded as a joke by them and others in the organisation as they provide little in the way of guidance.

Alongside concerns that many mission statements are rather idealized statements which could apply to virtually every organization and that others are hopelessly unrealistic, they found that

> a careful analysis of statements of purpose (mission and vision statements)—particularly those more detailed versions—demonstrates incoherency, emanating from unrecognised conflict between aspirations, opaque reasoning, and incompatibility of goals statements—where some are aspirational and others' statements of what currently exist.

As with any specific example of communication, we need to 'look behind' the words on the page to uncover the underlying reality. Think about your own organisation. Does it have a mission or vision statement? What is it and what does it really mean? Does it make a difference? Who is it aimed at?

New technology might offer some opportunities here, enabling an organisation to gain contributions and commitment through a more interactive and collaborative process leading up to a mission statement or policy.

## Social and cultural background

A range of important cultural and social differences affect the way we interpret what is meant. Some degree of common background is essential for exchanging messages. Sometimes, practical problems crop up because the communicators fail to establish early on what that common background might be.

### Codes

A code is a coherent set of symbols plus the rules you need to structure a message. Our language is the most important code we use, but gestures, illustrations and mathematics are all codes that have important roles in communication.

### Situation and relationships

Situation is the context in which a message is sent and received – it has both physical and relational aspects. For example, communication in a lecture room is influenced both by the layout of the room and by the relationship between the lecturer and the students.

We always interpret communication in terms of the type of relationship we have with the other person. In many business situations, the status relationship is particularly important. For example, consider the message: 'Please bring me the Smith file.' What does this mean when said by a manager to an administrator or secretary, and what does it mean when said between two administrators of equal status? In the first case, we hear an instruction or command presented in polite language. Between administrators, we hear a request for help which can be turned down: 'Sorry, I am busy, you'll have to find it.' This could be accepted as a reasonable response in the second case (depending on the style and the relationship), but what about the first case? Would the manager see this as a 'challenge to authority'? This would depend on the specific relationship and working arrangements. The meaning of a message depends on the relationship between the people involved.

Reviewing these and other factors, this book aims to highlight the different reactions and potential ambiguities which can affect our communication.

## HOW THIS BOOK IS ORGANISED

The structure of this book reflects how we think business communication is best understood and how you can approach it to improve the ways you come across to colleagues and bosses.

Chapter 1 suggests that you start by *not* thinking about communication itself – communication is always a means to an end and if you do not have some idea about where you are heading in personal and professional terms, then you are unlikely be able to choose the communication methods and approach which will be effective. So we start by considering more general goals and objectives. You also need to understand your own approach to communication and how you can best develop your capacity and understanding – this is what Chapter 1 is all about.

Then you need to develop a more detailed appreciation of what communication means and what it involves. This is what Chapters 2 and 3 are about. As well as looking at how we can define communication (and the practical implications of that), we investigate the factors which comprise communication in more detail and suggest overall principles which we feel are critical aspects of communication for people working in twenty-first-century organisations.

Communication always takes place in a specific organisational context. Chapter 4 explores what this means in organisations by looking at different forms and levels of social context.

The dominant form of communication in many organisations is written, whether it ends up as a paper or online message. That is the focus of Chapters 5–8. As well as looking at practice and research on the advantages of plain language, we look at how effective design can influence how documents are understood. We also look at how documents can be best organised and look at the range of printed and online documents which are now used in most organisations.

Communicating face-to-face is as important, if not more important than written communication, and that is the focus of Chapters 9–13. After defining the major interpersonal skills, we look at how these can be used in a range of contexts, including formal presentations. We then look at group dynamics and team development, and how these principles can be applied to improve formal and informal meetings.

The final chapter (14) raises issues of organisational change as they apply to all forms and types of communication, and we wind up the book by offering a few cautionary words about the future of business communication.

## AND FINALLY

In the course of this book we make numerous references to websites and Web resources. As many of these change frequently, we have only included Web references in this print copy where we are absolutely confident that the website will have a longer shelf life than this book. All the weblinks quoted in this book were checked at the end of May 2014.

On the website, you will find notes for each chapter, which include all the links and websites, updated and expanded wherever we have found new materials. We look forward to meeting you there to carry on our discussion.

Chapter 1

# Developing your communication

## Deciding where to start

### INTRODUCTION

You want to improve your communication – where do you start? We suggest that you do *not* start by focusing on the specific details of communication itself. To make a significant change as far as your communication is concerned, you need to decide on your overall career and personal goals and then work on the following aspects of your professional development:

- Become self-sufficient in terms of your learning and personal development.
- Adopt a sceptical and self-critical approach to your own and your organisation's behaviour. Be proactive in searching for systematic research to analyse human behaviour and communication, and avoid the many myths about our behaviour and organisational life which are propagated by the media. We will try to 'explode' as many of these myths as we can in the course of this book.
- Self-monitor – i.e. understand and manage the ways you behave and present yourself; these days, you need to pay special attention to identifying and managing your digital identity.
- Review and, where necessary, expand the range of communication tools you use on a regular basis.

We cannot give you all the answers to effective communication because (as we illustrate in every chapter) the world is changing too fast and we cannot know the specific circumstances of your organisation. For example, virtually every recent text we have seen on business communication includes some discussion of email. But what if you decide to work for an organisation which has decided to *abandon* this technology?

We cannot give you all the answers but we *can* help you work out how and why you need to change – to become more self-reliant and self-sufficient. Use this book *and* the website as a springboard and starting point. If this sounds too abstract, then an analogy will help.

Suppose you decide to lose weight. You can rush to your local health shop and pick up a 'magic pill' – the latest best-selling diet book. Follow its instructions to the letter and you will probably lose weight. If you stay healthy (some diets have unfortunate side-effects), you only have a small chance of maintaining that weight loss *unless* you stick to that diet long-term *and* keep monitoring your progress. Effective schemes for weight loss usually mean changes to your lifestyle, not just to the specific food on your plate. So you must be able to accommodate these changes in your preferred lifestyle.

The importance of lifestyle and commitment may explain the success (in the UK at least) of the '5:2 diet', based on fasting two days a week, limiting your calories to 500 or 600 kcal (for women and men respectively). One proclaimed advantage is that you only need to concentrate on your food intake for two days a week. However, can you/we do that on a long-term basis?

Alternatively, another powerful strategy for weight loss is to examine how and why you eat as 'most of us are blissfully unaware of what influences how much we eat'. Then you can make small and achievable adjustments to your habits as 'the best diet is one you don't know you're on' (Wansink, 2010, pp. 1 and 219). Successful weight loss also depends upon social support; commercial enterprises often use the social group as a tool to support and encourage dieters. There is another important aspect of dieting which is relevant here – you need to work out your long-term target, the weight which you will consider as optimum and where you want to stick long-term.

We make the analogy here with improving your communication. This book is not a 'magic pill' which will immediately change your life. To make significant and lasting change to your communication, you can follow the same steps needed for lasting *and* healthy weight loss:

- commitment to a long-term 'ideal';
- commitment to long-term and sustainable change;
- finding and using the best available evidence (ignoring magic quick fixes);
- becoming more self-aware;
- changing your behaviour;
- gaining social support;
- continual review.

Our aim is to provide useful ideas and techniques which you can use as the springboard to personal change. First, you need to step back and reflect on your overall aims and priorities.

This chapter suggests three starting points – three distinct but interrelated aspects of communication and learning:

- reviewing your personal objectives and goals;
- adopting learning strategies to improve your communications, which include learning from others;
- reviewing (and deciding on) the tools and enhanced skills you will need to support your continual professional development.

We suggest that you consider these topics in the order presented here, but this does not imply that you do them in a rigid sequence. One key theme running through this book is the need for constant and continuous review/revision and we give examples of this later on.

**OBJECTIVES**

*This chapter will:*

- suggest how you can review your current approaches and perspectives as a first step to improving your communication;
- suggest some of the tools and opportunities you can consider as you review your learning approach and compile your personal development plan.

## REVIEWING YOUR OBJECTIVES AND GOALS

Virtually every book on business communication or business skills emphasises the importance of goals and objectives. However, different authors use this terminology differently and also focus on different levels. For example, in the text described on its sleeve as 'the field's leading text for more than two decades', Bovee and Thill (2014) suggest that 'All business messages have a general purpose: to inform, to persuade, or to collaborate . . . each message also has a specific purpose, which identifies what you hope to accomplish with your message' (p. 129). They only talk about goals in the sense of 'career goals' such as your 'career specialty' (p. 33). The problem here is deciding how you move from career goals to specific purposes.

Another common approach is to identify characteristics of goals/objectives which are likely to be achieved – typically SMART goals or, as Cameron (2010, p. 28) suggests, CSMART objectives, standing for:

- **C**hallenging
- **S**pecific
- **M**easurable
- **A**chievable
- **R**elevant
- **T**ime-defined.

Cameron also talks about a hierarchy of goals where you need to break down goals into their component parts. This is the approach we favour and use the terminology proposed by John Kay (2011). He distinguishes between high-level objectives, intermediate goals and basic actions. 'High-level goals are typically loose and unquantifiable – though this does not mean it is not evident whether or not they are being achieved.' As an example, he uses the high-level objective of ICI to retain their industrial leadership. One intermediate goal was then defined as 'the responsible commercial application of chemistry' and the resulting action was the 'launch of a pharmaceutical division (all quotes from p. 41). Thanks in part to this clear strategic perspective, ICI was 'Britain's leading industrial company for seventy years' (p. 63).

You can translate this hierarchy into personal individual terms and an example is given in Figure 1.1. If you have the high-level objective of 'being an effective manager', then this must be broken down into goals which relate to both productivity and social relationships (where it is useful to use the CSMART criteria) and then specific actions. There are two other important points to highlight from Kay's analysis:

- Problems are often best solved indirectly or obliquely as we live in unpredictable and fast-changing environments.
- Objectives, goals and actions must be constantly reviewed to ensure that they retain their importance and relevance. Becoming an effective manager is not something which can be defined absolutely as it will change. You will learn what it means by trying to do it, in the same way that skilled athletes understand what they do very differently from novices.

Figure 1.1 also gives us the opportunity to introduce our approach to concept mapping. You will see that concepts are shown in boxes which are linked to make propositions, as in – high-level objectives . . . must be translated into . . . goals . . . which can be achieved through . . . activities. This illustrates how you can 'read' the map. The overall structure depends on what we want to demonstrate – in this case, we have included two maps side by side – the abstract approach on the left hand of the page and practical illustrations on the right. The original versions of all the diagrams we use in this book are available for you to download either as image files or in their original format (we use the cmap software available from www.ihmc.us/cmaptools.php). At this website, you will also find links to tutorials and examples so that you can use this software effectively. It is both very useful and very easy to learn.

A particular variant of concept mapping which has been used in business situations is 'causal mapping' – 'a word-and-arrow diagram in which ideas and actions are causally linked' and 'the arrows indicate how one idea or action leads to another' (Bryson *et al.*, 2004, p. xii). Bryson *et al.* claim it is 'the most helpful way of gaining an important issue areas in such a way that we can figure our effective strategies and actions that will achieve our goals' (ibid., p. xv). It is worth looking at Bryson's book for the examples of this approach in action. They use a common structure which underpins all the maps in the book based on the key questions listed in Table 1.1. Applying these questions to your personal development plan would be a useful way of checking or complementing the process we suggest below.

**Table 1.1** *Key questions to build a causal map (from Bryson et al., 2004, p. 36)*

| |
|---|
| What would be your overall purpose or mission? |
| What would result from doing that? What would the consequences be of doing that? |
| What do you want to do? |
| How would you do that? What would it take to do that? |
| What are you assuming about the world? |

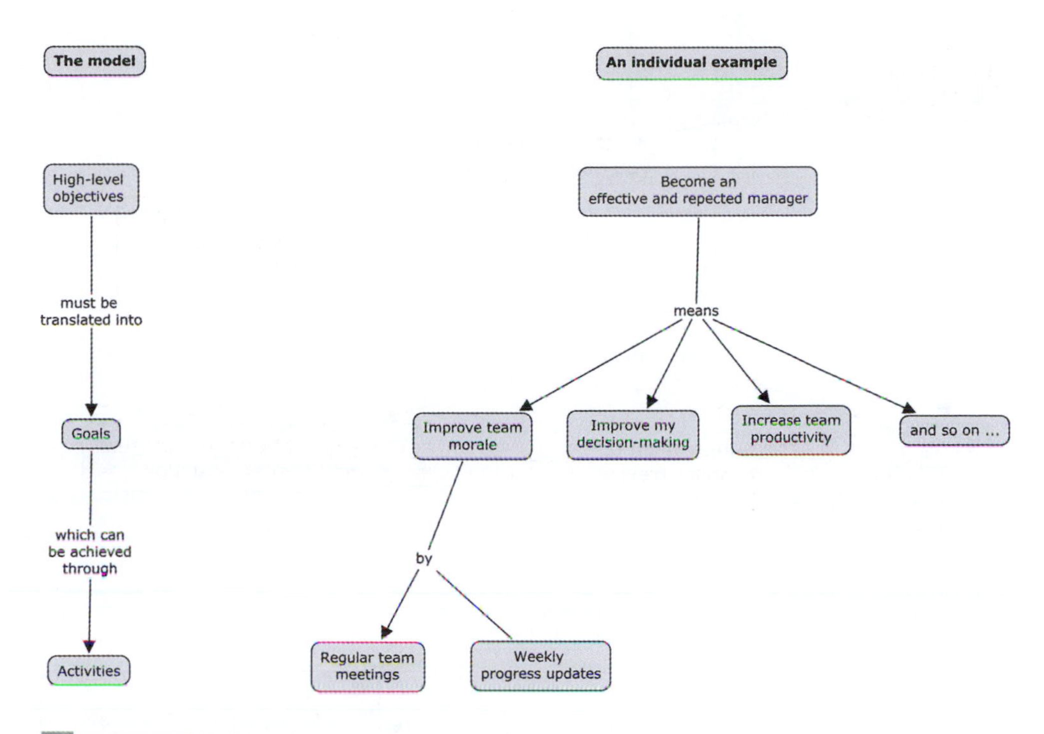


***Figure 1.1*** *Objectives, goals and activities*

As well as our own experience of the value of using mapping techniques, we can point to many examples of their value in education at various levels (e.g. Novak, 2010). However, we would hesitate to recommend them unreservedly. One of the main messages of this book is that you need to be flexible and select techniques to suit the situation and your own personal style.

Returning to the issues of goals and objectives, can we accept Figure 1.1 and move on? You may like to consider this question for a few moments.

We think there is one major problem with this analysis so far – it does not include an analysis of the starting point and the broader social context in which you operate. Looking back at the example in Figure 1.1, the activities of regular team meetings and weekly progress summaries seem to reflect the goals. However, they could be counter-productive in some circumstances. For example, if there are deep-seated personal conflicts between members of the group, then regular meetings may simply offer more opportunities to fight. The conflict may need to be resolved or at least weakened *before* meetings can become more amicable and productive. As a result, we want to revise Figure 1.1 to include a review stage.

Figure 1.2 includes several review loops, including reviewing the present situation in relation to the original goals and defining the gap between what is happening now and what you would like to see happen.

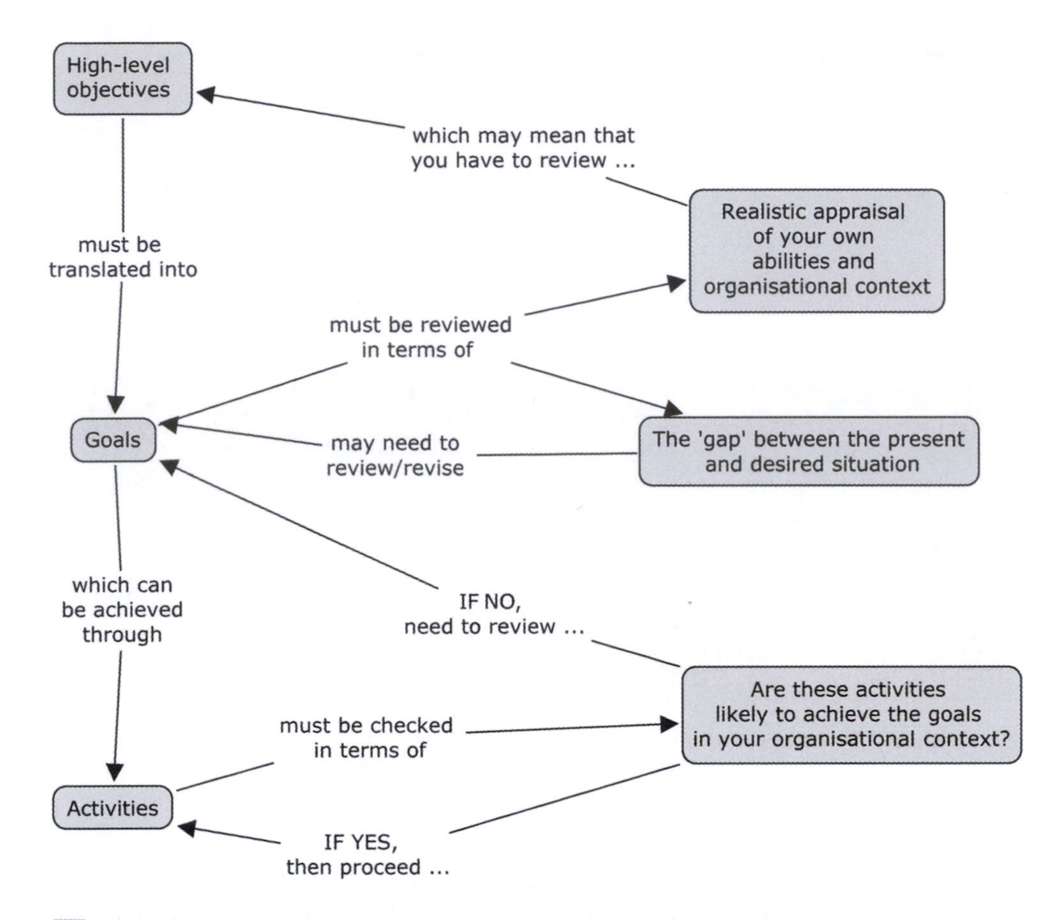


***Figure 1.2*** *Revised model of objectives, goals and activities*

## REFLECTING ON THE FUTURE OF WORK

As you consider your own future in your own organisation, you should also consider more general trends in the social and political context which may directly affect your long-term future. One of the most useful analyses we can point you to is the work by Professor Lynda Gratton from the London Business School, whose research has suggested five major forces which are changing the way we work and the three shifts she recommends to deal with these (Gratton, 2014). The five forces are: technology; globalisation; demography and longevity; society; and energy resources. The three shifts are summarised in Table 1.2.

Many of the recommendations later in this book reflect the trends shown in Table 1.2.

### Ways of setting those long-term improvement goals

There is no one best way of doing this. Here are some suggestions to get you started (and there are more ideas and practical suggestions on the website).

***Table 1.2** The future of work*

| *You need to shift from . . .* | *You need to shift to . . .* | *Because (rationale)* |
|---|---|---|
| 'shallow generalist' | 'serial master' | You will need in-depth knowledge and skills in a number of areas and these areas will change over time. The number of jobs that require very general skills at fairly superficial level will continue to shrink and disappear |
| 'isolated competitor' | 'innovative connector' | You will need to develop networks of colleagues who can provide support and expertise when you need it, rather than working as isolated individual |
| 'voracious consumer' | 'impassioned producer' | You will have the opportunity to engage with more meaningful work and to find a better 'work–life balance' |

1 Find approaches that suit your lifestyle and personality. We discuss ways of reviewing important personality characteristics later in this chapter.
2 Select evidence-based techniques. For example, Timothy Wilson (2011) uses research evidence to argue that private reflective writing over a period of days can be a more powerful technique for working through difficult experiences than professional counselling. However, some forms of writing have more impact than others. When reflecting on unpleasant or very negative experiences, you need to adopt a perspective which gives you 'some distance from the event' and which enables you to 'analyse why the event occurred' (p. 57) – a 'step-back-and-ask-why strategy' (p. 58).
3 Avoid self-help recipes which simply reflect the style or perspective of the author. There is no shortage of books which offer the promise of immediate and dramatic change. There are some which are strongly based on research evidence (e.g. Beattie, 2011; Wiseman, 2012) but many simply seem to offer '"remedies" (which) make people feel good but don't cure what ails them' (Wilson, 2011, p. 42).
4 Consider a programme which gives you the responsibility but also offer tools and social support. A good recent example of this in the UK is the Lifewide Education initiative – http://lifewideeducation.co.uk – and see further discussion on the website.

## ADOPTING LEARNING STRATEGIES TO IMPROVE YOUR COMMUNICATIONS: REVIEW, PLAN AND IMPROVE

The underpinning principle for this chapter (and the rest of this book) is 'communication can always be improved', which might appear obvious, although it is often neglected in practice. We suggest a 'review, plan and improve' philosophy, based on 'continuous improvement' approaches used in many business sectors. The key to this is reviewing the impact of your own behaviour on others (including the influence of your own assumptions

### BOX 1.1 PRACTICAL TIPS ON GOAL-SETTING

*Be realistic*

It will take more than a few weeks to transform your communication skills – there are practical limits in what you can achieve in a short space of time. Be realistic about your goals and recognise that you will need practice, time and repetition.

*Prioritise your goals*

If you also follow the advice later in this chapter about self-review, getting feedback from others on your communications skills and analysing your personality, you will have a good picture of the skills and attributes you want to develop. It is important to prioritise those that will be of most use to you and work on these first before moving on to the others. To get started, it is a good idea to focus on just one goal.

*Phrase your goals to be achievable and practical*

Use our model (Figure 1.2) or a similar approach to avoid very open-ended goals such as 'I want to improve my communications in meetings'. Select more focused goals. For example, if colleagues have suggested that you are not the best listener, then you could focus on specific behaviours such as summarising or building, as discussed in Chapters 9 and 10.

*Plan 'small steps'*

Once you have identified an achievable goal, recognise that achieving it will be the result of taking small steps – aim to create regular, practical and achievable activities that you can undertake to reach the goal.

and possible prejudices/stereotypes), and seeking out feedback to help inform your strategies and plans to improve your communications.

Continuous improvement philosophies are now well established in many sectors. For instance, Kaizen (Japanese for 'improvement' or 'change for the better') philosophy is used in many industries for improving processes and eliminating waste. It is meant to be practised daily among staff at all levels in an organisation and should result in small improvements which can collectively result in significant overall improvements. At the heart of the Kaizen approach is a cyclic process of making improvements and reviewing the results. As well as organisational development (e.g. Miller *et al.*, 2013), this philosophy has also been applied to personal development where people are encouraged to take small steps towards improvement.

This sort of approach is not new and you may think we have simply repeated existing wisdom. However, we want to highlight two aspects which we think have been neglected in previous analyses:

- Do *not* regard review, plan and improve as separate or discrete stages. We are advocating a *continuous* review – keeping alert at all times for feedback which suggests

**Figure 1.3** *Using Kaizen in this chapter*

that all is well or not, and responding flexibly and immediately. This emphasis does not come across in other well-known approaches. For example, Bovee and Thill (2014) advocate a three-step approach to business messages where you plan (including 'analyse the situation' and 'defining your purpose'), you write (including 'adapt to your audience' and 'compose the message'), and finally you complete (where you 'produce the message', proofread, revise and distribute – pp. 127ff.). They go on to suggest a general rule that you should use 'half your available time for planning, one-quarter for writing, and one-quarter for completing your messages' (p. 128). Our approach is to see these stages as a continuous process (see Figure 1.3) and adopt new technology which allows us to work much more flexibly.

- We must update our approaches to reflect the opportunities and challenges of the digital world. For example, we shall shortly discuss the concept of 'digital identity' that people acquire as they engage with digital media (e.g. social networks) and how such digital identities influence communications, in both positive and negative senses.

With these caveats in mind, you can use the Kaizen philosophy to improve your communications, using the 'review, plan and improve' cycle in our daily practice.

## Self-review

Reviewing your own skills is harder than it first appears. This is perhaps not surprising as our education systems typically see assessment and feedback as something 'done' to students, rather than students being in the driving seat of self-assessment and review. When students make the transition to the workplace, there is no tutor to assess their performance and provide feedback. Instead, there may be CPD (continuing professional development) programmes and appraisals as well as opportunities for feedback from supervisors, managers and colleagues. However, these often do not address communications skills and they rarely follow the Kaizen philosophy of regular small improvements. Performance review, which relies on the 'annual appraisal interview', is very far from the process we are proposing.

The capability of 'self-review' is a key capability that all professionals should develop. There are a number of ways of doing this – see the website for further suggestions – but consider these objectives as a starter for ten:

***Table 1.3*** *Useful objectives*

| *Objective* | *Explanation* |
|---|---|
| There is a clear purpose to my communication | Do you understand what you want to happen as a result of your communication – e.g. what do you want your audience to do? |
| I have taken steps to understand my target audience and listen to their perspectives. | Can you visualise yourself in their position? How you would feel about the communication? |
| I understand the specific social, cultural, historical and technological context to the communication | These contexts can enhance or constrain communication. For instance, assertive behaviour can be interpreted as aggressive in some cultures |
| I have evaluated several options for achieving my purpose and selected the one most likely to succeed | Given the ever-increasing ways of communicating (both face-to-face and with technology), which will be most effective in your situation? |
| I've tried to ensure that there is consistency between what I say, my behaviour and my body language – as well as no ambiguity | Research into the impact of body language on communications provides varied results, and we discuss this in Chapters 9 and 10 |
| I've looked for non-verbal clues to see how my communication has been understood and interpreted | Interpreting non-verbal behaviour is both important and complex. You need to be continually looking for clues which might help you to improve your communication |
| I have taken steps to get feedback to see how well the target audience has understood the communication and how they interpreted its meaning | You can only find out how people have interpreted and understood your communication by getting feedback – e.g. through engaging in a discussion |
| I have followed through on promised actions | While this is not communication in itself, it is very important in maintaining your credibility |
| I keep up-to-date with new forms of digital communications and have spent time using them in order to assess their value | This is now a critical aspect of communication in organisations. See the discussion of digital literacy later in this chapter |

Now think of a typical and recent work situation you are involved in and rate yourself (1 = low; 5 = high).

***Table 1.4*** *Reviewing your objectives*

| *Objective* | *Rate your skill* | | | | |
|---|---|---|---|---|---|
| There is a clear purpose to my communication | 1 | 2 | 3 | 4 | 5 |
| I have taken steps to understand my target audience and listen to their perspectives | 1 | 2 | 3 | 4 | 5 |
| I understand the specific social, cultural, historical and technological context to the communication | 1 | 2 | 3 | 4 | 5 |
| I have evaluated several options for achieving my purpose and selected the one most likely to succeed | 1 | 2 | 3 | 4 | 5 |
| I've tried to ensure that there is consistency between what I say, my behaviour and my body language – as well as no ambiguity | 1 | 2 | 3 | 4 | 5 |
| Where feasible, I've looked for non-verbal clues to see how my communication has been understood and interpreted | 1 | 2 | 3 | 4 | 5 |
| I have taken steps to get feedback to see how well the target audience has understood the communication and how they interpreted its meaning | 1 | 2 | 3 | 4 | 5 |
| I have followed through on promised actions | 1 | 2 | 3 | 4 | 5 |
| I keep up to date with new forms of digital communications and have spent time using them in order to assess their value | 1 | 2 | 3 | 4 | 5 |

In a perfect world, you will have rated yourself as 5 on all these characteristics. If you have, then we respectfully suggest that you are fooling yourself. Ask a friend or colleague to rate you on the same basis and compare your results. You are much more likely to end up with a variety of scores and this gives you some ideas for priorities and immediate action.

## Personality analysis

We are not always good at making judgements on how others see us. Our behaviour and body language give off all sorts of clues to our personalities and we may not be fully aware of the impressions we are presenting to others. This area is covered in more detail in other chapters, but we can start by asking how good we are at judging ourselves. Unfortunately, psychological studies have shown that we often misjudge our own personality and capabilities. For example, are you a good multitasker? Judging by their behaviour, many people seem to think so, but recent research suggests that very few of us can effectively multitask. Most of us would be more effective if we deliberately focused on one thing at a time.

It is also worth thinking about your more fundamental personality characteristics. Large organisations often employ a range of personality tests to help their staff recruitment and continual professional development programmes. Some tests focus on the individual and others on teams in order to help organisations in selecting and blending together different and complementary personality types. More recently, such tests have become available as online services and it is possible to use these to help in the analysis of your personality and your team abilities. However, such tests come with a word of caution. Ideally, they should be overseen by a skilled psychologist, particularly with the analysis and interpretation of results. Furthermore, they are best used within a context of 'review, plan and improve', although sometimes they are used in less positive contexts – e.g. for staff screening. There are also a range of complex issues in terms of people responding to and acting on the results. For instance, how people respond to tests can be influenced by the 'authority' of the evaluator, whether the person believes that they are undertaking a personalised test and whether the test includes mainly positive traits. There is also the risk of subject validation where the subject only hears what they want to hear. It is also possible for people to become dependent upon the personality traits that the test reveals about them and this can lead to them abandoning attempts to improve those areas of 'weakness'.

However, if you bear these health warnings in mind, there is value in considering broad aspects of your personality without professional support. You can (and should) always 'check' your results with close friends and colleagues. We suggest three specific areas you can pursue:

1 *Overall personality measures*. Possibly the most well-known is the Myers Briggs test which measures psychological preferences, based on Carl Jung's theories of psychological types and their different perceptions of the world. Various versions are available online – see the website for details. A particularly important dimension is introversion–extroversion where 'introverts and extroverts differ in the level of outside stimulation that they need to function well' (Cain, 2012, p. 10). This leads to differences in behaviours such as preferred work practices and decision-making. Susan Cain argues that 'many of the most important institutions of contemporary life are designed for those who enjoy group projects and high levels of stimulation' (p. 6). In other words, we have constructed our school and workplaces to explicitly favour extrovert personalities. The consequence is that we may be losing valuable contributions from more introverted people (about one-third to one-half of the population in the USA according to the studies that Cain researched). They have to adapt to be successful. She argues that organisations can be more sensitive to introverts' needs and adopt strategies which enable them to make more of a contribution – including several uses of new technology which we talk about later. She also emphasises the importance of recognising your own tendencies and working to accommodate these.

2 *Mindset*. Dictionary definitions of this term tend to focus on a 'fixed state of mind' which influences or determines our behaviour. But which mindsets do we need to worry about? Which preconceptions might hinder your learning and progress? To stimulate your thinking on this we summarise two recent studies below and include more links on the website:

   Carol Dweck has popularised the term and her studies have focused on differences between the fixed mindset – 'believing that your qualities are carved in stone' – and the growth mindset – 'based on the belief that your basic qualities are things you can cultivate through your efforts' (Dweck, 2006, pp. 6–7). Her studies have shown the damaging impact of the fixed mindset. She offers tools and techniques to support change to the growth mindset and concludes in ways that parallel our approach to communication – that mindset change is 'about seeing things in a new way. When people . . . change to a growth mindset, they change from a *judge-and-be-judged* framework to a *learn-and-help-learn* framework. Their commitment is to growth and growth takes plenty of time, effort, and mutual support' (p. 244).

James Reed and Paul Stoltz claim to have found the mindset which top employers really want and that they 'picked *mindset* over skill set as the key element in those they seek and retain' (2011, p. 7). They list the 'Top 20' mindset qualities, with the top six being honesty, trustworthiness, commitment, adaptability, accountability and flexibility. They have distilled these qualities into a model with three categories to produce the 3G Mindset – Global, Good and Grit – and offer suggestions on development (and a one-off free survey if you buy the book!)

3 *Team roles*. There are various inventories designed to establish how you operate in teams – one of the most well known is the Belbin test. This is discussed in detail in Chapter 13.

## Feedback from colleagues

Feedback from colleagues – if it is candid, open and honest – can and should inform your review of your communications capabilities, though there are potential pitfalls. While formal organisational appraisals can provide useful feedback, in practice they occur infrequently and are typically provided by a limited number of colleagues – though it is increasingly common for organisations to arrange '360-degree feedback' exercises. These aim to evaluate and provide useful feedback from a range of colleagues on performance. However, all these processes are 'done to you' rather than proactively seeking out feedback from colleagues on a regular and frequent basis.

One of the advantages of more proactive approaches to getting feedback from colleagues is that it can be timed when you need it. For instance, you could ask your colleagues to identify examples of when you are good and not so good at communications – as they happen. In this way, you will get immediate feedback on real situations. You can also explore with them different facets of your communication skills, relating to what you say, your listening skills, your body language, etc. There are caveats about this process, though – for instance, any feedback you receive must be interpreted in context. What is the relationship between you and your colleagues – will they be open and balanced in their comments? Many people, when asked to provide feedback, are likely to tell people what they want to hear and thus reinforce self-delusion, so it is important to stress that you would *really* like candid and honest feedback. Furthermore, to interpret feedback you also need to understand the strengths and weaknesses of your colleagues and the boundaries of their skills and capabilities – choose feedback from colleagues who you and others see as having particular strengths in the area in which you are looking for feedback. Although receiving feedback from colleagues has all sorts of traps, the best way of teasing out any biases and prejudices to use the feedback as a starting point for dialogue with colleagues where you can ask them to explain further and help you to develop approaches for improvement. Many people will be flattered to help out and only too willing to help you to improve.

This discussion assumes that you are ready and able to accept feedback. Useful advice on this comes from Heen and Stone (2014). They suggest a number of techniques which can help you to become better at taking feedback on board, including the following (with explanation and our comments in the parentheses):

1 'Know your tendencies' (you may have a particular pattern in the way you receive comments which will get in the way of considering them fully – e.g. going on the defensive and arguing back).
2 'Disentangle the "what" from the "who"' (you need to consider both the content of feedback and the relationship you have with the 'giver').
3 'Unpack the feedback' (you need to make sure you really understand what they are saying to you rather than accept general and possibly vague comments).
4 'Ask for just one thing' (requesting feedback on specific areas can be really useful).
5 'Engage in small experiments' (make small changes and see if they work in the desired direction).

Spontaneous and unrequested feedback from colleagues can also be useful, but this can often be clouded with self-interest – you may have to tease such self-interests out. Their motivation might be more to do with boosting their own self-worth or political/personal agendas.

## Your digital identity

Nowadays, anyone can create their own identity on the Internet, which may be far removed from their real identity and fraudsters regularly take advantage of this ability. While such criminal activity is an extreme, there are significant implications for everyone using the Internet. First of all, you just don't know who you are dealing with, and this puts up barriers to how well you can communicate with them. You can overcome this to some extent by engaging in dialogue with them and trying to pick up clues, but it is not easy.

There is also the issue of how others perceive you and, of course, people will be making assumptions about who you are, based on the clues and trails you leave on the Internet. For instance, your postings and profiles on social networks, your Twitter postings, what you say in discussion groups, what's been published about you on websites – all these help others to build up a picture of your personality, traits, preferences and attributes – in other words, your digital identity. But there will be other pieces of information that are posted that you have no control over – e.g. postings from friends and colleagues and even potentially malicious postings from those who don't have your best interests at heart. There are two unfortunate consequences of all this: first, the information that builds up about you, rather like a jigsaw, is created in a rather unplanned, haphazard way and sometimes without any control from you; second, it is often very difficult (and sometimes impossible) to get rid of an unwanted information about you – e.g. on social networks. This all means that your digital identify – how others perceive you online – is not that much in your control and there are serious consequences and implications for your professional life.

Employers and job recruiters actively research your digital identity and look for clues as to how you will perform in your work. They will base decisions on whether or not to recruit on what they find. So while social networks such as Twitter, Facebook and LinkedIn are being increasingly used to find jobs, it is a double-edged sword. A recent study suggested that a clear majority of employers screen job applicants via these networks. Numerous news stories relate how people failed to get a job based on what the employer found out about them – in one case, a job applicant tweeted 'Company X offered me a job! Now I have to weigh the utility of a fatty paycheck against the daily commute to San Jose and hating the work' and the company withdrew the job offer. However, it is not all bad: one survey suggested that 68 per cent of employers have hired a candidate because of something that the candidate said on a social networking site. The solution to influencing your digital identity is not to avoid posting. People expect you to be part of the digital world – a digital citizen – and not participating says a great deal about you.

You need to influence your digital identity – we deliberately do not use words such as 'manage' or 'control' as it is probably not realistic to have a great deal of control in this area. However, you can influence your digital identity and the first step is to review what this currently is. You can start on this by searching out all references to yourself on social networks such as Twitter, Facebook and LinkedIn as well as on websites, discussion groups, etc. Remember to look for images, audio and video as well as text. Try to put out of your mind your own personality and review the postings as if it were another person. You can then begin to see how others see you who have never met you and how your digital identity will shape how they communicate with you.

There are a number of ways in which you can influence your digital identity. Perhaps the most important (and safest) overall principle is to treat *every* digital communication – and this includes every email and every Facebook entry – as potentially a public message. Are you happy to make this information known to the world at large? Box 1.2 gives some practical suggestions on this and Box 1.3 shows how a couple of individuals have used digital media to develop and promote their new careers.

## BOX 1.2 MANAGING YOUR DIGITAL IDENTITY: PRACTICAL SUGGESTIONS

- *Develop your social media strategy for your 'brand'.* Think of yourself as a 'brand' and work out what are the key attributes about yourself you want to convey.
- *Choose social media.* Consider using a range of social media applications such as LinkedIn, Facebook, Twitter, blogs such as WordPress, picture and video sites such as Flickr, YouTube.
- *Claim your IDs.* Claim your unique ID at sites even if you don't use it – for instance, if you have a Twitter name, you may want to have the same name on other sites – e.g. Skype, Facebook. In choosing an ID, make sure it aligns with your 'brand'.
- *Have separate private and professional accounts.* As a general rule, keep your private life private (within limits) and create separate professional and private accounts.
- *Keep on top of privacy and copyright rules, settings and terms.* Pay attention to privacy/copyright settings/terms of service/preference settings and keep abreast of changes in them. Many social media sites change their privacy settings from time to time and are not always good at proclaiming this. Bear in mind copyright terms – e.g. Google Docs claim certain rights to use anything in your online documents.

*continued . . .*

## BOX 1.2 *Continued*

- *Be selective in choosing 'friends'.* Be choosy who you select as 'friends' or 'colleagues' and don't automatically accept all 'friend/colleague' requests.
- *Be proactive in using social media to build your identity.* Use social media sites to support your professional work – e.g. for research, networking, ideas generation, discussions, etc. – but keep in mind your 'brand'.
- *Keep abreast of opportunities for learning and knowledge creation.* The Web also provides a wealth of opportunities for learning and knowledge creation.
- *Follow netiquette.* Follow sensible rules of net etiquette – and remember that all those out there in the digital landscape are human beings even if it is difficult to picture them.
- *Be vigilant for fraudsters, scammers and bullies.* Remember that social media is also used unscrupulously – e.g. for employee screening, harassment and bullying, spamming, spying, etc.
- *Engage on a regular basis.* Maintain your digital presence/network on a regular basis and always respond to feedback and messages.
- *Keep others informed of your progress, news and ideas.* Use the network to share your professional news and ideas, although avoid blatant self-promotion.

## BOX 1.3 CREATING DIGITAL IDENTITY

These two case studies demonstrate how people can successfully create digital identities using a range of online tools (and that it is never too late to start).

### *Iain Cameron*

Iain Cameron's LinkedIn profile was in the 5 per cent most viewed in 2012. He writes a regular monthly article on industrial strategy and skills policy issues for a business improvement organisation and always promotes each article through LinkedIn. His prompts on LinkedIn take the form of a question posed with the link to the article as a putative answer to tease potential readers into clicking on the link.

With over 25 years' experience in the UK Industry Department and the Civil Service College and 10 years working on policy and research for an automotive trade association, Iain became interested in the growing debate across the developed world on what industrial strategies will be most effective in the face of rapid growth in emerging economies. Rapid development of advanced manufacturing is seen by both the United States and the European Community as the right strategic response to this situation. Surprisingly, even in the present relatively depressed state of the world economy, ambitious manufacturing firms across the globe are finding it hard to recruit people with the right skills.

*continued . . .*

**BOX 1.3 *Continued***

Iain promotes his articles on Twitter but found it easier to build his readership on LinkedIn. Twitter has proved its worth in learning of new research and conferences on industrial and skills strategy issues. It has also proved effective as an alert for new business opportunities.

Location – living in London – is another important factor. A number of organisations based in London ('think-tanks') mount presentations, conferences and discussions, which are mostly free to attend. The key is getting an early alert of what is coming up as popular topics quickly get booked up. Twitter is also a useful tool here. Many think-tanks issue a regular e-newsletter and subscription to these is another useful channel.

### *Caroline Gurney*

Caroline Gurney spent 18 years in public service – first as a diplomat and then in the Cabinet Office – before stopping work to look after a son with learning difficulties. Then, 20 years later and following a successful battle with cancer, she decided to return to work in a totally different career. She established her own business, Caroline Gurney Historical Research Services, working as a professional genealogist and house historian.

Caroline's business grew directly out of her already established online reputation as a 'hobbyist' genealogist and came after several years of turning down offers of paid work. All her marketing takes place online, using a variety of websites and social media. She built her own website using Weebly, has a blog on Blogger, business page on Facebook, a profile on LinkedIn and is an active Twitter user. She also uses sites such as Free Index, Speaker Mix and This Is Bristol to promote her business. She uses Brand Yourself for SEO and Vizify to link the various aspects of her Web presence, using her Vizify 'visual thumbprint' as her email signature.

Caroline devotes regular time each week to keeping all these sites up to date and so far has never been without a client. Her biggest project – tracing the descendants of the men who sailed on the *Cutty Sark* – came through a friend who had read the genealogy blog posts which Caroline shares on Facebook. This in turn led to work for the BBC. She has prepared two house histories for a client who found her on Free Index and receives numerous enquiries through her website. Her clients are international, with work during the past year having come from Canada, Australia and Norway as well as the UK. Caroline receives over 1,000 unique visitors a month to her websites and nine out of the top ten Google search results for her name point to her. Despite already having this high profile online, she saw a significant rise in enquiries the week she signed up with Brand Yourself.

Looking to the future, Caroline is planning to launch a new business offering tailor-made family trees as gifts for new babies, incorporating bespoke artwork and family photographs. She also has ambitions to expand into the world of heritage tours. She has already secured the domain names for these new projects.

## Developing your digital literacy

The UK higher education sector is now working hard to develop the concept of digital literacies, equipping graduates with digital skills, although there is still some variation in the understanding of the term and very different interpretations by employers on graduate digital skills. Some employers simply talk in terms of being able to use word-processing and/or spreadsheets. Others have a more sophisticated understanding – wanting their graduates to apply key management/professional skills in the selection, adoption and application of new technologies. Some go even further to talk about the ability of graduates to have the skill to 'influence' colleagues in the strategic/operational adoption of new technologies. So-called 'digital influence' has been identified as a key skill for managers in the next few years.

Our model of digital literacy (Figure 1.4) reflects this position and suggests that we need to give graduates far more than expertise with a few mainstream software packages to prepare for employment.

You can see that this model emphasises that we need to develop an overall understanding of technology to underpin our skill development and then we must apply this not just to our own development but in our work with colleagues and broader organisation. And all of this must be self-critical and ethical. Figure 1.5 offers a more detailed version. How far do you 'tick all the boxes'? How would you assess your digital literacy against this recipe?

There are, of course, other models of digital literacy and this term is debated/contested. For a good example of research which explores these arguments, see the work by Ibrar Bhatt on adult learners coming to terms with the technical and academic demands of their college environment (Bhatt, 2012). He illustrates how specific learners 'successfully make the link between their own everyday digital literacy practices and the requirements of their course' (ibid., p. 289). If we add 'and/or organisation' to this last sentence, then this is something we all have to do.

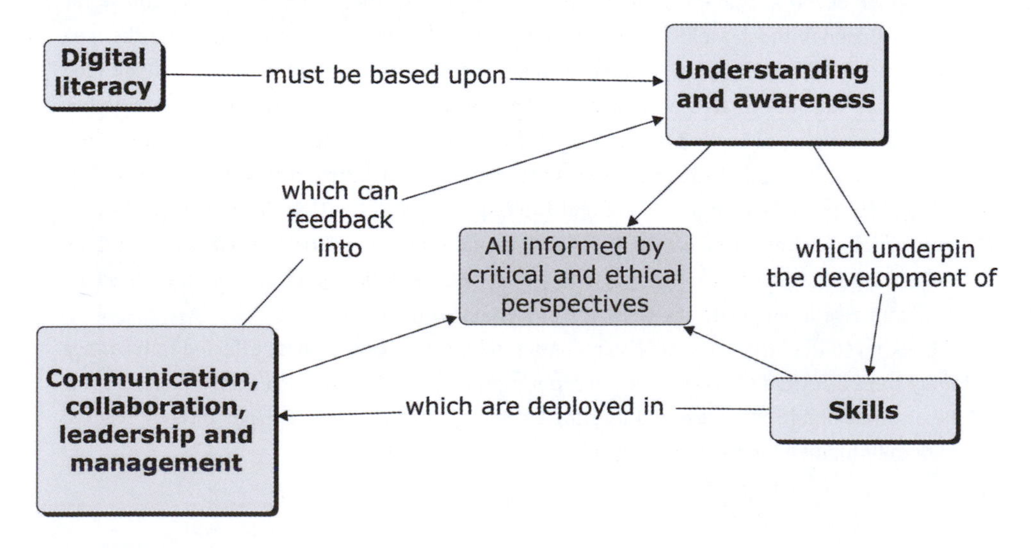


***Figure 1.4*** *Overall model of digital literacy*

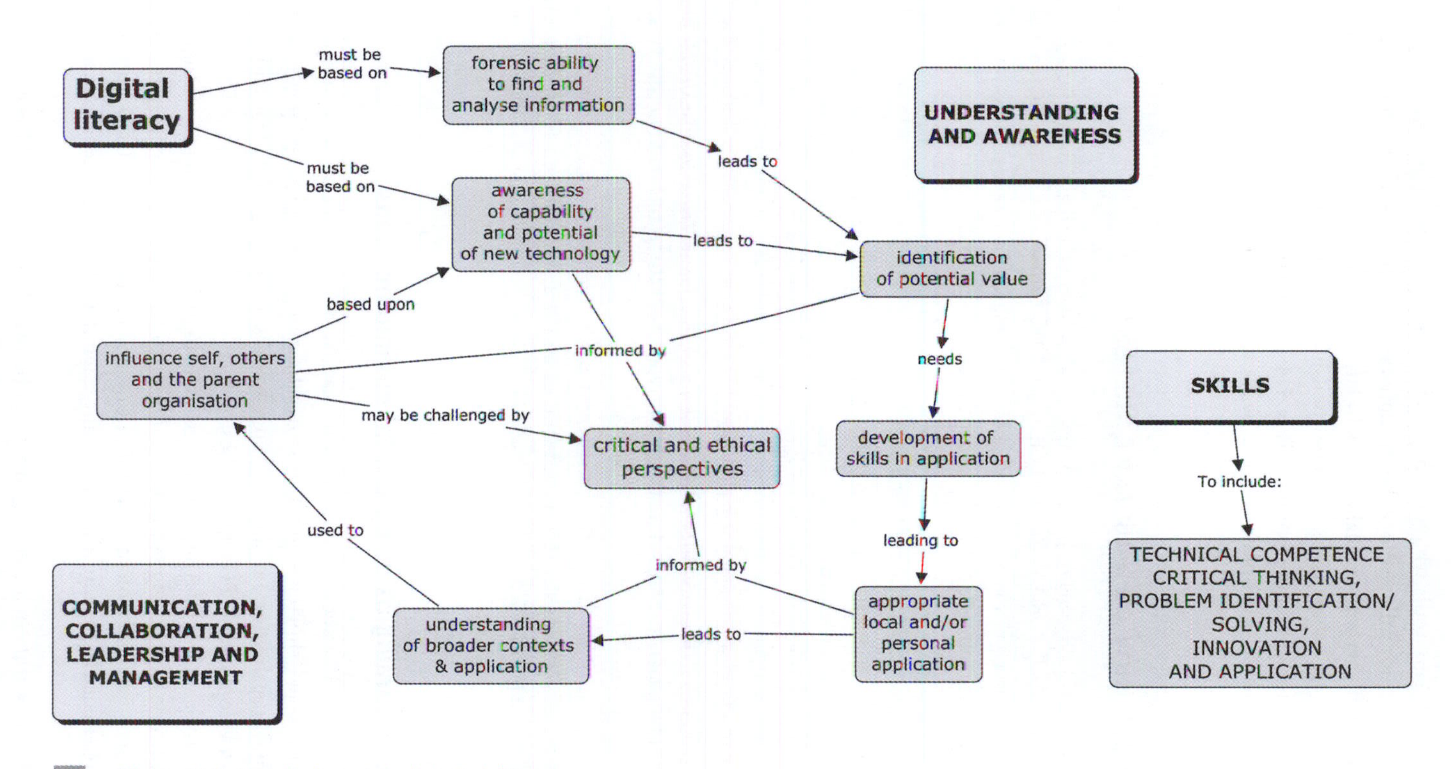


**Figure 1.5** *Detailed model of digital literacy*

## CHOOSING APPROPRIATE COMMUNICATION TOOLS

We now have too many tools which we can use to communicate. This can be a good thing, but it can mean we don't fully explore the strengths and weaknesses of each tool. We highlight various attributes of currently available tools in later chapters. For the moment, we ask you to consider the range of tools you are currently using and ask yourself whether this range is the most effective for your development. Box 1.4 shows how even a very simple task like taking notes can now be done in a variety of ways using different mixes of technology.

### BOX 1.4 HOW DO YOU TAKE NOTES?

Every manager and professional in organisations has to take notes in meetings, presentations, interviews, etc. What is your preferred technology? The following list suggests possibilities and we return to some of these in later chapters. The most effective method will depend on your working style, your budget and your organisational context:

- pen and paper, using dedicated notebook;
- pen and paper using some planning/diary system like Filofax or Day-Timer;
- speech recognition technology like Dragon Dictate;
- handwriting recognition directly on a tablet such as an iPad;
- notetaking application on smartphone, laptop or tablet like Evernote, which allow you to synchronise your notes across devices;
- electronic pen like Livescribe. Early versions of this pen allowed you to take notes on special notepaper and record audio so that you could listen to the audio afterwards which related to particular notes you made. The most recent version works in sync with iPads or iPods so that the notes transfer automatically into electronic form. This new version uses the recording facilities on the synced device rather than relying on its own internal mic.

### New learning paradigms using digital communications

A Motor Company HR executive recently told us that 'the half-life of an engineering degree is getting shorter and shorter – graduates therefore need to regularly update their skills, knowledge and capabilities on an on-going basis via lifelong learning and continuing professional development (CPD) approaches'.

The emergence of the Internet and low-cost computing is helping to change the CPD paradigm from one of teaching (something 'done' to the learner) to concepts such as self-directed learning and assessment. Organisations are changing their CPD approaches and techniques, particularly in how they are using digital technologies to support their CPD strategies.

Some of the new approaches arising are given below. A more detailed version is available on the website.

***Table 1.5*** *Approaches to CPD*

| *Concept* | *Details* | *Typical technologies* |
|---|---|---|
| Work-based learning | Companies deliver education and training in-house which is integrated into everyday working activities | e-portfolios<br>Social networks<br>Wikis<br>Blended learning<br>Technology-enhanced learning (TEL)<br>Apps on mobile phones/tablets, etc. |
| Self-directed learning and assessment | Individuals take more control over planning their learning, seeking out knowledge (e.g. from the Internet) with tutors playing more of a role of coach | e-portfolios, usually linked to "personal development plans" (PDPs)<br>online diagnostic tools<br>e-APEL (experiential learning for potential accreditation) |
| 'Do-it-yourself' learning materials | Low-cost multimedia technologies has enabled materials which can be either distributed for stand-alone use (including use on mobile devices) or made available online, using Cloud-based hosting services for hosting video, audio, etc. | Vodcasts and podcasts<br>Screencasts<br>e-book authoring<br>Mind/concept maps<br>Interactive multimedia authoring<br>Animation<br>Open educational resources (OERs) – content that is made freely available to others to use<br>MOOCs (Massive Open Online Course) where free courses are delivered in a totally online format |

### Using this technology re communication

The main implication of this explosion in technology is that we should be taking full advantage of it to support our own professional development in communication. For example, we can write our own development plan using free/open source software or commercial software, much of which is modestly priced. The table below highlights a few new technologies which we think have important applications and which we feel are currently underused in many organisations. Our argument is that everyone with supervisory or management responsibilities in a modern organisation of any size should be familiar with this range of technologies, using some of them to support both themselves and their team.

## A FINAL WORD ON OPEN BADGES

One recent development with significant potential is Open Badges. The idea behind this development by Mozilla is to offer a way of accrediting your skills and expertise outside the confines of conventional certification. You can earn and display 'badges', which contain information and evidence about your skills and achievements, which you can display and

**Table 1.6** *Taking advantage of new technology*

| *Technology* | *Features and examples* |
|---|---|
| Interactive multimedia editing and authoring tools | Individual media editing/production tools are becoming less expensive (or even free) and much easier to use – e.g. Adobe Premier for video editing; Audacity for audio editing/production (open source); and Camtasia or Jing for screencasting |
| Mind mapping and concept mapping | Mind maps and concept maps are very effective tools to use in communications as they can team to distil key ideas and concepts. Examples are Cmap (all the diagrams in this book are available from the website in this format), Mindjet, MindManager and MindMeister (an online tool which has recently added a range of new Internet facilities) |
| Web conferencing/Web collaboration | Web-conferencing and web-collaboration systems include basic tools such as Skype and Google HangOut; more advanced tools include Adobe Connect and Blackboard Collaborate |
| Wikis | Wikis are used typically by groups to construct knowledge bases – the most well-known being Wikipedia. There are a range of wiki tools available – e.g. PBWorks and Wikispaces |
| OER resources | There are a range of online repositories for open educational resources (OERs) – e.g. Jorum, OER Commons, ITunesU |
| Survey and polling tools | Survey tools provide the ability to create online surveys which can be used as part of learning programmes. Examples include SurveyMonkey and Poll Everywhere |

make available to prospective employers or customers and organisations can use them for staff development. On the website, we will show how you can take advantage of this development to review your own progress in communication.

You should also have a look at the Open Badges website itself – http://openbadges.org – and become familiar with the approach and philosophy so you can make the most of our suggestions.

## SUMMARY

- Review your more general goals and objectives as a starting point for reviewing your communication.
- Self-review is a key capability that all professionals should develop.
- Feedback from colleagues and co-workers can be especially valuable, but you need to make sure that it is helpful and focused.
- You need to review and manage your digital identity as best you can.
- A range of tools and new technologies are now available to support your professional development – you need to choose the ones which will give you the necessary support. At the very least, consider the opportunities offered by the Open Badges development.

## FURTHER READING

Gratton, L. (2014) *The Shift: The future of work is already here.* London: Williams Collins. You can find links to further resources and developments at www.lyndagratton.com.

Given our theme of reflecting more generally about your behaviour and aspirations before we look at communication specifics, all the following books offer useful ideas about how we can learn and change our behaviour:

Beattie, G. (2011) *Get the Edge: How simple changes will transform your life.* London: Headline.

Burkeman, O. (2011) *Help! How to become slightly happier and get a bit more done.* Edinburgh: Canongate.

Wiseman, R. (2012) *Rip it Up: The radically new approach to changing your life.* London: Macmillan.

These three books are good examples of self-help books based on recent research evidence – two written by professional psychologists and one by a commentator who always bases his analysis on current studies. Even so, you have to approach their conclusions with a critical perspective – for example, compare Beattie's analysis of the Mozart effect with other more critical discussions.

Dean, J. (2013) *Making Habits, Breaking Habits.* London: Oneworld. Also written by a psychologist, this book provides both research evidence and practical steps on changing our habits. Also worth consulting Dean's online blog: www.psyblog.co.uk.

Dweck, C.S. (2008) *Mindset: The new psychology of success.* New York: Ballantine. This book gives a full account of her work on the concept of mindset which you can follow up at http://mindsetonline.com/index.html.

Wilson, T.D. (2011) *Redirect: The surprising new science of psychological change.* London: Allen Lane.

This book suggests that we can make significant positive changes by 'learning to redirect the stories we tell ourselves' and offers various practical steps supported by research.

## Chapter 2

# How should we analyse communication?

## INTRODUCTION

We are concerned that many popular guides to 'improving your communication' (*and* some management training courses) do not spend enough time considering what is *meant* by 'communication'. We neglect this issue at our peril. Our understanding of what communication 'is' influences how we act, and influences how we analyse situations. It is important, both practically and theoretically, to work out what communication involves. So this chapter looks at how we define communication and how we can best understand the way communication 'works'.

We argue that you need to examine communication from two contrasting perspectives – analysing the process and interpreting the meanings. You *always* need to contrast and integrate these perspectives to decide what is happening. To demonstrate our approach, we analyse an example of a situation which virtually everyone has experienced – the first few hours of a new job. This shows that even simple everyday interactions are worth analysing in depth to unravel the complexities of communication.

We shall also use this situation to illustrate basic principles which inform the rest of this book and to introduce some thoughts on the use of new technology – how we can use new software both in preparation for and to support face-to-face communication.

### OBJECTIVES

*This chapter will*:

- show how our personal definitions of communication influence how we act;
- review popular models of communication and explain why we need a more complex approach;
- introduce our approach and basic principles which inform the rest of this book;
- outline a practical example of communication in the workplace and show how we can analyse it.

## COMMUNICATION AND ACTION

Deciding what we mean by communication is not just an academic exercise. As human beings, we *act* on the basis of our perceptions and beliefs. So if we have a particular view of human communication, then we will *act* on that view. If we have a faulty view, then our behaviour may cause problems. An example of how managers act on their perceptions and cause problems will make this point clearer.

Consider Fred Davis, recently promoted telecommunications manager, who is responsible for implementing new telephone, voicemail and email systems in a large organisation which has recently gone through a merger. We used this case in the first edition of this book, as described by Finn (1999), based on experiences with organisations implementing new technology. We are using it again to highlight the fact that some issues and problems are almost timeless – in today's world, Fred would consider different technologies but this would not resolve his difficulties. For example, as we see in Chapter 8, some organisations have abandoned email or are actively considering other methods. However, the problem here is not the technology – it is Fred's approach. He would suffer much the same problems whatever technology he decides on.

Back to the actual case. Fred did not have a good time: he received several messages from senior management who were unhappy with the new voicemail system; he found 700 complaints about the system in its first week; less than half the employees turned up for training sessions; and some units within the organisation purchased answering machines and cancelled their voicemail service. Fred was also worried because he knew that the organisation would have to switch to a new email system in the very near future or the computer network would not cope with the traffic. What made it even more frustrating for Fred was that he could not see where he had gone wrong. From the technical point of view, the changeover went very smoothly and the system can achieve everything which the organisation wants – but only if people use it properly.

### What was Fred's problem?

The main problem was his failure to manage. This was based on his *perception* of his role and his belief about how he should act and communicate as a manager. He sees himself as an expert and as a 'doer'. He makes decisions on his expert knowledge and then concentrates on making those decisions happen. During the planning and installation, he arranged everything in precise detail. What he did *not* do was communicate in any meaningful way with the prospective users of the new system. He did not make sure that the users knew exactly what was happening, why it was happening and how they could benefit from the new system. He had not built a consensus within the organisation which supported his plans. Of course, such communication would have slowed him down and he would not have been able to implement the system in such a short time. However, a system which is not used cannot be effective. In terms of the approach which we advocate, he failed on both counts – he did not consider the process of communication which could have assisted him and he did not think about the meanings which others in the organisations would read into his actions.

Unless managers like Fred reconsider their role very quickly, their careers will come to an abrupt end. Fred needed to think what managing really means and what he can achieve by working *with* and *through* other influential members of the organisation. Only by adopting a new managerial style will he be able to rescue the situation – 'he has not yet begun to shed his *doer* role to become an *enabler*' (Rogers *et al.*, 1999, p. 580). In the same way that we all have views about how to manage, which may be more or less effective, we also have views on how to communicate. In other words, we have an *implicit* view or theory of communication.

Compare Fred's approach with the strategy used by the developers of the Post-It note. This originated because scientists at 3M had developed a glue which was not very sticky. Rather than throw all their hard work away, the originator took time to investigate possible uses for a 'temporary' glue. He developed some trial products and gave them to colleagues to try them. They clamoured for more and he was able to develop a business plan which showed that there was already demand for the product. A new and very successful product line was launched.

## DIFFERENT VIEWS OF COMMUNICATION

If different views of communication have very real practical consequences, what are the main differences? Philip Clampitt (2010) suggests that managers typically use one of three different approaches to communication: the 'arrow', the 'circuit' and the 'dance'.

Arrow managers believe that communication operates one way, as in firing an arrow. If your aim is good, then you will hit the target. If you have a clear message, then you will communicate. On the positive side, arrow managers may well spend time working out their ideas and making sure that their messages and instructions are as specific as possible. However, as we shall see throughout this book, it can be very dangerous to see listeners as passive processors of information. It is also very difficult to construct messages which are absolutely unambiguous. Arrow managers can be insensitive to possible ambiguities in what they say and how they say it.

In contrast, circuit managers concentrate on communication as a two-way process, emphasising the importance of feedback. They usually emphasise the importance of good listening and trust in relationships. Clampitt argues that this approach also has some weaknesses. In particular, he feels that circuit managers can over-emphasise agreement and fail to recognise real differences in views which people can hold in the workplace. Circuit managers may assume that disagreement is simply a matter of poor communication and that more communication will almost automatically lead to agreement. It may be that more communication is necessary to work out *how and why* we have different opinions and values.

Clampitt concludes (and we agree) that the metaphor of dance is the most appropriate way of describing communication. To support this metaphor, he discusses a number of similarities between communication and dance, including:

- *Both are used for multiple purposes*. You can dance to entertain others, to impress your partner, to express yourself, and so on. In the same way, you can communicate for different reasons – to inform, to persuade, to impress, etc.
- *Both involve the co-ordination of meanings*. The importance of co-ordination is an obvious feature of dance. You have to know what your partner thinks is the best way of doing

the dance – you have to know what they are going to do next. When we communicate we also have to recognise how other people see the situation, recognise what they are doing and respond accordingly. We shall see how important this is in communication when we look at interpersonal skills.

- *Both are governed by rules*. There are sets of rules which apply to different types of dance: what sort of steps to use, how these steps are organised in sequence, what dress is appropriate. Again, in this book we shall see how different rules apply to different communication situations – ranging from the rules and conventions of grammar through to social rules and expectations. Also, these rules can change over time and be negotiated by the participants.

This analysis has very important practical implications – these different views of communication influence how we behave. Confronted by a similar situation, these three different types of manager will respond very differently. And this is why it is important to think very clearly about how we define communication and what that definition involves. How we think about communication will influence what we do. Confronted by misunderstanding or conflict, the arrow manager will perhaps focus on developing a 'clearer message'. If that manager has a misleading picture of the employees' assumptions, then this effort may be completely wasted or even lead to further conflict.

So you need to check how you think about situations (and be prepared to revise our thinking) before you decide how to act in them. The importance of our perceptions and beliefs is a theme which will be repeated many times in this book.

## ANALYSING COMMUNICATION

We suggest that you need to think about communication by putting together two different perspectives and working out if this is creating any gaps in understanding between the parties involved:

- Define the process: examine major components of the communication process and the sequence of events which is taking place.
- Interpret the meanings: investigate the social and cultural context, and the historical background to see how the participants *interpret* what is going on.

Once you can identify any differences in perceptions, you can develop your communication hypotheses and an appropriate action plan, as in Figure 2.1.

These two perspectives – process and meaning – are an extremely simplified version of communication theory. You can find much more complicated accounts from scholars such as Robert T. Craig or Stephen Littlejohn which you may wish to follow up (details are on the website). However, we want to home in on what we think is one of the most fundamental distinctions which causes practical difficulties – between an approach which assumes the importance of 'the message' and an approach which focuses on 'meaning'. In the rest of this chapter, we shall explain these different perspectives and show how you can put them together to arrive at a clearer picture of what communication involves.

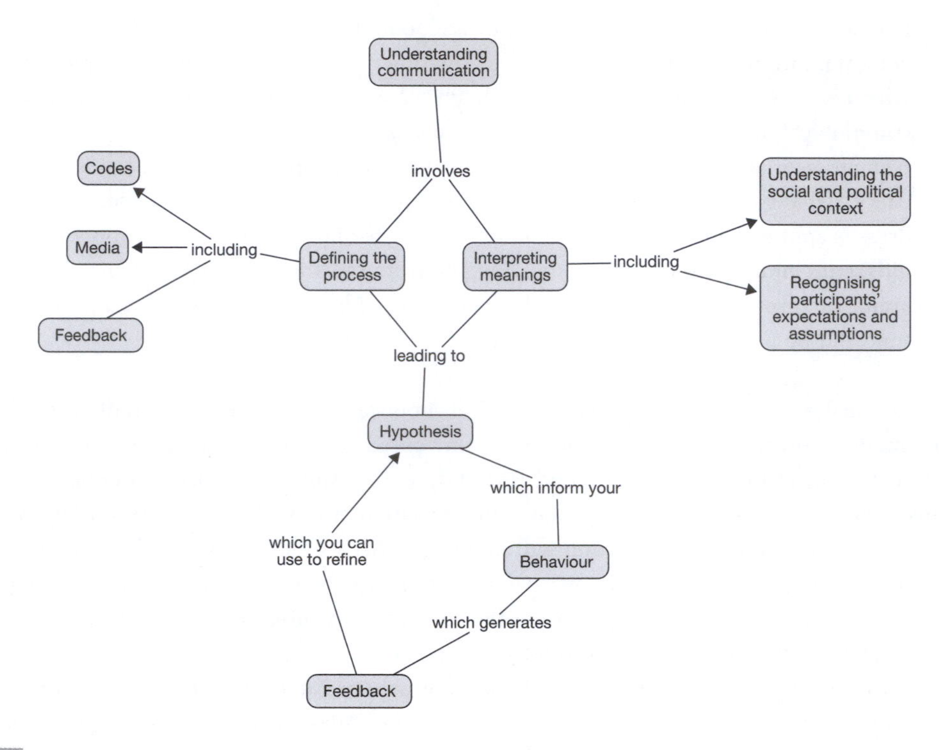


**Figure 2.1** *An integrated approach to analysing communication*

## Communication as process

The definition of communication in many management texts is based on a model first popularised in the 1950s, the so-called 'mathematical theory of communication'. This was developed from work on telecommunications systems. It aimed to show how information is transmitted from source to destination and to analyse what can affect the quality of the information during this process. The model then became very influential with researchers in human communication (see Littlejohn, 1983, or Mattelart and Mattelart, 1998, for a more extended account). This early model saw communication as essentially a one-way process with information passing from sender to receiver. The most important early development added a feedback loop. Various authors have added slightly different emphases but this basic model is still very common. For example, Bovee and Thill (2014) talk about different meanings which people can take from the same message but they offer an eight-step process model, which includes the following main concepts.

### *Codes*

A code is a coherent set of symbols plus the rules needed to structure a message. For example, a language code consists essentially of a list of words, and a set of rules for preparing a text. These rules are the grammar or syntax of the language.

### *Encoding and decoding*

Encoding is using a code to structure a message in an effort to achieve our communicative objective. Decoding is the reverse – we use our knowledge of the code to work out the meaning of a received message.

### *Media/channel*

This is the physical system which carries the message from sender to receiver, which can vary from the air carrying the voice between two speakers to something like an email where the author is separated from the reader by complicated electronic processes. Some texts use 'channel' for this concept and there is often confusion as to what constitutes a medium or a channel. Bovee and Thill use both concepts to distinguish between the '*form* a message takes (such as a Twitter update) and the channel as the system used to deliver the message (such as the Internet)' (ibid., p. 49).

### *Feedback*

Feedback refers to any signals which are received by the sender. In a face-to-face meeting this could include facial expression, gestures or other forms of body language.

One concept which you can often see in process models but which is not explicit in Bovee and Thill's is 'noise' – usually defined as any random input which distorts or which interferes with the transmission or reception of a message. This was a very important component of early models of communication systems which were used to consider the process of electronic communication. Noise may be external or internal. Examples of external noise are traffic noise making conversation difficult or electrical interference on a telephone line. An example of internal noise is a temporary irritation which causes a communicator to lose concentration, such as feeling tired or a headache. We have reservations about using this concept in human communication on the grounds that factors like the loss of concentration are not really random.

## Limitations of the process approach

The process approach has been fiercely criticised. We would highlight three criticisms which have very real practical implications:

- It does not take sufficient account of social or historical factors.
- It seems to assume that the meaning of an event is 'given', as opposed to 'negotiated' between the participants.
- It does not take account of business realities – it suggests one sender and one receiver, whereas most business communication involves 'multiple senders and multiple receivers' (Waller and Polonsky, 1998).

One response to these criticisms is to create a more complex model (as Waller and Polonsky did). However, more complex models still tend to imply that there is *one central message* which we can define unambiguously. This approach is not sufficient. We also need to emphasise the social and cultural background, and look at how meaning is developed and negotiated through interaction – we need to interpret the meanings.

## Interpreting the meanings

In order to fully understand how people communicate, we need to understand not just the immediate background but the much broader social context and history of their relationship. Not only do we have to examine how people *come to agree* on what is happening, but we also have to look at how they *feel* about events. The following two examples illustrate some of this complexity.

### *The case of the confused trainees*

A colleague of ours was invited to run residential training events for managers in a large manufacturing organisation. He came back from the first of these looking very dispirited, and complained that he could not understand the reactions from the group of managers, who were supposed to be very committed to personal development. There seemed to be at least three different reactions:

- some managers looked really interested and spent the weekend frantically scribbling notes;
- some managers seemed over-anxious and did not seem to be concentrating on the events;
- some managers seemed to see the event as a 'bit of a holiday'.

At the next event, he asked the managers *why* they had come, and found that *none* of the managers had been explicitly told why – their 'commitment' was a senior management *assumption*. As a result, they had tried to devise a meaning based on their own experience, which then coloured their reactions to the event.

The first group thought it was some kind of test which would influence their next promotion or regarding. They were doing all they could to impress the trainer as they were convinced that he was reporting back on them. The second group were worried that this training reflected problems with their performance and were mentally checking what they had done over the last six months to work out where/how they had failed. The third group saw the event as a reward for good behaviour which need not be taken too seriously.

Our colleague was only able to communicate with these groups *after* these expectations and assumptions had been uncovered and discussed openly. In other words, the training could not begin until the participants had *negotiated* the meaning of the training event.

### *War in the training room*

One of our colleagues was invited by the head of a training department to run a staff workshop on effective communication. The head was very insistent that the staff had requested this event. Arriving at the training room for the evening session, our colleague's first impression was of unease and tension. Although he delivered a session which usually received very positive feedback, he was unable to achieve any real dialogue with the staff who attended.

Over coffee, he started a conversation with one of the more friendly participants and eventually discovered what was going on. Staff had definitely *not* requested the event. In fact, they were involved in a longstanding and bitter dispute with the head over staffing and workload. This event was seen as the head asserting his authority. He was seen by staff as dogmatic, authoritarian and insensitive. We later discovered that the head felt that the staff were lazy and incompetent. Our colleague had inadvertently put himself in the firing line. The training session was a complete waste of time and only intensified the conflict. In this case it was not possible to negotiate an acceptable definition of the event, and our colleague retired hurt.

In both these cases, communication depended on a complicated history of events. People had developed shared meanings over time, which meant that communication was based on *very different* assumptions and expectations. Potential consequences in both situations were further misunderstanding and possible conflict.

If we look at the way people develop shared meanings, then we can also look at the way people express those meanings. In the last decade, organisational researchers have become very interested in the way people in organisations tell stories, tell jokes and use metaphors to describe what is going on in their organisation. These stories and metaphors can provide very useful insights into the way people typically behave and communicate in that organisation. Story-telling has now become a useful technique for uncovering organisational dynamics as well as being recommended to managers as a useful if not essential skill (Denning, 2011) – 'stories can be used to create change, build culture, disseminate learning, and capture knowledge' (Hutchens, 2009).

For an example of the power of these metaphors and how they can influence communication, consider the case of the Disney Corporation in the 1980s. Smith and Eisenberg (1987) analysed the metaphors then used by Disney employees and found two very strong metaphors in place – drama and family. Employees saw themselves as 'actors' using costumes to play out stories which would entertain the customers. They also used the concept of family not only to describe their relationship with customers, but also to characterise the relationship between management and employees. The strength of these feelings led to difficulties when, faced by increasing competition and other economic pressures, management cut various costs and benefits. For some employees, the way this was done destroyed the metaphor. The depth and strength of feeling led to union action and conflict. Smith and Eisenberg argued that the way for management to rescue this situation was by reconsidering these metaphors.

## CASE STUDY: FIRST DAY ON THE JOB

You have accepted a new job as a technical writer for a large engineering company. Read through the following account of what happens on your first day. We shall give our analysis later. As you read through it, note your opinions on:

- how you feel about the way you are treated;
- how the other members of the organisation communicate to you;
- how you would analyse the communication 'habits' of this organisation;
- how you could improve the communication to new members if you were the manager.

You arrive at the main entrance on the morning of your first day as requested in the formal letter you received offering you the job. You are somewhat apprehensive as you have been told by friends (after you accepted the job, unfortunately) that the company has a reputation for being rather formal and bureaucratic, and is rather old-fashioned in its use of technology. When you report to the security desk, the receptionist checks your details very carefully and then gives you directions.

After some time hunting round the large open office, you find the desk, chair, a small filing cabinet and a desktop computer (not quite as powerful as you hoped for) with an opening screen asking you to enter your network password. On the desk is a handwritten post-it note asking you to telephone the department head, Jan Thompson, when you arrive.

*How do you feel about the organisation so far?*

In a few minutes, Thompson walks in carrying a stack of printed manuals and a USB stick, gives you a handshake and smiles. The following conversation takes place.

THOMPSON: Welcome to Ace Products. Hope you like your new office space. Here are half a dozen manuals so you can see the kind of things we need to produce. The project briefs are on the USB stick. You won't be on our network yet so you won't be able to access them from the desktop. Read the stuff to get an idea of the work we do. Our administrator will bring over material on our new dump truck project which you will be working on. Tomorrow you will meet the engineer in charge of the project. Oh yes, please go down to the staff office some time today; they want to complete your records. If you have any questions, don't hesitate to ask, but I have to go to a meeting.

YOU: Thank you, I look forward to getting into the project. Also, I wonder if I could meet some of the salespeople who work with the kind of customers I will be writing for?

Thompson hesitates for a few moments, then looks away with a slight tilt of the head. You wonder what this means – could it be surprise? Does Thompson now think that you seem a little over-eager to make a good impression? Thompson says 'In due time' and leaves the room. You are convinced by Thompson's tone of voice that you have spoken out of turn.

*How do you feel about the organisation now?*

A little later you receive the following phone call from the administrator, who you have not met:

| | |
|---|---|
| DU TOIT: | This is Bobby du Toit speaking. I'm the administrator that Jan Thompson mentioned. |
| YOU: | Thank you. And can I have the file on the dump truck project? |
| DU TOIT: | I don't have the file. |
| YOU: | Oh, but Jan Thompson said you would let me have it. |
| DU TOIT: | Jan may have said that, but I haven't received it. When I receive it, you can be assured that you will get it immediately. |

*Looking back on these two conversations, how do you feel now about the organisation and your colleagues?*

## Returning to the first day at work – key issues from the process perspective

*Sender*: as both the initiator of the communication and the senior person, Thompson is the 'sender' and must take responsibility for the progress of the communication. But did he seem prepared and 'in charge'?

*Media*: Thompson used two media for his communication: a note and then face-to-face discussion. Is a hastily scribbled note appropriate first contact for a new employee? Face-to-face discussion is surely better but is undermined by Thompson's need to rush away.

Though close by, Du Toit chose to telephone. Was this a deliberate choice of media or a reflection of a very busy colleague?

*Message*: superficially, the messages exchanged are clear. But what attitudes did you see in the actions? Does Thompson see you as 'over-eager'? Did Du Toit really resent your request?

*Noise*: there is little by the way of physical noise to interfere with the message. You might consider your apprehension as internal or psychological noise.

*Feedback*: has Thompson received adequate feedback from you? Can you be sure that you have interpreted Thompson's feedback correctly?

## Outcomes of the process

The objective of initial communication with any new staff member is to help you become productive and contented in the shortest possible time. So the communication was unsuccessful.

There were several negative results:

- Several messages seem to confirm the view that the organisation is impersonal and bureaucratic.

- Thompson seems to consider that you are 'pushy' and over-eager, but there has been no additional feedback to confirm or disconfirm this.
- Du Toit seems to consider that you are 'pushy'.
- You feel Du Toit is officious and unfriendly.

The more fundamental problem is that most of these outcomes (if not all of them) are probably misconceptions which will take some time to dispel. And we have also ignored your own behaviour – how far did this influence the actions and reactions?

Going back to our earlier model, you also have to accept that all of these possible conclusions are based on hypotheses which you need to test or check. For example, you should not 'write off' Du Toit as 'unfriendly' – there may be a number of different reasons for the behaviours you observed.

## Analysing the meanings in the first day

Going back to our case study, think about how you would have felt in that situation. After your first hour in the office, which of the following statements would summarise your reactions so far?

a I feel disappointed that I have not been able to make a better impression. I did not realise that Thomson would be taken aback by my request about meeting the staff. I also did not intend to upset the secretary. Tomorrow I shall have to be a bit more cautious.

b I am angry that the organisation seems to care so little about new staff. The people at the reception desk did not know who I was and spent ages checking my papers. Thomson gave me an impossible task – reading all these manuals today – and then got upset because I showed some initiative. I was also annoyed because our administrator was so abrupt and inefficient. If things don't get better quickly, I shall be looking out for a better opportunity.

c I am puzzled by the confusion and lack of organisation. There did not seem to be any systematic preparation for my arrival and I am not sure what impression I made on the other staff. Thomson seems pleasant but does not seem to know how I am supposed to fit in. There seem to be issues about status and formality which I need to work out.

Of course, there are other possible interpretations of the situation, but these three show how you can arrive at very different meanings by adopting a different perspective on the same series of events. These different perspectives reflect:

- different emphases on different events;
- different interpretations of the motives behind other people's behaviour;
- different personal priorities and agendas ('I want to be accepted' in (a), compared with 'I deserve to be well-treated' in (c)).

Another implication of these three different accounts is their very different implications for future behaviour: perception – creates expectations – leads to specific behaviour and communication. The first person will be trying harder tomorrow but will also be guarded about what they say and what they do. The second person will be looking for further evidence of poor treatment and perhaps being a bit impatient. The third person will be looking for more evidence to work out what is really going on.

These differences also reflect more broader expectations – remember you had heard that the organisation was formal and bureaucratic. With a different expectation, the first day could have had more or less impact on you. And this is why we always need to consider communication from these two perspectives – defining the process and analysing the meaning. To add to the complexity, we have not fully discussed the meanings which Thompson or du Toit interpreted from the day's events. What implications could these have for future working relationships?

### What were your assumptions?

When you imagined how you would feel about the first day at this office, what were your images of the people involved? We deliberately left their identities ambiguous. For example, did you *assume* that the manager was male and the administrator was female? Would your perceptions change if the genders were different? Would it make any difference if they came from different social or cultural backgrounds – would this change your expectations? We examine complexities of communication caused by different social backgrounds later in this book.

As a final example, you will see that we have not fully explained one part of the case study – Thompson's reaction to your request to meet the sales staff. Was this simply surprise at an unexpected question? Could it be that Thompson was trying to be informal and 'low-key' as a deliberate tactic to make you feel welcome? Or did Thompson's reaction indicate something more significant? Suppose there has been some conflict in the recent past between the sales staff and Thompson's department. Have you unwittingly implied that you already know the politics of the organisation? You can only decide between these alternatives by more detailed investigation.

So we must beware of simple models of communication and try to take account of the full range of historical and cultural factors which influence how we think and behave. We must be critical of our own models and presuppositions.

## PLANNING COMMUNICATION: WHAT COULD/SHOULD HAVE HAPPENED?

Induction can be done in various ways – e.g. by personal discussion, arranging for a mentor, and supplying policy and procedure manuals online in advance. Departments should have clear procedures on the induction of staff.

However, remember the meaning: a highly planned process like this *should* improve the organisation's chances of building positive attitudes in new employees. But it could be carried out very mechanically and actually send the wrong message – e.g. 'this is something we have to do but we do not really care about you'. So we must always watch out for the way that meanings are developed and negotiated, as we shall see in later chapters.

This case study highlighted the importance of communication within the induction process. There is evidence from recent surveys that induction is often done very badly. This is an area where we need more research on the ways new staff are integrated (or not) into the organisation, especially on how the organisation communicates the 'content' of socialisation – the values, norms, beliefs, skills and knowledge which are expected of the organisation's members.

## AND SO TO BASIC PRINCIPLES

This case study illustrates basic principles which underpin all our other chapters. There is more discussion of the principles on the website.

### Principle 1

*You can improve (but not guarantee) your chances of 'success' in communication if you have clear purpose(s) and select appropriate strategies.*

Your chances of effective communication can be improved if you can decide what you really want to achieve and then selecting the best strategy to make this happen. However, this cannot guarantee success and there is no 'one best way' which will work all the time.

One of our starting points is the fact that humans are *always* interpreting the meaning of events on the basis of the information available. Whatever our message it will have *some* effect on our audience and we should at least be clear in our own minds what outcome we wish to achieve. If we are unclear, then our audience will be more so.

We can also cause difficulties in two ways: by having vague or inconsistent objectives and/or by choosing an inappropriate strategy.

### Principle 2

*Communication always means more than 'the message'.*

To communicate effectively, you need to anticipate how 'messages' will be interpreted in context. And there is never 'just one message'. No matter how simple the situation, you can always think of a number of different messages which can be exchanged. You need to consider the meanings which will be 'taken' from your behaviour. Ambiguity is an inherent feature of both language and non-verbal communication.

Ambiguity can be worse if some forms of digital communications are used as there can be less opportunity to interpret meaning through signals which we take for granted in face-to-face communication – e.g. voice tone, body language, etc. Hence, it is important to ensure clarity and use of plain language when using digital forms like email or Twitter.

This also suggests some very simple approaches we can use to support this principle:

- recognising that ambiguity is an inevitable feature of human communication;
- looking for feedback and checking understanding;
- accepting that others' interpretations are legitimate;
- realising that discussion is essential to arrive at clear, shared meaning;
- recognising that some forms of digital communication provide limited opportunities for effective discussion and interpreting messages through non-verbal cues.

Do these approaches characterise everyday interactions in your organisation?

## Principle 3

*Communication is always based in a specific social, cultural and technological context.*

We need to recognise the constraints which influence communication because of the social, historical and technological context in which it occurs, and respond accordingly. We will criticise attempts to provide guidelines or techniques for communication which ignore the context. For example, many management texts endorse the values of assertiveness without referring to the research which shows that assertive behaviour may be seen as aggressive or inappropriate in certain cultural settings or by certain individuals.

This principle is very important in a situation of change. Management who wish to introduce new processes or procedures should be sensitive to the meaning of the existing patterns of behaviour.

## Principle 4

*Communication and action must 'match'.*

Your verbal and non-verbal communication must express the same meaning if you are to be believed. If your body language contradicts what you say, then the other person will have to choose which channel to believe. Early research suggested that the non-verbal channel would always be believed and many popular handbooks simply repeat this conclusion. We now know that it is more complicated, but we do know that we are very sensitive to this sort of ambiguity. If your speech and body language do not agree, then this will almost certainly be noticed and interpreted by your audience.

Linked to this idea is the oft-quoted statement that 'you cannot not communicate'. In other words, failing to act can be seen as meaningful. For example, how do staff feel about the chief executive who always stresses the importance of communication in public meetings and media interviews but who never contributes anything to the staff newsletter?

And this suggests how to follow this principle – act in the way that you say that you do. Of course, there may be some issues of interpretation and these should be sorted out as soon as possible. The management team who announce that they have an 'open door' policy to all employees should clarify what they mean with some examples or through discussion. It is very easy to set up expectations with a snappy slogan which makes claims that are obviously over-optimistic when you consider the likely interpretation by the audience.

The use of email and social media in organisations makes this even more important as it is so easy for anything that is digitally distributed to reach large audiences instantaneously and for large groups to discuss what you have said and done (or not done) – even if they were not part of your intended audience. Generally, it is best to assume that anything you say or send electronically can reach people who you did not intend to communicate with.

## Principle 5

*Communication can always be improved.*

Although we accept that some people are inherently more skilled in their communication, we can all improve our skills with the right coaching or preparation.

As we said in the previous chapter, if you believe that communication can be improved, then you will devote time to at least some of the following activities:

- reviewing the impact of your own behaviour on others;
- requesting feedback from others;
- developing strategies or plans to improve your communication;
- developing your digital literacy, including the ability to choose the appropriate means of traditional or digital communications for a specific context and audience;
- developing your skills in self-review;
- trying new techniques and reviewing their effectiveness.

## Principle 6

*Communication is a fundamental management responsibility (which we must all share).*

If management do not accept responsibility for the quantity and quality of communication (both traditional and digital) in the organisation, then who will? Management must take responsibility – but this does not absolve us all from our responsibility to behave effectively and ethically.

This principle can be translated into practice in various ways. For example, we can ask how far the behaviour of managers at all levels throughout the organisation reflects concern for and commitment to communication.

This has been a longstanding concern for organisation theorists. Our first edition referred to Werner David's (1995) five fundamental steps:

- making a senior manager formally responsible for 'linking every employee into the communication network' (p. 4);
- systematic training in communication;
- building the organisation's communication network in a way which uses all the available media and which is especially sensitive to information which indicates the need for change;
- continually monitoring the network to make sure it works effectively;
- costing communication so that its effectiveness can be measured.

As with all general strategies, there are possible pitfalls. For example, the notion of making one senior manager 'responsible' could lead to other managers 'leaving it to him or her' rather than taking equal responsibility. Costing is difficult to organise and monitor. Furthermore, these ideas were developed in 1995, before the advent of social media and mobile devices. We now work in a world where business and technology are tightly integrated, allowing individuals to communicate in a multitude of ways with large audiences, both within the boundaries of 'corporate' systems and externally with the world at large. This places an even greater need for management to take responsibility and be able to balance open communications with communication protocols that address corporate needs relating to, for example, confidentiality, intellectual property, privacy, data protection and other compliance agendas. At the very least, the fundamental steps listed above need to be enlarged with, for example, systematic staff training in digital literacies and development of communications protocols for staff. Although we have reservations about some aspects of David's approach, we wholeheartedly agree with the overall concept – that management should have an explicit strategy which is regularly reviewed.

## Principle 7

*New media can and should enhance communication.*

We now have a wider choice of communication media than at any time in history. These media can make a profound and positive impact if they are carefully introduced and maintained.

We will discuss various aspects of new media throughout the book, including:

- The use of intranet and Internet technologies to distribute information both within and outside the organisation.
- The use of social media, such as blogs, wikis, social networks, etc. For example, tools such as Twitter can support teams in sharing ideas and information, building knowledge-bases and task management.
- The potential of all these technologies and media to support cost-efficient (or 'lean') ways of working and new business relationships – e.g. global teams, partnership working, supply chain working.
- The application of real-time conferencing – e.g. audio/video-conferencing, web-conferencing – to enable meetings which might otherwise be too expensive to sustain.

All of these examples depend on management strategy – management will invest to provide the facilities and then the commitment to sustain the appropriate use of this technology. We do not have to look far to find examples of computer failures and the repercussions for the organisation.

However, we can learn from the mistakes of the past and devise effective ways of using new technology to augment human aptitudes. And the same is true of communication in general. Reflecting on some of the problems and pitfalls of human communication in organisations can show us how to avoid them, provided we are prepared to take the responsibility.

## Principle 8

*Digital literacy should be a core part of staff professional development.*

Digital communications are becoming so integral to business operations and working practices that what is now known as 'digital literacy' must be considered a prerequisite for staff skills.

Professional development in organisations has to place more emphasis on:

- self-directed awareness and learning about new technologies, particularly awareness of the capability and potential of new technology;
- forensic ability in finding, analysing, using and managing information;
- effective practices of digital communication – e.g. collaboration and participation in networks, sharing, facilitation, mentoring, coaching, critiquing, group learning etc.;
- effective practices of critical reading, creative production, persuasion, argument, expressing and sharing ideas;
- knowing how to choose and apply technologies to cost-effective business practices – e.g. project management, product innovation, sales and marketing, finance, lean working, team working – with an understanding of broader contexts;
- ability to influence colleagues and the organisation in adoption of appropriate communication technologies.

## Principle 9

*The ability to influence has become a key communication skill in modern organisations.*

Most current working practices are predicated on group-working with the days of the isolated lone-worker long gone. To be an effective team-worker requires the specific communications skill to influence others towards achieving goals.

### SUMMARY

- Our understanding of communication influences the way we behave.
- Some managers define communication as a linear process which may or may not incorporate feedback. This definition is not sufficient and can be misleading in many situations.
- You can analyse human communication from at least two different perspectives – the process perspective and the interpretive perspective.
- The process perspective emphasises the way messages are constructed and delivered, and the various factors which influence how those messages are received.
- The interpretive perspective emphasises the meaning which we perceive in situations. This meaning is often the result of complicated historical and cultural processes.
- We need to consider both process and interpretive perspectives when we examine specific examples of business communication. And we need to define both the intended and the received meanings.

## FURTHER READING

Clampitt, P.G. (2010) *Communicating for Managerial Effectiveness* (4th edn). Thousand Oaks, CA: Sage.

Chapter 1 provides a set of propositions which can help us understand communication. Chapter 2 gives a detailed explanation of the three views which managers seem to adopt. As well as this and other useful texts, Philip has produced an excellent website with useful resources: www.uwgb.edu/clampitp/Phils%20Site/Internet_Broadcast/index.html. We hope that our book also endorses and reflects his teaching philosophy, quoted on the website as 'to help you become a thoughtful, strategic, and professional communicator'.

Hargie, O. and Tourish, D. (eds) (2009) *Auditing Organizational Communication: A handbook of research, theory and practice.* London: Routledge.

If you want to investigate broader perspectives on the role of communication in organisations, this is a good place to start.

Chapter 3

# What does communication mean?

## INTRODUCTION

You cannot transmit your mental images, ideas and feelings directly to another person, unless you believe in telepathic communication. We have to translate or encode our thoughts in such a way that others can receive and interpret what we think.

This encoding is the focus of this chapter. We introduced the notion of codes in the last chapter but we need to analyse the variety of codes we use in everyday communication. We focus on both verbal and non-verbal codes and consider how much scope there is for ambiguity and interpretation. If we can anticipate how other people will interpret what we say and do, then we can make our communication more effective. We now have a range of new media we can use for communication which we can employ to both reinforce and extend our face-to-face contact.

Of course, we also need to bear in mind the implications of the last chapter – communication is not just the transmission and reception of information. No matter how carefully we feel we have 'encoded our message', we need to be aware of all the factors which can influence how other people will interpret our behaviour.

**OBJECTIVES**

*This chapter will*:

- introduce the range and variety of human communication codes;
- explain why we need to think of human language as a collection of multiple and overlapping codes;
- examine the nature and scope of non-verbal communication, and its relationship with language;
- identify practical implications for the appropriate use of language and non-verbal codes in business communication;
- identify some new possibilities created by the use of new technology.

## WHAT ARE THE DIFFERENT CODES WE USE TO COMMUNICATE?

There are several ways of categorising the different codes we use to communicate with each other. For example, Ellis and Beattie (1986) identified 'five primary systems of communication' which occur in face-to-face interactions (p. 17):

- *Verbal* – i.e. all the words, clauses and sentences which we use in speech and writing.
- *Prosodic* – i.e. all the stress and pitch patterns such as pauses and intonation which we use in speech and which are 'linguistically determined' – we use them to punctuate the speech and make its meaning clear. Ellis and Beattie give the simple phrase, 'old men and women', as an example. If you leave a silent pause after 'men' when you say this sentence, then it changes the meaning.
- *Paralinguistic* – i.e. all the pauses, 'ums', 'ahs' and other sounds which are not 'real' words and which do not have a clear linguistic function.
- *Kinesic* – i.e. all the ways we move our bodies during communication, including our posture, gestures, and so on.
- *Standing features* – i.e. more static non-verbal features such as appearance, orientation (the angle at which you stand to the other person) or distance.

There are two main issues with this and with other systems of classification:

- Does this mean that the different systems 'work' in different ways? Do we somehow interpret or process them differently?
- Do the different systems have different functions? For example, it is often suggested that non-verbal signals communicate our emotions better than words.

Both these issues have important practical implications. For example, what do you attend to when you are meeting someone for the first time? Do you concentrate on what they are saying or on some aspect of their non-verbal behaviour? How would you give them some clues that you liked them – what signals would you use?

As we shall see in the rest of this chapter, these issues are not easily resolved. For example, based on more recent research, Beattie suggested that gesture is one code with particular characteristics which we explain later. For the moment, we shall use the distinction between verbal and non-verbal codes but emphasise that the most important issue is how they work together to create a particular meaning.

## UNDERSTANDING HUMAN LANGUAGE

We agree with Michael Clyne (1994) who suggested that language has four main functions. We use language as:

1. Our most important medium of human communication.
2. A means of identification. We use language to express our membership of social groups, which may be national, ethnic, social, religious, etc.

3 A means of intellectual development. The way that children learn and develop their language skills is very strongly related to the way they experience their surrounding environment. In adulthood, we use language to develop new ways of thinking and new concepts.
4 An instrument of action. Much of what we say is directly linked to what we do. When we promise or apologise, we are not simply passing on information.

Although this book concentrates on function (1), we must recognise the practical implications of the other functions. People who concentrate on function (2) may have very strong views on what language use is appropriate in a given situation – see later and in Chapter 9 for a further discussion of this. Function (4) can cause difficulties if we do not recognise the action implications of what we say. This may be especially important in cross-cultural encounters, as we see in Chapter 6 when we discuss business English as an international language.

## Language and social identity

You can see the importance of language as a symbol of broader social identities in the following examples:

- The campaign for 'official English' in the USA aims to ensure that English is the only language used for official functions. As their website explains: 'U.S.ENGLISH, Inc. is the nation's oldest, largest citizens' action group dedicated to preserving the unifying role of the English language in the United States. Founded in 1983 by the late Senator S.I. Hayakawa, an immigrant himself, U.S. English now has 1.8 million members nationwide' (www.us-english.org/view/3).
- The French Academy has attempted to protect the French language from 'foreign' words and expressions. For example, they tried to stop female ministers in the French government from using the female prefix to describe themselves (*la ministre*) as this departed from the traditional masculine form (*le ministre*). More recently, the Academy has tried to thwart the attempt by some French universities to teach all their courses in English (www.thedailybeast.com/articles/2013/05/30/france-s-pointless-hopeless-battle-against-english.html).

These movements are based on the idea that some varieties of language are inherently inferior. They try to define one version of the language which can be accepted as the ideal or standard. They face serious challenges on both these counts. All languages grow and develop. Any attempt to 'police' a language which does not recognise these processes is unlikely to succeed.

## Codes within language

Language is not just a carrier of information – it can convey various levels of meaning depending on the situation. In even a simple conversation, there may be several different codes which we can recognise:

A: I'm getting an error message – could be a driver problem.
B: OK, Bones, what are you going to do about it? They're all supposed to have the 3.5 upgrade.
A: Obviously you need to try it on the other two machines first.

In this brief conversation between two people trying to get a computer program to work properly for a demonstration, we can see various codes at work:

- technical jargon as in 'driver problem';
- the joke based on a Star Trek character;
- the private joke over who does what – 'you' do this.

All of these depend upon the relationship between A and B, recognising that they both understand the jargon, recognising the joke and the verbal sparring. B would have adopted a very different tone with a relative stranger or a new boss.

This example illustrates Kurt Danziger's view that all communication simultaneously works on two levels:

- the presentation of information (he calls this representation);
- the presentation of a particular relationship which is implied in what is said and how it is expressed (he calls this presentation) (Danziger, 1976).

He shows how certain individuals are very conscious of this distinction and manipulate what they say to entrap the other person in a particular relationship. His examples include sales representatives and interrogators. This is *not* the same as the distinction between verbal and non-verbal codes as we can express a relationship both verbally and non-verbally. One very important practical implication here is that we need to review both *what* we communicate and *how* we do it. We need to establish the appropriate relationship as well as convey the appropriate information.

## Language variety

Here we need to introduce three main concepts: register, dialect and accent. All of these have important practical implications – people have expectations about the 'correct' register for a particular occasion and will make judgements about the people they meet on the basis of their dialect and accent.

### *Register*

The English language is not a single coherent body. Different groups use different subsets of the language to suit their purposes, so we can identify the characteristics of different subsets or registers. For example, one early study of scientific reports found common features which were very rare in everyday conversation, such as compound nouns, passives, conditionals, prepositional verbs, and so on.

Without going too far into these linguistic technicalities, you can recognise the main features of the different registers, as in Box 3.1. The important implication is that certain registers are accepted as the norm in certain situations even if they are not very 'efficient', as we shall show later in the discussion of plain English in Chapter 6. If you select the wrong register, then you can very easily create the wrong impression. A personal anecdote to illustrate – the university selection panel for the new Web design consultancy included senior, experienced academics and managers, both male and female. The young Web designer who started his pitch with 'we can really do a good job for you guys' and then kept referring to the panel as 'guys' effectively lost the job for his company. His choice of register was interpreted as insensitive and pushy, not the basis for effective collaboration and communication.

## BOX 3.1 A COMPILATION OF REGISTERS

How would you describe the register of the following extracts? Which is the closest to your idea of 'good' business writing? And why?

- Did you like the previous version? Did you? Well? We would have liked it a lot more if it was, um, a bit better.
- Gold discoveries were like No. 11 buses yesterday. None came for ages, then three arrived at once.
- ABC Industries, the financial services conglomerate which is breaking itself up, is poised to go out with more of a whimper than a bang.
- Fed up with the same old job? Then it's time for a change! Full training and uniform provided plus above average rates.
- If you think we are just another high street retailer, allow us to open your eyes. This is a company that leads the field in many different sectors of retail, from small electrical goods to toys, from jewellery to furniture. Our computer technology is among the most sophisticated in the business, our stock- control systems are the best around and we offer convenient shopping along with convenient service that keeps the customers coming back.

The first extract is from a computer games magazine; the rest are from a mass circulation British newspaper – the first two from the editorial in the business section and the last two from job advertisements (security guards and store managers respectively). All are from UK sources. What differences would you expect to see in, say, North American examples?

### *Dialect*

A dialect is a language variety which is characteristic of a region or a socioeconomic group. In England, for example, there are a wide variety of regional dialects such as Cockney, Liverpool (Scouse).

Over the years in Britain there has been considerable pressure to achieve what has been known as 'Standard English'. Despite growing acceptance of regional dialects, most people still consider some dialects 'better' than others. This is also true in other parts of the world with other languages – we cannot look at the way language is used without investigating the *opinions* people have about language variety. We can illustrate the problems this may cause by looking at the impact of different accents.

### *Accent*

Accent is often confused with dialect because a non-standard accent is often associated with a non-standard dialect. Accent refers to the distinctive pronunciation which characterises a group or a geographical area. In a country like Great Britain, accents tend to be regional – e.g. Scots, Welsh, Irish, Yorkshire, etc.

Research confirms that certain accents are more highly regarded than others, and some organisations are deliberately selecting staff to deal with customers on the basis of these perceptions. This regard for certain accents may vary from country to country and from group to group. Of course, many people deliberately cultivate an accent as a means of reinforcing group or cultural identity.

The great danger in our attitude to people with an accent that differs from our own is that we stereotype them with attributes that have little or nothing to do with ways of speaking, as in the British examples a few paragraphs above. For example, we tend to consider people less well (or better) educated merely because they speak with a different accent. Of course, people may also discriminate against a particular accent in order to discriminate on racial or class grounds.

## Structural features of language

Every language has certain structural features which have implications for how we communicate in (and how we learn) that language. For example, if I tell you 'it rained last night', you have no way of knowing from this whether I know this because I was there, or because I heard the weather forecast, or from some other source. If I was speaking to you in the Hopi language, the source of my information would be clear from what I said. In other words, the language specifies the context as well as the event or information.

Among the most interesting features of the English language are the following.

### *Expanding and developing vocabulary*

We can find many English words that appear in dictionaries but which are virtually extinct as far as everyday use is concerned. Does it matter if we no longer use terms such as velleity, aposiopesis or the mycoclonic jerk, two of which are highlighted as errors by my Microsoft spell-checker (Bryson, 1990, p. 60)? There is the regular debate in the British media over which new words should be recognised in the next edition of the *Oxford English Dictionary*. As with many aspects of language, this can generate heated debate.

The important principle for our purposes is that new expressions are appearing all the time in various ways:

- We borrow words from other languages, such as 'shampoo' from India or 'ketchup' from China.
- We put new meanings into old words. An obvious example here is the word 'gay'.
- We add or subtract parts from old words, usually by abbreviating them. So examination becomes exam, television becomes TV, and so on. Sometimes we can take a longstanding word (such as political) and add to it to create a new expression. According to Bill Bryson, the word 'apolitical' appeared in 1952 (ibid., p. 76)
- We create new words, usually by making some analogy. So we now talk of politicians talking in 'sound bites' to mean short snatches of political rhetoric, a phrase that first became popular during the 1988 American elections.
- Oxford Dictionaries issue a quarterly newsletter with 'new words' which have become accepted in everyday speech and writing. For example, the November 2013 update includes 'merch', 'slow jam' and 'frack' (www.oxforddictionaries.com).

### *Multiple meanings for words*

An example here would be 'set' – this has 58 uses as a noun, 126 uses as a verb and 10 uses as an adjective. Many other words have multiple meanings and we have to work out how they are being used from the context.

### *Variety in pronunciation*

The English language has more sounds than many others. This can be a particular problem for many language learners, especially when we find that many spellings and pronunciations do not match (e.g. how would you pronounce 'chough'?) There are also changes in pronunciation which seem to reflect changing fashion and the obvious variations in dialect. These variations can be quite dramatic.

### *Variety in spelling*

According to linguistics expert David Crystal, 'English spelling is difficult, but is not as chaotic as is often claimed' (Crystal, 2013, p. 6). He explains the ways that English spelling has gone through several historical changes and that understanding these changes provides important clues to correct spelling and explains many of the seeming inconsistencies.

### *Flexible syntax*

We do have rules of grammar but no formal ruling body to enforce them. As we shall see in Chapter 8, some rules are more 'powerful' than others and they are subject to change over time.

The important practical implication of these features is that we cannot simply rely on a dictionary to choose the most effective language in a given situation. We need to assess the situation and context. For example, how can we recognise when a word or expression has become sufficiently accepted so that it can be used, especially in more formal situations such as a written report or a public meeting? This depends on the audience. For example, are they familiar with expressions which arise from popular culture? In a business document, would you use any of the following phrases which we picked out of recent British daily papers: 'road rage', 'spin doctor', 'trend towards retro' and 'prosecution of spam king'? Or do you have an audience which is openly hostile to 'trendy catch-phrases' or to 'Americanisms'? There is also the question of business jargon and we now have several guides to jargon which has now gone 'past its sell-by date' and is probably best avoided (e.g. Taggart, 2011).

## Speaking versus writing

There is a longstanding academic debate about the differences between spoken and written language. The following table gives some common distinctions.

**Table 3.1** *Spoken vs. written language*

| *Characteristic* | *Spoken language* | *Written language* |
|---|---|---|
| Universality | Everyone can speak | Still some problems of literacy which can exclude certain individuals and groups |
| Complexity | Tends to be less complex, using simpler sentences | Often uses complex sentences and expressions |
| Rate of change | More likely to change, and at a faster rate | Less change, likely to change much slower |
| Formality | Likely to use many colloquial terms | Likely to use more 'official' terms and avoid colloquial or slang expressions |

This comparison uses ideas from analyses published by the Linguistics Society of America etc. For a more detailed analysis, see Baron (2008). But how far are these differences affected by context? And what about new media, which seem to muddy the distinction between spoken and written language. For example, text messages are delivered as written messages but often read more like extracts from a conversation. If you then add in all the abbreviations in common use, how do you classify a text message? Naomi Baron concludes that instant messaging is more like speech than text in terms of overall characteristics, but she found some interesting gender differences to complicate the issue – e.g. that females tended to use a style that was more similar to their writing style. And this debate has important practical significance when we consider the impressions we make on each other. We return to this issue when we look at business messages in Chapter 8. For the moment, we can highlight some of the issues and emotions related to texting in Box 3.2.

**BOX 3.2 'TEXT MESSAGES DESTROYING OUR LANGUAGE'**

David Crystal uses this headline from an American paper in 2007 to illustrate some of the negative reactions to texting (Crystal, 2009, p.8). As well as being surprised by 'the extraordinary antipathy to texting' from certain commentators, Crystal suggests that many common beliefs about texting are simply 'wrong, or at least debatable' (ibid., p. 9), including that:

- It is only used by young people. In fact, texting is used by a wide age range.
- It hinders literacy. He reports a number of studies, which suggests that texting helps or supports literacy.
- Text language is increasingly having an impact on language in general. He suggests that the relatively small number of text messages in comparison to all messages means that 'its long-term impact on the already existing varieties of language is likely to be negligible' (ibid., p. 10).

## OTHER BUSINESS CODES

There are other important codes to mention, especially re written communication. Numerical and mathematical conventions and systems can be analysed as examples of communication codes. Graphic codes, such as illustrations and diagrams, are widely used to avoid problems associated with communicating to people of different languages, but we cannot always assume that graphic symbols will be universally understood and this can be very important, especially with health and safety information. (We examine issues of graphic codes in Chapter 7.)

## NON-VERBAL CODES

When the media talk about non-verbal communication or body language, they often focus on what is known as kinesics – the fourth communication system we introduced at the beginning of this chapter. Signals which have been studied under this heading include facial expression, eye contact, gesture and body posture. Much of the time, such communication is unconscious. The face in particular signals a wide range of emotions and there seems to be a range of 'basic emotions' which are very similar across many cultures. A number of classic studies and analyses suggest that there are six fundamental emotional states: happiness, surprise, fear, sadness, anger, and disgust/contempt (for example, see the work of Paul Ekman at: www.paulekman.com/paul-ekman/). There are a number of training courses and resources which use these categories to help you interpret emotions correctly. However, this has been challenged by recent research at the University of Glasgow using new techniques and software (Jack *et al.*, 2014). This research suggests four 'biologically basic emotions' and a hierarchy which has developed over time to signal other emotional states. For example, they suggest that fear/surprise is one basic category. These two emotions can be confused by viewers as they start from the same bodily movement – raised eye-lid – but then are distinguished by different following movements. The same applies to anger/disgust, starting from the nose wrinkle. The researchers are now extending this work to look at cultural differences. The important practical consequence of this is that we may need to re-examine some training methods to give a more sophisticated insight into how we judge these emotional states. And it is worth questioning your own assumptions about the meaning of non-verbal signals, as we explore further in Chapter 9.

We do seem to interpret facial expressions in terms of clear categories rather than as a continuum. This can have unusual consequences. If you suffer a particular brain injury, you will find it difficult to recognise certain facial expressions but not others. You may recognise happiness and surprise but not fear or anger.

There is an enormous amount of research on different non-verbal signals. This has focused on how different signals are used and what they usually mean. For example, eye contact signals interest and helps to control social interaction. Body posture often signals the attitude towards the interaction, whether it is tense, relaxed, interested or bored. Gestures are often used for submission. Sometimes gestures become ritualised as in an army salute. Body posture can also become ritualised as in bowing, kneeling, etc.

In this chapter, we shall highlight important aspects of non-verbal codes, as follows.

### *Non-verbal codes may contradict the verbal*

Often body language contradicts a spoken message and we say that the sender does not 'mean what he says' and is insincere. This raises another fundamental question which we return to later – how far can you become skilled at reading body language?

### *Non-verbal messages can be very important*

Many books about NVC which are aimed at general readers make similar claims about its 'power'. For example, Judi James (1995) suggested that certain research did 'discover exactly what it is that contributes to the total message' (p. 9), as follows:

- Verbal – 7 per cent
- Tone of voice – 38 per cent
- Visual – 55 per cent.

These statistics are based on studies from the 1960s and are typically used to support claims like 'most of the messages in any interaction with another person (face-to- face) are revealed through body signals or "bodytalk"' (Borg, 2013, p. 61) or that 'eye contact can account for as much as 55 per cent of information transmission in a given conversation' (Dutton, 2011, p. 72). Unfortunately this does *not* reflect how NVC really works in everyday practice and we will explain why in Chapter 9. See the website for further analysis.

Despite the fact that subsequent research has painted a much more complicated picture, this finding is still regularly repeated and often without any attempt to suggest any reservations (e.g. Hasson, 2014). Do *not* rely upon these statistics, which are actually difficult to interpret. Research has shown that non-verbal signals *can* be very important but they may not be so dominant in every situation. We must *always* consider the relationship between the words and the non-verbal cues.

### *Non-verbal communication cannot be avoided*

You cannot avoid sending non-verbal signals. Even the purposeful avoidance of contact by one or both parties sends a signal that they do not wish to communicate. Eye contact, a smile or a proffered handshake all signal/varying degrees of willingness to communicate.

### *Much non-verbal communication is culture-bound*

Some non-verbal behaviour appears to be universal – we have already mentioned the 'basic, strong emotions' such as fear, surprise, sadness, and so on. However, the expression of less intense emotions and general social feelings is much more culture-bound. For example, in many situations in British and American culture, failure to 'look a person in the eye' is interpreted as shiftiness. However, in many African and Hispanic cultures averting the eyes is a mark of respect for a person of higher status. Similarly, the American 'OK' hand sign has an obscene or vulgar meaning in other countries as diverse as Brazil and Greece.

As a result, we now have books which offer dictionaries of non-verbal signs and guides to 'correct' non-verbal expression in a range of cultures. There are obvious problems with all these generalisations, including whether they apply equally across a culture and whether they are changing. There is also the problem of deciding which rules are current and which are really important. For example, Morris (1994) observed that, in England, 'men's shirts should not have pockets' (p. 114) – which means that both of us have to buy a new wardrobe!

But how can we make sense of these differences? McDaniel (1997) argues that non-verbal behaviour reflects or represents dominant cultural themes. He uses the example of Japanese culture where there are a number of clear themes, including social balance and harmony, strong group and collective loyalty, formality, humility and hierarchy. He then shows how Japanese non-verbal behaviour both illustrates and reinforces these cultural themes. For example, the Japanese tend to avoid direct eye contact except 'unless a superior wants to admonish a subordinate' (p. 259). Thus, the typical behaviour reflects the norm of humility – this norm is only broken to reinforce another cultural theme, hierarchy.

As McDaniel acknowledges, this form of analysis is easier in cultures which have very strong themes such as Japan. It is much more difficult in more diverse cultures. And we have the problem of measuring cultural themes, which we revisit in the next chapter.

## The meaning of non-verbal behaviour depends on the context

Even within the same culture, we cannot expect a particular non-verbal signal to mean the same thing in different situations. For example, Mark Knapp and Judith Hall (2010) review research on the non-verbal signals associated with dominance. A non-smiling face is seen as dominant but does this mean that dominant people smile less? Some studies have found that dominant members of a group smile more! They suggest that people who are *trying to achieve* dominance may use a different set of non-verbal signals from those who have already achieved high status.

### *You can improve your interpretation of non-verbal communication*

It is possible to improve your skill in interpreting body language. One key principle here is to look for 'leakage' where the person tries to control their expression in certain parts of their body but the true emotion leaks out elsewhere. I may feel very angry and put on a poker face but you may be able to spot my anger in my gestures, or the way my foot is furiously tapping, or some other leak which I cannot control. Linked to this is the notion of 'micro-expressions' – small and very quick changes of facial expression or bodily movements which are claimed to reveal the 'true' emotion that you are feeling. This idea has led to practical training courses and even a fictional TV series – *Lie To Me* – where the body language experts resolve crimes by judging the authenticity of the feelings expressed by suspects and villains.

## How non-verbal signals can communicate (or not) in everyday business situations

One point that we will repeat as it is so important – you should interpret communication in a holistic way – you should interpret the total picture before you, looking at all the verbal and non-verbal codes together. However, there are situations where a particular non-verbal code can have particular significance.

### *The importance of paralinguistics as a special clue*

In the work situation, the paralinguistic message can be the most important. Thus, when a subordinate says 'everything is going well', the hesitancy in the voice may show that everything is *not* going well.

The reverse can also happen. You may have a perfectly sound proposal to put forward to management, but if your behaviour is badly affected by nervousness, then the proposal may come over as uncertain and hesitant. As a result, you may not be taken seriously. If you have an important verbal message to put across, you need to ensure that the paralinguistic message supports and does not detract from it.

### *Appearance*

A person's appearance is often taken as an indicator, not only of that person's attitude, but also of the organisation's attitude to the people he or she communicates with. Thus, a waiter in nondescript, dirty clothes sends a negative message about himself and the organisation. One study has even shown that overweight people have trouble in getting job offers.

Clothing can have a significant effect on whether a person is employed, makes a sale or is believed by those with whom he or she communicates. Many organisations provide uniforms to ensure that employees project an appropriate image, as in the travel industry. Almost all airline employees who are in contact with customers have a uniform of some sort. This is intended to convey an image of discipline, reliability and orderliness to reassure passengers. Other organisations do not go to the extent of having uniforms, but have written or unwritten dress codes which define what is acceptable.

Dress also has a cultural dimension and can sometimes be a source of discord or discrimination. Certain groups signal their affiliation by clothes. Examples are the turbans of Sikhs and the yarmulkes of certain Jewish groups. In addition, certain minority groups have their own dress codes which may clash with prescribed codes. As dress can be a source of miscommunication and friction in organisations, management should develop a sensible policy which should be reviewed regularly as attitudes and fashions do change with time.

### *Eye contact*

Barbara Shimko surveyed 38 general managers of fast-food restaurants about their employment practices and found that 9 per cent of applicants were rejected because of 'inappropriate eye contact' (Shimko, 1990). She also noted the success of Project Transition in Philadelphia which trained people on welfare to work in the fast-food industry. One part of the training helped trainees to rehearse their interview behaviour – they were instructed to adopt the typical non-verbal behaviours of a 'middle-class, mainstream candidate'.

This study illustrates how people in organisations do have norms and expectations about non-verbal behaviour. People who want to gain entry to a particular organisation may have to comply with these norms to get through the selection procedure. Posture may be very important here – it is usually seen as a strong indicator of a person's attitude to the situation and audience. In high-stake situations such as job interviews, the interviewee is unlikely to create a good impression with an 'over-relaxed' posture. In superior–subordinate interactions, the subordinate who wants to impress will probably try to take up a posture that is slightly more rigid than the power-holder. Of course, there are dangers here – an over-rigid posture can signal lack of confidence.

### *Personal space and distance*

The effect of personal space and distance in communication is complex and depends on a number of factors which include the social relationship, the situation, the status relationship and the culture. Edward Hall (1959) identified four distance zones for middle-class Americans:

- intimate – physical contact to 45 cm;
- casual-personal – 45 cm to 120 cm;
- social-consultative – 120 cm to 365 cm;
- public – over 365 cm.

In cultures which follow this pattern, business interactions tend to take place at the casual-personal or social-consultative levels. Bur expectations of the type of interaction influence the distance – if we expect an unfavourable message, we will distance ourselves from the sender. So, depending on the level of formality, we tend to alter the distance to where we feel comfortable.

One general rule is that the person with power or status controls the interaction distance, particularly in the intimate and casual-personal interactions. In your organisation, is it acceptable for a manager to pat a junior on the back as an accompaniment to encouragement or praise? And would the reverse be resented?

Comfortable interaction distances vary from culture to culture, and you need to understand this when working in intercultural situations. The 'comfortable' distance for Arabs and Latin Americans is much closer than those for South Africans, British or Americans.

## CAN WE DEVELOP PRACTICAL GUIDELINES ON COMMUNICATION CODES?

One of the themes running through this chapter is that we make judgements about people who are communicating to us based on various features of their behaviour – their accent, dialect, appearance, etc. Can we somehow 'control' these judgements or at least eliminate possible negative judgements? Chris Cooke (1999) suggests that organisations can take some steps to eliminate what he calls 'unconscious stereotyping' where people make unconscious judgements based on certain language features in a message.

Cooke gives the example of the UK company who produced guidelines to help their managers adopt a communication style which 'would encourage positive attitudes among the workforce' (ibid., p. 184). They did this in three main stages:

- identifying linguistic features which could create the desired impression;
- identifying 'key audience groups' and deciding which linguistic features were important to each group;
- training managers to follow the guidelines and monitoring how they were being used.

This raises the general issue of how language codes can be used to control behaviour. This issue will crop up several times in this book – Box 3.3 introduces the concept of corporate-speak.

To return to Cooke's example, general linguistic features were identified from previous surveys of employee communications and by a workshop with a group of staff looking at a specific publication. These features included formality (using formal language rather than more conversational or colloquial expressions); jargon; propaganda features (features which made it 'look like sales talk'); use of the first or third person; and headlines or leaders (using catchy slogans or more formal titles and subtitles).

Specific guidelines were then identified for specific groups of employees (e.g. middle managers, frontline staff, etc.) on the basis of further research. Cooke concludes by identifying four 'general features which will probably apply to most organisations' (ibid., p. 185). Two of these echo much of the advice on written communication summarised in later chapters of this book:

- technical or business jargon can be very intimidating to a general audience and should be used carefully and always explained;
- you should avoid language features which suggest 'propaganda' or 'sales talk', such as buzzwords, euphemisms and cliches.

The other two are more controversial. First, Cooke suggests that 'in general communication it is better to use the third person – e.g. "it is thought, they do this" rather than using the first person ("I think this") as the first person can be seen as "patronising, or less dominant"' (ibid., p.185). Of course, this is advice for management but we are not so sure that this emphasis on control will 'work'. The workforce may see such an obvious linguistic tactic as manipulative. It also assumes that the target groups are reasonably homogenous in their response to language. We return to this issue in Chapter 7.

Second, he advises that 'important topics dealt with in briefings or publications lend themselves to more formal language to ensure they are taken seriously' (ibid., p. 185). Again, we wonder how the workforce responded to such formality.

**BOX 3.3 CORPORATE-SPEAK: NEW WORDS OR NEW ACTIONS?**

If company management start using new terms and expressions to describe aspects of the business, what impact does this have? Fiona Czerniawska suggests the company language ('corporate-speak') 'is a powerful way of instilling a common outlook and ideology' (Czerniawska, 1997, p. 26). However, she also argues that it is neither possible nor desirable for management to have absolute control through their use of language. She notes how many organisations followed Disney's lead in the USA and developed their own jargon.

With both of these recommendations, we wonder whether the background research has managed to uncover all the *meanings* which are presently circulating in this organisation. It seems to have investigated the process but perhaps not questioned the context and history. For example, if there is an issue about management being patronising, then how was this impression created? If management did behave in a patronising way in the past, then a more formal or official style of language may *emphasise* that impression. The workforce will respond to language in relation to the overall context. Language does not work in isolation.

Of course, *we* may be making assumptions about this organisation which are not warranted. Unfortunately, Cooke's article is relatively brief so he does not discuss the detail of how the scheme developed and whether it was successful in the long term. He also does not give any detail on the *level* of formality which is recommended. There is not an absolute distinction between formal and informal language – it is a continuum which has degrees of change.

We have given this article particular attention because it highlights important issues from this chapter, and relates back to the approaches we used in Chapter 1. It raises important issues – organisations can research and review their communication practices and change them if they wish. It also shows that communication codes are not just an abstract concept – they have everyday practical relevance for all of us.

## POSSIBILITIES OFFERED BY NEW TECHNOLOGY

We now have new ways of communicating which can augment the codes we use in face-to-face contact, and new methods/media are appearing. Nancy Baym suggests that the new media 'allow us to communicate personally within what used to be prohibitively large groups. This blurs the boundary between mass and interpersonal communication in ways that disrupt both' (Baym, 2010, p. 4). She suggests that we can use 'seven key concepts' to differentiate between the new forms, as summarised in Table 3.2.

**Table 3.2** *Key concepts for new communications media*

| *Concept* | *Meaning* |
|---|---|
| Interactivity | The forms of interaction which are supported |
| Temporal | The nature of the timing involved. For example, text messages can be either synchronous (immediate response) or asynchronous (delayed response) |
| Social cues | The range of cues such as tone of voice, facial expression, etc. |
| Storage | Can you keep the messages? |
| Replicability | Can you save and pass on the message? |
| Reach | Size of the audience you can reach |
| Mobility | Portability |

We shall look at these characteristics in more detail in later chapters. For the moment, we can bring out some of the main implications of this analysis:

- We now have techniques which allow us to make contact and reinforce relationships with relatively few limitations of time and place.
- This access to mobile contact has potential issues. It means we have to think about how much access people have to us. For example, do you need to consider 'strategically limiting your availability' (Baym, 2010, p. 11)?
- We can use asynchronous media when we want to plan our message and when we might need a fairly quick response.
- We can also keep records and store certain conversations where we need to. Of course, you have to then think about how and where any records are stored. There is the recent cautionary tale of the college head who recorded a 'private' meeting on his Livescribe digital pen and then distributed the notes of the meeting to colleagues, complete with the recorded conversation. The complaint from the other person recorded led to the head's resignation.

The growth of videoconferencing systems means that we can simulate face-to-face conversation relatively easily and inexpensively (e.g. through Skype, Facetime, etc.), so we need to think very carefully about the best media for particular forms of communication.

## SUMMARY

- We use a variety of codes to communicate, including verbal and non-verbal codes.
- Social rules and expectations are associated with these codes and they influence how the codes are interpreted (e.g. perceptions of accent).
- Our communication will reflect our attitudes and feelings and we need to make sure that we do not send out ambiguous or misleading signals.
- Although there have been exaggerated claims about the importance and meaning of non-verbal communication, we must make sure that our non-verbal signals create the appropriate relationship.
- *All* human codes are fuzzy and potentially ambiguous. As a result, we always need to consider their meaning in context.
- We must pay attention to the whole range of communication codes when we try to detect emotional states such as deception.
- Using the concept of codes, organisations can research and review their communication practices and change them if they wish. An example of this work shows that communication codes are not just an abstract concept – they have everyday practical relevance for all of us.
- New possibilities are offered by developments in digital technology, both to manage the information which others have about us and to maintain contact through online media.

## FURTHER READING

Baron, N.S. (2008) *Always On: Language in an online and mobile world.* New York: Oxford University Press.

Baym, N.K. (2010) *Personal Connections in the Digital Age.* Cambridge: Polity Press.

These two books offer a very comprehensive introduction to major issues and theories in this area.

Bhatia, V. and Bremner, S. (2014) *The Routledge Handbook of Language and Professional Communication.* London: Routledge.

Jackson, J. (ed.) (2012) *Introducing Language and Intercultural Communication.* London: Routledge.

Two recent and useful analyses of language in communication which explore in more detail many of the issues raised in this chapter.

Bryson, B. (1990) *Mother Tongue: The English language.* London: Penguin.

This remains one of the most entertaining introductions to the complexities of language, focusing on how English has become 'the undisputed global language'.

Cameron, D. (1995) *Verbal Hygiene.* London: Routledge.

Essential reading for anyone who wants to explore the debates about what makes language 'good or bad' and the various attempts to control how people express themselves.

Crystal, D. (2013) *Spell it Out: The singular story of English spelling.* London: Profile Books.

Crystal demonstrates that English spelling is not as 'difficult' or as 'chaotic' as many people think, by analysing how it has evolved over time. He argues that understanding this historical development helps us understand why/how words are spelled as they are and so can develop our practical skills.

Hartley, P. (1999) *Interpersonal Communication* (2nd edn). London: Routledge.

Solomon, D. and Theiss, J. (2013) *Interpersonal Communication: Putting theory into practice.* London: Routledge.

See Hartley, Chapters 8 and 9 especially, for further analysis of the relationship between language and non-verbal communication. The book by Solomon and Theiss offers an updated review of this area.

Knapp, M.L. and Hall, J.A. (2010) *Non-verbal Behaviour in Human Interaction* (9th edn). Fort Worth, TX: Harcourt Brace.

A comprehensive overview of research into non-verbal communication.

## Chapter 4

# How is communication affected by the organisational context?

## INTRODUCTION

This chapter discusses three characteristics of organisations which have profound implications for the ways we communicate: the organisational culture, the organisation structure and the technology. These all influence how you communicate and how others respond to your communication.

The notion of organisational culture did not become prominent in the management literature until the 1980s, possibly as a reaction to models of organisations which were seen as 'over-rational' or 'over-mechanical' (Albrow, 1997). Since then, many large organisations have spent large sums of money, both investigating and trying to improve their internal culture. Communication has been a central concern of all these initiatives.

Organisational structures have also seen considerable change and innovation. Do particular organisational structures encourage or impede organisational communication? One very important issue is whether traditional hierarchical structures have 'had their day'.

Finally, we need to consider the technology adopted by the organisation. This will make different forms of communication either more or less practicable. The technology has seen dramatic changes over the last 30 years: 'computers' transformed into 'information technology (IT)', then into 'information and communications technology (ICT)', and then into the 'network of networks' supported by the Internet and World Wide Web. These are fundamental shifts in terms of what the technology can do, although we must not ignore social and political influences on the way the technology is applied. Organisations which fully embrace new technology do have significant opportunities which have not been available before. This has a profound impact on the way we communicate.

## OBJECTIVES

*This chapter will*:

- explain what we mean by organisational culture and show how/why it is important for communication;
- explain major dimensions of organisational structure and discuss their implications for communication;
- identify major characteristics of new technology in organisations and their implications for communication;
- highlight significant examples of organisations using new technology to develop their structures, cultures and communication.

## CASE STUDY: USING AN ONLINE INFORMATION MANAGEMENT SYSTEM TO COMMUNICATE

This case study analyses how a virtual college/university partnership – the Automotive College – used an online information management system as its principal means of digital communications, information management and knowledge building. It responded to a need from industry for education providers to meet their specific needs for graduate competencies and capabilities and has evolved into the National Skills Academy for Manufacturing. Members of the partnership were located all over the UK and needed to operate efficiently and virtually. The college developed an online information management system (known as the 'OIM' system), which became their principal means of digital communications, information management and knowledge-building, and was one of the first organisations to adopt such an approach in preference to other ways of exchanging information – e.g. using email.

The system was based on Lotus Notes and accessed via a Web browser. It was designed to match information needs to partnership workflows. For instance, when developing new learning materials, design teams would upload new drafts of their materials to which others could feed back suggestions and the OIM system would manage version control and 'signing-off' by those authorised to do so. The OIM system also featured tools to support meeting management and documents, task allocation and management as well as various course and student management functions. What was unique was that email, while not being totally 'banned', was greatly discouraged and the phase 'it's on (or "use") the OIM' became almost a mantra. Members of the partnership would log on every day to find the latest updates and the system would highlight any new postings that matched the member's profile (the concept of 'roles'was adopted whereby different roles had different privileges, and also allowed members to decide who could and could not see any of their postings).

Many of the features of the OIM can be found in more recent cloud-based project management systems – the Automotive College's new approach, using cloud-based services, overcame many of the weaknesses inherent when using email (i.e. overload of information and everyone keeping private information records). A major advantage of the OIM was that it developed an extremely valuable knowledge base for the college. New personnel joining could have access to this rich knowledge resource, which would not happen using email as a principal means of communication. The implementation of OIM was not without its difficulties – some members of the partnership did not like the openness of the system and were more comfortable with the use of private email. However, the college had a director who was firmly behind the approach and insisted that all participants adopt the OIM system. A major benefit for both the college Board of Directors and operational teams was that the system freed up their meetings to be much more focused on creative brainstorming, and all the administrative and project-chasing activities were undertaken using the OIM in a more asynchronous mode.

We can use this case study as an example of where communication did 'work' because the three aspects of context were in harmony:

- The technology was effective in supplying the members of the different organisations the information and support they needed.
- The communication was not impeded by the fact that different institutional cultures were involved. Communication took place in a common (and neutral) environment which was accessible to everyone.
- There were no barriers related to organisational structure as everyone had equal access to the system and all the information.

This information system was successful because it met the organisational needs and priorities of the time. But just making information available does not mean it will be used effectively. Vermeulen (2010) advises organisations to 'Shut down your expensive document databases; they tend to do more harm than good' (p. 156). His main supporting evidence is studies of accountancy firms and consultancy groups where the availability of massive information banks overloaded rather than helped the users.

## ORGANISATIONAL CULTURE AND COMMUNICATION

Definitions of organisational culture usually echo definitions of national culture, talking about typical or traditional ways of thinking, believing and acting. They talk about the way ideas are shared by members of the group and the way they must be learnt by new members. Consider how you feel when you join a new organisation. You are very keen to find out 'the way they do things round here' and you probably behave rather cautiously to make sure you do not offend anyone by breaking one of the 'unwritten rules'. So how can we define the components of an organisational culture in more detail?

Compare the two lists of components in Table 4.1 (adapted from different definitions in Senior, 1997).

Although they have a lot in common, there are important differences between these two lists. List A covers more of the ways that culture is communicated – e.g. myths, heroes etc. – whereas list B focuses more on underlying principles – e.g. how far the organisation uses teams. List B includes many formal organisational rules – e.g. the reward criteria, the way in

**Table 4.1** *Components of organisational culture*

| *List A* | *List B* |
|---|---|
| Examples of common language: jokes, metaphors, stories, myths and legends | Member's identity |
| | Group and team emphasis |
| Behaviour patterns: rites, rituals, ceremonies and celebrations | People focus |
| Behaviour norms | Unit or department co-ordination |
| Heroes | Control |
| Symbols and symbolic action | Tolerance of risk |
| Beliefs and values and attitudes | Reward criteria |
| Ethical codes | Conflict and co-operation |
| Basic assumptions | Company focus on goals |
| History | Relationships with external systems |

which salary increases and promotions are decided. It also focuses on notions of identity, the degree to which employees identify with the organisation as opposed to identifying with their job or professional background. You can use a list like this to develop a checklist to review and compare different organisational cultures (Senior, 1997, p. 103). List A focuses more on informal characteristics like jokes and stories, and also highlights the historical dimension.

Both of these lists are long and detailed. Which aspects should we concentrate on? How do we decide what is most important? And what details should influence our interpretation? After all, we can observe lots of details even within one room in an organisation:

> [Meeting] rooms generally reflect and reproduce the structures of interaction expected in the organisation. Straight lines of chairs and note pads, each guarded by a water glass as erect as a sentry, communicate a sense of conformity and order.
>
> (Morgan, 1997, p. 135)

## Levels of organisational culture

Edgar Schein (2009, 2010) suggests that there are three levels of organisational culture:

- 'Artefacts' – visible structures and processes in the organisation. This includes the language people use, stories that circulate around the organisation, rituals and ceremonies, and the organisation's environment (including the buildings and the way space is allocated).
- 'Espoused values' – values which the organisation *claims* to follow. These are expressed in the business plans, the annual report, the mission statement, and so on.
- The third and deepest level is what he calls the 'basic underlying assumptions'. These are the taken-for-granted beliefs which are the *real* source of values and actions within the organisation and which may be accepted subconsciously or unconsciously. Box 4.1 shows how an organisation can be designed on very explicit values.

## BOX 4.1 ORGANISATIONAL CULTURE FROM BASIC PRINCIPLES

Jerry Hirshberg (1998) explained the development of Nissan Design International (NDI) from his perspective as founder and company president: 'that began by identifying idea making as the centermost concern of a business' (p. 237).

Nissan had decided to incorporate Western design skills into their car-building to become more attractive to Western audiences. Determined to establish a new design operation which would be organised 'around the priorities of the creative process' (p. 15), Hirschberg identified four themes which underpin creative activity:

- polarities – i.e. all those 'opposites' and ambiguities that encourage people to think creatively;
- unprecedented thinking;
- breaking down boundaries;
- emphasis on synthesising and integrating ideas.

These themes were used to generate 11 key strategies – e.g. hiring designers not as individuals but in pairs who were deliberately different from one another.

An example of a new working practice was the evaluation of a prototype. Traditional Detroit practice used a very selective audience and only expected comments from designers and major executives. In NDI, *anyone* could attend and comment. At one review, an executive secretary blurted out that the car looked 'fat, dumb and ugly' (p. 58). After the initial shock of this blunt reaction, the designers realised she was right. The design needed major revision.

Hirshberg retired in the year 2000 and NDI became Nissan Design America, one part of Nissan's global design activities, moving to new premises in 2005. But did the culture survive these changes?

The obvious implication of Schein's definition is that there can be important differences between what an organisation *says* it does and what it actually does. The organisation that claims to value and support its employees in the mission statement may be extremely ruthless when it comes to hiring and firing people. The basic underlying assumption may be 'survival of the fittest' whereas the mission statement portrays a 'happy family'. Employees will believe the actions and not the rhetoric. For an example of debate (and major disagreement) over the realities of an organisational culture, see the example of the Jack Welch management era in the GE company in the USA we discuss in Chapter 14. For an interesting contrast between managers on a central component of organisational culture, see Box 4.2.

## BOX 4.2 THE BOSS WANTS US TO COLLABORATE

A leaked internal email from Yahoo to all employees proclaimed that 'communication and collaboration will be important, so we need to be working side-by-side. That is why it is critical that we are all present in our offices' (Swisher, 2013). It seems ironic that the chief of such a large technology company should institute a policy to constrain remote working when the technology has become so accessible. This also illustrated our point that anything you publish within an organisation may be broadcast to the world. If you Google 'yahoo no work from home memo', you can read over a million results, including the full text of the memo.

A completely contrasting view on virtual working and collaboration came from one manager we interviewed in a UK company:

> We do not really need an office except to impress some clients. I encourage my staff to work from home if they wish and have given them the technology to do so (including personal tablets). That policy, plus getting staff to work in pairs with clients, has paid off in terms of productivity and collaboration.

There may also be significant differences between groups in the way they perceive the same event. These differences can give us clues to how these groups view the organisation in more general terms. Daniels and Spiker (1994, p. 10) contrasted administrators' views of the registration process at University X – an 'orderly, necessary set of procedures' – with those of the students. Students called the event 'the Gauntlet' and delighted in jokes and grim tales ('war stories') of how tedious and inefficient the process was: 'Sign up for at least twice as many classes as you really need. That way, you may actually get something.' Through these stories, new students were introduced to shared perceptions about the administration.

The culture can have very clear and important practical consequences. Philip Clampitt (2010) suggests four key consequences:

- 'Culture affects the bottom line' (p. 73).
- Culture influences how the organisation both analyses and solves problems.
- Culture influences how the company responds to change.
- Culture has a profound impact on employee motivation.

### How do the workers experience the culture?

Rick Delbridge spent four months working on the production line in two factories: one Japanese-run and one British operation trying to introduce Japanese methods (Delbridge, 1998). He found dramatic differences between the espoused values, such as worker participation, open communication and team involvement, and the actual practice. For example, 'counselling' sessions with workers who were having difficulties turned out to be one-way communication from the management to 'do better' with little if any genuine dialogue. There were also 'team meetings' where only managers ever spoke.

## Major models of organisational culture

Other models have emerged from research and business consultants and we offer a couple of popular examples below. These and other models are described in more detail on our website.

### *Harrison's four cultures*

This was proposed by Roger Harrison in the 1970s and later popularised in the work of Charles Handy. He suggested four main organisational cultures:

- *Role* – where there is strong emphasis on defining roles for each worker and manager.
- *Achievement* – where individuals are all directly involved in the work and the focus is on getting the job done, with very little time spent writing down procedures or rules. Examples include a small family business or small firm of management consultants.
- *Power* – where all the important decisions emerge from and are taken by the few powerful individuals at the centre.
- *Support* – which is based upon mutual support and commitment. Members feel that they have a personal stake in the organisation and work hard to maintain it. An example would be a workers' co-operative.

### *Corporate cultures (Deal and Kennedy)*

This model made an immediate impact in the 1980s. Deal and Kennedy (1982) examined hundreds of companies and identified four main cultures.

#### Tough guy, macho culture

Individuals work hard and fast, often take risks, and expect to receive quick feedback and awards. This culture favours the young and is very competitive. As a result, it may be difficult to get staff to co-operate.

#### Work hard/play hard culture

Staff are rewarded for hard work and there is an emphasis on 'team play' and conforming to recognised procedures.

#### The 'bet your company' culture

Here we have large businesses which invest a lot of money in projects that take a long time to complete. Staff are valued for their commitment, technical competence and stamina/endurance.

PROCESS CULTURE

There is strong emphasis on how things are done – getting the procedures right and attending to the detail.

## Contrasting different models of organisational culture

One common theme is that certain cultures are more or less suited to a particular business/economic environment. One influential management text of the 1980s took this further to say that some cultures were *inherently* better than others (Peters and Waterman, 1982). They claimed that effective organisations shared specific values, including a 'bias for action' and 'closeness to the customer'. Unfortunately for this analysis, some of the organisations they labelled as successful went on to struggle in the 1990s and Vermeulen (2010) suggests that only three or four of the organisations listed in 1982 would be candidates for excellent ratings today.

This raises the question of how far organisational culture is related to broader social and political issues. One controversial proposal is that many modern organisations are taking on the values of efficiency and predictability which were first promoted in the American fast-food industry. Box 4.3 looks at this proposal in more detail.

### BOX 4.3 THE 'MCDONALDIZATION' THESIS

George Ritzer introduced the term 'McDonaldization' to suggest: 'the process by which the principles of the fast food restaurant are coming to dominate more and more sectors of American society as well as of the rest of the world' (Ritzer, 1996, p. 1).

Ritzer suggests that many organisations have adopted four major principles which have been taken to their logical extreme in fast-food chains:

- *Efficiency.*
- *Accountability.* The quantitative aspects of both the product and the service are calculated in great detail. Fast-food restaurants emphasise exact measures of ingredients/helpings and speedy delivery to the customer.
- *Predictability.* The products in New York will be exactly the same as the ones in London or Paris, and they will be the exactly the same tomorrow as they were today. This predictability also applies to workers' behaviour and the scripts of the service staff.
- *Control.* Technology is used to control both the staff and the customer.

Ritzer does not ignore possible advantages. For example, organisations have used these principles to deliver a wider range of goods and services to a wider range of people. However, he is concerned about negative features, contrasting these with the early attempts to build 'rational, scientific organisations' and ideas of bureaucracy. Even the founding father of bureaucracy, Max Weber, later commented on the 'iron cage of rationality'. Bureaucracies

*continued . . .*

**BOX 4.3 *Continued***

can be dispiriting and unsatisfying places to work. Similarly, Ritzer suggests that McDonaldization can have negative and dehumanising consequences. He concludes that customers do not recognise some of the factors which make the organisation inefficient from their point of view. For example, many of these systems make the customers do a lot of the work. They may also be rather expensive and may create a lot of waste in packaging etc. He is also very critical of their values, accusing them of double standards. Whereas those at the top of the organisation value their own freedom, they simultaneously 'want to control subordinates through the imposition of rational systems' (pp. 123–124). Ritzer has regularly updated the book (7th edition in 2013) possibly even more relevant in today's society.

This work received very powerful reactions, not least from the organisations which are obvious targets of his criticism. See our website for further debate. For the moment, we must emphasise the important issue of possible conflicts between value systems, which are highlighted by Ritzer's analysis.

Given the current economic recession, we must also question what happens to organisational culture when its economic environment changes. For example, in the 1990s, Deal and Kennedy returned to their categories and concluded they were still valid. But they also concluded that 'within any single real-world company, a mix of all four types of cultures will be found' and that 'companies with very strong cultures . . . fit this mould hardly at all' (Deal and Kennedy, 1999, p. 14). They agree with other research that 'sustaining visions are . . . the driving force in strong-culture companies' (p. 27). In other words, if there is a long-term vision from the company leadership which is supported by action, then the company is likely to be successful. This conclusion is supported by other important studies of the relationship between company culture and performance. However, more recent studies also confirm that different types are commonly found and also suggest that typologies are useful – e.g. Cameron and Quinn (2011).

In the discussion so far, we have mostly implied that a single organisation fits one culture. This is one problem with many cultural models – the assumption that the organisation is a unified whole. A number of factors argue against this assumption:

- Some cultures are stronger than others. Employees' acceptance of the general culture can vary.
- Different parts of the organisation may reflect different cultures.
- Cultures can and do change.

Another possible misconception is that culture only develops in large organisations. In fact, we can observe and analyse culture in organisations of all sizes, including the very small indeed.

## How is organisational culture communicated and expressed?

Early research on organisational culture tended to focus on management attempts to communicate corporate values to their employees. But, of course, this may not accurately reflect what happens in the workplace. As a result, researchers have paid increasing attention to the ways in which organisational culture can be revealed in more personal communication. For example, there is research on:

- stories people tell about the organisation and about heroes in the organisation;
- slogans, catch phrases and graffiti in the organisation;
- jokes and metaphors which people use to describe their experience of the organisation.

This research uncovers values which are accepted by members of the organisation and also conflict which may exist between subgroups. The examples given below illustrate these points.

### *The power of metaphor*

Smith and Eisenberg (1987) concluded from employee interviews that two fundamental metaphors represented the Disney approach: Disneyland was a 'drama' and a 'family'. Employees saw themselves as 'actors' putting on 'costumes' to act out a 'show' for their 'audience' (customers). The family metaphor described management/worker relationships and attitudes. When management responded to increasing competition by adopting hard economic measures, the workers felt that this was 'a breach of Disney's caring philosophy' (p. 374).

### *Lists versus stories*

Another continuing theme in the literature on organisational culture is the comparison between organisations. Browning (1992) suggests two broad types of cultures, identified by their preference for lists or stories. The 'lists' organisation will tend to issue written lists to staff to tell them what to do and how to do it. This reflects organisational values such as maintenance of standards and accountability. The 'stories' organisation will rely on face-to-face interaction and story-telling to communicate to staff. This is an organisation which values humour and performance.

## Cultural differences

Much of the research to date on organisational stories has looked at Western organisations using English as the dominant language. In other cultures, members of the organisation may have different ways of expressing themselves through stories. For example, whereas stories in UK or US organisations often use images, jokes and metaphors drawn from popular television programmes, films and music, a study of story-telling in a Malaysian organisation found that most stories used traditional legends and historical characters (Ahmed and Hartley, 1999). The one major exception was a story in several parts which also used Power Rangers characters to comment on current management preoccupations.

## Analysing your organisation's culture

A range of factors influence the culture which an organisation develops. We developed the following diagram to summarise these factors. Practical tools and techniques you can use to analyse your organisation's culture can be found in the work of analysts we have already cited, such as Schein (2010), Senior and Swailes (2010) and Cameron and Quinn (2011). There are also online inventories such as OCAI (based on Cameron and Quinn). You need to consider whether you are comfortable in your organisation's culture and what this means for your communication. Uncovering negative information about your organisational culture can be a very difficult experience, as we see in Box 4.4.

### BOX 4.4 WHEN CULTURE GOES WRONG

Michael Woodford was appointed President of the Japanese Olympus corporation, one of a very small number of non-Japanese natives to achieve a senior position in a large Japanese company. Shortly after taking up his post he was made aware of magazine articles accusing the company of 'posting mountainous losses on account of management carelessness of momentous proportions and funnelling cash behind the scenes to antisocial forces' (Woodford, 2012, p. 41). So accusations of 'white-collar fraud' were tied up with links to organised crime. When Woodford tried to investigate these charges, he was opposed by other senior managers. This opposition included the previous president, a longstanding Olympus employee, who had taken on the role of CEO after appointing Woodford and who had been implicated in the allegations of fraud. Despite strong support from some other Olympus managers and an independent audit report which supported his suspicions, Woodford was unable to work through the issues. The extraordinary board meeting where he intended to distribute a statement listing his concerns was cancelled and replaced by a meeting where the other board members unanimously voted for his dismissal. This was a short meeting lasting about eight minutes and only comprised the formal motion and then a vote where 'all fifteen members simultaneously raised their hands in approval. . . . There was to be no discussion, no debate, just acquiescence' (ibid., p. 66). This was not the end of the story by any means as the subsequent publicity surrounding these events led to investigations, legal proceedings and further financial difficulties for Olympus alongside international awards for Woodford to recognise his personal bravery and integrity. His subsequent account of these events was described by one reviewer as having 'all the hallmarks of a John Grisham novel' and is a fascinating if depressing insight into corporate chicanery.

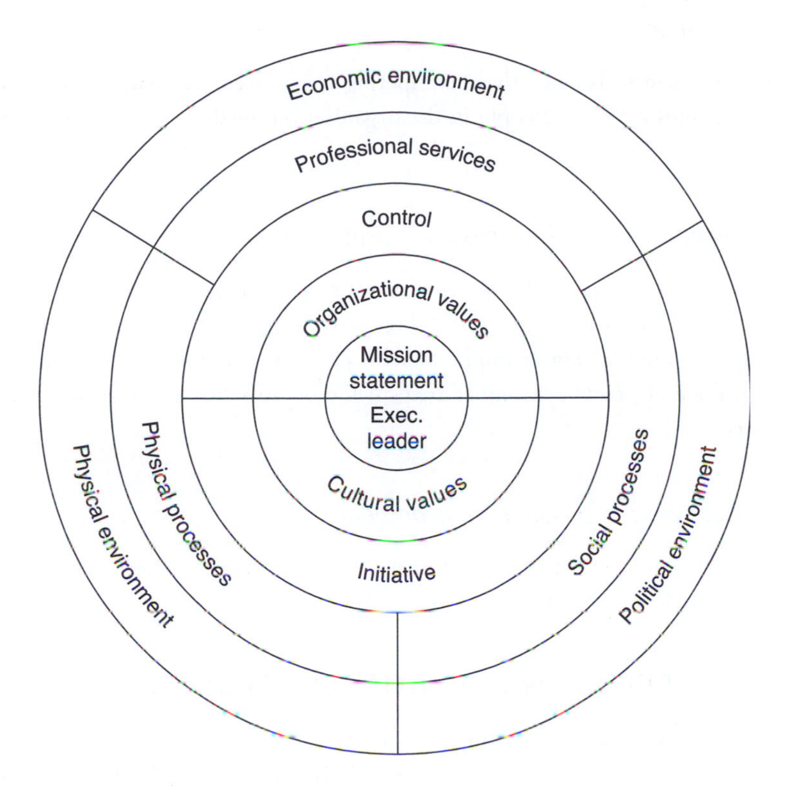


**Figure 4.1** *Determinants of organisational culture*

The key point for this chapter is Woodford's evaluation of the organisational culture at Olympus. This culture reflected long-standing national values and norms which he and others have argued have become counterproductive in the current economic climate. The commitment to harmony and cohesion which helped Japanese industry become powerful in the 1970s and 1980s did not allow new ideas to surface when other countries caught up on the manufacturing and technology. Woodford quotes from a Japanese nuclear accident report which attributed accidents to *'the ingrained conventions of Japanese culture; our reflexive obedience; our reluctance to challenge authority; our devotion to "sticking with the programme"; and our "insularity"'* (ibid., p. 225, italics in the original). He suggests that these same traits were responsible for his treatment at Olympus where his attempts to uncover wrongdoing were thwarted at the time by unquestioning loyalty to the previous hierarchy.

### *Organisational mission – executive attitudes – organisational values – cultural values*

In theory, the core of the organisational culture should be the organisational vision or mission. However, this may not be the case if this mission is not 'echoed' by these other factors. If these four factors are not aligned, then some level of conflict is inevitable.

### *Control – initiative*

All organisations have to balance these competing tendencies. The larger the organisation, the more it becomes an issue. People in the organisation need to 'know where they stand' on these issues.

### *Physical processes – social processes – professional services*

A business may focus on one of these – a chemical processing plant would be an example of physical process – but is likely to contain all three to some degree. The mix of people involved will be an important factor. For example, many organisations employ professionals who have a professional code of practice. Conflict arises if the organisation's demands clash with that professional code.

### *Political – economic – physical environments*

This may be especially important for international organisations where the parent culture may clash with the laws or customs of a particular country.

## HOW CAN WE DEFINE ORGANISATIONAL STRUCTURE?

The most common way of representing the structure of an organisation is the organisation chart and a simple example is given in Figure 4.2. But what does this tell us? The vertical dimension shows the hierarchy and status relations, and the horizontal dimension shows the range of activities which the company is involved in. In this example of a manufacturing company, these activities include production, research and development, finance, marketing, and so on.

This diagram is one way of representing an organisation, and it can be criticised. For example, it provides an image of the organisation as a well-ordered system with clearly structured authority relations. This can be very misleading. If management see the organisation

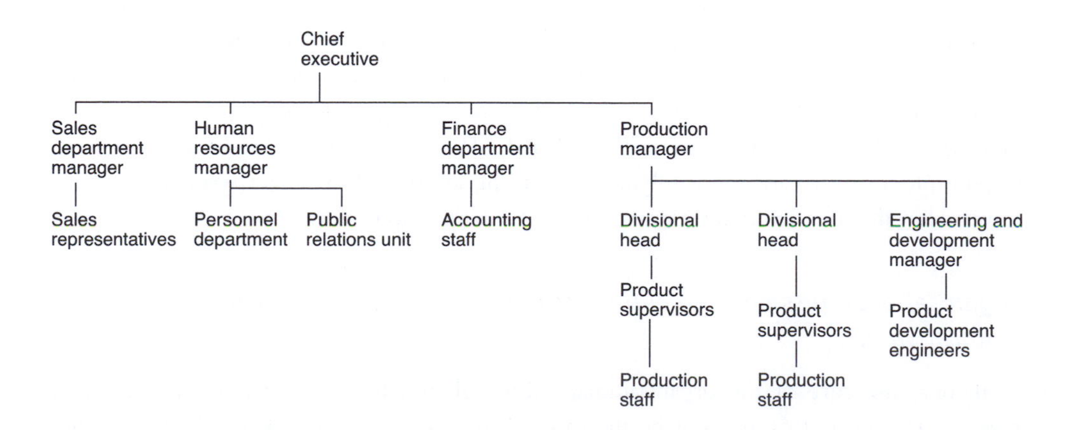


***Figure 4.2*** *Simple organisation chart of a manufacturing company*

in this 'clear-cut' way, they may implement policies which do not work because the organisation does not actually work in such a systematic way.

Different ways of representing the structure of the organisation are not just matters of technical detail. They represent fundamentally different approaches and different theoretical assumptions. If you review some of the classic texts on organisations, you will find very different starting points. These range from the organisation's contribution to the wider society, through approaches based upon how power and authority is organised, and on to approaches which reflect how the organisation is structured to meet the demands of its environment. One very influential management text argued that: 'all theories of organization and management are based on implicit images or metaphors that lead us to see, understand, and manage organizations in distinctive yet partial ways' (Morgan, 1997, p. 4).

As our main purpose is to focus on communication, we will not provide detailed analysis of different theories and metaphors. What we will do is show how different structural perspectives have important implications for the role of communication by offering three different ways of describing the organisation's structure:

- An organisation is a set of stakeholder groups who are connected through communication.
- An organisation is a set of managed subsystems.
- An organisation is a command hierarchy which can be realised in different ways.

## Defining the stakeholders

Stakeholders are usually defined as 'people who have an interest in the organisation, which may cause them to seek to influence managers' actions' (Stewart, 1991, p. 80).

Other commentators have argued that this model of business communication is much more relevant to modern organisations because they need to consider far more than simple economic motives. They must consider broader issues and implications, so communication with both suppliers and the local community must forge long-term relationships for the common good. This analysis has also generated new forms of communication, as described in Box 4.5.

### BOX 4.5 COMMUNICATING WITH STAKEHOLDERS

Future search conferences have developed as a method to improve connections and relationships between the different stakeholder groups, especially in periods of change or economic turmoil. They are based on three essential features:

- bringing together the 'whole system' in one place to work through an agenda which focuses on the organisation's task;
- emphasising connections between the stakeholders;

*continued . . .*

**BOX 4.5 *Continued***

- encouraging stakeholders to 'take ownership' of future development of the company and to commit themselves to future action.

With up to 80 participants, lasting up to 3 days and involving external facilitators, these are expensive and significant events for a company. They need to be carefully planned beforehand to create an agenda which all participants will commit to.

If you adopt this view of an organisation's structure, then you will consider communication primarily in terms of the links and connections between the stakeholder groups.

## Defining the organisation's subsystems

The executive group in charge of an organisation is responsible for maintaining a number of communication systems. These systems are interdependent, but they are described independently in Figure 4.3 where we try to show the relationship of the executive group to these various communication systems. If you adopt this view of an organisation's structure, then you will consider communication primarily in terms of how the executive group manages and/or controls these different communication systems.

## Defining the hierarchy

We have already suggested that there are different forms of hierarchy in modern organisations. One fairly typical set of definitions comes from Andrews and Herschel (1996). They suggest six prominent forms of organisation:

- traditional centralised structure;
- centralised structure with decentralised management;
- divisional form;
- decentralised structure;
- matrix structure;
- 'type D' organisation.

The first two have strong control from the senior management group and a very clear hierarchy. In forms three and four, the senior management have devolved authority in rather different ways. Within a divisional structure, the organisation has a central office which coordinates and controls, but the main work of the organisation is carried out in its divisions. In the matrix structure, we have a dual command structure so that employees report to senior staff in terms of their specialist role. The final form – type D – is characterised by 'distributed work arrangements' where the work is distributed between the organisation's

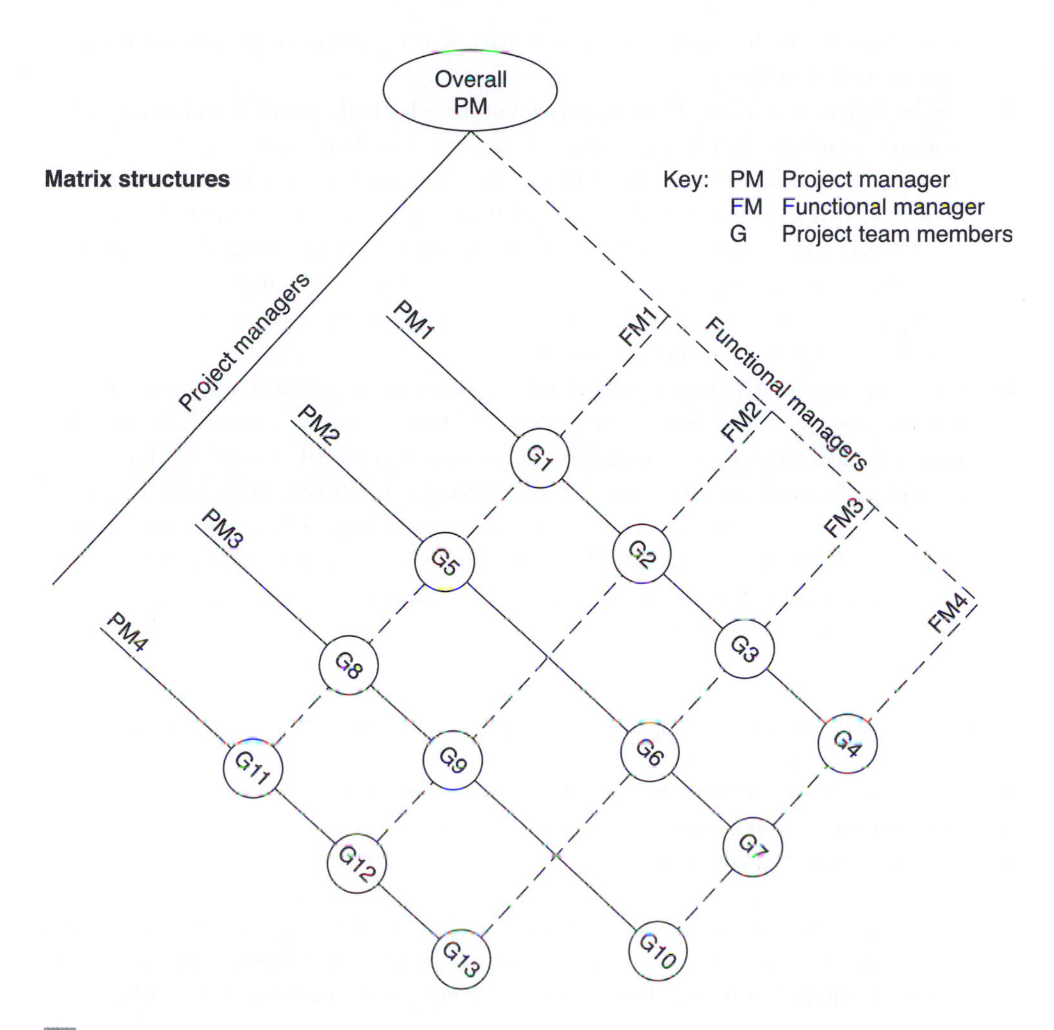


***Figure 4.3*** *Basic matrix structure of an organisation*

'core' and peripheral units which might involve external subcontracting and various other mechanisms based on the use of information technology.

## Defining structures within structures

Although broad characterisations of a hierarchy are useful, we can argue that few organisations (especially larger ones) conform entirely to a single basic structure. Any large organisation can include a mix of:

- *Line structure*. This is based on the idea that at each level people control and administer the work of a group in the level below them. Over the last 20 years, many organisations have restructured to reduce the layers of middle management (downsizing). This has often been done as part of a 're-engineering' exercise, using ideas described in Box 4.4.

- *Staff or functional structure*. Here, management includes both specialist and functional managers, each one instructing workers on an aspect of their work.
  A version of this model was advocated by one of the early management theorists, Frederick Taylor, who is usually associated with breaking down manual tasks into small functional tasks. He actually suggested that management should also operate in this way, but the management of his day did not wish to lose their power base and simply applied his logic to the workers. Matrix management is probably the most common example of this form of structure
- *Committee structure*. Clubs and professional organisations are often run by committees which try to operate on democratic principles. Decision-making is usually by majority vote, although they often try to achieve consensus. Traditional universities, for example, often operate on a system of interlocking committees, and membership of these committees is often determined by status or invitation. Increasing managerialism in higher education has weakened these structures. Most business organisations appoint committees for co-ordination and special purposes. Although committees can work well with a good chair, they are often associated with bureaucracy and inefficiency.

There are a further range of complexities which have implications for communication:

- distinctions between employment and representative roles;
- the nature of advisory roles;
- the role of informal communication.

This raises important issues about how we define the 'real' organisation structure. We can also look at the relationship between structure and culture as many if not most planned changes to organisational culture involve significant structural change, as we illustrate in Box 4.6.

## BOX 4.6 ANYONE FOR RE-ENGINEERING?

Business process re-engineering (BPR) was defined by its founders as 'the fundamental rethinking and radical design of business processes to achieve dramatic improvements in critical, contemporary measures of performance, such as cost, quality, service, and speed' (Hammer and Champy, 1993, p. 32). They suggested that radical rethinking of what the organisation is about would lead to:

- changes in organisational structure such as a move to teamworking;
- changes in job and role definitions with increased sharing of responsibility;
- managers becoming advisers/facilitators;
- far fewer levels of management – the hierarchy becomes flatter.

Large organisations may have particular issues and complexities. Fisman and Sullivan (2014) suggest that Procter & Gamble introduced matrix management and ended up with 'a three-dimensional matrix, with separate reporting lines and hierarchies for products, functions *and* geographies' (ibid., p. 88). This proved too complex and P&G have been through several restructures since 1998, suggesting that finding the right structure is not simply a case of adopting a model advocated in the textbooks but 'a much more subtle storyline of the trial-and-error grasping for a better way of organising' (ibid., p. 91).

But does it work? Since the mid-1990s, re-engineering has attracted very serious criticism on the grounds that:

- many re-engineering projects fail to deliver;
- re-engineering fails to take account of the softer human factors which influence business performance.

Even articles which suggested that BPR had a more impressive record of success also suggested that it would not work without a strong emphasis on the skills of cultural change, including clear communications and the development of trust.

## Complexities within structures

### *The growing organisation*

Sometimes textbooks give the impression that these are only issues for large firms. Structure is just as much an issue for a small and developing company although there are obvious differences in scale. Structure may become especially important when the company tries to grow.

Consider the case of a small service organisation set up by two partners. How many extra staff can they recruit before they need to establish a layer of management? What if they decide to open a second site? How will this be managed? This development might also create strains in the relationship between the two partners. At the start, they may be able to share the work out equally and not worry about specialisation. But once they have a significant workforce, they will have a number of additional concerns. For example, how will they deal with the complexities of employment law and welfare rights? Will they employ some advisory staff or will they ask some outside firm to handle these aspects? All of these are critical issues of organisation structure.

### *The 'informal organisation' and 'grapevine'?*

Many authors distinguish the 'formal' organisation from the 'informal' organisation: the formal organisation as expressed in the organisation chart – the informal organisation being the network of relationships which co-exists, based on personal and political relationships.

Communication across this informal organisation is often dismissed as of low quality, being a mixture of leaks, rumour and speculation. However, sometimes very accurate information (and sometimes very embarrassing to management) can reach employees through this network, which can be defined in various ways, including the grapevine, the 'old boy' network and company social gatherings.

### BOX 4.7 CULTURAL AND STRUCTURAL CHANGE AT MICROSOFT

In 2013, Microsoft announced plans to reorganise the company and transform into a 'leaner, meaner devices and services machine' (Foley, 2013). Table 4.2 below summarises some of the main issues, structural changes and cultural aims behind this reorganisation. We will see how far this 'worked' over the next few years. Reports so far do suggest that these changes are having positive outcomes, with accounts of better relationships developing between teams across the organisation (Foley, 2014).

**Table 4.2** *Cultural and structural change at Microsoft*

| *Organisational issue* | *Cultural and business aims* | *Major structural changes* |
|---|---|---|
| Company seen as 'working in silos' and not co-operating across divisional boundaries | Company not reacting quickly enough to change | Five previous business units disbanded |
| | More collaboration and sharing – e.g. of technologies and components across the company | All three operating systems merged into one unit |
| | | Marketing and business strategy becomes one central unit |
| | Teams will deliver more quickly | Four new engineering groups |
| | Distinction between customer and enterprise services will be become more blurred to reflect market changes | |

## THE TECHNOLOGICAL INFRASTRUCTURE: HOW FAR ADVANCED IS THE 'DIGITAL REVOLUTION'?

Technological hardware advances and improvements in software have combined to turn some very long-established ideas from computing into everyday realities which most of us can afford in affluent societies. It is worth summarising these ideas (for a detailed discussion of the history, see Winston, 1998) as they suggest how electronic communication will further develop:

- *Remote/distant operation*. This was achieved to some degree as early as 1940. Nowadays you can access your home or office computer from your mobile phone.
- *Sharing resources*. Early computers of the 1950s and 1960s – large machines in large rooms – usually controlled networks. Users in distant offices used keyboard and

monitor to connect to the main processor. Nowadays we have access to networks through a variety of devices and in multiple locations. The development of cloud computing is a recent example.

- *Flexible messaging*. Demands for secure military communication prompted the development of the Internet's predecessor – the Arpanet – breaking messages down into packets which were sent separately through the network in the most efficient way possible. The rise of the smartphone has supported a dramatic increase in messaging and we now have new forms such as Twitter.
- *Information organised as a Web of associations*. In 1945, Vannevar Bush argued that it was possible to construct a machine which would enable the user to search through all available knowledge, following an 'intricate web of trails' through the information. Another related idea – hypertext – was also first established in the 1940s. Ted Nelson developed the idea of a text which did not have the structure of conventional books, enabling you to jump from an idea on one page to a related idea or illustration somewhere else in the document. This is the pattern of navigation which we now take for granted when we use multimedia and search the Web. The inventor of the Web, Tim Berners-Lee, wanted to use hypertext so that computer users could free associate between ideas in the same way that the human mind does. Berners-Lee also wanted to reproduce the informal collaboration which you would find in the coffee area of a research department – somewhere where people could get together and share ideas. In 1994, he set up the World Wide Web Consortium (W3C) to take on the job of managing the Web. This is not managing in the sense of controlling but maintaining his original principles: common standards and openness.
- *Computers can exchange all types of information provided they share standard rules (usually called protocols)*. The fact that there are standard rules has enabled the Web to become an international system. However, it is also one of the Web's problems. The Web uses a standard publishing language – HTML (Hypertext Markup Language) which allows you to specify which part of the text are headings, subheadings, bullet lists, and so on. But HTML is continually being developed to allow writers to produce more complex Web pages. Browsers like Explorer and Safari need constant revision to keep up with HTML development. Different browsers are better at 'reading' certain pages.

Combining these ideas with developments in portability and computing power, we can anticipate further developments along the lines that we come back to in Chapter 14, including:

- better ways of representing information;
- different ways of accessing and exchanging information;
- more flexible messaging.

## Key developments

Many commentators identify the key change as the way that computers and communication systems have combined. We think there are other important processes:

- technology has developed new roles;
- technology is 'embedded'.

## Changing roles

Computers can obviously automate processes. The example of the check-out suggests a second main function: they can *monitor and control* processes. One challenging implication of computer control is the role of the human operator. For example, would you happily travel in an aircraft which was *completely* computer controlled from take-off right through to landing? And what if there were no human pilots on board?

When computers do take charge of a process, then you have to consider what happens if something goes wrong. The near-disaster at Three Mile Island is the classic illustration of what happens when human operators do not fully understand how the computer responds to emergencies. The computer took emergency action which the operators did not understand. They reversed the (correct) computer actions and very nearly caused a major accident.

### *Integrating*

Computer technology can also integrate processes in new ways. A commercial example of data integration is the way that supermarkets develop customer profiles.

### *Informating*

Another critical process is what Zuboff calls 'informating'. This is based on the notion that computers generate a lot of additional information as a by-product of their main function. In her own words:

> the . . . technology simultaneously generates information about the underlying productive and administrative processes through which an organisation accomplishes its work. It provides a deeper level of transparency to activities that had been either partially or completely opaque. In this way information technology supersedes the traditional logic of automation.
>
> (Zuboff, 1988, p. 10)

This principle of informating applies to *all* applications of computers. An example of how this can be used to control and monitor workers' performance would be the computerised telephone system used in a call centre. Management can discover at the press of a key exactly how many calls any operator has dealt with and how long they took. The quality of service provided in a phone call can be difficult to measure, so these crude statistics may be used (perhaps unfortunately for the customer) as measures of productivity.

One consequence of these technological and role changes is that some business and organisational processes have been completely transformed. A few examples to illustrate this are as follows (for more details, see the website):

- *British national newspapers in the late 1980s*: from a concentration in Fleet Street based on mechanical production to distributed companies based on computers with very reduced staffing and role changes.
- *The demise of bookshelf encyclopedias*: from multi-volume paper encyclopedias as prized possessions in many UK homes to free access on the Web.
- *The death of the record album?* Will downloading mean that all record shops and certain formats like the album disappear? Or does the current revival of vinyl sales signify a new long-term change for the record industry?

### IT has become embedded

The microchip is already becoming an embedded technology. There are microprocessors in many domestic appliances with functions which were not feasible before digital technology. Combining computer and communications technology means that devices can offer new functions. Linking sensors to computers which can communicate offers a range of new possibilities, including the car which diagnoses its own breakdown and calls a breakdown service without the driver's intervention. As we went to press, we noted the opening of Amazon's 'wearable technology store'.

**BOX 4.8 THE COMPUTER IS IN CHARGE: NOTHING CAN GO WRONG, GO WRONG, GO WRONG . . .**

While the technology has developed at an astonishing rate, the human capacity to manage it has not advanced at the same rate. Back in 1996, Stephen Flowers analysed 'failed' computer systems and highlighted a number of common factors, many of which relate to communication. These factors are still relevant and include:

- 'Hostile culture' – where staff feel unable to comment openly on errors and possible problems. Staff may still try to continue a project which is failing rather than admit the problems. And this will usually make things worse in the long run.
- 'Poor reporting structure' – a situation where senior management do not have a clear idea of the progress of the computer project.
- 'Technology-focused developments' – where system design has focused on technological possibilities and has ignored important human factors.
- 'Poor consultation' with users and other stakeholders.

## NEW FORMS OF BUSINESS ORGANISATIONS

We have moved into an information age, where the dominant form of employment and production is no longer manufacturing. This move demands new organisational structures and new patterns of communication.

## Moving away from the pyramid

Many organisations have adopted flatter structures with fewer layers of management. However, simply removing layers of management cannot be an end in itself, although this did seem true of many downsizing operations. Many writers suggest that this delayering will only work well if staff further down the pyramid are allowed to increase their capabilities and competence. This will have particular implications for those middle managers who remain.

Another related recommendation is that these new organisations must become less rigid and mechanistic. They must become more 'organic': the clear distinctions between roles which characterise formal organisational charts will become blurred as people co-operate to achieve the necessary tasks.

## Does this mean a paradigm shift?

One interpretation is that many organisations are moving towards new ways of working, and this has been happening for a while. For example, Henning (1998) described the engineering company which has only 35 employees, with no staff in finance, personnel, manufacturing or public relations. All of these functions were subcontracted to outside organisations. The rationale is that employees concentrate on what they do best: developing solutions to engineering problems and forging marketing relationships. Everything else is done from outside.

### *The networked organisation*

This can be visualised as a cluster or federation of business units which is co-ordinated by the central core of the organisation – potentially very different from the classic hierarchical organisation structure. The central core provides the broad overall vision and strategy, a coherent administration and ensures that the subunits work together to support the common purpose. The network will constantly change to serve the needs of customers and to adapt to changes in the business environment. Electronic communication is absolutely central to this model.

### *Teleworking*

Debates about the value of teleworking have reflected different national cultures. Early European debates tended to view telework as simply unskilled, low-paid office work which was done at home. This assumed that the work was organised by a distant but central office. In the United States, the debate mainly focused on the costs and benefits of eliminating commuting (Qvortrup, 1998, pp. 22–23). More recently, there has been more systematic debate on the international level which has recognised that there are very different forms of teleworking. This makes measurement and comparison quite difficult. For example, possibilities include supporting staff to set up their own electronic home offices, shared facility centres where a building, equipped with IT facilities, is used by various workers from different companies, or providing very flexible work facilities where workers are given the tools to operate at a distance from the main organisation's facilities.

Different forms of telework and telecommuting have not grown at the rate expected by some enthusiasts, as reflected in the statistics from the USA. However, this growth has made work more demanding and stressful for some homeworkers. For example, Glass and Noonan (2012) report that telecommuting has led to 'the general expansion of work hours . . . and/or the ability of employers to increase or intensify work demands among their salaried employees' (ibid., p. 38).

## How fast are organisations really changing?

Although the advocates of new organisational forms may offer persuasive examples, we cannot assume that all organisations are so progressive. Nor can we ignore the political implications of new forms of working. A more pessimistic picture was painted in papers from the annual International Labour Process Conference (Thompson and Warhurst, 1998). These suggested that claims of 'revolutionary' and wholesale change were exaggerated when we consider that:

- much 'knowledge work' is in fact extremely routine and repetitive;
- organisations may wish to ensure consistency and 'quality' by using strong control principles akin to the ideas of 'McDonaldization' (see Box 4.3);
- some modern human relations practices which claim to 'empower' workers are devices 'to achieve nothing less than the total colonisation of the . . . workforce' (p. 7);
- 'most companies in the US remain traditionally managed, wedded to a low-trust, low-skill, authoritarian route to competitiveness' (p. 9);
- relatively few workers are currently able to take advantage of the flexibilities which are offered by ICT.

However, they also pointed to situations where there has been significant positive change.

There is a further complication: larger organisations may contain a number of different structures within them – some based on older forms and some based on new principles and/or new technologies. For example, Harris quoted examples as diverse as the Japanese Ministry of International Trade and Industry and the BBC to illustrate the point that 'markets, hierarchies and networks may co-exist as complementary alternatives *within the same institutional setting*' (Harris, 1998, p. 85, his italics). He goes on to complain that theorists often ignore this diversity, especially those who advocate the virtual organisation.

## What these changes mean for communication

If organisation structures do change (if only partly) in the ways advocated in the previous sections, then business communication must also change. For example, if we assume a broadly networked organisation with lots of external links and subcontracting, then the managers in the 'core' of the organisation will have to adopt a much more co-operative and less directive style. There will also be increased needs for horizontal co-operation and the need to manage the growing importance of teamwork.

However, there are inherent contradictions which are difficult to reconcile. Fisman and Sullivan (2014) argue that, by providing more information to everyone in the organisation, computer technology enabled the flattening of many corporate hierarchies. At the same time, 'improved communication systems . . . actually push decisions back up the hierarchy' (ibid., p. 259). When the boss is available 24/7 on her mobile, why do I need to take responsibility to make that decision? The answer to this question depends on the broader organisational culture.

Given these contradictions and tensions, perhaps the best way to conclude this chapter is to highlight recent organisational initiatives in workspace and office design/redesign which reflect very diverse approaches to the complex relationship between culture, structure and technology:

- The Barbarian Group, a New York advertising agency, have refurbished their office space to include 'an undulating 1,100 feet long desk that would seat all 125 employees' (http://twistedsifter.com/2014/02/1100-ft-undulating-office-desk/).
- Jacquelyn Smith highlights 10 office designs which claim to 'offer employees much more creative, colorful and conducive workspaces' (www.forbes.com/sites/jacquelynsmith/2013*/03/08/10-cool-office-spaces/*)
- Google and FaceBook are often quoted as innovative examples of workspace design, and you can find pictures of their and other environments at: www.hongkiat.com/blog/creative-modern-office-designs/. For further examples of both creative design and user research, see the Cabe report at: http://webarchive.nationalarchives.gov.uk/20110118095356/http:/www.cabe.org.uk/files/impact-office-design-full-research.pdf.

We shall monitor these development to see which (if any) provide key pointers to the future shape and working environment of successful organisations. The next few years are likely to see further major changes in flexible working and learning spaces. As the rate of change of organisations, their people, their needs, their tools, their spaces, etc. continue to increase in often unpredictable ways, it is important to build flexible spaces to allow for unpredictable change.

## SUMMARY

- You need to understand the culture (or multiple cultures) within your organisation to anticipate how colleagues and management will respond to particular messages and ways of working.
- You need to consider the way you define your organisation's structure and its implications for communication.
- Technological change means that the ambitions of early pioneers can now be realised.

## FURTHER READING

Fisman, R. and Sullivan, T. (2014) *The Org: How the office really works.* London: John Murray.

Using approaches from organisational economics, this book focuses on the realities of current organisational operations and structures. Their examples and case studies illustrate the communications which shape the 'compromises' and 'trade-offs' that characterise the ways we work. We need to consider their argument that 'the highly imperfect office of today may nonetheless represent the least dysfunctional of all possible worlds, however depressing the idea of "least dysfunctional" may be' (p. 4).

Schmidt, E. and Cohen, J. (2014) *The New Digital Age: Reshaping the future of people, nations and business.* London: John Murray.

At the time of writing, Eric Schmidt is Executive Chairman of Google and Jared Cohen is Director of Google Ideas. They do not say much on very specific activities in organisations but we all need to consider the implications of their more general themes such as changing power relationships following greater access to information – 'The spread of connectivity, particularly through Internet-enabled mobile phones, is certainly the most common and perhaps the most profound example of this shift in power, if only because of the scale' (p. 6).

Senior, B. and Swailes, S. (2010) *Organisational Change* (4th edn). London: Prentice Hall.

This is a very readable introduction (with companion website) to major theories and change practices.

Vermeulen, F. (2010) *Business Exposed: The naked truth about what really goes on in the world of business.* Harlow: Pearson.

At the time of writing, Freek Vermeulen is an Associate Professor of Strategy and Entrepreneurship at the London Business School. His ongoing blog, FREEKY BUSINESS, also 'probes what really goes on in the world of business, once you get beneath the airbrushed façade. It examines the people that run companies – CEOs, managers, directors – and dissects the temptations, the influences and the sometimes ill-advised liaisons and strategies of corporate life.' This quote is taken from the front page of the blog: http://freekvermeulen.blogspot.co.uk.

Chapter 5

# How should we plan and organise professional and business writing?

## INTRODUCTION

Many books on business writing start by offering advice on the most appropriate business style. For example, Albert Joseph's book, *Put It In Writing!*, which described itself as 'the most widely used writing course in the English-speaking world', starts by emphasising that good business writers should write so that readers receive a clear and accurate impression of the writer's message. It then moves on immediately to five principles of clear writing, where principle one is 'to prefer clear, familiar words' (Joseph, 1998, p. 12). We comment on principles like this in the next chapter but we think that all writers need to start by taking a step back to reflect on their approach to writing and the way they organise information. This will also raise questions about what sort of document is needed and we focus on that in Chapter 8.

Our starting point is represented in the following quote from two well-known British researchers and consultants in communication, Turk and Kirkman:

> the real effort in writing is in the thinking required for planning and preparing, in the judgement required for organising and laying out, and in the continual need for sensitivity in the encoding of ideas in words and phrases.
>
> (1989, p. 126)

This quote identifies *three* critical steps which we reflect in this book: planning, organising the material, and choosing the best way to express yourself. It also puts the initial emphasis on planning and preparing. So how do you plan and prepare to write? Is there a best way of going about this process? For example, in this chapter, we emphasise the importance of clear objectives. A document can be beautifully written but if it does not have clear objectives and does not satisfy the needs or expectations of its readers, it is *not* an effective business document.

This chapter starts by examining different approaches to writing. We highlight the way that structure affects our perception and demonstrate that the organisation of a document influences how readers respond to it. This reinforces the need for clear objectives and we suggest ways in which these might be prepared and phrased. Finally, we discuss different methods and techniques for planning the structure of documents, and give examples to show how particular structures can support particular objectives.

**OBJECTIVES**

*This chapter will:*

- review different approaches to writing and suggest that you need to decide which approach suits you best;
- explain why organising and structuring information is so important;
- discuss how to establish clear objectives;
- explain different methods and principles for structuring information, including the use of outliners and other relevant software, and show how these can be used to plan documents;
- show how we can also use these principles to organise information at different levels, including how to construct paragraphs and link them into a well-organised text;
- show how the structure of a document can and should support its objectives.

## IS THERE A BEST WAY TO APPROACH BUSINESS WRITING?

Many texts on business communication recommend that writing is best achieved through a definite sequence of steps. Different writers use different labels for the steps but the ideas are very similar, as Table 5.1 shows. The recommendations are usually applied to both word-processed/printed and online documents. Stages of testing and maintenance are also often added to the timeline for online documents.

***Table 5.1*** *Stages of the writing process*

| *Steps involved in creating business documents* | | |
|---|---|---|
| *Authors* | | |
| *Bovee and Thill, 2014* | *Timm and Bienvenu, 2011* | *Barker, 1999* |
| Decide what you want to say | Define the context (including your objectives) | Create a message |
| | Consider your media, source and timing options | |
| Research information | Select and organise your information | Organise the information |
| Write your draft | | Write a first draft |
| Edit and revise | Deliver your message | Edit and revise |
| | Evaluate feedback for continued success | |

## Should we always follow the suggested steps?

If the *advice* from business communicators is clear, is this advice supported by research evidence? Can we assure success by following these steps?

As with most aspects of human communication, reality is more complex than some of the advice. In one of the most accessible and interesting reviews of what we know about the writing process, Mike Sharples concluded that there are three 'core activities' in writing – planning, composing and revising – but the 'flow of activity, however, is not just in one direction' (Sharples, 1999, p. 72). His model is reproduced in Figure 5.1. It shows a flow of material in a clockwise direction – from notes and plans to draft to final copy – *and* a flow of ideas in the opposite direction. For example, reading a draft may generate an idea which alters the plan.

Sharples also reviews specific studies on the impact of the initial planning phase, as well as looking at some of the methods we cover in this chapter. He concludes that 'time spent on planning is time well spent' (p. 88) but that there are different ways to plan. Writers need to find the combination of methods that suit their situation rather than relying on a single 'model approach'.

We can extract practical conclusions from this brief review:

- It is important to develop plans and objectives.
- You do not have to write in a rigid sequence of steps.

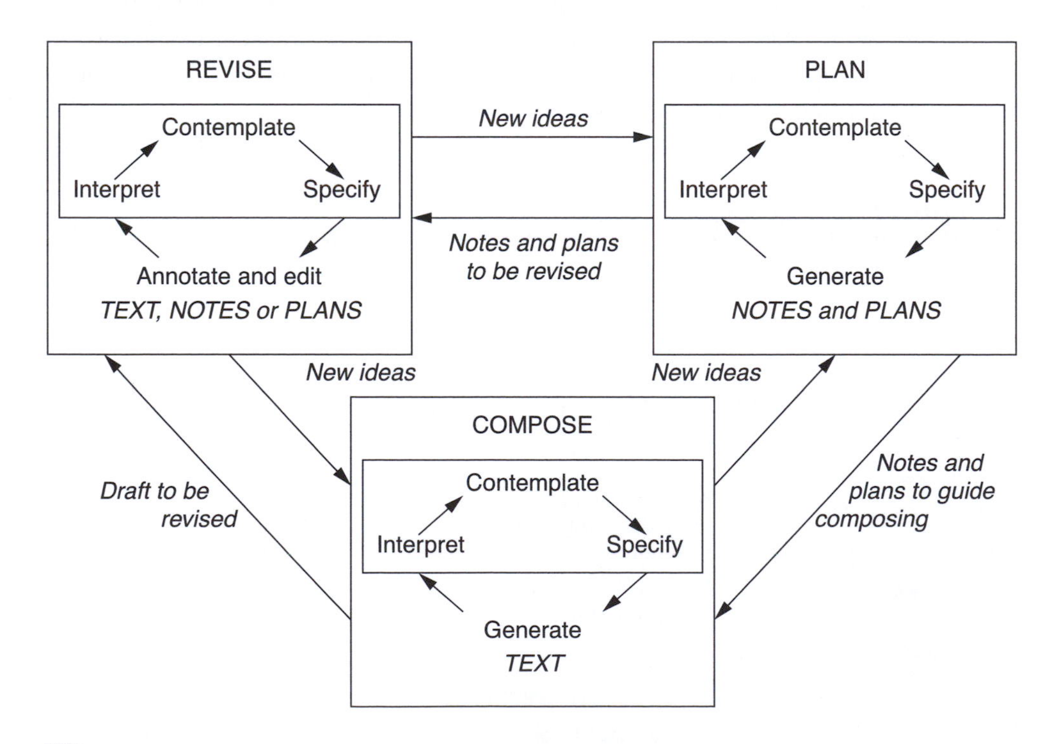


**Figure 5.1** *Sharples's model of writing as creative design*

Source: Sharples, 1999, p. 72.

- You should continually review your initial plans and objectives as your writing develops.
- You need to find an approach to planning and organising your writing which suits you.

An important research finding is that writers have very different ways of approaching all three main components of the writing process, and we summarise some of the important differences in Box 5.1.

## BOX 5.1 ARE YOU A BRICKLAYER OR AN OIL PAINTER?

Several research studies have tried to investigate the main strategies used by writers. Sharples identifies two major studies which came up with very similar results (Sharples, 1999, pp. 114ff.). The table below highlights major differences between strategies.

***Table 5.2** Writing strategies*

| *Writing strategies* | | | | |
|---|---|---|---|---|
| *'Watercolourist'* | *'Architect'* | *'Bricklayer'* | *'Sketcher'* | *'Oil painter'* |
| Tend to write 'in one pass' from mental plan | Make detailed plan | Build the text up, sentence by sentence | Produce rough plan | Start by drafting rather than planning, working from broad headings |
| Tend to review and revise on screen rather than print out drafts | Do a draft, then print out. Revise paper version and then return to computer | Revise on screen as they go | Make frequent revisions and review/ revise both on screen and from paper draft | Review drafts on paper |

Some writers seem to use one strategy almost exclusively; other writers adopt different strategies for different tasks. We can find examples of successful professional authors who use each of these strategies. The key to successful writing is being aware of what you need to produce rather than following a specific process. As Sharples concludes: 'Being a writer is, above all, having control over how you write and trust in your ability to make progress' (Sharples, 1999, p. 128).

### Planning is more than the text

Another important point which is not always emphasised is that planning should not just be about the words or the text – it should consider the whole of what we call 'document design'. You need to consider *four* interlinked aspects which will create the finished document:

- *Style of writing* – i.e. choice of words, jargon, the way you address the reader and so on. We cover this in Chapter 6.
- *Layout and design* – i.e. the design of the page whether printed, online or both, and the use of any visual aids such as illustrations or diagrams, and so on. We cover this in Chapter 8.
- *Structure of information* – which is the focus of the rest of this chapter.
- *Choice of media* – for example, it is not enough to simply think of the distinction between print and online. There are different possibilities depending on which type of print or online document you may choose and we say more on this in Chapter 8.

One advantage of a clear plan is that the completed document should be easier to understand from the reader's point of view.

## WHY IS STRUCTURING INFORMATION SO IMPORTANT IN BUSINESS COMMUNICATION?

We know from decades of research into human perception, cognition and memory that our brain continuously anticipates, organises and reorganises the information it receives. A lot of the time we are not conscious of the amount or extent of this processing. As a result, we can be misled by the way information is presented. Scott Plous demonstrated this very convincingly in his summary of research on human decision-making and problem-solving. For example, he quotes research which asked students to comment on film clips of road accidents. Students who were asked how fast the cars were going when they 'smashed' estimated an average speed which was 30 per cent higher than students who were asked about the speed when the cars 'hit'. Students who were asked about 'smashed' cars were also likely to 'remember' a week later that the accident involved broken glass, something which was *not* on the film clips. In other words, these students had not just remembered – they had *reconstructed* an image of the accident based on the notion of a 'smash' and subconsciously exaggerated elements of what they had actually seen. Other research has shown the power of suggestions in particular formats of questions – for example, it makes a difference to people's estimates if you ask 'how *long* was the movie?' rather than 'how *short* was the movie?' (Plous, 1993, pp. 32ff. and 66ff.).

More recent studies have emphasised the way we actively construct our interpretation of events. For example, we can be influenced in our thinking and judgements by perceptual biases such as anchoring and priming.

Perhaps the best way to appreciate the idea of priming is to imagine that you have volunteered to participate in a psychology experiment. Your first task is to assemble four-word sentences from a set of five words. You are then asked to walk to another room to do another task. Suppose the words that you were working with in the first task contained a lot of words relating to old age and getting old. Would that influence your later behaviour?

The short answer is 'yes', as the researchers compared the behaviour of participants who worked with a lot of 'elderly' words and those who did not. They measured the time it took them to walk to the next room and discovered that those participants who had been 'primed' to think about associations with old age walked slower down the corridor. This classic experiment and other similar studies are discussed in detail by Daniel Kahneman (see Kahneman, 2011, Chapter 4).

Anchoring is a similar process where you subconsciously use an estimate that you already have in your mind to make a decision or solve a problem. Again, the best way to understand this is to use an example. Consider your response to the following two questions:

1 Is the height of the tallest redwood tree more or less than 1,200 feet?
What is your best guess about the height of the tallest redwood tree?

2 Is the height of the tallest redwood tree more or less than 180 feet?
What is your best guess about the height of the tallest redwood tree?

These are variations of the same problem – how tall is the tallest redwood tree? But the first variation gives you a much bigger anchor – 1,200 feet – and this has a significant impact on the way that most people answer the question. When these questions were presented to different visitors at San Francisco Exploratorium, the answers were 844 and 282 feet respectively – in other words, the average answer added over 50 per cent of the anchor figure (Kahneman, 2011, pp.123ff.).

The important practical implication of these studies is that we have to be very aware of possible interpretations which our readers may make and which could be avoided by different structuring. We should aim to enhance what Kahneman refers to as the 'cognitive ease' of the reader's task and we illustrate that by using his analysis of tactics for a persuasive message in Box 5.4.

So our retention and understanding of messages depends on how they are presented. We cannot easily absorb or remember information which is not clearly structured. For a simple example, read the following list of animals once and try to remember and repeat them before you read on:

chacma
cheetah
gorilla
impala
leopard
vervet
wildebeest
wolf
zebra.

Most people find this list difficult to remember. It is organised – it is arranged in alphabetical order – but this does not help you to structure the list in any meaningful way. It does not give you much help remembering the information, especially as some of the animals are not very widely known. A meaningful structure would make recall much easier. Consider the following reorganisation.

| *Herbivores* | *Carnivores* | *Primates* |
|---|---|---|
| impala | cheetah | chacma |
| wildebeest | leopard | gorilla |
| zebra | wolf | vervet |

Recall of this classification is easier for two reasons:

- a long list has been subdivided into three short lists;
- there is some logic in the subdivision.

However, we must use sensible structures. If we examine these three sublists closely, the logic is not consistent. 'Herbivores' and 'carnivores' refer to eating habits while 'primates' refers to a zoological order. If we added 'bear' to the list it would not fit into any of the classifications as it is neither a herbivore, a carnivore nor a primate. To get a logically consistent classification we would either have one based on eating habits (herbivores, carnivores and omnivores), or one based on zoology (primate and non-primate).

This illustrates the point that, while classification helps us to order our information, we need to use a system of classification which is consistent – it should use one criterion at a time. It is, of course, possible to have subclassification. We can classify the animals into primates and non-primates and then again subdivide each group into herbivores, carnivores and omnivores.

If you were trying to help people remember a list of this sort, you would also need to choose criteria to suit the subject matter and the needs of the audience. For example, an animal nutritionist would be more interested in a dietary classification than a zoological one.

The practical point here is that, if we can present information which is clearly organised *and* organised in a way which makes sense to the audience, then that audience will find the information easier to understand and remember.

## DEFINING OBJECTIVES

Many discussions of objectives imply that you must have them 'perfectly' worked out before you do anything else. We see objectives as more flexible in line with the more fluid description of the writing process we gave earlier. There are two aspects of objectives we want to highlight in this chapter:

- phrasing your objectives in a particular way can help you decide what information to provide;
- clear objectives help you to improve the document by revising or redesigning it.

After we have discussed these we will look at one common business objective – to persuade – and show some of the complexities of translating this into writing.

## Phrasing objectives

Ros Jay gives an example of how useful it is to refine your objectives and make them more specific – suppose you had to write a proposal which would convince a customer to 'buy one of our swimming pools' (Jay, 1995, p. 14ff.). This could cover a range of different models – suppose we believe that the 'deluxe' model would suit the customer's needs best. But what needs are they? Jay suggests 'quality' and 'ease of maintenance' as needs but, of course, we could be more specific. We could develop an objective which helps to structure the communication – e.g. to demonstrate that the deluxe model would satisfy customer X by being well built and reliable, easy to maintain, safe for all the family members to use and economical to run. We can use a simple layout to show how this objective is structured.

The deluxe model would satisfy customer X by being:

- well built and reliable;
- easy to maintain;
- safe for all the family members to use;
- economical to run.

This layout demonstrates that this objective is structured in two parts:

- the overall purpose;
- a list of the main criteria or arguments which support this purpose.

You can structure the main objective for an investigation or report in the same way.

Replacing our current management information system with the Genesis system will:

- improve our management decisions;
- give operating staff more satisfying jobs;
- save on running costs.

Once again, this is an objective which then supplies the main structure of the argument. You would expect this report to have three main sections – one about management decisions, one about staff jobs and one about running costs.

## Clear objectives can lead to new (and better) documents

David Sless analysed how a large company used several rounds of customer testing to refine the format of what had been a complex multi-page document – a traditional letter plus several forms (Sless, 1999). The single page which resulted satisfied all the necessary objectives:

- telling the customer that their insurance policy would be cancelled if payment was not received by a certain date;
- reminding the customer of the details of the policy in question;
- providing a payment slip which customers could use by mail or at a post office.

The previous design put these objectives on separate pages. This created practical problems – all the customer needed to do was separate the letter and the forms and they had no idea which policy was being chased up. Using a single sheet eliminated this problem. The layout of the new form also clearly highlighted the three sections by the use of shading behind the text.

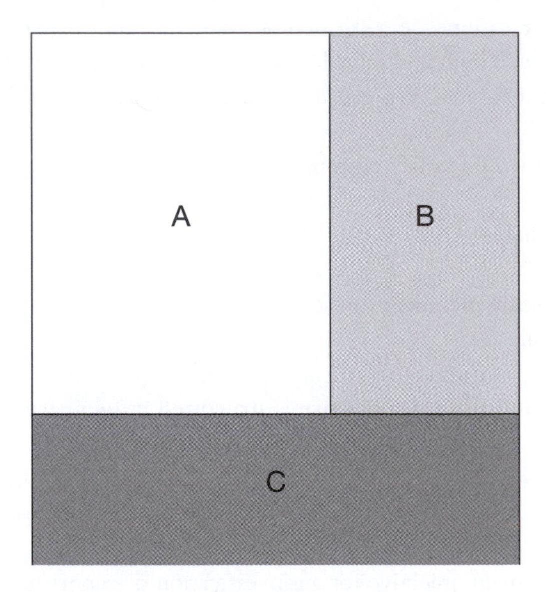


***Figure 5.2*** *Sections in a printed document*

Section A was the 'letter' explaining the timetable for cancellation, section B summarised the policy and section C was the payment slip.

For examples of similar restructuring and simplification, see the work of the Simplification Centre in the UK (and especially their 'Simple Actions' reworkings) at: www.simplificationcentre.org.uk.

## WHEN THE OBJECTIVE IS TO PERSUADE

The study of persuasion goes back about 2,500 years to the time when the Greek Sophists taught people to argue their cases in courts and in a public forum. For example, Aristotle recognised that there was more to persuasion than logical argument: 'We ought in fairness to fight our case with no help beyond the basic facts . . . other things affect the result considerably owing to the defects of our hearers.'

Aristotle recognised that there were three basic elements:

- *ethos* – establishment of sender credibility, or believability;
- *logos* – appeal to reason;
- *pathos* – appeal to the emotions.

These three basic elements still underpin many modern theories of persuasion.

## Sender credibility

Aristotle correctly reasoned that if people could impress an audience with their credibility, then what they said was likely to be accepted. In the business context, sender credibility operates at a number of levels. For example, a group within an organisation can achieve credibility by reaching its targets and individuals within the organisation by living up to their promises, e.g. 'If Juliet Smith says it will be ready tomorrow, you can rely on that.' We are also inclined to believe in communication from presentable and helpful staff. Outward appearances can give an impression of credibility.

## Rational argument

We cannot just rely on the strict rules of logic which the ancient Greeks used. In most business situations, you do not progress from irrefutable facts to logical conclusions; rather, you have a mass of evidence, often contradictory, which has to be weighed before a decision is taken. You have to show that the weight of the evidence favours certain conclusions, and that these conclusions suggest certain actions.

So, persuasive argument in business writing usually consists of:

- a clear presentation of facts and inferences;
- an objective analysis of this information;
- reasoned conclusions from the analysis
- a proposed course of action based on these conclusions.

There are some further issues to worry about, described below.

### *Emotional appeal*

It is important to realise that the audience will often react emotionally to a message. It is important to know those areas where an audience is influenced by strong emotion, particularly where political, religious, and moral beliefs and values are concerned.

### *Audience analysis*

Persuasion aims to change the audience's world view in some way, so it is important to have some idea of the audience's *present world view* and the factors that are likely to *motivate* the audience to adopt the desired view.

### *Format of correspondence*

All writing should encourage the audience to read it as there is usually no compulsion to do so. The minimum requirement for a persuasive letter is that it is clear and well set out.

## Deciding on the content of persuasive writing

You can use all three of Aristotle's principles. For example, when applying by correspondence for financial support, sender credibility (*ethos*) can be established by a number of methods, such as:

- the high status of the writer or the organisation;
- the obvious legality of the document – e.g. proper organisational stationery, fund-raising number, etc.;
- stating (briefly) some achievements of the organisation.

We must also use logical argument and provide some evidence that the appeal is necessary. Such evidence can come from:

- facts and figures;
- expert opinion.

The emotive appeal must be carefully handled. It has been shown that overly emotional appeals do not necessarily result in the desired action, although they may often elicit an emotional response – e.g. people usually want to forget unpleasant emotions as soon as possible. Charities have found that focusing on a bad situation during appeals is less successful than placing some emphasis on the potentially happy outcome of a successful appeal.

Modern techniques and approaches to persuasion (e.g. Perloff, 2013) emphasise the importance of building conducive relationships. For example, Robert Cialdini (2007) suggests six principles: reciprocation, commitment and consistency, social proof, liking, authority and scarcity.

Kevin Dutton reviews a wide range of studies and his own analysis of persuasive techniques in action proposes 'five major axes of persuasion': simplicity, perceived self-interest, incongruity, confidence and empathy (Dutton, 2011). We have summarised these in Table 5.3 below. You can use this as a checklist for your own persuasive messages, both written and oral.

# METHODS AND PRINCIPLES FOR STRUCTURING INFORMATION

There are several different ways of looking at structure.

## Chunking, ordering and signposting

Much of the communication skills training that we have been involved in over the last twenty plus years has used these three basic principles (Hartley, 1984):

**Table 5.3** *Characteristics of persuasive messages*

| *Characteristic of persuasive messages* | *Meaning* | *Checklist question* |
|---|---|---|
| Simplicity | Simple messages are more memorable | Can you summarise your main message in a simple phrase or sentence?<br><br>Does your use of language make the main message easy to remember? |
| Perceived self-interest | Your main message should appeal to what the audience sees as its own advantage | What does your audience want?<br><br>Does your main message offer them an advantage? |
| Incongruity | Persuasive messages contain an element of surprise which captures attention | Does your presentation contain any novel elements which will catch your audience's attention? |
| Confidence | Persuasive messages are expressed confidently | How does your presentation inspire confidence? |
| Empathy | Persuasive messages demonstrate that you appreciate the feelings and circumstances of your audience | How does your presentation demonstrate that you have recognised the main issues or interests of your audience? |

## BOX 5.2 WHO IS YOUR 'MODEL COMMUNICATOR'?

One interesting category of management texts uses historical and sometimes fictional figures to act as role models for management behaviour. So we have had texts on management and leadership based on Moses, Genghis Khan, Superman and even *Star Trek*. If you want a more sensitive or controversial example, consider the claim that Jesus Christ provides a model of effective marketing and communications (Finan, 1998). The argument here is that communication was one of the major tools used by Jesus and his life illustrates the power of some basic principles:

- clear and simple objectives;
- careful planning for long-term success – one of Finan's main points is that all of Jesus's reported actions contributed to his overall strategy;
- using each and every opportunity to explain his message;
- assembling a committed team to 'spread the word' and support him.

- *Chunking* is the way that information can be broken down into sections or 'chunks' which make the information easier to digest. An example would be the way we sorted the list of animals above into three chunks to make it easier to remember.
- *Ordering* is the way we put those chunks into an order which will make them more or less useful or meaningful.
- *Signposting* is the way we can offer clues or signals to explain or demonstrate the way the information is structured.

We can illustrate these principles with an everyday example. The news bulletin on US or UK television is usually clearly organised along the following lines:

- The bulletin is presented in a series of specific events with some use of overall categories – e.g. the sports stories are clustered together towards the end (chunking).
- The introduction at the beginning lists the main stories (signposting). This is repeated at the end and sometimes also about halfway through.
- The most 'important' stories come first (ordering). There is often a short amusing story at the end to provide light relief.

All of the methods we go on to describe use some combination of these three basic principles. They often use some visual analogy as a basic idea and so we start with the 'magic' of pyramids.

## The pyramid principle

This is explained in detail in the book of the same name by Barbara Minto, which was first published in the USA in 1987 and has since been published in several different editions. It is based on the idea that the human mind will look for patterns in the information presented, as we have suggested above, and that the pyramid is a common and convenient pattern. So she suggests that 'the clearest written documents will be those that consistently present their information from the top down, in a pyramidal structure' (Minto, 2002, p. 11). She explains how to construct pyramids which can then be translated into documents, emphasising that any level in the pyramid must summarise the ideas grouped below it *and* that you must logically order and cluster ideas into sensible groups (what we would call chunking). She recommends a top-down approach, although she also shows how you can build a pyramid from bottom-up, where you have a collection of information but do not have a clear idea of how to put it together.

With a clear objective, you can use the top-down approach. You start by defining the top-level of the pyramid. To do this you need to decide what question you are dealing with and what is your recommended answer. This answer then fills the box at the top of the pyramid. For example, suppose that you have been asked to produce a written report which evaluates a proposal to replace an existing information system with a new one. If you decide that the new information system is a good idea, then this proposition becomes the top box in the pyramid. You then have to ask yourself how to convince your reader to go along with the proposition. For example, you may want to argue that a new system will actually provide more comprehensive information than the present one. It may be cheaper to run. It may be easier to use and allow staff to spend more time on other more important jobs. You can see from Figure 5.3 below that you can use these ideas to build the second layer of the pyramid.

By generating a logical question which follows from these three propositions, you can produce of the third layer of the pyramid. The key question here is 'how?'. How will the new system deliver more comprehensive information? How will it be cheaper to run? How will it allow staff to spend more time doing more important jobs? To construct the complete pyramid, you simply repeat this question and answer sequence to generate as many levels as appropriate.

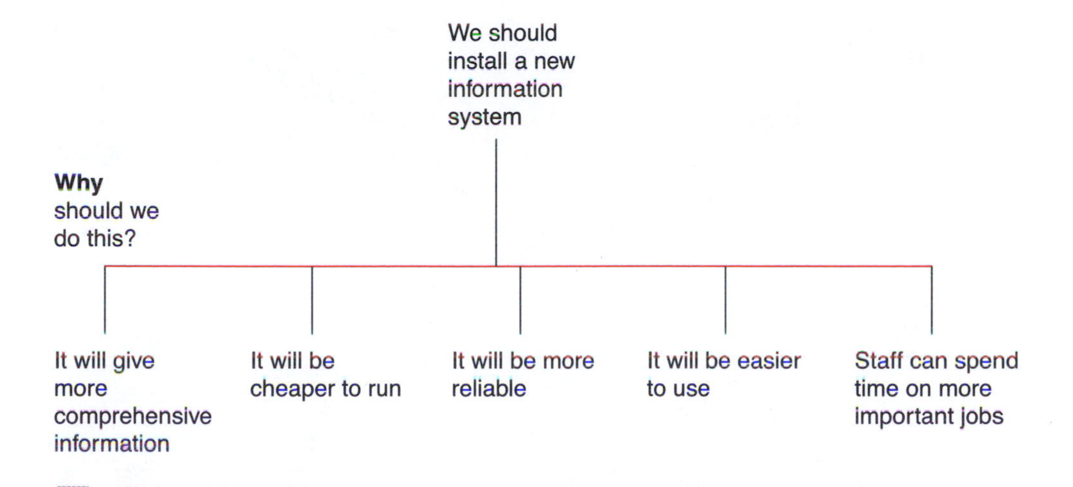


**Figure 5.3** *Pyramid example*

Minto also provides a very interesting model to form the introduction to any document. This is based on her suggestion that we need to spell out the history of events which have led up to the document. This can be represented by what she calls a 'classic pattern of story-telling' – situation, complication, question, answer. This sequence is explained in more detail below.

## Spider diagrams and mind maps

The pyramid principle advocates that we should visualise the structure of our argument as a pyramid. But what other visual analogies can we use?

### *The spider diagram*

Another way of developing a structure of ideas is to create a spider diagram. You write your central idea or topic in the middle of the page and then build a 'spider's web' of associated ideas which link from it. This then gives you a structure which you can amend and revise until it covers what you want. We have used this very simple method of summarising ideas in various ways – to take notes of lectures, to plan lectures, to give as handouts, to plan reports and papers, and so on (as in Figure 5.4 – our early notes for this chapter). The spider diagram has a number of potential advantages over linear notes or a full transcription:

- it is quick and easy to do;
- it gives a visual map of the topic which can make it easy to remember;
- it can summarise complicated ideas.

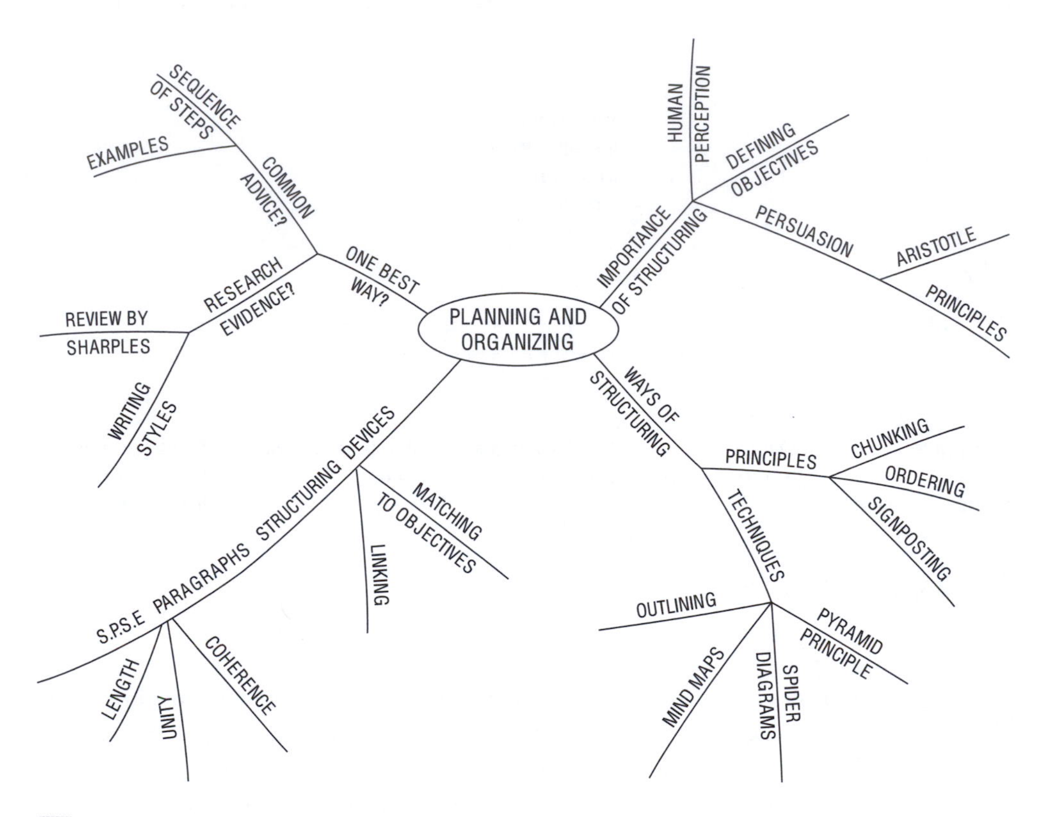


***Figure 5.4*** *Spider diagram*

## *Mind maps*

A more sophisticated development of this idea comes from Tony Buzan, one of the leading advocates of the Mind Map®, which he describes as 'a powerful graphic technique which provides a universal key to unlocking the potential of the brain' (Buzan, 1995, p. 59). He argues that these maps work best when you incorporate a variety of techniques, such as:

- *emphasis* – by including images, colours and spacing on the page, and by variations in the size of lines, text and images;
- *association* – by making links across the diagram and by developing your own codes to represent ideas.

As a result, many of the examples in his main book are much more visually complex and colourful than the diagrams we have tended to use in this book.

### *Building electronic maps*

There are now various software packages which allow you to build different types of spider diagrams and mind maps, including packages from Buzan himself.

## Outlining

We have tried to show that even the simplest of written communications needs some form of planned structure. This can vary from a three- or four-point outline for a response to an enquiry letter, to an outline with headings and subheadings for an investigative report. We show examples of this in later chapters. Modern word-processing software includes an outliner so you can either type in your text in normal page fashion or directly into the outliner. Provided you have used the hierarchy of headings which your word processor allows, you can also review your text in outline at any time. You can also move the text around in outline view, which can be easier than using 'cut and paste' in normal view.

You can therefore produce an outline straight into the word processor to see if your plan looks sensible and then expand it. For example, one junior administrator was asked to produce a short report on replacing the carpeting in the main office. He started with the following outline:

- carpet qualities available and suitability for various types of work areas;
- cost of the various grades;
- colours available (need pamphlet showing colours);
- fitting services offered by local firms
- guarantees.

For longer documents, such as reports on investigations, you can use the outliner function to produce a plan of action as a guide before you start your investigation. Once the investigation is complete, this can be expanded in the outline for the report. For example, if you were asked to investigate the copier needs of your organisation for the next five years, your plan could look something like this:

- present copying facilities;
- estimate of future requirements;
- technology – current and developing;
- operating costs;
- back-up service and spares.

Once the information has been collected and examined, you could develop this plan into a more comprehensive outline. For example, under operating costs you would want to investigate the comparative costs of purchase or lease and the different forms of lease available.

In the next few years, we are likely to see further advances in the way computer software supports our writing through functions like outliners. And you should check whether your default word-processor software is offering you the facilities you really need as in Box 5.3.

### BOX 5.3 ARE YOU USING THE 'RIGHT' WORD PROCESSOR?

If you have been through a school/college/university career where these institutions used Microsoft Office, you may never have considered using an alternative word processor to Microsoft Word on your desktop or laptop. There are a number of alternatives which offer a different range of facilities. For example:

- Google Docs allows collaboration online but does not have such a wide range of formatting.
- Microsoft Word is now available online and on tablets such as the iPad.
- One of us (PH) prefers Apple's Pages to Word because of the way it uses templates and styles.
- Some word processors offer particular advantages for particular tasks.

See the website for an update and further discussion.

## STRUCTURING DEVICES IN WRITTEN DOCUMENTS

There are a range of devices we can use in documents to make the structure clear to readers. To illustrate how this can be done we shall concentrate on features of the paragraph: structure, length, unity, coherence and linking devices. In later chapters, we show how features like typefaces and page design can supply similar cues, including the use of headings and subheadings linked to layout on the page.

### Structure of paragraphs

One common structure in paragraphs in business writing presents the following a logical progression:

Situation
⇓
Problem
⇓
Solution
⇓
Evaluation

This sort of structure is also used as a model for structuring documents – see Box 5.4 for some examples. Often only two or three of the components are present but they follow the same sequence:

- situation – problem – evaluation;
- situation – evaluation.

For example, the following paragraph follows the 'situation – evaluation' pattern.

> Any substantial written business text contains a number of different pieces of information that are part of a presentation to achieve some communication objective. These pieces are usually related in a structured way.

Another common structure is to follow the time sequence.

> We were travelling by car to Springfield. Near Halfway House the left-front tyre burst and the car skidded off the road into a barrier. We were extremely lucky to escape without injury.

This paragraph also follows the 'situation – problem – evaluation' sequence.

You can also use physical or spatial arrangements as the basis for paragraph structure. For example, you can describe a house in terms of its downstairs features, followed by its upstairs features. The most important point to emphasise is that paragraphs should have a clear and consistent structure.

## Length of paragraphs

As you have just seen, a paragraph can consist of a single sentence. Short, one-sentence paragraphs are often used to emphasise a point.

There is no upper limit to the number of words in a paragraph. Good business writing tends to have short paragraphs compared with literary writing. For long documents like reports, a maximum of 100 words per paragraph is a rough guideline. For shorter documents like letters and memos, about 60 words is suitable, but you must not destroy the unity of a paragraph in an effort to reduce its length.

To maintain the reader's interest, you should use paragraphs of varying lengths.

## Unity

Unity here means that the paragraph deals with a single topic and contains no irrelevant material. Any sentence that does not refer to the topic should be excluded and moved to a new paragraph. This enables the reader to follow your train of thought one step at a time. However, a paragraph may have linking sentences which link it to preceding or following paragraphs and we will look at those later.

## Coherence

It is not sufficient that all sentences in a paragraph refer to the topic; they should also develop the theme in a logical way. Each sentence should follow on naturally from the previous one.

### BOX 5.4 STRUCTURING DOCUMENTS TO ASSIST 'COGNITIVE EASE'

Kahneman (2011) suggests a number of practical steps which should reduce cognitive strain and help make messages more persuasive, including:

- Maximise legibility.
- If you are using colour in the document, then use it appropriately. Apparently, text in 'bright blue' is 'more likely to be believed' than 'pale blue'.
- Use simple language.
- Make the language as memorable as possible by using techniques like verse and rhyming to get across main points.

However, he also says that these techniques will not necessarily guarantee success.

A typical practical translation of these sorts of ideas comes from Suzanne Sparks who advises that you should 'structure your writing to reach your reader' (Sparks, 1999, p. 48). She offers five possible structures for letters and memos which are similar to the paragraph structures we discussed above. For example, she suggests that a persuasive communication should be based on the following five paragraphs:

1. You try to establish some common ground.
2. You explain the problem which will be resolved if the reader agrees to your request.
3. You explain the solution and show how it has significant advantages for the reader which outweigh any disadvantages.
4. You list all the benefits for the reader.
5. You clearly specify what you want the reader to do.

## Linking devices

We can use linking to help the reader follow our train of thought. Linking can apply to the sentences within a paragraph and to the paragraphs within a text. Various ways of linking are:

- linking punctuation;
- linking words;
- linking phrases;
- linking sentences.

Linking can slow down the reader, so avoid excessive use. It can also be irritating, particularly where the linkage is obvious.

### *Linking punctuation*

The semicolon is commonly used to show that two statements which could have been written as separate sentences are closely related – e.g. 'The company has applied for an overdraft to finance increased stock levels; this will be essential for the continued expansion of the business.' The clause after the semicolon could have been written as a separate sentence, but the use of the semicolon emphasises the close relation of the two ideas.

### *Linking words and phrases*

Linking words are those such as thus, therefore, also, but, first . . . second, etc. – e.g. 'The programme has been designed to meet the needs of large businesses.' However, it can be adapted for small businesses.[1]

Repeating key words can also provide linking, as in 'The programme has been designed to meet the needs of large businesses. The programme can also be adapted for small businesses.

Similarly, phrases like 'next in importance is. . .', 'we conclude therefore. . .', 'to sum up' . . . etc. can all help the transition between sentences and paragraphs.

### *Linking sentences*

Where one topic has been dealt with in detail and a completely new topic is to be explored, it is sometimes necessary to signal this with a transitional sentence at the end of a paragraph. For example, if we have been considering the causes of inflation and wish to move to the cure for inflation, a transitional sentence can make this clear: 'Having examined the causes of inflation we will now examine the possible cures.'

## MATCHING STRUCTURE TO OBJECTIVES

The most important point to conclude this chapter is that the structure of your written communication should support your objectives (this also applies to face-to-face communication as we shall discuss later). We can illustrate this by looking at possible structures for a persuasive letter. The following are some of the elements that may be included. Not all of these elements will suit every case and they do not necessarily follow the sequence given:

- attention-getting introduction;
- statement of problem or situation;
- statement of needs of or advantages to receiver;
- statement of needs of sender;
- visualisation of outcome;
- reconciliation of sender's and receiver's needs;
- call for action.

For example, consider the appeal letter below which we used in our first edition – it is based on a real letter from an animal charity which has been slightly modified to illustrate the above points.

**Table 5.4** *Letter using structure which aims to persuade*

| *What each paragraph does* | *Text of the letter* |
|---|---|
| Attention-getting introduction | When a dog lies crippled and crying on the roadside, the call automatically goes out for the ANIMALCARE ambulance. |
| Needs of receiver | When a stray is found – a family pet, abandoned by its owners and left to fend for itself – everyone reacts in the same way: 'Get ANIMALCARE on to it.' Even a child knows that if his beloved pet is sick or in pain, there'll always be someone at ANIMALCARE to help. |
| Statement of situation | But how many people know what goes on behind the scenes – or even realise where the money comes from for the care and attention of the animals who cannot speak for themselves? |
| Background to sender's needs<br>Statement of situation | Last year, because of lack of funds, it was touch-and-go as to whether we would be forced to close our doors, but miraculously, through the help of many generous friends in the community, we've managed to stay open. |
| Background to sender's needs<br>Statement of situation | We receive no State Aid, and because 90% of our work is done free of charge, our funds are stretched to the limit. We battle to cope with escalating costs and the frightening increase in the number of animals needing attention. |
| Sender's need | But the crisis is by no means over. |
| Sender's need | Frankly, the situation is desperate. Which is why I am writing to you – as someone living in an area covered by the ANIMALCARE service – for your support. |
| Visualisation of outcome<br>Receiver's need | Your gift, whatever the size, will not only help to eliminate suffering among animals, but will assist your local ANIMALCARE to protect you and your family from health hazards such as rabies. |
| Reconciling sender's and receiver's need | You can assist in the elimination of animal suffering by supporting our work. A donation of 50 ecus will support a dog for two months. |
| Call to action | We have enclosed a donation form and an addressed envelope. |
| | Please help us, as we rely entirely on kind people such as you. |
| | Yours sincerely |
| | J Jones Organising Secretary |
| Attention-getting | PS This region's only Bird Hospital is run by ANIMALCARE. Wouldn't it be a tragedy if it had to be abandoned due to lack of funds? |

This letter does follow a sensible structure, but we can still ask questions about its likely impact:

- Will people take the time to read it? Don't most of us tend to throw away circular letters unless they come from organisations we are already committed to?
- Will it be read by people who are not already committed to the cause of animal welfare?
- Will reading it lead to action? Does the donation form make donating easy enough?
- Is a letter the best form of communication for this sort of appeal nowadays?

Perhaps we need a different or additional approach based on a more fundamental review of the document aims? We return to this issue in Chapter 8 (also see further discussion on the website).

## SUMMARY

- Many texts divide the writing process into a series of steps and suggest you follow them in that order, moving from preparation and research, to organising the material, and on to writing and revising.
- Research suggests that life is more complex. Writers need to find the combination of methods that suit their situation – it is important to develop plans and objectives but this does not mean that you have to write in a rigid sequence of steps.
- Research shows that if we can present information which is clearly organised *and* organised in a way that makes sense to the audience, then that audience will find the information easier to understand and remember.
- Clear objectives are an important part of planning. Phrasing your objectives in a particular way can help you decide what information you then need to provide.
- Persuasion is an important function of many documents. We need to consider whether our writing can use appropriate tactics and techniques.
- There are various ways of structuring information which you can use as the basis for a written document. They are all based on three basic principles: chunking, ordering and signposting.
- There are many useful techniques for structuring material which often use some visual analogy as a basic idea. It is worth considering the pyramid principle, the use of concept and mind maps, and the use of outliners.
- There are also devices we can use in documents to make the structure clear to readers. To illustrate this, we concentrated on features of the paragraph: argument structure, length, unity, coherence and linking devices.
- The structure of your written communication should support your objectives, and we illustrated this by looking at possible structures for a persuasive letter. However, this raises the question of the appropriate media for particular messages.

## FURTHER READING

Chabris, C. and Simons. D. (2011) *The Invisible Gorilla: And other ways our intuition deceives us*. London: HarperCollins.

The Invisible Gorilla study demonstrates the 'power' of our attention to focus on some things while ignoring other important stimuli. This book brings out the practical implications of this and related research.

Dutton, K. (2011) *Flipnosis: The art of split-second persuasion*. Croydon: Arrow.

Don't be put off by the gimmicky title. This book summarises a wide range of relevant research studies as well as Dutton's own studies of persuasive techniques in everyday life.

Minto, B. (2002) *The Pyramid Principle: Logic in writing and thinking* (3rd edn) London: Pearson.

This gives the complete description of this principle and its practical application, and includes lots of relevant business examples. Minto has now written an updated version (2010) which is available from her website: www.barbaraminto.com. You can also find a summary of her course concepts at the Apple iTunes store: https://itunes.apple.com/us/app/minto/id538500088?mt=8.

Plous, S. (1993) *The Psychology of Judgment and Decision Making*. New York: McGraw-Hill.

Probably the best (and certainly one of the most entertaining and thought-provoking) introduction to the complex ways we process information.

Sharples, M. (1999) *How We Write: Writing as creative design*. London: Routledge.

An excellent summary of what we know about the writing process (and what we don't) which raises many interesting practical questions.

Chapter 6

# What is an effective writing style?

## INTRODUCTION

As we said in the last chapter, business writing should achieve some business objective – it should help to get some necessary job done. For example, you might be writing to give someone accurate information (as in a product information sheet) or to persuade someone to set up a project (as in a project proposal).

How effectively you achieve your objective will depend in part on your writing style. So we need strategies which will increase the likely effectiveness of business language. These strategies are what this chapter is all about – how to write in an effective style for business communication.

We start by identifying some common criticisms of official and business language and then work through the main criteria we use to identify effective style – appropriate content and appropriate tone. Many business communicators advocate plain English as the appropriate style to meet these criteria and we review both the main supporting claims and the criticisms of this approach.

Finally, we look at some detailed strategies for improving writing and assess the value of methods which are supposed to measure the readability of a document. However, we cannot offer a 'magic solution' to language problems. Throughout this chapter we shall point out the difficulties and pitfalls of relying on simple or absolute rules of 'effective' language. As we keep saying, communication is both complex and dependent on context.

### OBJECTIVES

*This chapter will:*

- identify common criticisms of business writing;
- explain the main criteria we use to identify an effective business writing style;
- outline the main characteristics, potential advantages, and possible limitations of the plain English or plain language approach;
- summarise important strategies of 'plain language' and suggest how to improve your style by using appropriate words and effective sentences;
- evaluate methods to measure the readability of a document.

## WHAT DO WE NEED TO 'FIX' IN BUSINESS WRITING?

There are two main aspects of business communication – how the business communicates to its customers and to the general public, and how the business communicates within its own walls. Both aspects of business writing have come in for their fair share of criticism. For current examples of baffling prose, we only need to consult the Golden Bull awards from the UK Plain English Campaign. Among recent 'winners' from 2012 and 2013 were the following.

### Example A

UBS believe that the 'new normal' economic environment of relatively low growth means that the ability to differentiate between secular and cyclical growth opportunities becomes more important and that for the foreseeable future the main driving influence on market sentiment will be the structural adjustments and political capital required to help mitigate the contractionary influence of low growth.

What this means for portfolio construction is that in a low-growth, low-return, capital-constrained environment, competitive advantage favours a combination of income generative, conservatively funded, self-sustaining businesses – groups that UBS class as 'dividend aristocrats' and who are experiencing secular growth. This leads UBS to their long-term core investment objective of being invested in high quality businesses.

### Example B

The committee concluded, having regard to the totality of the factors considered above, that choice could not be given significant weight and that there was not currently a gap on the spectrum of adequacy sufficient to conclude that the provision of pharmaceutical services is not currently secured to the standard of adequacy. Accordingly, the committee concluded that the application was neither necessary nor expedient to secure the adequate provision of services in the neighbourhood, and therefore dismissed the appeal in this respect.

### Example C

The sale is very much in line with our ongoing focus on recycling capital out of assets at the appropriate time in the cycle in order to crystallise gains from higher value uses and redeploy into other profitable growth opportunities in our core markets.

### Example D

The submission of this document has failed due to departmental specific business logic in the body tag. Your submission contains an unrecognised namespace.

Example A came from the 2011 Investors' Report from The Children's Mutual. Example B was the explanation from the NHS Litigation Authority for rejecting an application to open a pharmacy – their Appeals Manager is quoted as admitting the error and promising to do better in future. Example C was a quote from a Chief Investment Office who also accepted that he was 'guilty as charged'. Example D came from an email from Her Majesty's Revenue & Customs.

These awards do generate considerable adverse publicity and can have an immediate impact. Many other equally illuminating/baffling examples can be found at the Plain English website: www.plainenglish.co.uk. All these examples would have been seen both inside and outside the organisations concerned.

Criticisms of the written materials which circulate only *within* organisations can be equally scathing. Again, this is nothing new. At the height of the Battle of Britain during the Second World War, the British Prime Minister, Winston Churchill, still found time to write a memo to his staff recommending 'reports which set out the main points in a series of short, crisp paragraphs'. He complained that the majority of official papers were 'far too long', wasted time and energy by not highlighting the main points, and contained too many 'woolly phrases'.

If business writing is still often ambiguous, over-complex and unattractive, what can we do about it? Perhaps we should accept William Horton's suggestion that we need a new type of business document – 'one that answers questions in a hurry' (Horton, 2007, p. 3). One common response has been to adopt plain English. Before we investigate this in detail, we need to examine the general criteria for good style which are often applied to business writing.

## WHAT IS 'GOOD STYLE' IN BUSINESS WRITING?

'Style in writing is concerned with choice' (Kirkman, 1992, p. 6). Even if you work in an organisation which has very strict rules about how letters and reports are presented, you will still have to make choices about which words and phrases to use, how to organise your paragraphs, and so on. You will have to make stylistic choices to create a document which has the appropriate content and tone, and we shall investigate these two aspects in search of the 'best' business style. Our comments reflect those of many other business analysts – for another set of rules or guidelines, see Box 6.1 and further links on the website.

### BOX 6.1 RULES FOR EFFECTIVE WRITING

Frank Luntz has an impressive track record of work with corporations and political leaders on their use of language. His 2007 book is based on the following 'basic advice' which we would echo: 'It's not what you say, it's what people hear.' So 'The key to successful communication is to take the imaginative step of stuffing yourself right into your listener's shoes to know what they are thinking and feeling' (p. xi). His ten rules of effective language are summarised in single words (p. 28) as:

*continued . . .*

**BOX 6.1 *Continued***

- simplicity
- brevity
- credibility
- consistency
- novelty
- sound
- aspiration
- visualisation
- questioning
- context.

This introduces some ideas which are not in our recipe and which are worth considering in your own context, such as the value of explaining things in a way which your audience can visualise.

These techniques can, of course, be used to mislead the reader. Steven Poole (2007) highlights a leaked memo from Luntz in 2003 which advises US Republican politicians to 'refine' the terminology they should use in an environmental debate – 'It's time for us to start talking about "climate change" instead of global warming' as '"Climate change" is less frightening . . .' Poole continues by discussing the effectiveness of this strategy of 'redefining labels' to serve political and economic ends (pp. 42ff.).

## Content criteria

What criteria can we use to evaluate the content of a business text? We suggest the most common criteria are listed below, although many texts on business communication focus on the first three:

- accuracy
- brevity
- clarity
- emphasis.

### *Accuracy*

In business writing, accuracy is the most important criterion. Inaccurate and incorrect information can often be more harmful than no information at all. Would you wish to travel on an aircraft that had been serviced according to an inaccurate manual?

However, this raises a problem: *how* accurate must your writing be? A high degree of accuracy often requires considerable detail and qualification of the information. The result could be long and turgid texts which nobody can bring themselves to read. So you need to strike the right balance in terms of level of detail.

### *Brevity*

Overlong documents are usually caused by unnecessary material and/or long-winded writing. In any communication situation, the writer usually has more information than is necessary and must therefore determine:

- what the audience already knows;
- what the audience needs to know;
- what the audience wants to know.

Once you have a clear idea of this, you can trim the message without leaving out important information. However, this is not as easy as it sounds as your audience may contain distinct subgroups with different needs.

### *Clarity*

Lack of clarity is often due to poor style rather than difficult subject matter, and may be caused by:

- stilted phrases and clichés;
- too much detail and repetition;
- lack of logical structure;
- excessive use of abstract and generic terms.

### *Emphasis*

Important information should be emphasised. But how do we decide what is important'? It is:

- information that is important to the audience;
- information that will support your arguments as writer.

Less important information should be left out or placed later in the text.

Apart from ranking items in order of importance, emphasis can be achieved by other methods, such as:

- *Format and typography*. The layout and typography of a document can be used to highlight important points. We say more on this in Chapter 7. Techniques include use of white space, use of lists and bullet points, use of headings, etc.
- *Grammatical structure*. We can emphasise a word by making it the subject of a sentence. For example, rather than 'The temperature was measured by an optical pyrometer', you can say 'An optical pyrometer measured the temperature'. This puts the emphasis on the means of measurement.

Of course, emphasis should not be carried to the point where information is distorted or where important facts are concealed.

## Balancing the content criteria

A good text depends on achieving a successful *balance* of the four criteria in order to meet the reader's needs. In the simple examples we have used above, the criteria are relatively easy to apply. However, even in simple examples we can dig deeper and discover possible ambiguities. For example, suppose you receive an email about a recent survey of your organisation's canteen facilities which discovered that most of the staff 'were in favour'. What exactly does that mean? What sort of facility did they want? And how often would they use it? This general approval might mask very strong differences in terms of what particular groups of staff want from a canteen. Of course, this detail may be in the attached report but the email should highlight the key findings. At the moment, this does not give a very clear pointer to any management action. So the criteria must always be applied in relation to what the written communication needs to achieve.

## Tone criteria

Even if the content of a message is good, business writing can still fail to achieve its objectives if its tone offends or upsets readers. We have already argued that communication always conveys two simultaneous messages – information and relationship. We can examine the style of business writing to see if it establishes or reinforces an appropriate relationship. This is especially important because everything you write can be taken to be writing on behalf of your organisation (or your part of the organisation in an internal communication). Any attitudes you express are assumed to be those of the organisation. Be aware of the image your organisation wishes to project and write accordingly.

For a simple illustration, compare the following sentences from letters to customers and decide which organisation is projecting the most 'professional' and positive image:

a 'If this does not sort out your gripes give me a ring.'
b 'If this does not solve your problems, communicate with the undersigned at your earliest convenience.'
c 'If this does not solve the problem, please telephone me at . . .'

Of course, the different relations that exist in business mean that you must be sensitive to the requirements of these situations. Therefore, you do not use the same tone when writing to a customer who has not paid his account for six months as you would to a potential customer. There are, however, certain tonal requirements that almost invariably apply to written communication. The fact that written communication constitutes a permanent record means that writers should:

- avoid undue familiarity;
- adopt a professional tone;

- use a tone appropriate to the status of the receiver;
- be sensitive to the existence of different business practices;
- be sensitive to cultural differences.

The last two points are particularly important in international business where there is always the danger of unintentionally giving offence. A common example would be the use of American conventions in messages for British readers – phrases like 'have a nice day' would often be seen as insincere and formulaic.

If we are searching for a business style which satisfies these criteria of content and tone, can plain English provide the answer?

## THE RISE OF PLAIN ENGLISH

Criticisms of official and business writing are nothing new. Equally long-standing are the pleas for plain and understandable writing – Martin Cutts (2013) notes the pleas going back to the sixteenth century. He offers a more detailed history, so we shall simply highlight some major landmarks in the rise of plain English in the United Kingdom as a fairly typical case study.

One of the major issues which prompted the rise of plain English in the UK was the poor quality of official forms and government publications. Earlier in the twentieth century, there were several attempts to simplify the language of government, including the very influential book by Sir Ernest Gowers, *Plain Words* (later revised and extended into *The Complete Plain Words*, Gowers, 1987). Another influential article, which is still quoted in the modern guide books, came from George Orwell in 1946 ('Politics and the English language'). See Box 6.2 for discussion of some of the broader implications of his approach. His six elementary rules are worth repeating as a useful summary of early plain English thinking which has had lasting influence:

1. Never use a metaphor, simile or other figure of speech which you are used to seeing in print.
2. Never use a long word where a short one will do.
3. If it is possible to cut a word out, always cut it out.
4. Never use the passive where you can use the active.
5. Never use a foreign phrase, a scientific word or a jargon word if you can think of an everyday English equivalent.
6. Break any of these rules sooner than say anything outright barbarous.

These rules have been consistently echoed in more recent guides to effective business language. For example, in a book published by the British Industrial Society, Alan Barker offers three 'golden rules of effective writing':

- use words your reader will recognize easily;
- construct straightforward sentences;
- make your point, then support it.

(Barker, 1999, p. 1)

An equivalent American book offers five main principles:

1 Prefer clear, familiar words.
2 Keep most sentences short and simple.
3 Prefer active voice verbs; avoid passives.
4 Use conversational style as a guide.
5 Revise, revise, and revise again.

(Joseph, 1998, p. 12)

There is a lot of common ground between these sets of principles, and this is also reflected in more recent and current texts. We shall explore the most important recommendations in more detail later in this chapter.

**BOX 6.2 THE POLITICS OF LANGUAGE STYLE**

George Orwell was not simply interested in improving the quality of official documents. One of his main concerns was the way that totalitarian states used 'corrupt' forms of language in order to disguise the true intentions behind political dogma. One of the key weapons used by the state in his classic novel *1984* is the language – Newspeak. This language systematically destroys the link between words and meanings and is used to make the dogma of the ruling party both meaningless and indisputable at the same time. Orwell's arguments for clear and transparent language were all arguments to prevent specific linguistic features being used to confuse and dominate.

Another important aspect of Orwell's thinking is also very relevant to modern thinking on plain English – the notion that plain language will be 'automatically transparent.' This assumes that there is a fixed code whereby a word corresponds to a fixed meaning. This is not our view. As we discussed in Chapter 3, language is a fuzzy code where flexibility is the norm. Although plain English may assist understanding, it can *never* guarantee it.

## Developments in plain language

One major difference between modern plain English recommendations and previous writers such as Gowers is the attention paid to the organisation, design and layout of documents – good writing is not just about 'getting the words right'. We also follow this philosophy, which is why we look at organisation and layout in the next chapter.

## Current agreement on plain language

If you read a selection of current texts on business communication, then you may be struck by the consensus that emerges over language style. Table 6.1 illustrates this agreement – and

**BOX 6.3 THIS ORGANISATION HAS RULES**

Some organisations publish very definite rules to control their staff's writing. And there are now many official publications endorsing ideas we discuss in this chapter. For example:

- The US Securities and Exchange Commission published their *Plain English Handbook* in 1998 to help staff 'free yourself of . . . impediments to effective communication' such as 'stilted jargon and complex constructions' (www.sec.gov/pdf/handbook.pdf).
- The National Adult Literacy Agency in Ireland published their *Policy Brief on Use of Plain English in Written Communications* in 2009 (www.nala.ie/sites/default/files/publications/NALA%20policy%20paper%20on%20plain%20English_1.pdf).

What is your organisation's approach or 'rule book' (implicit or explicit)? And how is this expressed and enforced?

also suggests some differences in emphasis – by listing eight major characteristics of plain language style and showing how they are summarised in three recent texts: one of the best recent British summaries of the plain English approach by Martin Cutts and two American texts.

You can evaluate your writing against the characteristics listed in the first column.

Another option which we can safely recommend on modern PCs/Macs is the use of speech recognition software to prepare documents. This software has been available for some time but earlier versions demanded significant dedication and patience from users. We have used Dragon software on both PC and Mac. Now that it is achieving impressive accuracy levels more or less straight out of the box, it is worth considering as it will enable you to see if a more conversational approach improves your documents (as well as helping cut down keyboard time and the attendant health risks).

## BUT IS PLAIN ENGLISH ALWAYS THE ANSWER?

A range of studies and examples make a persuasive argument in favour of plain English/plain language (e.g. the 50 studies summarised by Kimble, 2012). But plain English also has its critics. Robyn Penman argues that we need to consider the context when we write and we cannot rely on a universal principle of plain or simple English. He reviewed evidence that plain English revisions do not always work, such as an Australian study which compared versions of a tax form and found that the revised version was 'virtually as demanding for the taxpayer as the old form' (Penman, 1993, p. 128).

We agree with Penman's main point – that we need to design appropriate documents – but we still think that *all* business writers should consider the recommendations coming from

***Table 6.1*** *Agreement on plain English*

| *Language characteristic* | *Cutts (2013)** | *Timm and Bienvenu (2011)* | *Bovee and Thrill (2013)* |
|---|---|---|---|
| Use short sentences | Average 15–20 words | 'sentences should average about 16 to 18 words in length' (p. 16) | 'Look for ways to combine a mixture of sentences that are short (up to 15 words or so), medium (15–25 words), and long (more than 25 words)' (p. 108) |
| Use familiar words | 'Use words your readers are likely to understand' | 'Use simple, everyday wording' (p. 21) | 'Choose familiar words' (p. 89) |
| No unnecessary words | 'Use only as many words as you need' | 'A sentence should contain no unnecessary words' (p. 1) | 'readers want messages that convey important content clearly and quickly' (p. 105) |
| Prefer active to passive voice | 'Prefer the active voice unless there's a good reason for using the passive' | 'Minimise the use of passive voice in workplace writing' (p. 218) | 'In most cases, the active voice is the better choice' (p. 86) |
| Direct style | 'Put your points positively when you can'<br>'Use clear, crisp, lively verbs to express the actions in your document' | 'write the way you would talk in a planned, purposeful conversation' (p. 19) | 'achieve a tone that is conversational but still businesslike' (p. 85) |
| 'Good' grammar and punctuation | 'Put accurate punctuation at the heart of your writing' | 'We conspicuously display our professionalism in our writing' This includes 'Avoiding common grammar, punctuation and usage mistakes (p. 194) | 'If you make errors of grammar or usage, you lose credibility with your audience' (p. 87) |

* All quotes are taken from his summary of guidelines on p. xxxi.

plain English sources. Unless you have clear contrary evidence, they are the 'safest bet', especially if you have a general or mixed audience. For the rest of this book, we shall talk of 'plain language' to refer to this approach, using the simplest and clearest expression which is appropriate for the audience.

A recent research contribution may give us further clues as to how we decide on the most appropriate language style for any given situation. Julie Baker looked at the comparison between traditional legal language and plain legal language using the concept of cognitive fluency which 'relates to the level of confidence a person has regarding his or her understanding of an object or piece of information. Simply put, a reader more quickly and easily processes fluent communications' (2011, p. 12). She concludes that 'plain language is, in fact, the right way to write, as it is "fluent" and thereby inspires feelings of ease, confidence, and trust in readers (whereas legalese is "disfluent", engendering feelings of dislike and mistrust). . . . however, . . . there are times when the legal writer's analytical or persuasive goals may be served by more difficult, less fluent language' (pp. 1–2). While this may be difficult to translate into specific recommendations for a given situation, it is worthwhile thinking in terms of the levels of cognitive fluency which you are assuming in the readers of the documents you are writing – how much effort will they have to put in to understand what you are saying?

It is also worth remembering that even simple language may not tell the whole story. Martin Cutts, one of the co-founders of the UK Plain English Campaign, now runs the Plain Language Commission. A recent edition of their Newsletter (Pikestaff number 60 – available free on subscription from the commission website – www.clearest.co.uk) gave a good example in the announcement from Instagram, responding to customer complaints about a change in conditions which implied that they would have the right to sell their users' photos without prior permission. They apologised and confirmed: 'To be clear: it is not our intention to sell your photos.' But Pikestaff also report the reaction to this from a UK designer-writer partnership, Ashbury and Ashbury, who suggest that this response 'isn't the same as saying "we won't sell your photos"'. As the Pikestaff editorial concludes: 'corporate language should be not only plain in style but also plain in intention and in content'.

There is one further word of caution we need to emphasise – changing language styles in an organisation does not just change the language. Language use reflects important aspects of organisation culture. There may also be specific implication for organisation relationships, as the study in Box 6.4 illustrates.

## BOX 6.4 WHERE PLAIN ENGLISH DISRUPTED THE ORGANISATION STRUCTURE

Jim Suchan studied how Report Assessors (RAs) in a government agency made decisions based on information in written reports from subordinates (with whom they had no direct contact). The RAs felt the reports were badly organised and difficult to read but they had various strategies to 'make sense of all the garbled stuff in these reports' (Suchan, 1998, p. 312). Despite these criticisms, they did not suggest that their subordinates should change their writing style – it was accepted as part of the job. The RAs had 'become very skilful in the manoeuvring through the reports to find the information they needed to make a decision. They were proud of that skill: it differentiated them from others.'

A few reports were rewritten using techniques such as headings and subheadings, bulleted lists, active verbs, shorter paragraphs, etc. However, these revised reports did not lead to better decisions. They were disliked and described as 'abnormal discourse'. The new report style was seen as a deskilling the RAs and 'usurping their authority'. Rumours circulating in the organisation about possible cutbacks and restructuring were an obvious factor in these perceptions.

This study shows that we cannot simply impose a new language style on an organisation without considering the broader impact and implications.

## APPLYING PLAIN LANGUAGE STRATEGIES

In this final section, we summarise plain language strategies which you can consider in your own writing.

### Hit the right point on the 'word scales'

You need to use appropriate words in a specific situation. Some organisations have tried to control word choices by introducing simplified English. Unfortunately, this can bring other problems. Assuming you have free choice, consider where your words fit on the following four scales.

#### *Abstract – concrete*

The main problem with abstract terminology is its vagueness. It often requires a concrete example to clarify it. Although a statement like 'Inflation is affecting our administration costs' may be true, it is vague. The statement could include a concrete example like 'Inflation is affecting our administration costs – the costs of printing and stationery have risen by around 7 per cent per year for the last three years.'

#### *Generic – specific*

'Vehicle' is a generic term, as it covers a variety of things. There is a range from generic to specific, as in: vehicle – motor vehicle – motor car – Toyota car – 1998 Toyota Corolla – 1998 green, 1.6 L Toyota Corolla – and so on. Business writing tends to be too generic.

#### *Formal – colloquial*

'The company is in financial difficulties' is more formal; while 'The company is going down the drain' is more colloquial. It is very important to pitch your writing at the point on the scale which is appropriate to your audience.

#### *Emotive – referential*

Emotive words may be considered as words that convey both facts and attitudes or dispositions. Referential terms convey facts rather than attitudes. Therefore, 'The shop floor was covered with sawdust' is essentially factual, whereas 'The shop floor was filthy' conveys the writer's attitude.

### Avoid jargon and technical slang

Jargon is technical language which is usually unintelligible to a wide audience. A term like 'discounted cash flow' would be unacceptable jargon to a general audience if no explanation was given. Technical slang covers slang terms that are used in technical conversation – e.g. expressions such as 'the bottom line'.

## Avoid clichés

Clichés are expressions which were once fresh and insightful, but have become stale through constant use. Some current phrases which have probably now gone 'past their sell-by date' include 'address the critical issues', 'action the problems', 'on a learning curve'.

## Avoid piled-up nouns

Nouns are often 'piled up' making it difficult to disentangle the meaning, as in 'staff induction emergency training procedures'. Apart from the difficulty of disentangling the meaning, there is always the danger of ambiguity. In this example it is not clear whether we are dealing with emergency-training procedures (how to train people to deal with an emergency), or emergency training-procedures (how to organise the training if there is some sort of crisis).

## Simplify sentence structure

While there is no set formula for writing sentences in business English, simple straightforward structures make for easy reading. The most common structure is to start the sentence with the subject – e.g. '*The company* increased its profits by 25 per cent compared with the last financial year.'

A common alternative structure is an adverbial opening such as '*In the last financial year*, the company increased its profits by 25 per cent.'

Adverbial beginnings are particularly useful when you wish to link the sentence to something that has gone before, as in '*However*, unfavourable trading conditions may not continue after the first quarter.'

It requires considerable skill to structure long sentences. Modern word-processing software has built-in spelling and grammar checks which will identify 'poor' or over-long sentences. But these checks can give some strange results, as we illustrate in Box 6.5.

### BOX 6.5 MICROSOFT MAY NOT KNOW WHAT YOU MEAN!

The following table gives examples of corrections to sentences and phrases which are recommended by the grammar checker in Word 2011 (set for British English) and which range from the unnecessary to the completely nonsensical.

This shows that you should approach these automatic devices with some caution. Often their recommendations are based on rather strict interpretation of grammatical rules, or on misinterpreting the context, or on slavish obedience to supposed 'good practice' (like avoiding the passive at all costs). There are also problems with different cultural norms.

*continued . . .*

**BOX 6.5 *Continued***

***Table 6.2*** *Feedback from grammar checker*

| | *Original phrase or sentence* | *What Word for Mac 2011 recommends* | *Comment* |
|---|---|---|---|
| 1 | The idea for the silicon chip was developed by two different research teams | Two different research teams developed the idea for the silicon chip | This changes the emphasis; it does not improve the clarity |
| 2 | You are described by a colleague as the single most important figure in popular music | A colleague as the single most important figure in popular music describes you | The recommendation is gibberish! |
| 3 | First the journalist would type up his or her notes; then these notes would be typed up by a compositor on a linotype machine to create the lines of lead type | First the journalist would type up his or her notes; then a compositor on a linotype machine to create the lines of lead type would type these notes up | To avoid the passive, Word produces a very tortuous sentence |

## Use the appropriate balance of active and passive sentences

There is a common misconception that the passive form is the 'preferred' business style for official documents. However, active sentences are usually preferred in plain language. In practice, you need a sensible mix of active and passive.

The criterion for choosing between active and passive should be emphasis. Consider the following sentences:

1 *The company* gave each employee a bonus.
2 *Each employee* was given a bonus by the company.

In (1) the emphasis is on 'the company'; in (2) the emphasis is on 'each employee'. Both sentences are perfectly clear. Your choice depends on whether you wish to emphasise 'the company' or 'each employee'.

## Use clear and simple punctuation

Punctuation is an important code – it can change the meaning or emphasis within a sentence. Consider the difference between these two simple examples:

1 Insert the ID card into the slot, with the label on the top right.
2 Insert the ID card into the slot with the label on the top right.

In (1) the punctuation tells you that the label is part of the ID card; in (2) the punctuation tells you that the label relates to the slot.

In more complicated instructions, possible ambiguities of this sort could be very dangerous. You could punctuate the following to give very different meanings: 'Send replacement mother board if the system fails again we will need to shut it down.'

How do we decide which punctuation to use and when to use it? Here the situation becomes more complicated. Different punctuation marks have different rules attached to them. For example: 'There are simple, definite rules about the use of the full stop at the end of sentences. There are no equally simple rules for all the various uses of the comma' (Collinson *et al.*, 1992, p. 19).

So how do we decide how to use the comma? Although guide books on English grammar offer extensive guidelines, they may not offer absolute rules:

> Commas are in a no man's land of punctuation, where few routes are charted and mostly we have to find our own away. It was easier before World War Two, when commas could be used all over the place. But the style now is to use them as sparingly as possible, so there is more reason to hesitate before slipping one in.
>
> (Howard, 1993, p. 87)

This highlights the importance of changes in taste and style. There are several useful and entertaining guides to modern punctuation, including one recent best-seller from Lynne Truss (2003) which illustrates how sensitive many of us are to the punctuation we see around us. Another good example of this sensitivity is the Apostrophe Protection Society whose website shows both how to use them properly and how many businesses fail to do so (www.apostrophe.org.uk). At the very least, you should:

- make sure that you are familiar with the conventional uses of the main punctuation marks;
- use these main punctuation marks consistently;
- recognise that punctuation marks are very important signals to the reader about when to pause and which parts of the sentence go together.

One strategy is to use only a limited set of punctuation marks. We do not agree with some advice which suggests that you only really need to use the full stop and the comma. However, we could write virtually every type of business document using only the punctuation marks discussed in one of the well-known British advice books which is now available online – *The Economist Style Guide* – where you can find specific advice on apostrophes, brackets, colons, commas, dashes, full stops, quotation marks, question marks and semicolons, and a useful discussion of different uses in American and British English (www.economist.com/styleguide/introduction).

This raises the question of which grammar/punctuation guide to use – there are many on the market and they do not always agree on specific points:

> Generations of schoolchildren were taught grammar as an arbitrary set of dos and don'ts laid down by people who knew, or thought they knew, best. Nowadays, grammar might be more helpfully defined as the set of rules followed by speakers of a language.
>
> (Marsh and Dodson, 2010, p. 7)

The problem is that different users may follow different rules, depending on their background, and some guide books on the market still offer 'rules' which are suspect or arbitrary. We suggest you stick with established texts on plain language which are based on research and/or practical application (such as work by Martin Cutts or David Crystal, or the useful chapter on grammar and punctuation by Marsh and Dodson, 2010) and avoid texts which adopt a more dogmatic stance. For example, we cannot recommend *Gwynne's Grammar* (Gwynne, 2013), although it has recently sold well in the UK. It makes the claim that grammar is a 'science' but then offers no method for its scientific investigation! Look for reviews of this text on the Web and you will find very different opinions, reflecting the strong feelings that many people have about what counts as good or acceptable grammar.

As additional help, most modern word- processing packages offer some help. This chapter was prepared with Word which:

- automatically puts a capital letter after every full stop – at the beginning of every sentence;
- highlights incorrect or unknown spellings;
- suggests when our sentences 'fail' its in-built grammar checker.

However, do not be tempted to rely too heavily on these automatic systems – they only offer very crude guidance, which can be misleading (see Box 6.6).

## Readability

There are several readability formulas which claim to predict how easy or difficult it is to read a particular text. These usually combine some measure of sentence length with some measure of average word length. Examples include the Fog index and the Flesch formula. One or more of these formlas is supplied as an automatic feature in many word processors – e.g. as one of the spelling and grammar tools in Microsoft Word. See our website for further examples.

Readability formulas can give a useful check – they can be used to revise texts to make them easier to understand. However, the results must be interpreted with caution as they ignore some critical points (Hartley, 1994):

- some short sentences can be difficult to understand;
- short technical abbreviations may be very difficult to understand;
- some long words are very familiar (e.g. communication);
- the formulas ignore any graphics or visual aids which can help readers to understand;
- the formulas ignore the impact of any layout, such as headings and subheadings;

## BOX 6.6 WHY DOESN'T MY WORD PROCESSOR KNOW I'M ENGLISH?

Another problem with computerised grammar checkers is that they may be insensitive to cultural variations. Microsoft Word continually criticises us as we do not follow one of the rules laid down by one of the main American authorities on written style – the *Chicago Manual of Style*. According to this manual, you should use the word 'that' to introduce a restrictive clause and the word 'which' to introduce a non-restrictive clause. For example, the manual approves of the following sentences:

a The book that Nigel gave me was no good.
b The book, which Nigel gave me, was no good.

In example (a), the clause is restrictive because I'm talking only about the specific book which Nigel gave me and not any of the other books which I own. In example (b), the clause is non-restrictive as the fact that Nigel gave me the book is simply added as extra information – the clause is not used to identify which book we are talking about.

Native English speakers do not usually make this distinction, although it does crop up in some well-known guides to good English which are used in Britain. This is an interesting example of a stylistic rule which makes little or no difference to communication. This reinforces the point made by Deborah Cameron that 'statements about "good writing" are not self-evident truths about language but value judgements upon it'. Her book on popular attitudes towards language should be required reading for anyone who advises others how to write good English (Cameron, 1995).

- the formulas ignore the readers' past experience and knowledge;
- the formulas ignore the readers' motivation.

James Hartley has also shown that you can increase the readability of text according to the scales and make it *more* difficult to understand (Hartley, 1999). Our favourite example of a short text which would pass a readability test but which is difficult to understand is the following notice, stuck by the elevator doors in a large multistorey American office block:

> Please
> Walk up one floor
> Walk down two floors
> To improve elevator service

If you take the notice at face value and walk up one floor, you discover the same notice by the elevator doors on the next floor (in fact, on every floor). The writer managed to construct a very tortuous way of advising users not to take the elevator for very short journeys! For more examples of this type of problem, see Chapanis (1988).

Another of our favourites in the same vein is the following notice on a fence in the middle of a large national park in the UK:

The land within is outside open land.

## SUMMARY

- Business writing often fails to communicate because of poor expression.
- We need to evaluate our writing using both content and tone criteria, bearing in mind the demands of the situation.
- The plain English movement has made a significant impact on official writing, but we need to consider research studies which suggest that this approach is not as straightforward as might first appear.
- 'Plain language' should be considered as a personal and company strategy, remembering that this argues for an *appropriate* style of language and *not* the same simple style for every document. Also, it is not just about using the right words – we also need to examine organisation and layout and consider the needs of users/audiences.
- We should follow standard conventions on punctuation while remembering that the rules are both flexible and changing.
- Readability tests offer some useful information but should be interpreted cautiously.

## FURTHER READING

Martin Cutts (2013) *Oxford Guide to Plain English* (4th edn). Oxford: Oxford University Press.

David Crystal (2004) *Rediscover Grammar* (3rd edn). London: Longman.

Cutts offers probably the best British book to date which explains both the purposes and techniques of plain English. If you want to explore grammar in more depth, then Crystal offers a good place to start.

Christopher Turk and John Kirkman (1994) *Effective Writing: Improving scientific, technical and business communication* (2nd edn). London: E. & F. Spon.

This book is quite old but still worth reading for lots of useful examples and illustrations from scientific and engineering contexts.

Joseph Kimble (2012) *Writing for Dollars, Writing to Please: The case for plain language in business, government, and law.* Durham, NC: Carolina Academic Press.

Contains 50 studies which demonstrate the value of a plain language approach from one of its longstanding advocates.

Chapter 7

# Effective design and visual aids

## INTRODUCTION

It is worth emphasising how quickly the process of producing business documents has been transformed. Back in the 1980s, many if not most business documents in large organisations were produced on electric or electronic typewriters. These offered very limited scope for page design and virtually no flexibility to use visual aids. The 'death of the typewriter' was publicised in various news reports and articles in 2011 as the last major manufacturer announced that production had ceased. Within 30 years the typewriter had gone from essential office technology to museum piece.

Word-processing software has copied and incorporated many of the technique and facilities which were first introduced by desktop publishing software on personal computers around 1985. Professional designers still use dedicated desktop publishing software as they need very precise control over page layout and design, but the key functions for most professional documents have been incorporated into all the major word-processing applications. As a result, we now have access to many techniques which had previously only been available to professional typesetters and printers: a very wide range of fonts; clip art and graphics; and relatively inexpensive laser and/or inkjet printers to achieve near-professional print quality. Other software has also added many useful features. For example, all the graphs included in this chapter can be produced from a spreadsheet table with a few mouse clicks.

The publishing revolution has continued on the Web where we can now all send messages and construct Web pages without the detailed programming knowledge which was previously required, although complicated websites linked to databases still need significant technical support.

Because of these technical developments and the associated changes in office structures, *all* business writers now need to understand basic principles of document design, and need to know how to construct simple and effective visual aids. These are the main themes of this chapter.

## OBJECTIVES

*This chapter will*:

- explain why effective design and layout is such an important part of effective business writing;
- review the main design features which we need to consider when we produce business documents;
- explain what business writers need to know about typography;
- show how page layout can be used to show the reader how the document is structured;
- analyse when and where you need to incorporate a visual aid into a business document;
- review the main types of visual aids used in documents and highlight their main advantages and disadvantages;
- show some of the dangers of using inappropriate visual aids and how you can avoid misrepresentation;
- discuss the potential of infographics which may become more important in organisations over the next few years.

## WHY IS EFFECTIVE DESIGN AND LAYOUT NOW SUCH AN IMPORTANT ASPECT OF EFFECTIVE WRITING?

Our answer to this question reflects the views of many graphic designers:

> Any one looking at the printed message will be influenced, within a split second of making eye contact, by everything on the page: the arrangement of various elements as well as the individual look of each one. In other words, an overall impression is created in our mind before we even start reading the first word.
>
> (Spiekermann and Ginger, 1993, p. 37)

Psychological research supports the designers' view that the 'look' of a document influences how it is read (Hartley, 1994). However, despite the importance of good design, many organisations are still content to treat their desktop computers as 'just a typewriter' – a view which can be easily challenged (Williams, 1992, 2003). One example of this misguided approach is the way that word processing is still sometimes taught in a way which simply reflects old typing conventions. But many old typing habits simply do not make sense when you are word processing. More seriously, the real advantages of word processing – using styles and templates – are treated as advanced features and ignored by many users. See Box 7.1 for a brief discussion of these problems.

**BOX 7.1 THE PC IS NOT A TYPEWRITER**

Although the typewriter is now obsolete, some interesting habits which were part of traditional typing practice still survive in many organisations using modern word processing. For example, leaving two spaces after a full stop (period) made sense on an old typewriter where all the characters take up the same amount of space (monospaced). The two spaces helped to separate the sentences. But on a computer we now use typefaces where each character is proportionally spaced – for example, the letter 'i' takes up less space than the letter 'm' – so you do not need more than one space to separate sentences. There are other habits in many printed documents we have seen in organisations which seem to be a legacy of typing, such as the use of underlining – professional printing avoids underlining and uses italics or bold for emphasis.

The most effective way to word process is to take full advantage of its automatic features such as styles and templates. Yet these features are often discussed later in the manuals as if they were more advanced features rather than part of the fundamental logic of the system. We have visited several large organisations where the administrative staff were unaware of styles and were formatting each new heading or subheading on its own – a complete waste of time, especially if someone later needs to change the overall format of the document. Changing the style characteristics of 'Heading 1' takes a few seconds – every Heading 1 in the document will then change automatically. Changing every heading individually in a long document can take some time. You can quickly work out whether a document has been effectively word processed by looking at the styles associated with headings and subheadings. If they are simply the 'normal' style with extra formatting, you have uncovered an example of using the PC as a typewriter (and wasting a lot of time and effort in the process).

## WHAT ARE THE MAIN DESIGN FEATURES OF BUSINESS DOCUMENTS?

We think of newspapers and magazines being professionally designed. Can we apply similar criteria to business documents? Every business document has a characteristic layout, which can range from the simple layout of an internal briefing paper to that of a glossy multicolour annual report from a large company. Only the latter may have received much attention from professional designers but all documents have been put together with some attention to their design. And design is important no matter how humble the document. A well-designed document has two main advantages over a poorly designed one:

- It makes a good impression on the reader by suggesting a professional and competent approach. So it can enhance the credibility of the person who prepared the document. In this way, it improves the chances of its message being accepted.
- The content or information is easier to understand.

Conversely, poorly presented material can put the reader off and create a poor image. A simple example would be coursework assignments which students have to complete at college or university. A well-prepared word-processed assignment is likely to gain more marks not because the tutor is consciously awarding marks for presentation but because the word-processed assignment is easier and quicker to read and looks as if it has been carefully prepared. Conversely, the poorly word-processed assignment – no page numbers, no sub-headings, poor quality print etc. – can lose marks because it gives the impression of having been 'knocked together' at the last minute. Memos and reports in business can create similar impressions on the reader, depending on the way these look.

There is now no excuse for poorly formatted documents. We can use word-processing software to produce most of the characteristics of professional typesetting. As a result, readers have come to expect documents which satisfy the criteria traditionally used by graphic designers (Lichty, 1989):

- *Proportion* – where all the elements of the page are clearly in proportion to each other.
- *Balance* – where there is a clear sense of balance to the design of each page.
- *Contrast* – where contrasting parts of the design are used to focus the reader's interest on the page.
- *Rhythm* – where the reader's attention is drawn smoothly down the page without distraction.
- *Unity* – where the various components of the page fit together to give a coherent impression.

## WHAT DO BUSINESS WRITERS NEED TO KNOW ABOUT TYPOGRAPHY?

Modern word processing offers writers a wide variety of typefaces. When this started to become standard practice, many writers abused this facility and produced documents containing many different typefaces. The result was usually messy – for most purposes, two typefaces are sufficient. The choice of a typeface is largely subjective, but you need to consider the conventional image and likely impact of the chosen typefaces – we shall discuss some of the main types below. Also, see Box 7.2 for some further possible choices.

There are a few technical aspects of typefaces and page layout which are worth knowing so you can make sensible choices. You also have to understand some technical terms with rather odd names – much of the terminology has been carried forward from the days when printing was a mechanical process using letters made from 'hot metal'. We outline these terms below before returning to the issue of which type is 'best' for particular business documents.

### Type families

Any single typeface can appear in different styles, which make up its 'family'. For example, Arial can appear as Arial, **Arial Black**, Arial Narrow. A specific size and style of typeface is usually called a font, as in '**this font is 12 point Times New Roman Bold**'.

One important type style is italic – this is not a separate typeface but a right sloping version of the basic font. It has several main uses:

- to *emphasise* a particular word or phrase;
- to indicate the name of a book;
- to indicate technical terms or foreign words;
- to indicate a quotation.

## Type size

Type size is usually measured in 'points', one point being approximately 1⁄72nd of an inch. However, this does *not* mean that different typefaces which are the same point size will look the same. The points measurement is taken from the top of a capital letter to the bottom of a lower case letter which extends below the baseline. However, when we look at a typeface we are more inclined to notice its 'x-height' – the distance from the baseline to the top of a lower case letter like x. The example below shows the difference between two fonts which have the same point size but different x-heights.

This is Times Roman in 12 point.

This is Arial in 12 point.

Despite these differences, we can make reasonable generalisations: 11 or 12 point is common for body text, with larger sizes usually used for headings; 8 or 10 point is often used for less important information as well as the 'small print' which you are always advised to read before signing a document. Consider your audience before you finally decide on the type size. For an older audience it is worth avoiding small print completely.

## Space between lines

This is called leading after the old printing practice of putting extra slices of lead between lines of metal type to increase the spacing. It is measured in points so that 10 on 12 point Times Roman means a 10 point font with 2 extra points of leading. A rough rule of thumb is to use leading which is about 20 per cent of the font size and this is what word-processing software tends to do as the default on body text.

You can see the difference on this paragraph where we have put the leading back to zero. On the next paragraph, we have increased it to double the normal setting. Increasing the leading does not necessarily make the text easier to read beyond a certain point.

You can see the difference on this paragraph where we have put the leading to double the normal setting. Increasing the leading does not necessarily make the text easier to read beyond a certain point.

## Alignment

You can align your printing on the left-hand side and/or the right-hand side of the paper. Traditionally, professionally typeset material has been aligned on both sides. On early word processors, this usually left unsightly gaps between some words as the control of the space between letters (letter-spacing) was not very sophisticated (from a distance, you can see 'rivers' of white space winding down the page). Although this control of spacing has improved, we recommend that documents leave a ragged right margin, as there is some evidence that this improves readability (Hartley, 1994).

## Categories of typefaces

There are literally thousands of different typefaces and there are official classification systems. For practical everyday purposes, a simpler classification will do and we use five main categories (after Spiekermann and Ginger, 1993, p. 50):

- *Serif* – where the endings of the letter shapes are decorated in a way which harks back to the way that letters were carved out of stone in Roman times. Famous examples of serif type are Times Roman which was designed as a readable and economical typeface for the *Times* newspaper in London and its computer equivalent – Times New Roman – supplied with Microsoft Windows.
- *Sans serif* – where the letters are without (sans) serifs. Examples here are Helvetica and Arial.
- *Script* – where the typeface imitates the letterforms of handwriting.
- *Display* – where the typeface has been designed for use in displays such as advertising or posters.
- *Symbols* – where the alphabet is replaced by symbols. For example, the phrase 'I like zebras' would print in the typeface Wingdings as '✋ ●♓&♏ ⌘♏♌❒♋⬧'. As an example of the practical application of fonts like Wingdings we have often used the 'r' symbol when we have created a letter or form which needed a tick box. You can resize the symbols in exactly the same way that you can resize conventional letters.

## And which typeface is best?

This is an almost impossible question to answer. The traditional view for printed documents was to use serif typefaces for body text and sans serif for headings, and many graphic designers had very definite views. For example, McLean stated that one of the 'rules' of legibility for continuous reading was that 'Sans-serif type is intrinsically less legible than serifed type' (McLean, 1980, p. 44). The superiority of serif type for body text was often presented as 'fact' in this way and yet researchers were not so sure – 'the available research really gives no clear guidance on this issue' (Hartley, 1994, p. 29).

Many organisations have now adopted sans serif typefaces as standard and do not seem to have suffered as a result. This suggests that people do get used to a particular typeface over time and that any intrinsic advantages or disadvantages may be less important than designers have argued. We suggest that the choice of typeface should depend on a number of factors:

- the purpose of the document;
- what the readers are used to and what they might expect;
- how the document might be used – e.g. some fonts do not stand up to repeated photocopying or faxing as some of the letter shapes are too thin.

## BOX 7.2 TYPEFACES IN ACTION

Below we give some examples of typefaces which are readily available on your PC or Apple Mac. Which would you use in a business report, assuming that your organisation does not specify one?

This short paragraph is written in 12 point Times New Roman, a typeface which is often used in business as it is so widely available. It used to be the default font in Microsoft Word. As a serif font which was designed for body text in columns (originally for newspapers), you can argue that it is 'readable' as body text. But does it give an 'old-fashioned' impression?

This short paragraph is written in 12 point Arial, a typeface with short ascenders and descenders, which means that lines can be placed close together and which was originally designed for email. It is increasingly used in business as it is so widely available. It is a sans serif font, so you can argue whether it is 'readable' as body text. But it will photocopy well and looks 'modern'.

This short paragraph is written in 12 point Garamond, a typeface which is often used in books. It is also a serif font, so you can argue that it is 'readable' as body text. It appears 'thinner' and 'fainter' than Times New Roman so may well not photocopy as clearly. But what impression does it convey? There are also several different versions of Garamond with different x-heights for the same point size.

This short paragraph is written in 12 point Verdana, a typeface which is often recommended for body text on websites. It is also a sans serif font, so you can argue whether it is 'readable' as body text. It 'works' on screen where the resolution is poor, but what impression does it convey on paper?

There are a number of issues regarding fonts and typefaces which we explore further on the website. For example, can we accept the assertion (widely reported in national and international media in March, 2014) that the US Government could save millions of dollars by changing their default document typeface to Garamond and use less ink? And how do we react to the finding by educational researchers that presenting material in a more complex typeface (i.e. less readable) can lead to better retention by the reader?

## PAGE LAYOUT AND DOCUMENT STRUCTURE

Chapter 5 emphasised the importance of clear structure. As we know that appropriate spacing can increase the clarity of text (Hartley, 1994), we should make sure that the document design and page layout emphasise the structure of the document. This can be done in a number of ways.

### Clear numbering

The decimal numbering system is popular because it provides an easily identifiable hierarchy of headings:

1 Main heading
1.1 Subheading
1.1.1 Sub-subheading

There is obviously no limit to the degree of subdivision, but beware of using more than three levels for most business documents. Excessive numbering and subdivision can create a fragmented and difficult-to-read document.

It is also possible to use space on the page to further emphasise the hierarchy of headings, as below. We have mixed opinions on this as it can use up a lot of space on the page.

**1 Main heading in 14 point Arial bold**

The text under the main heading is in 12 point Times New Roman and will be set out like this on the page so that it lines up . . .

***1.1 Subheading in 12 point Arial italic bold***

The text under the subheading is in 12 point Times New Roman and will be set out like this on the page so that it lines up . . .

**1.1.1 Sub-subheading in 12 point Times New Roman bold**

The text under the sub-subheading is in 12 point Times New Roman and will be set out like this on the page so that it lines up . . .

The following table shows how the three levels of heading have been formatted in this book.

***Table 7.1*** *Levels of heading*

| | *Typeface* | *Size* | *Characters* | *Spacing* |
|---|---|---|---|---|
| Heading 1 | **BELL GOTHIC** | 11 pt | Black, Capitalised | Before 19.5 pt After 6.5 pt |
| Heading 2 | **Bell Gothic** | 11 pt | Black | Before 19.5 pt After 6.5 pt |
| Heading 3 | *Bell Gothic Light* | 11 pt | Italic | Before 19.5 pt After 6.5 pt |
| Body text | Perpetua | 11 pt | Normal | Standard line spacing |

The table shows how:

- different typefaces can distinguish main headings from body text;
- spacing can be used to emphasise the hierarchy of headings and subheadings.

Although these applications of spacing and numbering may seem fairly obvious, they are often ignored or not understood. For example, when undergraduate students (who were experienced in word processing) were asked to use space and typographic cues to improve the readability of a short text, they were often inconsistent or failed to use the variety of cues (Hartley, 1999).

## Using lists

Lists are a simple way of presenting information to make information more readable. For example, sometimes a sentence becomes long because a number of items are governed by the main verb – e.g. 'When leaving at the end of the day make sure that: all the windows are closed; the back and side doors are locked; the burglar alarms are set; and all the lights are switched off, except the one at the front door.'This sentence can be made more readable just by listing the items.

When leaving at the end of the day make sure that:

- all windows are closed;
- the back and side doors are locked;
- the burglar alarms are set;
- all lights are switched off, except the one at the front door.

You can also change the style:

When you leave at the end of the day, make sure that you:

- close all the windows;
- lock the back and side door;
- set the burglar alarms;
- switch off all the lights, except the one at the front door.

### Page grids

A good page layout can also contribute to ease of reading. Again, this reflects the traditions of graphic designers: 'All documents stand to benefit from the use of a grid . . . [which] . . . guarantees consistency throughout the document, identifies margins, and determines the orderly placement of columns and illustrations on the page' (Lichty, 1989, p. 99). In other words, you need to have a plan for your page design which shows where you are going to set your margins, how wide your columns will be, page numbering, use of white space on the page, and so on. For example, Box 7.3 shows the grid we used for the page design in this book. Of course, your word processor will provide default settings for all these features.

For correspondence, a common practice is to use 25 mm for the side margins and 35–40 mm for top and bottom margins. You need to decide whether these settings create the effect you want.

### Use of colour and texture

Colour and texture can be used to enhance the appearance of a document, but of course it is more expensive. If you produce diagrams or charts in colour, then you also have to consider whether anyone will want to photocopy the pages. At the moment, colour photocopiers are still too expensive for routine, everyday use in many organisations.

There are also a number of practical considerations which need to be reviewed before deciding on the format for a document that will be widely distributed, including:

- *Types of binding*. This can range from simple stapling to expensive book-type bindings, which often include covers.
- *Folding and packaging*. Frequently, documents require folding before they are packaged, so it is often advisable to design the document round the folds. For example, an A4 sheet, when folded into three, fits into a standard 220 x 110 mm envelope. By designing the document to fit into three or six panels, you can produce an attractive document with increased text.

## WHEN AND HOW DO YOU NEED TO INCORPORATE A VISUAL AID INTO A BUSINESS DOCUMENT?

One of the most respected academic writers on the presentation of statistical evidence and information design, Edward R. Tufte, argues that good graphics should '*reveal* data' (Tufte, 1983, p. 13). We extend this idea to all the visual aids that you might use in a business

## BOX 7.3 EXAMPLE OF A DESIGN GRID

The diagram below shows the grid which was used to prepare this book.

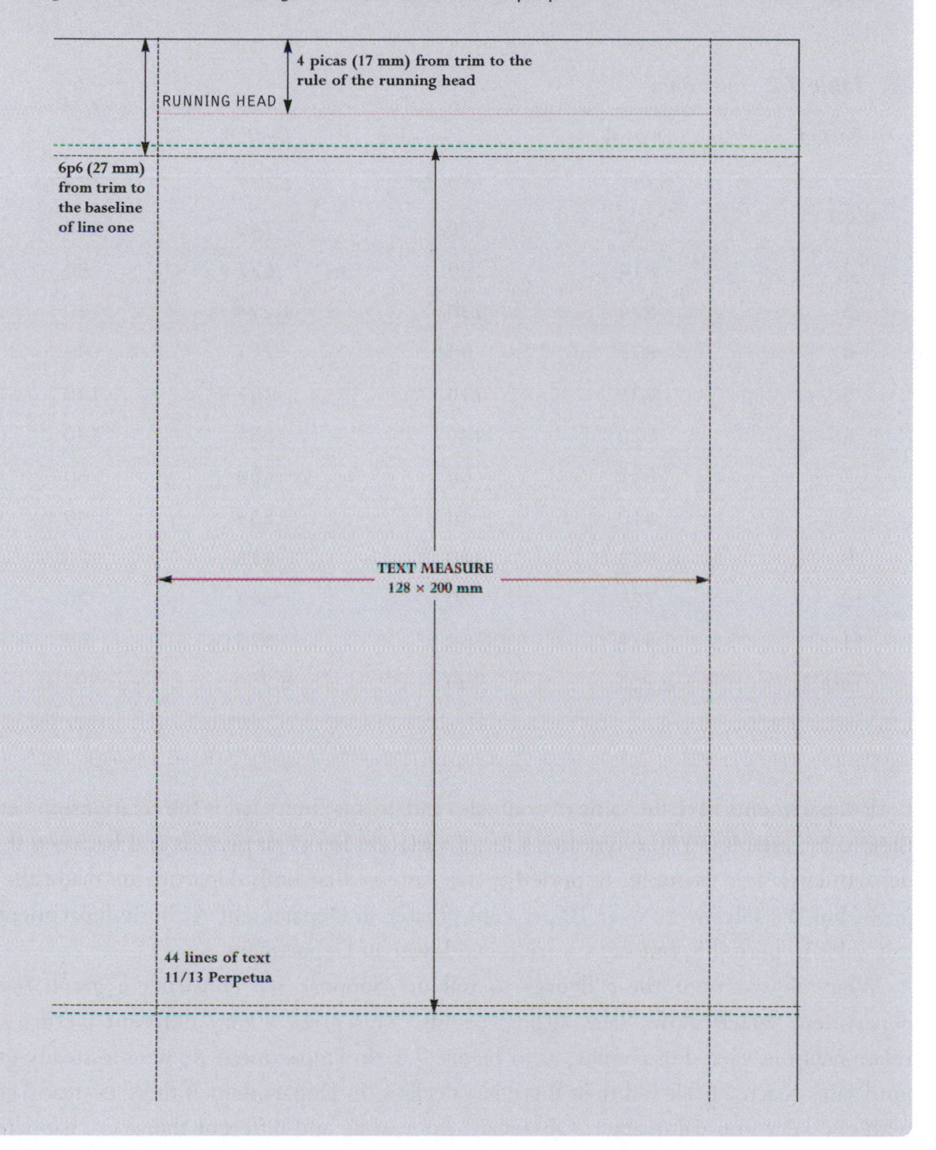


document. They should not simply display data, but they should *reveal* its importance and meaning. They should present an argument that supports the argument being expressed in the text.

Unfortunately, many visual aids in business documents fail to do this, either because they have been put in simply to make the document look 'attractive' or because the writer has not really worked out what the data means.

For example, consider this simple table of business data which gives the sales and profits of two departments in a large retailer over the same period of time. Before reading on, make a few notes on what this data tells you. If you were asked to comment on this data in a meeting, what would you say were the most important trends?

**Table 7.2** Sales data

| Period | Dept A | | Dept B | |
|---|---|---|---|---|
| | Sales | Profits | Sales | Profits |
| 1 | 914 | 100 | 746 | 100 |
| 2 | 814 | 80 | 677 | 80 |
| 3 | 874 | 130 | 1,274 | 130 |
| 4 | 877 | 90 | 711 | 90 |
| 5 | 926 | 110 | 781 | 110 |
| 6 | 810 | 140 | 884 | 140 |
| 7 | 613 | 60 | 608 | 60 |
| 8 | 310 | 40 | 539 | 40 |
| 9 | 913 | 120 | 815 | 120 |
| 10 | 726 | 70 | 642 | 70 |
| 11 | 474 | 50 | 573 | 50 |
| Totals | 8,251 | 990 | 8,250 | 990 |

Both departments have the same overall sales and profits, but what is the relationship between these two variables? You can notice a lot of variation between periods and between the two departments. For example, in period 9, we can see that both departments made the same profit but the sales were over 10 per cent greater in Department A. Both departments had low sales in period 8, but sales were much lower in Department A.

What do we want these figures to tell us? Suppose we construct a graph for each department which shows sales against profits. This gives a very different picture of the relationship in each department, as in Figure 7.1. In Department A, we see steady growth until sales reach a peak and then there is a decline. In Department B there is steady growth with one very unusual quarter. Obviously, interesting and different things are happening in these departments which need further investigation. And the initial format of presenting a table did *not* allow the reader to see the pattern in the data.

This example was not based on real sales data. We used part of data sets which Tufte uses to show how a graphic can often highlight aspects of data which are not easily spotted in the raw figures (Tufte, 1983, pp. 13–14).

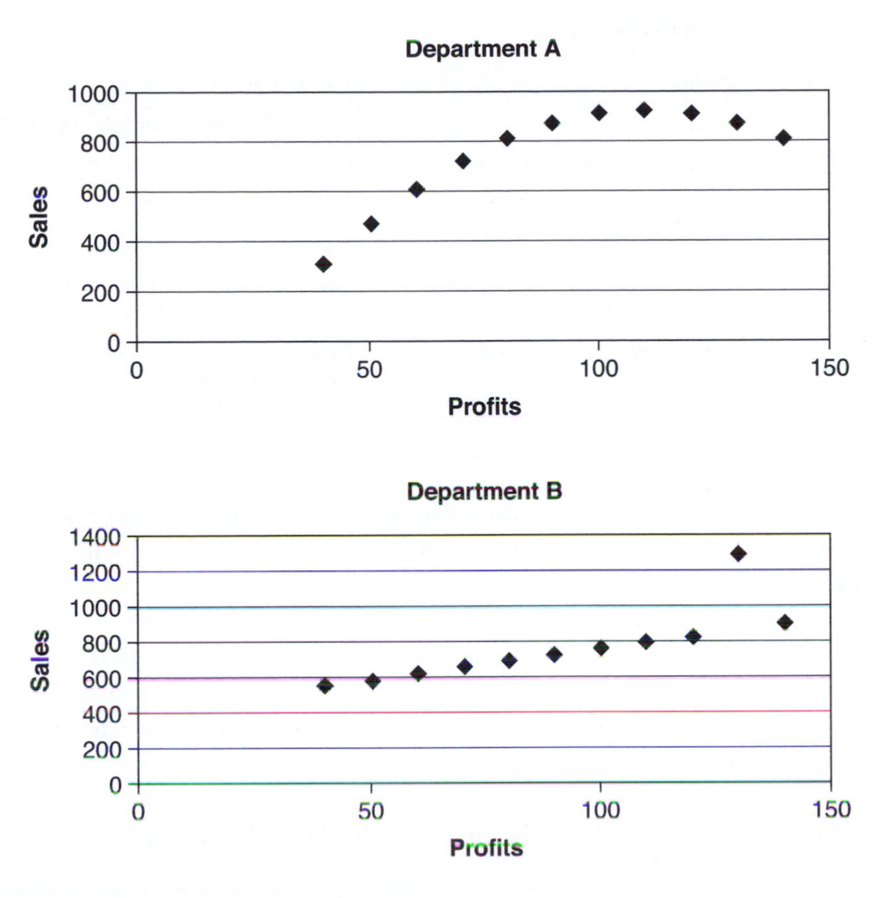


***Figure 7.1*** *Comparing sales and profits in Departments A and B*

## When are visuals needed?

If we argue that visual aids must contribute to the argument which is being made in the document, then we still have to decide *when* they are worth inserting. Of course, this depends on the context. The ultimate criterion is whether the visual aid helps the reader to understand the argument. We use one tool, borrowed from Eric Meyer. He discusses how newspapers use visuals like graphics and photos to help tell their stories. Depending on the type of story, different types of visuals are needed. For example, if it is a 'who' story which focuses on people, you might use photos or 'breakout boxes' which give potted biographies of the people involved. If it is a 'when' story which looks at events over time, a graphic which shows the timeline could be useful. The different types of story and possible visuals are summarised below in Table 7.3 (based on Meyer, 1997, pp. 36–38).

**Table 7.3** *Matching story to visuals*

| *Story type* | *Focus* | *Useful visuals* |
|---|---|---|
| Who? | People | Illustrations of the people involved |
| What? | Particular agreement or plan | Graphic of the main points of the plan |
| When? | Chain of events or schedule | Some sort of timeline |
| Where? | Place | Map or diagram of the location |
| Why? | Pros and cons of a particular position or argument | Table or chart which summarises and contrasts the pros and cons |
| How? | How things work or happen | Graphics, photos or diagrams which show the process |

You can apply the same logic to business documents. For example, a report might cover a number of these types – what? why? how? – and visuals will help the reader to understand the material.

Another important point from Meyer is that graphics should be *organised* to make a point. He argues that all graphics should employ the 'inverted pyramid' form, which is the classic form of newspaper narrative – you express the most important point first, then the second most important, and so on. Translating this idea to graphics, he recommends a three-step strategy for design:

- start with the main point and make sure this is 'loud and clear';
- go to the secondary point;
- offer supporting details.

If details do not support the main point, they should be omitted (Meyer, 1997, Chapter 3). We shall return to this point later when we look at some visual aids in action.

## WHAT ARE THE MAIN VISUAL AIDS AND HOW DO THEY WORK?

You can use a wide range of visual aids in business documents and need to be aware of their main advantages and disadvantages. There are three main types, which we have summarised in the following table. Even this division is not entirely watertight as a map is both pictorial and schematic.

### Visual representations of numerical data

If you have to present numerical data, then you have to decide whether to represent it in tables, charts and/or graphs. As we shall see, all the methods have potential disadvantages.

**Table 7.4** *Different forms of visual aid*

| *Type* | *Includes* | *Main advantages* | *Main disadvantages* |
|---|---|---|---|
| Visual representations of numerical data | Tables, charts and graphs | Can summarise a lot of data very effectively<br>Can show trends | Audience must have sufficient technical knowledge to interpret them |
| Schematic presentations | Diagrams, signs, flow charts, organisation charts and algorithms | Can convey information more efficiently than text | May rely on implicit knowledge which audience may not share |
| Pictorial presentations | Drawings, photographs, artistic illustrations, maps | Realistic representations | Can be expensive to produce |

## *Simple tables*

Readers find difficulty in absorbing numerical information when it is embedded in a sentence. It is often better to use a small table. Consider the following:

> Comparing the 2013 and 2014 results, it can be seen that while sales of electrical appliances decreased by 20 per cent from 3 million to 2.4 million, furniture sales only decreased by 10 per cent from 3 million to 2.7 million.

This can be rewritten as a simple table, as follows.

> The figures show that sales of electrical appliances decreased much more than furniture.

**Table 7.5** *Simple table to summarise data*

| | *2013 sales (in millions)* | *2014 sales* | *% decrease* |
|---|---|---|---|
| Electrical goods | 3 | 2.4 | 20 |
| Furniture | 3 | 2.7 | 10 |

The formatting feature in word-processing software means that you do not have to leave this as a simple set of boxes, as shown in Table 7.6.

**Table 7.6** *Table with simple formatting*

| | *2013 sales (in millions)* | *2014 sales* | *% decrease* |
|---|---|---|---|
| **Electrical goods** | 3 | 2.4 | 20 |
| **Furniture** | 3 | 2.7 | 10 |

As with all such automatic features, you should ensure that the formatting does not interfere with or detract from the main point you are trying to put across. You also need to consider how readers might use the document. Some of the formats offered for tables in packages like Microsoft Word do not photocopy very clearly.

Tables like the one above are intended to be read as part of the text. They usually obey the following conventions:

- they present a limited amount of numerical information;
- they are not identified by a table number and often do not have a title;
- they are not listed in the table of contents;
- they form part of the text and must not be moved for typographical convenience.

## Complex tables

Where you have more extensive datasets, you will need to insert a more formal table with the following characteristics:

- It appears in the text in a convenient position after its first mention in the text.
- It has an identifying number.
- It has a clear and informative title.
- The data is arranged in some rational order.
- Columns have clear descriptive headings.
- Where appropriate, the units of measurement are stated.
- Important data are emphasised by their positions in the table.

Unfortunately, many complex formal tables you will find in business documents are not well organised. Some of the most powerful criticisms of the way tables are used come from Ehrenberg (1977) who offers the following four principles for presenting data in tables:

1. Round off numbers so that readers can make comparisons quickly and easily.
2. Include averages for each set of data so that readers can quickly work out the spread of values.
3. Organise your table so the reader compares the columns. Figures in columns are easier to compare than figures in rows.
4. Order rows in columns by size with larger numbers placed at the top. Again, this helps the reader to compare the data.

## BOX 7.4 USING EHRENBERG'S PRINCIPLES

Consider the following table which compares the composition of the workforce in the ABC Corporation over the last few decades. All figures are in thousands employed.

**Table 7.7** *Trend table which makes the reader do all the work*

| | *1980* | *1990* | *2000* | *2010* |
|---|---|---|---|---|
| Total | 201.66 | 342.54 | 410.44 | 567.21 |
| Males | 150.64 | 278.50 | 323.22 | 441.16 |
| Females | 51.02 | 64.04 | 87.22 | 126.05 |

After revising the table using Ehrenberg's principles, it is much easier to see possible patterns in the data.

**Table 7.8** *Trend table which tries to analyse the data*

| | *Males* | *Females* | *Total* |
|---|---|---|---|
| 2010 | 441 | 126 | 567 |
| 2000 | 323 | 87 | 410 |
| 1990 | 278 | 64 | 342 |
| 1980 | 151 | 51 | 202 |
| Average | 298 | 82 | 380 |

Of course, we always need to question the purpose of a table like this. If the real purpose is to investigate whether there is any gender bias in ABC's employment practices, this should be the focus of the table.

**Table 7.9** *Trend table which highlights the key statistic*

| | *Total* | *Female numbers* | *Females as % of workforce* |
|---|---|---|---|
| 2010 | 567 | 126 | 22 |
| 2000 | 410 | 87 | 21 |
| 1990 | 342 | 64 | 19 |
| 1970 | 202 | 51 | 25 |
| Average | 380 | 82 | 22 |

## Charts and graphs

### *Which visual aid to use?*

Spreadsheet software will allow you to convert a spreadsheet table into a chart or graph. However, we can choose from an enormous variety of graphs, as the following list shows:

- line graphs
- scatter diagrams
- bar charts
- pie charts (area graphs)
- histograms
- frequency polygons
- cumulative frequency curves.

Which one is the best one to use in a given circumstance? We do not have space in this book to offer a comprehensive comparison of them all, but we can bring out the main issues by contrasting some of the main types (for further discussion and examples, see the website). For example, suppose that you need to present sales data which shows that a particular initiative has reversed a decline – would you use the line graph in Figure 7.2 or the bar chart in Figure 7.3? We suggest that the line graph is a more immediate visual demonstration of the trend, especially if you label the main point as in Figure 7.4.

### *How can we evaluate effectiveness and appropriateness of graphic messages?*

Graphic messages can be evaluated in terms of certain criteria, just as messages in written communication are evaluated: their content and tone. It is also worth emphasising the importance of a clear purpose and making sure that the audience will be able to interpret the visual aid in the way you intend.

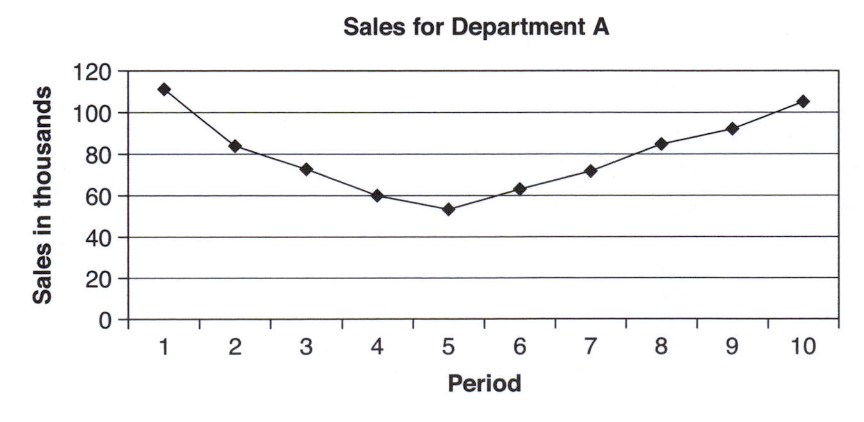


***Figure 7.2*** *Example of a line graph*

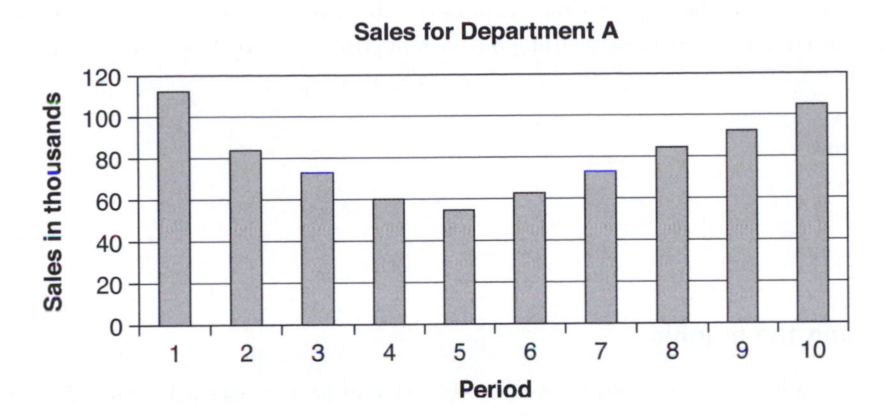


***Figure 7.3*** *Example of bar chart*

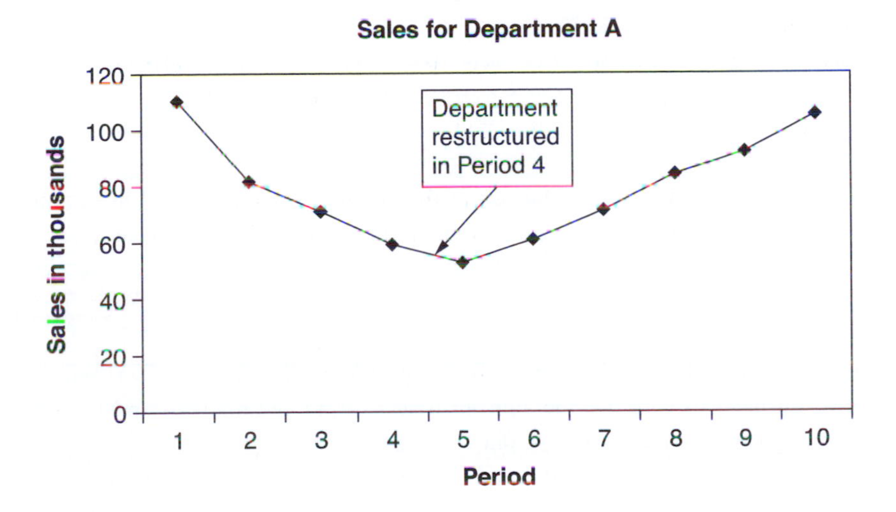


***Figure 7.4*** *Line graph with label to suggest the important conclusion*

## Checking the audience

You need to consider your audience's background whenever you choose a visual aid. For example, one important study found that information presented in a table was preferred by readers with a strong technical background, whereas less technical readers found a flowchart better for the same information (Wright and Reid, 1974). Unfortunately, we do not think that graphic literacy is as widely taught in our education systems as it should be, so, for most audiences, the simpler and more pictorial the device the better. Of course, many professions such as engineers, economists and architects do have their own graphic languages and conventions which can be used where appropriate.

In general, you have more information available than can be used in the visual aid, so the selection and processing of information is essential. Where the information is numerical, you need to use a form that matches the purpose and the needs of the audience. You can then decide the content of the message using the content criteria we have already discussed in this book:

- accuracy
- brevity
- clarity
- emphasis.

## Choosing the graphic

Once the audience analysis has been done, you should have a reasonably clear idea of the most suitable visual aid. You should then experiment with the factors listed below.

- *Type* – e.g. horizontal or vertical bar charts.
- *Scale* – this can affect the emphasis.
- *Complexity* – there is a trade-off between detail, and accuracy and clarity.
- *Use of colour* – certain colours are conventionally associated with certain attitudes and emotions, but beware of any cultural differences if they affect your audience.

You should also check whether the size of the graphic may be reduced to fit column or page sizes. If so, make sure your graphic can be reduced without loss of clarity.

## Tone

Graphic devices do not offer the same opportunity for tonal variation as written material. However, you need to consider the appropiateness of graphic material and the extent to which attitudes can be expressed in graphics.

Graphics that treat any part of the audience without respect for their essential human dignity are unacceptable. This is particularly the case where humour is used to make a point. A more subtle form of incorrect attitude to audience is stereotyping – for example, where supervisors are always portrayed as white and workers as black.

## Avoiding bias and misrepresentation in visual aids

Graphic devices can be used to deceive. Sometimes the line between honest emphasis and deceit is not always clear. In the final analysis, the author's or the professional illustrator's professional integrity is the best guide. The following are some of the methods that can, intentionally or unintentionally, deceive an audience.

### *Suppressing the zero*

The zero on a graph is sometimes suppressed to save space or to emphasise a small but significant change. Note that in Figure 7.5 there is no indication on the graph that the zero

## BOX 7.5 USING GRAPHICS: PRACTICAL GUIDELINES

If you intend to produce your own graphics, the following are some practical guidelines:

- Keep the graph simple. Bear in mind the purpose and the audience; provide no more detail than your purpose requires and your audience needs.
- Place titles either above or below the graph, but be consistent throughout the document or presentation.
- Without being long-winded, ensure that your title accurately reflects the contents of the graphic. Words like 'Graph of . . .' or 'Diagram of . . .' are unnecessary as this should be apparent. An explanatory note below the title can help the reader.
- See that your graph has some logic behind its presentation – e.g. largest to smallest, most important to least important, by provinces, or by time sequence. Use the ordering of information to emphasise the point you wish to make.
- Make the illustration attractive. It should provide a welcome break from the written word and not be a distraction or puzzle.
- Use specific devices to help your reader and to emphasise important points. Examples of such devices are: colour, arrows, heavy lines, distinctive plotting points, annotation and keys.
- Avoid bias in presenting information. This will be discussed in more detail later.
- Make sure that axes are clearly labelled and that units are unambiguous and consistent.
- Wherever possible, use horizontal labelling in preference to vertical labelling.
- Where possible, label line graphs directly rather than using a key, but do use a key if the graph becomes cluttered.
- Do not place a graphic before its first reference in the text, but place it as soon as practicable thereafter.
- Do not just repeat information from graphs in the text but rather use the text for comment, explanation or interpretation.
- For scales, use multiples or submultiples of 2, 5 or 10.

has been suppressed. The graph suggests that sales are rising much more steeply than if the full range was included, as in Figure 7.6.

### *Mixing the scales*

Often two- or three-dimensional presentations are used in pictographs, but the scale used is linear. Spreadsheets like Microsoft Excel offer you a range of 3-D presentations, but this can lead to distortion. The data in Figure 7.7 is turned into three-dimensional cylinders in Figure 7.8 to suggest that the difference between sales is much bigger than it actually is.

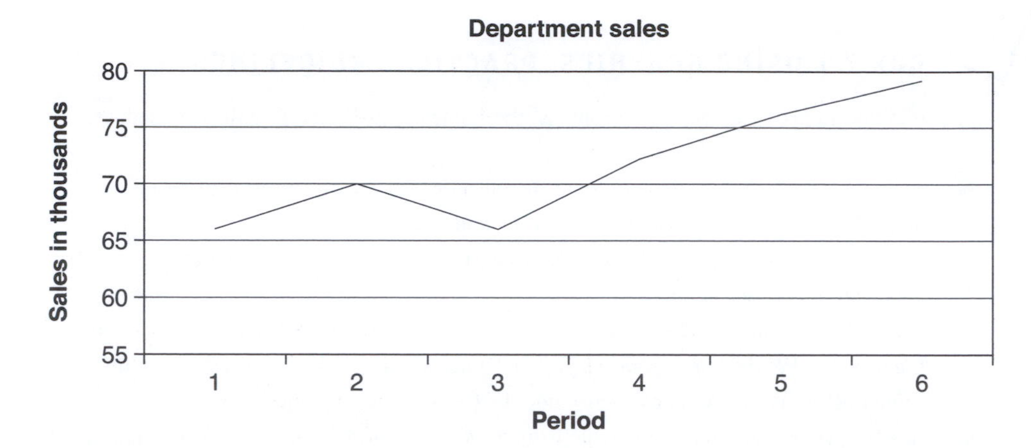


***Figure 7.5*** *Line graph with suppressed zero: the effect is to exaggerate the change*

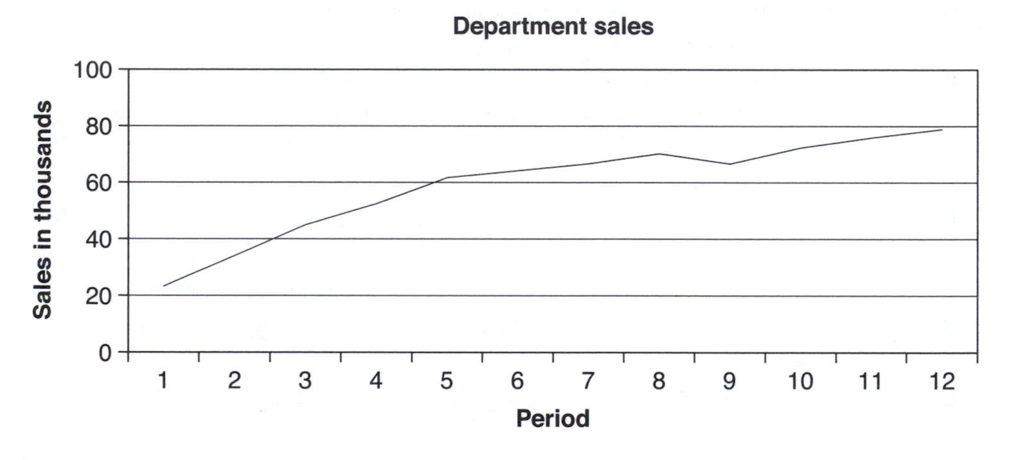


***Figure 7.6*** *Line graph without suppressed zero*

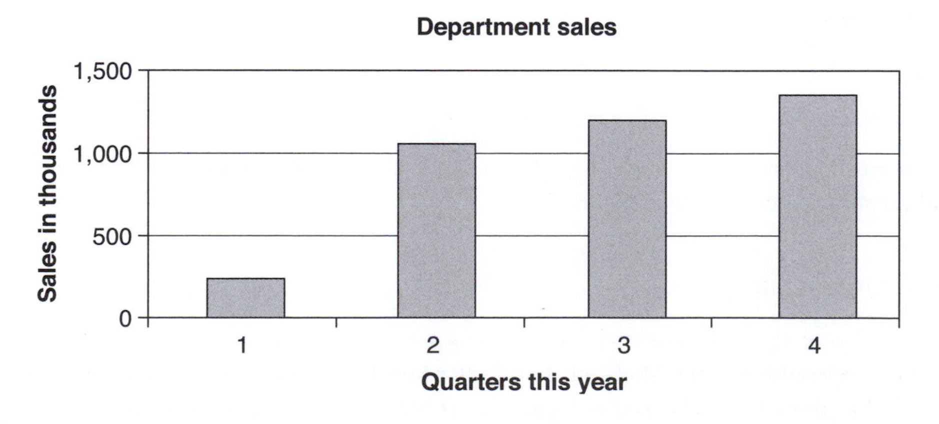


***Figure 7.7*** *Sales data expressed as a chart*

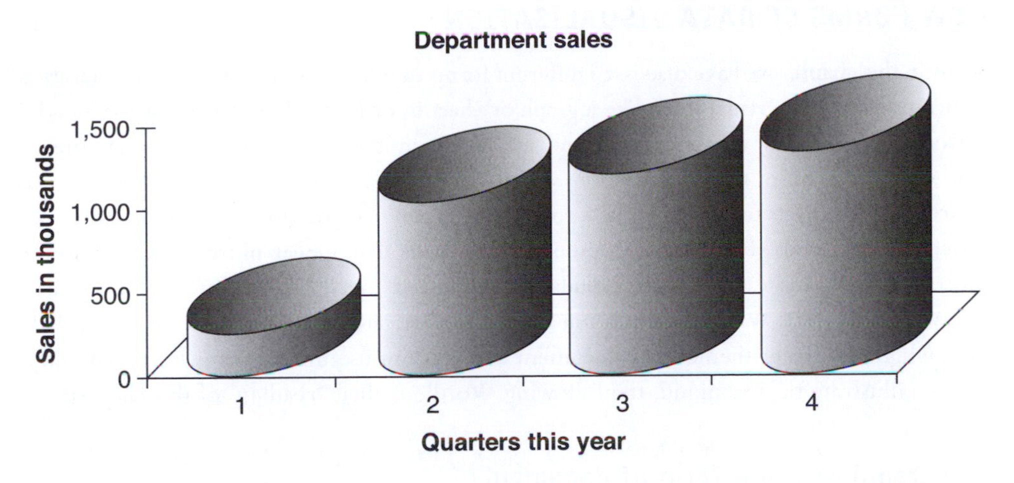


***Figure 7.8*** *Sales data in 3-D cylinders: the effect is to exaggerate the differences*

Tufte suggests that you can quantify the distortion by working out what he calls the 'lie factor' which is:

- size of effect in graphic;
- size of effect in data.

This formula is taken from Tufte, 1983, Chapter 2, which also contains many more examples of distorted graphics.

### *Unjustified line fitting*

Where the data shows a considerable scatter, there is a temptation to fit a line or curve which supports the particular hypothesis favoured by the author. Even where sophisticated curve-fitting methods are used, the result will not necessarily represent the best interpretation of the data. Ideally, any relationship derived from the data should be used as the basis for planning and testing further observations. This is, however, not always possible. Figure 7.9 shows that attempts can be made to fit both a straight line (AB) and a curve (CD) to the data.

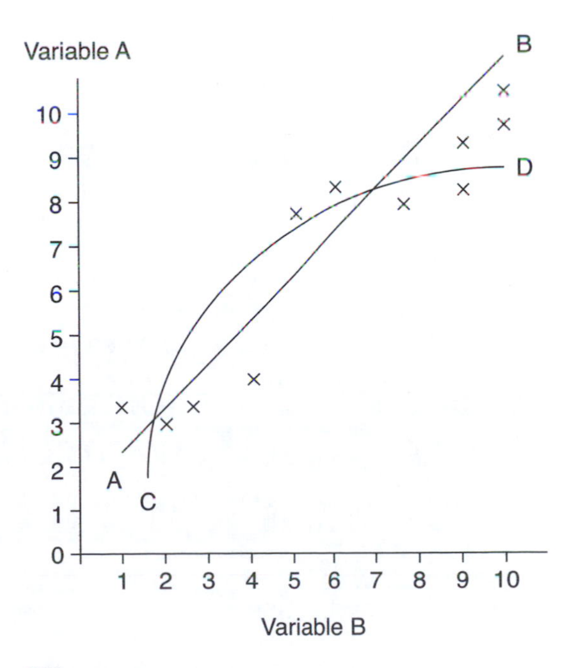


***Figure 7.9*** *Fitting a line*

## NEW FORMS OF DATA VISUALISATION

So far in this chapter we have discussed different forms of what is often called data visualisation – turning data into a visual form like a graph or chart in order to show trends or meaningful patterns. New forms are appearing and are likely in the near future. For example, if you want to identify major themes in a document, then you can use software such as Wordle which (in its own words) is 'a toy for generating "word clouds" from text that you provide. The clouds give greater prominence to words that appear more frequently in the source text. You can tweak your clouds with different fonts, layouts, and color scheme' (www.wordle.net). While this does not offer a sophisticated linguistic analysis, it can help to highlight the major themes in a document and you can use the diagrams in presentations etc. To illustrate the technique, the following Wordle is their 'reading' of this chapter.

### Infographics: a new form of document?

If you have done much Internet searching for information over the last few years, you are likely to have come across infographics. Randy Krum suggests that the emergence of this term as a household word is down to the influence of the Internet and cites the significant growth in people searching for the term word (Krum, 2013). Our experience echoes this and we can now find infographics on the Net to cover an enormous range of topics – see our website for some current examples which we have found useful. The ideas behind infographics have a much longer history and the Wikipedia page is a good place to start if you want to explore this.

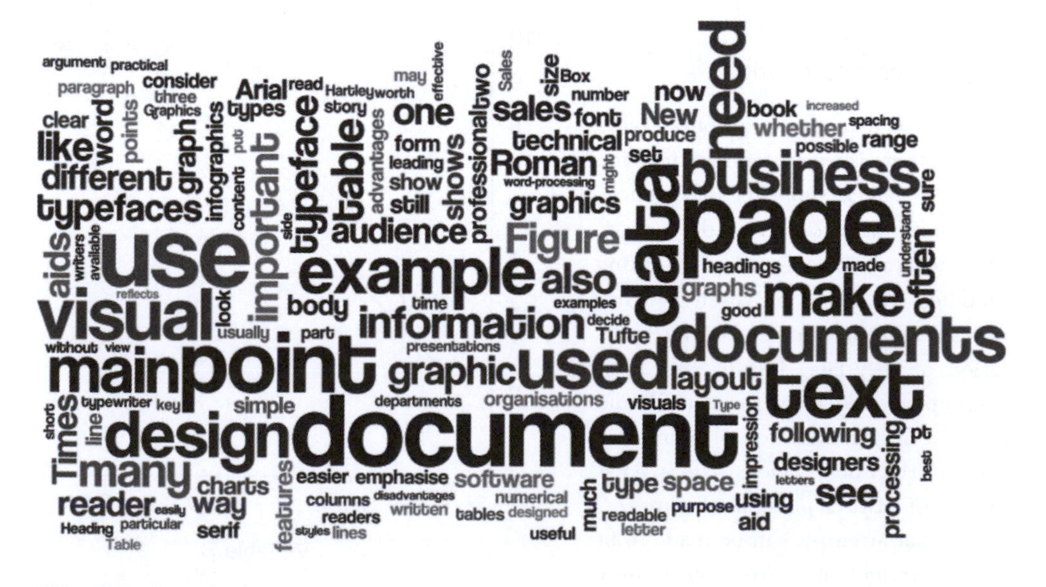


***Figure 7.10*** *Example of Wordle*

We agree with Randy's definition of infographics as 'a larger graphic design that combines data visualisations, illustrations, text and images together into a format that tells a complete story' (ibid., p. 6) The key feature is the use of a range of methods to tell a story, usually on a page so that you can view it as a printed document and which can easily be scrolled if you are viewing online.

The key issue for us is whether infographics are a specialised form of document which need specialist design and/or technical skills, or can be seen as documents which we can all produce. In the same sense that word processing evolved by borrowing techniques and facilities from desktop publishing, can we see infographics as a further stage in the development of business documents? Our current view (see the website for any updates) is that you should explore the possibilities offered by infographics as they can be useful, and you can achieve many of the effects through a combination of the range of templates and visual aids now incorporated into word-processing software.

## SUMMARY

- Psychological research supports designers' views that the 'look' of a document influences how it is read. But despite the importance of good design, many organisations are still content to treat the PC as 'just a typewriter'.
- A well-designed document has two main advantages: it makes a good impression on the reader by suggesting a professional and competent approach, and it makes the content or information easier to understand.
- Writers should consider basic technical aspects of typefaces and page layout so they can make sensible design choices, such as using page layout to emphasise the structure of the document.
- Good visual aids should *reveal* data. It is important to highlight the main points you wish to make in whatever visual aid you decide to use.
- There are three main types of visual aids you can use in documents: visual representations of numerical data (including tables, charts and graphs); schematic presentations like diagrams, flow charts etc.; and pictorial presentations like photographs. Although computer technology has made these easier to produce, there are still cost and production issues. These need to be weighed against the advantages.
- Graphic devices can be used to deceive. You must recognise the potential for misrepresentation and avoid it in your own documents.
- New forms of data visualisation are appearing which you can use – e.g. Wordle and similar applications.
- Infographics are worth investigating as a hybrid document which mixes text, graphics and visuals to create single page documents on a single theme or question.

## FURTHER READING

Hartley, J. (1994) *Designing Instructional Text* (3rd edn). London: Kogan Page.

Although this text is now a little dated and also only focuses on instructional text, it offers a very comprehensive survey of research and practical advice on document layout and design which is still relevant today.

Lupton, E. (2010) *Thinking with Type: A critical guide for designers, writers, editors, and students* (2nd revised and expanded edn). New York: Princeton Architectural Press.

This probably contains all the current and historical content you will ever need to know about typefaces.

Krum, R. (2013) *Cool Infographics: Effective communication with data visualization and design.* Indianapolis, IN: John Wiley & Sons.

McCandless, D. (2012) *Information is Beautiful.* London: Collins.

Randy Krum's book offers a useful introduction to this area. You can also find useful examples at his blog: www.coolinfographics.com. David McCandless offers a book full of infographics where you can also see some of the techniques used by professional designers. Also see his website at www.davidmccandless.com.

Tufte, E.R. (1983) *The Visual Display of Quantitative Information.* Cheshire, CT: Graphics Press.

Tufte, E.R. (1990) *Envisioning Information.* Cheshire, CT: Graphics Press.

These books by Tufte have been recognised as classic contributions to the debate on the impact of visual presentation. You can find further details of these and other works by him at www.edwardtufte.com/tufte/

Williams, R. (1992) *The PC is Not a Typewriter.* Berkeley, CA: Peachpit Press.

Williams, R. (2003) *The Mac is Not a Typewriter* (2nd edn). Berkeley, CA: Peachpit Press.

Although now dated in some of the technical references, these books make the important (and still very relevant) argument that we should approach our computers as word processor and 'page designer'.

Chapter 8

# What makes documents effective?

## INTRODUCTION

This chapter starts by raising general issues about the range and type of documents we now need in organisations and ponders the future of the paperless office.

We summarise principles of effective communication from the previous three chapters – structure, style and design – and then apply these principles to common business documents, ranging from the informal to the official, and from the individual to the corporate: memos, letters, reports, email and fax, Web pages, social media such as blogs and wikis. A further section on CVs and applications is available on our website. Even if you only want to read about particular documents rather than the whole chapter, we recommend you read this summary first.

Finally, we highlight general issues, such as the impact of change. For example, some institutions are abandoning or rethinking their use of email. Is this an indication of the future?

### OBJECTIVES

*This chapter will*:

- summarise the main principles we need to consider when preparing all business documents;
- review the typical characteristics of the main forms of business documents, using these principles;
- raise important issues about the changing nature of business documents, including the importance of new forms of communication.

## WHAT DOCUMENTS DO WE NEED?

There is no simple answer to this question. We can illustrate some of the potential diversity using two short case studies – one comparing our personal use of writing software and one based on a distinctive organisational approach.

## Personal use of writing software

To illustrate the point that you need to choose communication methods which suit your personal style, we can compare our own experience and preferences – we use very different techniques for personal note-taking and routine communications.

One of us (PH) uses concept maps as an alternative to note-taking in meetings. He explains his attachments to concept maps as follows:

> Where they are particularly useful in meetings is in their use as a tool to stimulate dialogue and focus attention on main points in meetings. I can develop a concept map as the meeting progresses and towards the end of the meeting present the map to the participants and will typically lead a discussion on the individual ideas as well as the bigger picture. This technique allows the participants to reflect on the ideas generated in the meeting and develop a consensus as well as building on the meeting ideas in a focused way, which are then added to the concept map. The graphical representation is most valuable in illustrating both the bigger picture and linkages between ideas.
>
> The concept maps can then be incorporated into reports and presentations, in either hard-copy form or in digital form. The inclusion of a concept map in, for instance, the beginning of a chapter of a report, can help me convey an initial "big picture" of the chapter and this can help the reader to contextualise the text of the chapter. Concept maps can also be used online in a similar way, and their usefulness can be extended by including hyperlinks to further information on each of the nodes of the concept map, thereby using it as a visual navigation aid – for an example of this see the website where you can download my favourite concept mapping software – Cmap – http://cmap.ihmc.us. I can also save the propositions which make up the map as a text file and load it into the word processor.

In contrast, PC needs software which reflects the amount of time he spends in meetings working with project groups, often meeting with colleagues who can only attend virtually.

> My usual approach is to create a shared online document (such as a Google Doc) and to type notes, ideas and actions as they arise. By setting the document sharing settings to allow others to edit the document, I can give the web address to others in the meeting and allow them to contribute as we go along. This helps to develop collective ownership of the notes, ideas and actions. This can work both in face-to-face meetings and in virtual meetings using e.g. Skype.

## Pyramid reporting as a company strategy

A large consulting company adopts a 'pyramid reporting' approach as a way of engaging its clients with both the detail and the 'big picture' aspects of its reports. We have already mentioned this company's use of mind-mapping software to support its consultants in collaboratively (and virtually) undertaking research analysis and report-writing activities.

The organisation has taken this approach a step further by adopting the pyramid approach to writing and presenting their reports.

Mind maps have an inherent hierarchical structure which supports the consultants in developing such a pyramid report – the consultants have to formulate the most important key messages first and then allow readers to drill down to get the next most important information and so on through various levels of detail. In such a pyramid report, the Table of Contents would take the shape of key message statements. An example would be: Level 1 'The project can be sustained and embedded in a number of ways to support the institution's key strategies' and Level 2 'Ensure key lessons from the project are embedded in staff development programmes'.

The approach has three main benefits:

- The consultants can collaboratively develop the key messages at each level of the pyramid.
- The pyramid approach forces the consultants to identify the most important messages from the research and analysis – which is not always easy to carry out – and it is not unknown for consultancy reports to disguise a lack of ability for such clear and rational thinking in an excessively long report.
- The approach helps to overcome the side effects of 'information overload', where readers, particularly senior managers, do not have the time to read long reports. Such a pyramid report can be more effective than the more common Executive Summary in that it provides the most important messages first and then allows the reader (or presenter) to drill down to whatever level of detail they wish to, in a highly efficient way.

The approach has additional flexibility if a presentation has to be offered to a client or senior manager. This can use the mind map as this software includes a presentation mode.

### Can we identify an ideal strategy?

Using these case studies as a starting point, you might like to consider what approach to documents has been adopted by your organisation and compare that with your own ideal approach.

## WHATEVER HAPPENED TO THE PAPERLESS OFFICE?

Before we look at specific documents, we should question the balance of activity in modern organisations.

In 2003, Abigail Sellen wrote that 'It seems that the promised "paperless office" is as much a mythical ideal today as it was thirty years ago' (Sellen and Harper, 2003, p. 2).

In January 2014, Greg Milliken wrote:

> After many monumental technology advances, we're not much closer to the paperless office than we were when Stevie Ray Vaughan was first laying down Texas

> Flood at Antone's in Austin in the early 80's when I was in college at the University of Texas.
>
> (www.wired.com/insights/2014/01/paperless-office-30-year-old-pipe-dream/)

A decade has passed and not much appears to have changed. Where will we be in 2024? Greg supports his conclusion with various current statistics including the facts that:

- The use of photocopiers is not shrinking.
- Companies' use of paper and the numbers of documents are both growing.

He suggests that we should accept that people are going to continue to want to use paper in some circumstances even when a reliable digital equivalent is feasible (e.g. the physical signature on an important contract) but we could move towards 'a pragmatic "paper-light" environment that can be achieved relatively quickly in any organization'.

Our own observations support this conclusion. Companies selling systems which support the paperless office can provide strong evidence for cost savings but also report limited progress. For example, an Iron Mountain company report suggested that only 1 per cent of EU companies had achieved a paperless state by 2014.

We doubt that a completely paperless solution is either practical or desirable, but you might like to review how many of your own practices could be reformed to avoid wasting paper. Table 8.1 suggests some common practices which have traditionally involved much exchange of paper and where technical solutions are now readily available. We have given examples of software we have used successfully but we must emphasise that other software is available which might suit you better.

However 'paper light' you are able to be, you need to consider the general principles which you can apply to all documents, and then understand the specific conventions and limitations of particular types of document.

***Table 8.1*** *Simple techniques for saving paper*

| *Activity* | *Technical possibility* |
|---|---|
| Drafting a report with input from colleagues | Use collaborative word-processing software (which allows everyone to edit the same document) like Google Docs |
| File sharing and storage | Save the document in a shared folder in DropBox or Sugar Sync |
| Preparing presentation slides and handouts | Use presentation software where you both prepare and store the slides online like Haiku Deck or use Powerpoint and upload to SlideShare |
| Scheduling a meeting | Use an online scheduler like Doodle |
| Taking minutes at a meeting | Use Google Docs and project the pages to get instant agreement on your notes |

## WHAT ARE THE GENERAL PRINCIPLES?

There are general principles to consider when preparing *all* business documents, whether print or online. We can offer two different but complementary ways of summarising this – one based on the detailed analyses from the last three chapters, and one extending the general principles which Geisler offers to increase users engagement on the Web.

### Specific principles

We summarise the specific principles using the main points from the last three chapters.

#### *Planning and structure*

- It is important to develop plans and objectives. This does not mean that you have to write in a rigid sequence of steps.
- Clear objectives are important in planning. Phrasing your objectives in a particular way can help you decide what information you need to provide.
- You must consider the particular needs of your audiences when you decide your objectives.
- If we can present information which is clearly organised *and* organised in a way which makes sense to the audience, then that audience will find the information easier to understand and remember.
- There are various ways of structuring information in written documents. They use three basic principles: chunking, ordering and signposting.
- The structure of your document should support your objectives.

#### *Style*

- Business writing often fails to communicate because of poor expression. We need to evaluate writing using both content and tone criteria.
- 'Plain language' should be considered as a company strategy, remembering that this argues for an *appropriate* style of language and *not* the same simple style for every document. We can use plain language ideas to evaluate and improve our words and sentences.
- We should follow standard conventions on punctuation while remembering that the rules are both flexible and changing

#### *Layout and visual aids*

- The 'look' of a document influences how it is read.
- A well-designed document has two main advantages: it makes a good impression on the reader by suggesting a professional and competent approach, and it makes the content or information easier to understand.

- Writers should understand the basic aspects of typefaces and page layout/design, and use them to make sensible design choices.
- Good visual aids should *reveal* data. It is important to highlight the main points you wish to make.
- Different types of visual aid have important advantages and disadvantages.
- Graphic devices can be used to deceive. You should avoid misrepresentation in your documents.

There are other general issues, described below.

### *You are the organisation!*

Whenever you write to another person, you are representing your organisation or your part of it. If you create a poor impression, the organisation suffers.

### *Format, image and house style*

Business documents project your image. Large organisations usually employ professional designers to design their corporate stationery. Although the current trend is towards simple stationery, you may have to work within a certain format dictated by the house style.

### *Legal and statutory requirements*

There are certain legal requirements which obviously vary from country to country. For example, in South Africa, letters *must* carry the company's registration number and the names of its directors. How this information appears depends on the image that the organisation is trying to project.

### *Document designs reflect organisational structures and culture*

Susan Katz suggests that 'every organization, and every department within an organization has its own conception of what makes "good writing"' (Katz, 1998, p. 109). She found that some managers very carefully coached new staff in their writing, explaining the importance and purpose of documents, providing models of good practice, and commenting on drafts and outlines.

Changing the design of documents may also change relationships between staff and their perceptions of their roles. Therefore, we cannot assume that making documents easier to read and understand will automatically make the organisation more effective.

## Increasing user engagement

Geisler offers a number of tried and tested principles which are designed to increase users' engagement with online and Web documents. In the table below, we explain these principles and discuss how you can extend their application to print documents.

**Table 8.2** *Engaging users*

| *Principle* | *Meaning and application to online documents* | *Application to print documents* |
|---|---|---|
| Design for diverse users | A Web system can provide various options in terms of navigation to suit different users | A well-designed and structured print document can suit different readers – e.g. the clear summary for readers under time pressures |
| Design for usability | Using familiar conventions and maintaining consistency are some of the techniques to make online documents more usable | You can also use familiar conventions and a consistent approach to help readers of print documents |
| Test the backbone | The technological backbone needs to make online documents easy to access | There isn't really a direct analogy here with print documents except that long documents should be easy to find your way around |
| Extend a welcome | Your website may attract users who are very different from your intended audience. How can you make them feel comfortable when they access the site? | The best way to make written documents accessible and welcoming is to use design and layout so that readers can easily see how to make their way through the document |
| Set the context | Any webspace is used in a particular context. Does the design of the webspace suit that context? For example, a wiki for collaborative writing needs to be set up to suit the overall context of collaboration | Printed documents also work in context. Are your documents suitable for the context you are working in? |
| Make a connection | Using techniques like story-telling can be a very useful way of establishing a connection with users | You can also use story-telling and personal case studies in written reports to bring home their relevance to readers |
| Share control | You can maximise user options and choices | This principle does not apply in the same way. You can design your documents so that readers can have some flexibility in their approach |
| Support interaction among users | You should offer ways for users to interact and collaborate through the webspace | You cannot do this directly with a printed document but you can put documents online to achieve the same end |
| Create a sense of place | Consistent design and layout creates a sense of place which users will find attractive | Consistent design and layout can also give a sense of a printed document as a coherent and attractive 'place to be' |
| Plan to continue the engagement | As well as supporting interaction on first use, the webspace can be designed to enable and encourage users to keep returning to the space and maintain their engagement | Again, this principle does not apply in the same way to a printed document but we can consider ways of blending the document into some online activity |

This table illustrates that online documents have some useful potential advantages over printed documents if you can use these principles. However, simply putting a printed document online will not necessarily realise these advantages unless you have accommodated all these principles.

## DIFFERENT TYPES OF PRINT DOCUMENTS

### Memos

The memo provides our first example of how technology is changing the way we communicate. In textbooks produced in the 1990s, the memo was described as 'a' or 'the' main method of written communication in business organisations. Nowadays, in many if not most organisations, memos have been virtually replaced by emails.

Memos may have disappeared, but you can still use some of the techniques used to construct 'good' memos. For example, if the message is more than a simple few lines, you should consider how you chunk it (as discussed in Chapter 6). Thomas Clark (1998) asked his students to draft business memos using these headings:

- Objectives
- Background
- Findings
- Issues
- Action steps.

He then suggests that you use a matrix, as in the figure below, so that you can check the relationships between the components. For example, do the findings relate clearly to the objectives? Do the action steps follow from the findings?

| Objectives | Findings | Actions |
|---|---|---|
| 1. | 1. | 1. |
| | 2. | 2. |
| | | |
| 2. | 1. | |
| | 2. | |
| | | |
| Background | | Issues |
| | | |
| | | |

***Figure 8.1*** *The memo matrix*
Source: based on Clark, 1998, p. 73.

The advantage of this system is that you can easily check if your memo is logically coherent. This structure can be used to think about reports.

## Letters

The writing of business letters has a long history. Their main advantage is that they provide a permanent record of what is said. On the other hand, letters are expensive, they have to be composed with care and feedback may be slow or non-existent. For these reasons, you always need to question whether a letter is appropriate in any given business situation.

### *Standard and circular letters*

The logic of a circular letter is that everyone receives exactly the same information (and the Arrow manager may assume that this gives everyone the same meaning) and at much the same time. In practice, this may have unanticipated consequences. For example, consider the following message in a circular letter from the relatively new general manager of a large multisite organisation: 'From September to December this year, we shall be holding consultations with all staff on the Greenfield site to consider proposals to amalgamate the departments on that site.'

Many staff on the Greenfield site received this news by word of mouth. However, the meaning of the grapevine message was more definite than the written message: 'The new general manager has decided to amalgamate the departments on that site.' This interpretation was strongly justified by its advocates. They pointed to several clues to management's 'real intentions':

- the way that the circular had been announced, out of the blue and just before the annual holiday period;
- the fact that the current department managers were completely unprepared for it;
- the 'fact' that the new general manager obviously wanted to establish her authority.

The important principle here is that a message which is designed to reach and mean the same for everyone (like circular letters) must take account of the context and anticipate different interpretations. In the last example, some of the problems could have been avoided, at least in part, by briefing department managers *and* by issuing the circular after the holiday period.

But is a printed circular the best method for this sort of message? Would an email have been greeted with more or less suspicion? That depends on the history and culture of the organisation. If it is a large distributed organisation, why not consider setting up a webinar led by the senior manager making the announcement?

### *Style in individual letters*

We can write individual letters of various types, including making/answering enquiries, appointing an employee, submitting or accepting a quotation, and so on. We can highlight main principles and issues with an example where the tone is particularly important: responding to a complaint.

### *Chunking in letters*

If you follow chunking principles from previous chapters, then each paragraph has a specific theme. We can think of business letters in terms of the basic begin–middle–end structure, as recommended by many trainers and teachers.

| | |
|---|---|
| Begin | Explain why you are writing. |
| Middle | Explain the detailed information. |
| End | Explain what action you are going to take. |

### *Deciding on the tone*

As well as making sure that the content was accurate, is the tone appropriate? For example, we would recommend a 'positive and neutral' tone for a letter of complaint to another person/organisation. One issue with any letter of complaint is the possible assumption that the other person is directly to blame. As accusations usually put the other person on the defensive, they are not a good strategy to resolve the problem, especially in the first letter. It is much safer to assume that your audience is someone who wishes to provide a good service, but that something has simply gone wrong.

### *A final word on style in letters*

A study published in 1987 compared a selection of business letters written in English, French and Japanese. The authors found many examples of what they called 'ritualized and formulaic writing' (Jenkins and Hinds, 1987, p. 328). We criticised this sort of language in Chapter 7. But how much has changed in the last 40 years? More recent studies have suggested a change towards the principles adopted in this book, but it is difficult to assess how widespread this change has been. The fact that organisations like the Plain English Campaign in the UK are still very active does suggest that we still have a lot to learn.

### *Layout conventions in letters*

Conventions have changed – for example, most organisations now use the block format of presentation:

- Everything starts at the left-hand margin, except possibly the company letterheading/logo at the top of the page.
- The right margin is either justified or ragged (we recommend the latter for word-processed documents).
- Punctuation is kept to a minimum with only the necessary full stops (periods) and commas.

You can see these rules applied in many of the templates now offered in word-processing software.

## REPORTS

A report is an official or formal statement, often made after an investigation and usually made to your immediate line manager, or to a working group or committee. The audience(s) may be either internal or external to the organisation, or, on rare occasions, both. The audience may not share the writer's expertise.

### Analysing the audiences

The structure and content of any report must meet the needs of up to four distinct categories of audience.

***Table 8.3*** *Audience analysis*

| *Your audience* | *Definition* |
|---|---|
| The primary audience | As a report aims to achieve action, these are people who have the authority to act on the recommendations. This may be a single person, such as a general manager, or a group, such as a committee or even the board of directors. Key parts of the report (especially the executive summary, conclusions and recommendations) should be targeted specifically at this primary audience |
| The secondary audience | Few decision-makers act entirely on their own; they seek advice from departments and specialists. This group of advisers is the secondary audience, which often has limited or special interests |
| The tertiary audience | If the recommendations of a report are approved, then it may be distributed to further readers who have to implement the recommendations. They will need details which were not necessary for decision-making, so make sure these are covered in the appendices |
| And other readers | There may be a fourth category of reader who, for policy reasons, 'need to know' (often senior staff in other parts of the organisation). Or there may be people at a later date who may find the report useful for similar investigations |

## TYPES OF REPORT

Three main categories cover most of the variation you will find in practice:

- form reports;
- short reports;
- long formal reports and proposals.

## Form reports, forms and questionnaires

These all share important features:

- They are designed to compile specific information from a variety of respondents.
- They collect information which can then be collated, analysed and interpreted.

Form reports are regular and standardised, such as production reports, sales reports, accident reports, progress reports, etc. There are definite advantages in having standardised forms for these:

- the same information is in the same place each time;
- we can check that all the required information is submitted.

Forms and form reports are increasingly online so that the information can be fed directly into the organisation's computer system. This can also lead to direct action if the system is set up for it.

Designing forms and questionnaires requires high levels of skill. It is all too easy to create ambiguous or misleading questions and collect data which is effectively useless.

## Short reports

These are internal reports, usually less than five pages, which do not require all the formalities of long reports. They often have simple subsections such as:

- Introduction
- Investigation
- Conclusion.

Descriptive reports of this sort are usually intended to supply information, rather than recommend specific action. In terms of effective style and structure, we echo what we said about memos, emails and letters, emphasising the importance of informative headings and subheadings to guide the reader through the text. You can also use techniques like Clark's memo matrix, as discussed earlier.

## Long formal reports and proposals

Long reports deal with a complex investigation or issue, often addressed to a number of different audiences. To cater for different audiences and to provide a logical structure, reports are subdivided into sections with distinct functions. A complete investigation (from problem definition through to recommendations) requires a logical sequence of actions, which are reflected in this sectional structure.

Proposals might be for a new company or departmental initiative. These have a similar format to reports but use some sections differently.

### *Objectives*

Writing a report is easier if you have a clear objective. You can use the approach to summarise your objective suggested in Chapter 7. Barker (1999, p. 99) offers another useful suggestion – summarising your objective in what he calls a 'function statement' as follows:

- the first part ('the aim of this report is to . . .') expresses the report's immediate aim;
- the second part ('so that . . .') looks to the *future*. What benefit, payoff or actions do you see as a result of producing the report?

Having a clear view of the objective is especially important with complicated reports which involve a lot of preparation. It is also useful to have a clear function statement like this as you can then check it with whoever commissioned the report.

### *Structure and report sections*

Basic report structure is an expansion of the begin–middle–end structure we have come across before, as in the following table. See our website for a more detailed description of each section and other links to useful guidance on the Web.

***Table 8.4*** *Variations in report structure*

| | *Report structure* | *Report sections* |
|---|---|---|
| Begin | Introduction | Title page<br>Synopsis or summary<br>Contents list<br>Introduction |
| Middle | Main body | Methods of investigation<br>Results<br>Discussion of results |
| End | Conclusions and recommendations | Conclusions<br>Recommendations<br>Appendices |

Not all reports will contain all these sections. How they are subdivided depends on the contents and the audience requirements. Table 8.5 gives a few variations to meet specific needs. The important principle is to choose a structure which supports your objectives and which readers will follow easily. For example, many writers advocate the SPQR approach:

**S** = the situation (this company is the leading producer of grommits)
**P** = the problem or problems which have arisen (sales of grommits are falling)
**Q** = the question which arises in the reader's mind (how can we restore the profit in grommit sales?)
**R** = response (solutions and recommendations, which may of course challenge the assumptions behind the original question. For example, it may be impossible to revive grommit sales as this technology is in long-term decline. What should the organisation do about this?)

**Table 8.5** *Different report structures*

| *Report which summarises the results of an investigation to arrive at a conclusion: 'the new manufacturing process does/does not meet Health and Safety standards'* | *Report which investigates three possible solutions to a specified problem and recommends the best course of action* | *Proposal which recommends that the department or organisation adopts new working practices (e.g. adopts new computer system)* |
|---|---|---|
| Title page<br>Title<br>Summary<br>Contents list<br>Introduction<br>Investigation, which comprises:<br>– method of information gathering<br>– results<br>– discussion<br>Conclusion<br>Appendices (e.g. detailed test results) | Title page<br>Title<br>Summary<br>Contents list<br>Introduction (which specifies the problem)<br>Solution 1:<br>– advantages<br>– disadvantages<br>Solution 2:<br>– advantages<br>– disadvantages<br>Solution 3:<br>– advantages<br>– disadvantages<br>Conclusion<br>Recommendations<br>Appendices | Title page<br>Title<br>Summary<br>Contents list<br>Introduction<br>Analysis of present working practices:<br>– problem 1<br>– problem 2<br>– and so on<br>How a new system would deal with these problems:<br>– advantages<br>– disadvantages<br>Conclusion and recommendation<br>Appendices |

Whatever the final structure in terms of headings and subheadings, it is essential that this reflects the structure of your argument. Having a visual summary of your argument can be very useful, perhaps using pyramid or spider diagram techniques as described in Chapter 7, or perhaps just summarising the building blocks of your argument.

## Report style

All the general issues of language style we discussed in Chapter 6 are relevant, but there are two issues which are worth emphasising.

### *Style and organisational structure*

A particular language style can reflect deep-rooted organisational attitudes which may be difficult to change.

### *Style and accuracy*

Some of the traditional conventions of formal reports, such as avoiding the first person and using the passive voice, were justified by the claim that this writing style was more 'accurate' or 'objective'. And some organisations still insist on some of these conventions. However, you cannot automatically assume that your writing will be accurate by adopting these strategies. In fact, these strategies can lead to tortuous expressions which can be vague or misleading.

The best practical solution is to make your reports compatible with the organisational house-style and avoid any constructions which can confuse. We still need to worry about the warnings from Kirkman (1992) of regular problems in more technical reports, including:

- *Excessive abstraction*. General and abstract terms are used instead of more specific and concrete terms which would clarify the meaning. This often leads to:
- *Excessive nominalisation*. A noun is used instead of the verb from which it comes. For example, we write 'the function of *allocation* and *distribution* of revenue will be performed by the Business Development Department' instead of 'the business development Department will *allocate* and *distribute* the revenue'. One way of checking for this is to review any sentence where you have used expressions like 'take place', 'carry out', 'perform', etc. as these often occur in sentences which can be simplified.

## EMAIL

Email dates from around 1970 when Ray Tomlinson wrote a couple of programs which allowed people in a computer lab to send messages between machines. His programs were incorporated into the early development of the Internet and by the mid-1970s people could send email across Internet connections and give immediate responses using the reply button. Email then provided an important stimulus to Internet development. Within a few years it was 'the driving force behind the network's expansion' (Naughton, 1999, p. 210).

This brief history is important because it explains the way email developed – as a simple message system which did not incorporate the formatting offered by word processing. It has developed over time so that modern email software can offer sophisticated ways of storing messages. However, the basic rationale has not changed.

Denise Murray suggested that this pattern of development created some problems. Because of the system's perceived simplicity, most users receive very little formal training or education in its best use (Murray, 1995, Chapter 5). This has had three important consequences:

- Senders often use the attachment facility to distribute long reports or other documents rather than summarise their content. Users can become overloaded with too much detailed information.
- As email was designed to exchange information, it is limited in what it can convey. Users have developed their own codes to supply additional meaning.
- Because it is so easy and quick, it is easy to send angry or rude messages before you have had a chance to think about it. We discuss this notion – that email inspires emotional outbursts, often called flaming – later in this chapter.

## Structure and layout

At first glance, emails look like electronic memos, with a space for the sender, the receiver and the title. The date and time of sending is automatically supplied. There are none of the politeness features that we expect in letters (yours sincerely, etc.).

The layout is restricted on most email systems:

- They use a single font.
- You can only highlight phrases by using bold or a different colour.
- You can use space to suggest subheadings or emphasis.
- You can use techniques like 'emoticons'. For example, the smiley face is a common signal of happiness, created by the following keyboard characters:-).

Users are increasingly swamped by emails (see Box 8.2), so it is very important that the title reflects the nature and urgency of the content. As some email systems have a word limit to the length of the title they show in the list of messages, a clear, short title can be very important. Apart from this specific issue, we suggest that emails are structured in terms of the principles outlined on pp. 169–170. Given that readers have to scroll long messages, organising the message in terms of descending importance – with the most important paragraph first – is a good rule of thumb.

## Style

Mulholland suggests that 'minimalism or brevity in language use . . . is becoming the preferred style for email messages' (Mulholland, 1999, p. 74). Is this just a further development of the concise style we see in written memos? Some writers believe that it is a more fundamental shift. This has even caused concern that computer-mediated-communication (C-m-C) may have long-term, negative effects on our use of language. At the very least there has been a shift to more conversational forms of writing. As an example of appropriate style for a specific audience, see Box 8.1.

## Is email talk or text?

Email and other forms of C-m-C do blur the distinction between talk and text. In other words, people adopt a style of communicating which is more conversational and does not

## BOX 8.1 HITTING THE RIGHT NOTE IN AN EMAIL

Imagine you are the owner of a small software company and you receive an email from one of the industry's most well-known and pioneering characters with the following subject line 'Get together?' Do you:

1. Email back immediately to suggest a meeting?
2. Ring him up or text him immediately?
3. Email him to say you are busy at the moment and will get back to him?

And what style would you use in your message?

(a) Formal and very 'business-like'.
(b) Formal but not too 'business-like'.
(c) Casual and chatty.

If you look up the detailed correspondence between Mark Zuckerberg of Facebook and of WhatsApp, you might be surprised at the casual tone of the messages – 3 and (c) in the above lists – especially when you realise that this led to a $19 billion-dollar business deal. However, the style was right for the context and established the right framework for the relationship.

have the more complicated features of written language. For example, Denise Murray suggests the following characteristics of email style (Murray, 1995, pp. 79ff.):

- use of abbreviations;
- use of simple words;
- use of simple syntax;
- disregard for 'surface errors' – in other words, people will ignore any spelling errors or typos or minor errors in syntax;
- symbols are used to represent non-linguistic use – for example, as well as the use of emoticons, you might write 'I *did* say', using asterisks to emphasise the word 'did'.

The obvious problem with these features is the assumption that the reader will recognise the code. For example, a reader may react to typos as evidence of a careless rather than hurried message. One of our colleagues once got himself into trouble by putting a sentence into capitals in an email. He meant to suggest irony/sarcasm; his reader interpreted this as 'bullying'. Luckily, their relationship was such that they could discuss and resolve this.

**BOX 8.2 SWAMPED BY EMAIL?**

In 2000/2001, email had become a standard office system and various survey results – e.g. that the average British worker received 171 messages per day – suggested that information overload was already a real problem. Researchers such as Charles Oppenheim suggested that this overload 'seems to screw people up. The sheer pressure is immense' (quoted in *PcPro*, March 1999, p. 56).

This problem has become worse. As well as the increase in genuine messages, there has been the growth of spam and hacking so that every organisation has to have appropriate protection and filtering in the system. Even then, you are likely to receive daily messages which are suspect but which can look surprisingly authentic. It is always worth taking a few precautions:

- never open an attachment unless you are confident that the email is genuine;
- check the sender's address even if the message looks authentic.

Even Richard Harper from Microsoft paints a picture of his colleagues overloaded and frustrated by the array of new media: 'Somehow the balance of things seems to have gone wrong . . . The tools designed to let them work better seem to have had the opposite effect' (Harper, 2010, p. 1).

There are some practical solutions (or at least things you can do to minimise the problems) and you need to choose the solution which suits your working practice:

- Some time-management texts recommend only answering emails at particular points in the day – say, at the beginning and end – so that you don't get continually distracted during the day.
- How often do you read any given email? Can you commit to only reading emails once and deciding what to do with them there and then?
- Using some form of filtering which automatically sorts incoming email and eliminates particular forms of message.

## Is 'flaming' inevitable?

Hargie *et al.* (1999, p. 182) reported one survey where over half of email users claimed to have 'received abusive e-mails . . . , which irreparably damaged working relationships'. Over half of these came from their managers and were much more likely to be written by men than women (five times more likely, according to this study). But how do we explain these abusive messages (originally known as 'flaming' but now often described in different ways for different contexts such as online discussion groups)? A number of factors could help to create this sort of abuse:

- Does computer-mediated-communication (C-m-C) inevitably create a lack of social restraint because of the absence of face-to-face cues and because of its immediacy (unlike memos or letters, you can reply instantly)?
- Was the culture of this organisation characterised by conflict and aggression anyway? Did email just provide a new arena for the conflict?
- Does the male–female difference reflect different management styles or power relationships?

Issues of flaming and email abuse have been debated by social scientists and in the mass media. Some have suggested that concern has been exaggerated and reflects people's lack of skill in using the medium. From a theoretical point of view, recent studies have found little evidence to suggest that the technology itself is to blame. Flaming may occur with particular users in particular contexts but we probably over-estimate the amount that exists and there is significant variance across different online groups (Baym, 2010). It is also worth remembering that concerns about antisocial behaviour also characterised the early days of the telephone (Baron, 1999).

## What is your individual style?

Individuals do develop their own style of writing emails. This covers such things as how politeness is expressed, the typical use of short sentences and abbreviations, and the absence of what linguists call 'metalanguage', where you use language to comment on itself as in the phrase '*can I ask* when the minutes will be distributed?'

Your style should be appropriate to your audience. Reviewing our own use of email, we noticed how our style varies from very conversational with close colleagues to a more impersonal style in messages which may reach a large group. You also need to consider your organisational culture. See Box 8.1 for an interesting example of matching your style to the other person.

## How is email used in your organisation?

This depends on your organisation's culture and working practices. For example, a study of email use in an Australian university, at a time when the organisation was experiencing significant changes, found a wide range of attitudes to C-m-C, both negative and positive (Mulholland, 1999). The introduction of email to support committee work had important consequences. For example, draft papers were circulated more quickly and this also allowed committee members to propose amendments, although some committee members lacked the skills to do this effectively – another example of the importance of training in this new technology. One potential long-term outcome could be to make the committee process more open and democratic.

There are other important issues to consider:

- *Emails may be kept on record*. In the last few years, several court cases have argued over responsibility for the content of particular emails. For example, one large oil company was taken to court by a group of women workers who complained about a 'joke' email which they found sexually offensive. The company lost the case as the court concluded that its email policy was inadequate. As a result, many large organisations have developed specific policies for the storage and archiving of email.

- *Emails may be monitored.* Partly for these legal reasons and partly because of concerns about staff 'wasting time' on personal concerns, many companies routinely monitor staff emails and this surveillance is becoming more common and sophisticated.

## FAX

In the 1990s, fax was described as the 'preferred form for electronic transmission among businesses' (Murray, 1995, p. 94), and the 'most widely distributed modern messaging system' (Chesher and Kaura, 1998). Back in 2000/2001, we noted that fax was still very important and useful despite the dramatic growth of email and Internet traffic, and that the market for fax machines was *growing* in the UK, with manufacturers commenting that staff often prefered hard copy to electronic documents (*PS Workplace*, July/August 2000).

There has now been a decline in the number of fax machines but significant growth in online faxing, as illustrated by the following infographic from 2013: http://fax87.com/fax-machines-dead-online-faxing-alive/. So the fax has adapted to the digital world and is likely to play a significant role in business and professional communication for some years to come. One major advantage is that you do not have to worry about the compatibility of file formats which you obviously need to check when sending computer files as attachments.

Messages specially written for fax seem to share many of the characteristics we discussed for email, although 'flaming' does not seem to be an issue. They are short (often less than one page, not counting the cover sheet with the contact information); they mainly supply or request information; and they are written in a more conversational style than traditional business letters.

## WRITING FOR THE WEB

Depending on your organisational context, you might have to write for the web in different ways, such as:

- Contributing to a wiki.
- Writing blog posts for the organisation or your own professional development.
- Setting up and/or managing an online discussion group.

Nowadays, none of these are likely to demand a high level of technical skill – all the technical detail will be managed by the system. For example, you can start a blog using Wordpress using one of their standard templates with very basic computer skills. So the key principles to worry about are those relating to the quality of our language, as we discussed in Chapter 6 – e.g. principles of clarity and appropriate purpose for the intended audience.

If you are using standard templates, you will probably have very limited, if any, influence on the page layout but you may need to choose appropriate illustrations and graphics.

## Effective online design

We have already suggested general principles of good online design, whether you are writing for an internal or an external audience. You can also use the specific guidelines we have used in previous chapters as they echo the recommendations you will find in the guides for online publishing. For example, Robert Tannenbaum includes the following in his list of general principles for screen design (Tannenbaum, 1998, p. 453):

- Develop clean, attractive, informative titles.
- Keep screens simple, conveying one major idea per screen.
- Choose type fonts and sizes that are clear and easy to read, yet direct emphases appropriately.
- Keep screen design uncluttered, using adequate margins and sufficient white space.

These design principles may need revising in some circumstances:

- As we become more familiar with reading on the Web, we can cope with more complex designs.
- Some cultures prefer much more activity on screen than preferred by Web designers in the UK and USA.

There are, of course, some important differences between print and screen information:

- Your screen design may be interpreted differently by different makes and different generations of browser. As a result, many Web designers recommend that you create websites which display the same on different machines. This is one major advantage of designing for an intranet as you should know exactly what equipment your pages will be displayed on.
- Web pages have to be assembled on the screen. They do not appear instantaneously. You need to ensure that the download time is slow and that the page components appear in an order which makes most sense to the viewer.

Nielsen suggests that the most important factors which determine the usability of public websites are what he calls 'learnability' – how quickly and easily you can work out how to find your way round the site – and 'subjective satisfaction'. He suggests that external users have to be 'kept happy' because they use the site at their own discretion. In contrast, employees using an intranet will do so because they *have* to gain important information and are also likely to be very regular users. As a result, he suggests that 'efficiency, memorability, and error reduction' are the most important attributes for an intranet. The important thing is to ensure that users can navigate the site efficiently without wasting time.

### Structure

Perhaps the most important feature of Web documents is that they use hyperlinks. The structure of the website has to be very carefully designed so that users do not 'get lost' and know where to find the information they are looking for.

## DEVELOPING WEB TECHNOLOGIES

One important development over the last decade is the increasing ability of the Web to carry audio and video information, which means multimedia can be delivered over the Internet. Other important developments have included:

- *Integrating Web and database technology*. Web pages can be constructed to respond to enquiries by lifting information out of a database. When the information in the database is updated, the Web page is automatically updated.
- *'Push' technology*. Surfing the Web is often described as 'pull' technology – you pull information from the website. Push technology is where the Web software 'pushes' information at you based on previous experience of your preferences and needs. A simple example is Internet retailers like Amazon who suggest new books based on analysis of your previous purchases.

All of these trends will continue and we see the development of what is called Web 3.0 where there will be a growing number of 'online personal assistants' to help with specific tasks and who have the capacity to learn your priorities and preferences.

## CHANGING PATTERNS OF BUSINESS CORRESPONDENCE

In 2000/2001, we were already beginning to see the 'transformation' of business communication through the Internet, quoting studies like the following:

- Hargie *et al*. (1999) pointed to the 'phenomenal' expansion in the number of email addresses and Web connections. They also highlighted a study of email traffic in one large company where '60 per cent of the messages . . . received by this means would not have been received by other channels' (p. 181).
- The survey finding that 53 per cent of UK business people felt that the use of email had increased their level of communication, and 28 per cent suggested that staff felt more involved in the company after the introduction of email (survey reported in *Mind Your Own Business*, March 2000, p. 19).
- Cultural differences in the patterns of business communication. The Pitney Bowes company found that US and Canadian staff preferred asynchronous or time-delayed communication, whereas European staff preferred real-time and more formal methods. There was very heavy use of voicemail in the USA (90 per cent of staff), less in the UK (58 per cent) and much less in Germany (32 per cent) (survey reported in *Mind Your Own Business*, July/August 1999, p. 30).

These trends have continued and information and email overload has become a significant issue, as we saw in Box 8.2. Changing patterns of business communication make it difficult to predict how things will develop over the next decade. From an individual point of view, you need to select a format that suits the meaning you wish to convey; from an organisational point of view, the messaging systems need to meet the needs of all the stakeholders in the enterprise.

At the moment, we can see organisations experimenting with different mixes of technology and not always making decisions which suit everyone's needs:

- Adrian Winscoe notes that many organisations are abandoning email for their customer services despite a strong preference for email by many customers: www.forbes.com/sites/adrianswinscoe/2014/03/02/abandon-email-as-a-customer-service-channel-at-your-peril/.
- Volkswagen stopped its Blackberry servers sending emails to workers outside standard office hours after discussion with the Workers' Council: www.forbes.com/sites/adrianswinscoe/2014/03/02/abandon-email-as-a-customer-service-channel-at-your-peril/.
- Atos, the French IT services company, decided to abandon email from 2014, noting their own survey that 'the average employee spends 40 per cent of their working week dealing with internal emails which add no value to the business'. This survey is quoted by Nick Atkin from Hatton Housing Trust which is also making this move: 'Our efforts to ban internal email mark a move towards an adult-to-adult relationship with our staff': www.theguardian.com/housing-network/2012/dec/17/ban-staff-email-halton-housing-trust.
- At the time of writing, Atos is sticking to its policy and has invested in an enterprise social network: www.ft.com/cms/s/0/11384220–8761–11e2-bde600144feabdc0.html#axzz2y6Bslo3F.

Other commentators are not so sure:

- www.information-age.com/it-management/strategy-and-innovation/123457303/-no-email–policies-will-not-last–says-gartner.

## SUMMARY

- General principles apply to *all* business documents whether print or online: deciding on appropriate objectives, meeting audience needs, organising the message, writing in an appropriate style, and using layout and design to support your message.
- Effective business correspondence meets both content and tone criteria.
- Written messages can be interpreted in different ways depending on the context in which they are received.

- The design of documents reflect aspects of organisational structure and culture, so there may be resistance to change.
- Each type of business document can be analysed in terms of structure, style and layout, and it is important to understand both the conventions which readers will expect and the potential problems caused by limitations of the system – for example, the limited formatting in email messages.
- You need to adapt the structure and style of your documents to the specific situation, as, for example, with the different ways of structuring long reports. Relying on a standardised approach will not usually be successful.
- Changing patterns of business communication make it difficult to predict how things will develop over the next decade. From an individual point of view, you need to select a format that suits the meaning you wish to convey; from an organisational point of view, the messaging systems need to meet the needs of all the stakeholders in the enterprise.

## FURTHER READING

Geisler, C. (2014) *Designing for User Engagement on the Web: 10 basic principles.* Abingdon: Routledge.

This is our favourite summary of the important principles you need to worry about in online documents.

Chapter 9

# What is effective interpersonal communication?

## INTRODUCTION

Various methods have been proposed over the years to develop interpersonal skills. For example, in the 1990s, many organisations were persuaded of the importance of personal understanding and interpersonal abilities by the best-selling books on 'emotional intelligence'. This concept emphasised self-awareness and the importance of handling relationships: 'a new competitive reality is putting emotional intelligence at a premium in the workplace and in the marketplace' (Goleman, 1996, p. 149). Goleman and others argued that organisations which failed to recognise or value these skills in their employees would simply not generate the trust, co-operation and creativity which are needed for long-term success.

Judging by the content of interpersonal skills training courses which are currently popular, business organisations have continued their interest in topics like assertiveness and building relationships with a particular emphasis on ideas from NeuroLinguistic Programming (NLP). Unfortunately, many of the central ideas in systems like NLP do not stand up to independent research scrutiny; we shall explode some of these myths in the next two chapters.

This chapter reviews research and theory, which suggests that effective face-to-face communication depends on interpersonal skills which *include* personal awareness and understanding. We shall examine what effective interpersonal communication involves, highlight the main characteristics of essential skills, and show how these skills can be used together in everyday situations. We shall also warn against the 'over-mechanical' use of certain techniques and we shall highlight the growing role of new technology in the way that we both create and receive impressions of others.

Our overall conclusion, however, suggests that we cannot simply rely on skills and technique to arrive at effective interpersonal communication. We need to become 'mindwise', as in the work of Nicholas Epley:

> The secret to understanding each other better seems to come not through an increased ability to read body language or improved perspective taking but, rather, through the hard relational work of putting people in a position where they can tell you their minds openly and honestly.
>
> (Epley, 2014, p. 183)

## OBJECTIVES

*This chapter will*:

- explain what effective interpersonal communication involves;
- identify and explain the most important interpersonal skills;
- comment on popular models of interpersonal skills and communication training;
- identify important implications of this analysis for your behaviour towards others at work;
- suggest some ways you can use technology to enhance your interpersonal effectiveness.

## WHAT DOES EFFECTIVE INTERPERSONAL COMMUNICATION INVOLVE?

One answer to this question is that we need 'good' interpersonal skills so we can respond or react to the other person or persons in ways which appear 'natural' and which are 'effective'. This suggests that we have accurately assessed what the other person is trying to communicate, and this depends on how we perceive that other person. But what if our perception is misleading? Suppose that you worked behind the counter in an English bank and were confronted by a male customer who handed over a cheque and said 'give me the money' with no change in intonation over these four words. Would you interpret this behaviour as 'rude'? Many native English speakers would – to them it sounds too abrupt or even aggressive. The most common 'polite' English expression would be to say this phrase with a slight rise in intonation on the last word (assuming that the person does not have a strong regional accent where different rules might apply).

If you interpreted the flat intonation as rude, does this mean that you would deal with this customer in a correspondingly abrupt way? Or perhaps you would not give him quite the same positive greeting you would give to other customers? But suppose your customer came from a Middle Eastern country. He has, in fact, used the pattern of intonation which is seen as polite in his native culture. Would you be sufficiently aware of this cultural difference to avoid an inappropriate reaction?

The definition also suggests that we know what the conversation is trying to achieve. Unless you know what the goals are, how can you judge what is effective? And most texts on business communication stress the importance of clear goals. This line of argument suggests that successful social interaction involves a lot more than just some 'correct' behaviours, and we shall return to this at the end of this chapter.

The process of interpersonal communication is complex. Unless you understand some basic features of this process, you can easily behave in ways which the other person will not accept or appreciate. For example, consider the model of interpersonal communication in Figure 9.1 (from Hartley, 1999). This suggests that there are a number of fundamental processes:

- Social perception: how person A interprets the behaviour and characteristics of person B. An example of this is the bank customer example we discussed above.
- Social identity: how person A sees him- or herself in terms of their role and status. We communicate in ways which support this sense of social identity.
- Coding – how A and B choose to express themselves. Do we use slang or jargon or technical words? What non-verbal signals do we use?
- The dual nature of 'the message' which always includes both information and relationship aspects.
- The influence of the social context.

We have already mentioned most of these processes in earlier chapters. We also need to emphasise the potential ambiguity which is inevitable in our everyday communication and which effective communicators anticipate and avoid. The more you investigate these processes, the more you realise that effective interpersonal communication demands both social understanding – recognising the processes – and social skills – being able to use the

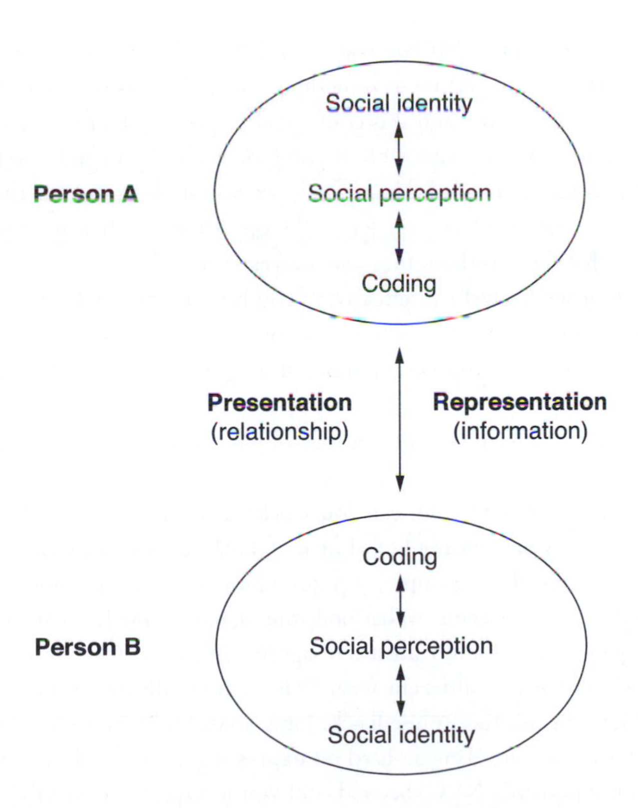


***Figure 9.1*** *Hartley's model of interpersonal communication*

behaviours and techniques. We shall look at fundamental behaviours and techniques before we return to this question of how they all 'fit together'.

This model was developed in a pre-digital age so we also need to consider the range of technologies which are now available to enhance or replace face-to-face interaction.

## WHAT DO WE MEAN BY INTERPERSONAL SKILLS?

Suppose you have been asked to nominate someone you know to lead a discussion group. Who would you choose? What do they do to make you think of them? What makes them good at getting people to talk? Do they make you feel that they really are listening and interested in what you are saying? How do they do this? How do they encourage you to contribute? What are the specific behaviours which make them successful? How and when do they smile, nod, invite you to speak, gesture, etc.? If you do this analysis in detail, then you will be doing a social skills analysis – you will define some of the social skills possessed by that individual.

This detailed approach to our social behaviour was pioneered in Britain by Michael Argyle in the 1970s. He developed the analogy between a motor or physical skill (like playing tennis or riding a bike) and a social skill like having a conversation with someone. He suggested that they had the following features in common (Argyle, 1994):

- *Goals.* You need to decide what you want to achieve. If you talk to someone, are you trying to persuade them, sell them something, make friends or what? Of course, my goals may differ from yours and this could lead to problems or conflict.
- *Perception.* You need to perceive what is going on around you and you need to do this accurately to achieve your goals. In a game, are you looking out for the opportunity to hit a winning shot? Will you recognise the opportunity when it comes? If you talk to someone, what do you think they are interested in?
- *Translation.* In order to perform effectively you have to 'translate' your idea of what you want to do into the correct action – if your customer is obviously not persuaded by your presentation, do you have another strategy? Can you think of another approach?
- *Responses.* Even if you have the correct idea of what you need to do, can you physically do it?
- *Feedback.* If you talk to someone, can you work out how interested they are? Can you recognise when they are getting bored or irritated? Can you accurately interpret the feedback you receive? For example, suppose you express your point of view and they lean back and cross their arms. What does this signal mean? Does it mean agreement or disagreement? If you think it means disagreement, do you try to restate what you think more clearly or in a different way? This example illustrates that there are several problems in reacting to feedback. First of all, did you notice the signals? You might have been concentrating so hard on expressing yourself clearly that you did not notice the other person's NVC. Second, did you interpret the signals correctly? And finally, were you able to respond effectively?

There are other important analogies between physical and interpersonal skills:

- We have to learn how to perform effectively and we can always learn something new or some improvement.
- We can benefit from good coaching and tuition.
- As we learn a motor skill, our actions become more fluent and better-timed. We become less aware of what we are doing – the action becomes subconscious. The same process can apply to interpersonal skills. For example, if you have to learn interviewing skills, your first interviews are likely to be hesitant and nervous until you gain some confidence. After some successful experience, you will no longer have to concentrate so hard as the behaviour has become more 'automatic'.
- We can let our skills 'lapse' by failing to practise. This is the downside of the previous point. As with a motor skill such as driving a car, we can become lazy and careless and fall into 'bad habits'.

One recent development of this approach comes from Owen Hargie (2011, p. 24). While endorsing Argyle's main ideas, he developed a more elaborate model – see Figure 9.2. This incorporates the following important ideas:

- The social context is an important influence on our behaviour. The skills that are effective in one context may not work in another.
- We gain feedback from our own actions as well as the other person's reactions. We are continually aware of our own behaviour and feelings and this can help us decide what to do next.

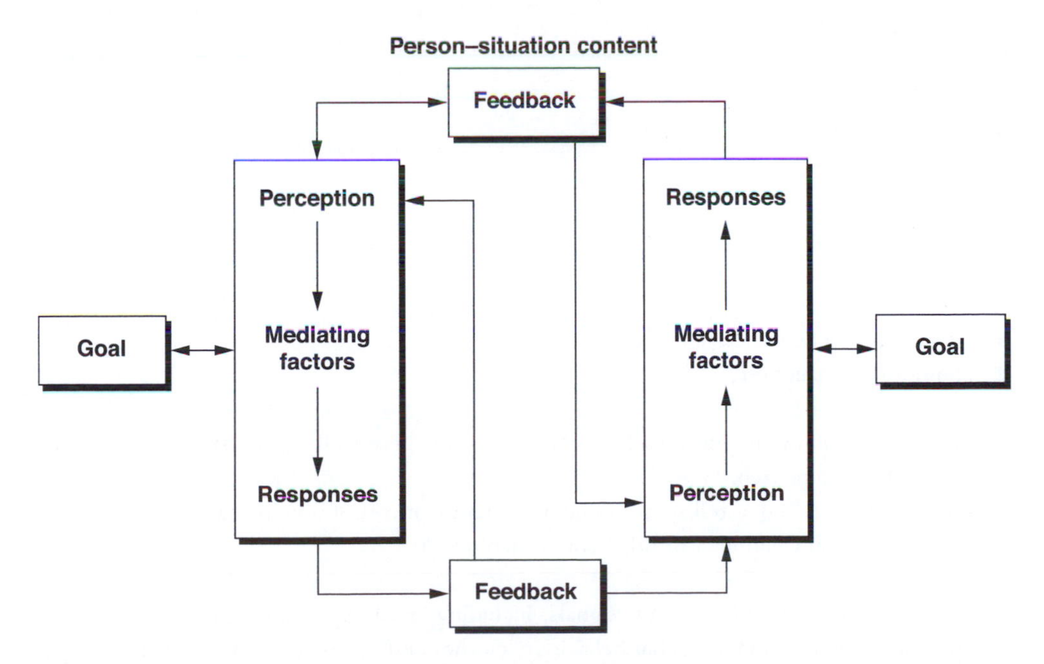


*Figure 9.2* *Hargie's model of social skills*

- We are influenced by our emotions as well as by our thoughts, so the term 'mediating factors' is used instead of 'translation'.

It is important to emphasise that these authors do *not* think that social skills are just the same as motor skills. We have already highlighted some important differences – the fact that other people may have different goals, the importance of feelings – and there is another more complex problem, as explained below.

### Metaperception

As well as directly perceiving our own behaviour and the behaviour of others, we can also reflect on how those other people are perceiving us. This has been called 'meta-perception' and has been shown to be an important factor in determining how people react to one another. For example, if we are having a conversation and I get the impression that you think I am being too 'chatty', then I might become more reserved to counteract this impression. If my initial impression is wrong, I will probably confuse you or even offend you with my sudden and unexplained change in behaviour.

## WHAT ARE THE MOST IMPORTANT INTERPERSONAL SKILLS?

One of the most comprehensive texts on interpersonal skills includes the following topics (Hargie, 2011):

- non-verbal communication (NVC)
- reinforcement
- questioning
- reflecting
- opening and closing
- explanation
- listening
- self-disclosure
- influencing
- assertiveness
- group interaction and leadership
- humour and laughter.

We summarise below the essential features of some of these to illustrate the importance of this analysis and approach.

We have already suggested some of the important features of non-verbal communication (NVC for short) in Chapter 3 of this book, notably that:

- There are a wide range of NVC signals, including facial expression, gaze, gestures, posture, bodily contact, spatial behaviour, clothes and appearance, non-verbal vocalisations (paralanguage) and smell.

- We usually react to the combination of these signals. For example, we may decide that someone is lying to us because they fidget, *and* avoid eye contact, *and* hesitate when they talk, etc.
- These signals are ambiguous. For example, the indicators of someone lying are very close to the signals of nerves and anxiety. This problem of ambiguity is very important if you are considering adopting particular NVC strategies.
- There are significant cultural differences in the meaning of non-verbal signals.
- When verbal and non-verbal signals seem to contradict each other, we are usually more inclined to believe the non-verbal 'message'.

Bearing these points in mind, we can suggest some recommendations for the skilled use of NVC in business situations.

### *Use a combination of signals to show what you mean*

Some texts, for example, suggest that managers should be very careful to choose the right seating position when they want to have a discussion with one of their staff. The usual recommendation is to avoid the direct frontal position, as this implies confrontation, and to talk 'at an angle' – across the corner of the desk rather than directly facing the other person across the desk. This will help to establish an atmosphere, but other cues are also important. To achieve co-operation you also need to use appropriate eye contact and gestures. Just sitting at the 'correct' angle will not help the manager who continues to belittle his staff verbally and non-verbally in other ways, perhaps by constantly interrupting them. These other signals will create the lasting impression in the staff.

### *Make sure that your verbal and non-verbal messages are 'in harmony'*

The boss who tells you he is listening to you while looking at his watch will not be believed!

### *Make sure your NVC is appropriate to the culture and the context*

The English manager who uses his 'native' pattern of eye gaze when dealing with Arabian colleagues may well be seen as 'shifty-eyed' and perhaps untrustworthy because he does not engage in sufficient eye contact.

### *Avoid NVC which has a popular interpretation you do not want*

Many popular books on NVC claim that particular signals definitely pass on a specific message. Even if this is not always true, what if the other person believes that it is? For example, one British guide for students preparing for selection interviews suggested that 'folded arms with the fists clenched . . . shows definite hostility' (McBride, 1993, p. 132). Another text suggests that crossed arms and a sideways glance will be perceived as 'suspicious' and that crossed arms indicate 'defensiveness'. Working on the assumption that many interviewers probably do believe this is what these gestures mean, the applicant should not use any of them.

### *Develop your awareness of your own NVC and its likely impact*

Perhaps the most important way of developing your NVC skills is through awareness of your own behaviour. Does your NVC always reflect what you want it to mean? You can only develop this awareness by reflecting on your own behaviour and by getting feedback from others who are prepared to give you an honest response. If you decide to change your behaviour, you also need to monitor the effect of change. You need to behave in a way which comes across as 'natural' for you rather than relying on 'textbook techniques'.

### *Look out for micro-expressions*

We introduced the concept of micro-expressions in Chapter 2 – very fleeting non-verbal expressions which are supposed to reveal the true emotional state. As we suggested earlier, there is some still some doubt about this but they can offer an additional clue to someone's feelings. You should also look out for any impressions you may be creating along these lines.

## Reinforcement

When you use reinforcing behaviours, you use behaviours which encourage the other person to carry on or repeat whatever they happen to be doing. Various experiments have shown how people respond to quite small expressions of praise, encouragement and support, including head nods, grunts and the 'uh-huh'. For a quick demonstration of the power of these simple cues, ask a friend to listen to you talking for a couple of minutes without showing any signs of support or agreement. First, they may find it very difficult, if not impossible, to do this. Second, you will find it very disconcerting to speak to what is effectively a 'blank wall'. And this bring us on to the importance of listening, which we discuss later.

## Questioning

If you have attended a series of job interviews you will know that some professional interviewers are much better than others at extracting information from you. This will be due in part to their question technique – whether they are asking the right sort of question at the right time. For example, texts on a person's interviewing technique usually distinguish between open and closed questions.

An open question allows the person to answer in whatever way they like – e.g. what do you think of the government's economic policy? A closed question asks for specific information or a yes/no response – e.g. do you agree with the government's economic policy? Open questions encourage people to talk and expand; closed questions encourage short answers. Inexperienced interviewers often ask too many closed questions and do not get the detailed answers which they really want. We say more on this in the next chapter.

## Reflecting

This skill is often used by counsellors and other people who have to conduct very personal interviews and who want the other person to talk in some detail about their own feelings and attitudes. Even the most open-ended questions can sometimes suggest the way that the other person should construct their answer. Reflections are more neutral – they feed back to the speaker some aspect of what they have just said. This invites them to elaborate or extend what they have been saying.

You can reflect in different ways and achieve different results. This will depend on whether you are interested in the factual statements that the other person has made or their feelings about what they are saying. Textbooks often distinguish at least three different forms of reflection:

- identifying a keyword or phrase which will encourage the speaker to say more;
- summarising what you have heard in your own words;
- identifying the feelings which seem to lie behind what the speaker is saying.

This last form of reflection is perhaps the most difficult and most skilful – you have to sense the underlying emotion accurately and read between the lines.

However, these different strategies focus on rather different aspects of the other person's communication – the first two relate to concentrate on what has been said; the third concentrates on how it was said, trying to interpret the non-verbal accompaniment.

## Opening and closing

This refers to the ways in which we establish the beginnings and endings of a particular interaction. For example, sales staff often receive very detailed training on how to start the interaction with the customer. Often this involves making conversation to establish the sales representative as more friendly and helpful than 'just a salesperson'. Consider all the different possible ways of starting a conversation with someone – some ways would be much more appropriate than others in particular circumstances.

The choice of opening can be very important in more formal situations such as an interview where the opening can establish either a positive or negative atmosphere. We shall give some examples of these in the next chapter.

## Listening

It is worth emphasising the importance of listening, as it is often taken for granted. Perhaps because we do it so much, it can be dismissed as a 'natural' behaviour which we have all learned. However, educators concerned with the development of interpersonal skills usually give it central importance: 'Listening is a core competence. People who cannot listen cannot relate. . . . Poor listening undermines the ability to communicate with others' (Hayes, 1991, p. 8).

Developing your skills as a listener involves two major steps:

- recognising (and eliminating) any barriers which prevent you listening with full attention;
- adopting and practising behaviours which help you listen (and which convince the other person that you are giving them your full attention).

Examples of important common barriers include being distracted by personal stereotypes or other perceptual biasses, such as listening selectively for what you expect to hear.

Detailed analysis of the skills which are used by people who are recognised as 'good listeners' shows that they use a variety of techniques. For example, Bolton (1986) talks about three clusters of skills:

- *Attending skills* – where you show the other person that you are attending to them. NVC can be especially important here.
- *Following skills* – where the listener uses a technique which encourages the speaker to give a full account of what they want to say. Reinforcing behaviour can be very important here, or what Bolton calls 'minimal prompts' like 'mmm', uh-uh', 'yes', 'and', etc.
- *Reflecting skills* – which we talk about in more detail below.

So the typical recommendations to support active or positive listening include (Hartley, 1999):

- Being receptive to the other person – showing that you are prepared to listen and accept what they are saying (of course, this does not mean that you automatically agree with it). Non-verbal signals are obviously important here and you need to avoid any signs of tension or impatience.
- Maintaining attention – using eye contact, head nods and appropriate facial expression.
- Removing distractions.
- Delaying evaluation of what you have heard until you fully understand it.

One research study which shows how important active listening can be in practical situations comes from Marquis and Cannell (1971). They compared the results of interviews about family illness when the interviewers used one of three techniques: active listening; sensitising the interviewee by reading out symptoms at the start; simply going through the questionnaire. Interviewees gave nearly 30 per cent more examples when the interviewer used active listening techniques.

## Self-disclosure

When you communicate with other people, you can tell them various things about yourself (or you can decide not to). Sidney Jourard (1971) coined the term 'self-disclosure' – the process of sharing information about ourselves with other people. When you self-disclose, you provide some information to the other person about yourself: how you are feeling; what your background is; what your attitudes and values are, and so on. Jourard was interested in how people came to reveal aspects of themselves to others and what this meant for the way that they developed relationships with others.

### *Self-disclosure and relationships*

You need to self-disclose to develop a relationship with another person. And this raises several practical issues:

- what do you tell them? What sort of information do you pass on? When is it 'safe' to reveal your personal feelings?
- How quickly do you reveal yourself? There are important social and cultural differences here. For example, in the USA, you are often expected to say a lot about yourself very early in a relationship. In the UK, a more leisurely pace is the norm.

In business, we have to develop good relationships with other people in the organisation, so self-disclosure is an important issue. How far can we (or should we) keep these relationships on a strictly formal basis and not self-disclose? If you develop a very close and open relationship with a group of staff and are then promoted to be their supervisor, can you maintain the relationship at the same level?

## Assertiveness

Over the last three decades, assertiveness training has become one of the most popular ways of developing social skills. As well as training courses and workshops, many popular books on business communication use assertiveness principles even if they do not use the term. And some of these endorse it very strongly, even claiming it can 'change your life' (see Hartley, 1999, Chapter 12).

### *What do we mean by assertive communication?*

The following quotes summarise essential points:

- 'Assertive behaviour . . . gives you the right to say what you think and feel calmly and clearly, without giving offence and denying the rights of others to have different views or expectations' (Wilcocks and Morris, 1996, p. 2).
- 'The aim of assertive behaviour is to satisfy the needs and wants of both parties involved in the situation' (Back and Back, 2005, p. 2).

### *What are the different styles of behaviour?*

Books on assertive behaviour usually define three styles of behaviour: assertion, aggression and submission (or non-assertion). These are often expressed as a continuum with assertion in the middle.

Aggression — Assertion — Submission

However, a better way of comparing styles of behaviour is to look out the two underlying dimensions:

- from indirect expression through to direct expression;
- from coercive behaviour through to non-coercive behaviour.

This gives Figure 9.3 below. The fourth style is where you express aggression in an indirect way without direct confrontation.

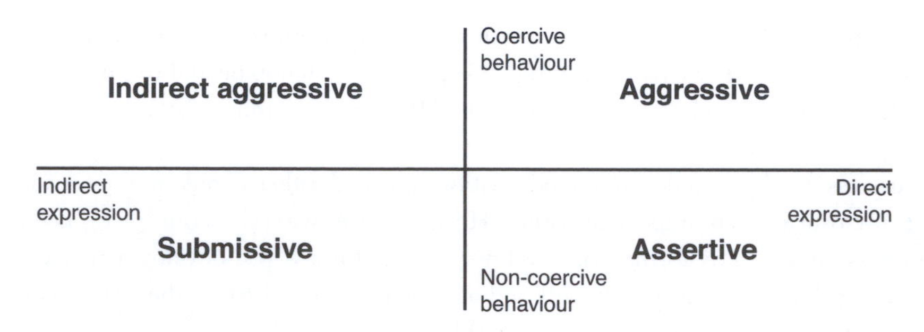


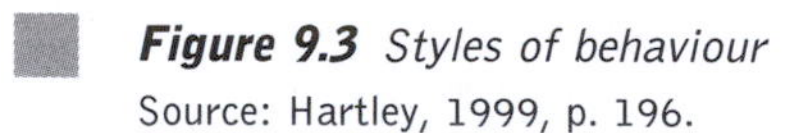

***Figure 9.3*** *Styles of behaviour*
Source: Hartley, 1999, p. 196.

Most texts concentrate on the three main styles, which we will do in this chapter (descriptions taken from Hartley, 1999).

### *Aggressive behaviour*

This includes some form of threat which undermines the rights of the other person. It is about winning, regardless of the other person's feelings. The verbal and non-verbal accompaniment to aggressive behaviour include loud and abusive talk, interruptions and glaring or staring eye contact.

### *Submissive behaviour*

This behaviour gives in to the demands of others by avoiding conflict and accepting being put upon. Verbal and non-verbal accompaniments include apologetic and hesitant speech, soft speech, nervous gestures and a reluctance to express opinions. Submissive individuals will be seen as weak and easily manipulated. They will certainly not inspire confidence in others.

The verbal and non-verbal behaviours associated with these styles have been demonstrated quite clearly in research studies as well as from observation of everyday life.

### *Assertive behaviour*

The characteristics are open and clear expression, firm and fluent conversation, and quick spontaneous answers. The non-verbal components include medium levels of eye contact, appropriate facial expressions, smooth gestures, relaxed but upright body posture, and appropriate paralinguistics.

## USING ASSERTIVE BEHAVIOUR

There are various ways of categorising assertive behaviour. For example, Ken and Kate Back define six main types of assertive behaviour which can be divided into two levels, and this is summarised in Box 9.1. The practical implications of this is that you should normally start by using a low-level assertion. If this is not successful, you try a high-level assertion. Other texts concentrate on what they regard as the main assertive techniques. To illustrate the approach, we can quote a typical example from Linehan and Egan (1983). They offer the 'broken record' technique as a way of resisting influence. This technique simply involves repeating your initial request or response without being side-tracked, until the other person accepts it. For example, suppose your boss asks you to work late one evening and you are already committed to an important social event. What do you say? If you say 'I'm sorry, but I cannot stay tonight', how do you respond if the boss says 'but it's really urgent and important'. Applying the broken record technique, you should say 'I'm sorry about that, but I really cannot work late tonight' and continue to do this until your point is accepted (see Linehan and Egan, 1983, pp. 80ff. for more discussion of this example).

### BOX 9.1 DIFFERENT TYPES OF ASSERTIVE BEHAVIOUR

Ken and Kate Back define six main types of assertive behaviour, which can be divided into two levels, listed below (Back and Back, 2005, Chapter 7). The practical implications of this are that you should normally start by using a low-level assertion. If this is not successful, you try a high-level assertion. The three types at the lower level are:

- *basic assertion* – a straightforward statement of what you need, want, believe or feel;
- *responsive assertion* – where you check what the other person needs or is feeling by asking them in a straightforward way;
- *empathetic assertion* – where you make a point of recognising the other person's point of view or feelings, before you state what you want.

The three high-level types are:

- *discrepancy assertion* – where you point out the discrepancy between what you have agreed previously on what seems to be happening or is about to happen;
- *negative feelings assertion* – where you point out the effect that the other person's behaviour is having upon you;
- *consequence* – (the strongest form of assertion) where you tell the other person what will happen to them if they do not change their behaviour.

They suggest that you should '*use the minimum degree of assertion for achieving your aim*' (p. 91, their emphasis). If you do not, you may be seen as aggressive and you will have fewer options if the other person does not wish to co-operate.

### Does assertiveness always work?

Most texts on assertiveness emphasise the possible benefits of this style of behaviour. However, there are also potential problems:

- Assertive behaviour may be 'misread'. It may be *seen* as aggressive, especially when the person is behaving differently from the way they have acted in the past.
- People have different definitions of assertiveness. For example, untrained women stress the importance of consideration for others, whereas untrained men seem to see assertiveness in terms of power and influence.
- There are issues of gender roles. Male assertion and female assertion can have different consequences, so reliance on the same techniques may actually work out differently.
- There are situational factors to consider. Certain types of assertiveness may well work better in some situations than others.
- There are cultural differences to consider. Behaviour which is culturally acceptable in the USA and Western Europe may not be accepted in cultures which place very different values upon humility and submission.

One final issue comes from work by Daniel Ames (2009) whose studies suggest that both under-assertiveness and over-assertiveness contribute to ineffective leadership and/or management. He found that under-assertive leadership can lead to 'failure to deliver on task objectives' whereas over-assertive leaders would be 'jeopardising their relationships with others. Getting assertiveness "right" appears to be a prevalent challenge for leaders' (ibid., p. 129).

## POPULAR THEORIES TO IMPROVE YOUR COMMUNICATION

Books on business communication often summarise specific theories of interpersonal communication which are often used on training courses but which you will not find in mainstream social science texts. In other words, they have achieved wide popular acceptance but have often been dismissed or neglected by professional and academic social scientists. To illustrate why this may have happened, we shall briefly introduce a few key concepts from one of these systems – Neurolinguistic Programming (NLP) – and highlight some important issues. See our website for an analysis of some other popular systems like Transactional Analysis (TA).

### Neurolinguistic Programming

Neurolinguistic Programming (NLP) was founded in the 1970s by two Americans, Richard Bandler and John Grinder. NLP ideas have since been incorporated into a number of popular management and communication texts, as well as being widely used in training. They claim that you only need three things to communicate well:

- a clear idea of the outcome you want;
- flexible behaviour – you need to find the behaviour which will work in the specific situation;
- the ability to recognise the responses you are getting from other people – if you can do this, you will be able to 'home in' on the behaviour which achieves the response you want from the other person.

They also emphasise the importance of non-verbal communication. They advocate specific non-verbal strategies and techniques, such as non-verbal mirroring, but they do *not* claim that each body language signal has a clear and specific meaning. They argue that body language can indicate how a person is responding rather than giving you specific signs or meanings.

### *Representational systems*

One fundamental idea from NLP is that we think using three main representational systems:

- *visual* – where you see visual images as you think;
- *auditory* – where you hear sounds inside your head;
- *kinaesthetic* – where you think in terms of feelings.

For example, if I asked you to tell me about your work, what would go on inside your head as you respond? Would you experience visual images or sounds, or would you experience some bodily sensations that represent how you feel? NLP claims that we think and *express* ourselves in terms of these systems. It also suggests that we have a favourite system.

Adler (1996) suggests four systems and offers lists of typical phrases used by someone with preferences for each as follows:

- *Visual* – as in 'I see', 'it appears', 'looking back', etc.
- *Auditory* – as in 'I hear what you say', 'rings a bell', etc.
- *Kinaesthetic* – as in 'I feel', 'I'll be in touch', etc.
- *Olfactory and gustatory* – as in 'fresh as a daisy', 'matter of taste' etc.

Adler goes on to say that you can increase rapport with someone by 'getting to know the thinking preference of the person you are communicating with, and changing your behaviour to literally make more sense to them' (p. 88). For example, if you are talking to a visual person, then you should use language which corresponds with that representational system. You should say things like 'I see what you mean' or 'that looks fine to me'. By using this technique, '*sometimes almost miraculously*, rapport increases as you share their experience' (Adler and Heather, 1999, p. 62, our italics).

Of course, to use this technique you have to be confident which representation system the other person is using. And that leads to another important idea – that there are reliable ways to recognise somebody's representational system.

Bandler and Grinder suggest that you can monitor someone's eye movements. You may like to try this out with friends or relatives to see if the generalisations offered by Bandler and Grinder reflect your experience (see Hartley 1999 for a fuller discussion; see Hott and Leeds, 2014 for a recent and typical explanation of NLP thinking). The snag with the analysis of eye movements (and with other NLP concepts) is that it has not been supported by systematic research.

## CAN WE BELIEVE THIS (AND ANY OTHER) POPULAR THEORY?

NLP does contain some interesting propositions and ideas, but we suggest that you approach it (and other popular systems you may come across) with some scepticism. We have some important concerns about NLP and similar approaches:

- It has suffered by being over-simplified and applied too 'mechanically'.
- It has been 'over-sold'. We believe some of the claims for their success are exaggerated.
- Probably because of the 'over-selling', it has not attracted the interest of independent researchers. As a result, there is little independent evidence to show that it really works over a wide range of circumstances.
- It seems to ignore cultural differences. And this is a general issue for all skills approaches.

So one way of looking at any popular analysis of human communication is to ask questions based on the following concerns:

- What are the ideas based on? (Do they come from systematic observation or what?)
- Are the ideas critically examined? (What are the recognised limitations to the ideas?)
- Are they applied in a way which recognises the specific social context? (Is any account taken of social and cultural difference?)
- Who are the gurus or advocates? (And what is their expertise based on in terms of experience, training, etc.?)

### BOX 9.2 ATTENDING TO CULTURE

So much of the research into interpersonal communication (and so many of the advice texts) is based on American and European examples that it is easy to forget the potential complications of cross-cultural communication. For example:

- patterns of self-disclosure and relationship development are very different in cultures with strong politeness norms and where the saving of face is critical, like Malaysia;
- NVC has strong cultural variations;
- assertive behaviour is seen very differently in cultures which do not share the individualistic values of the US and UK.

## THE ROLE OF NEW TECHNOLOGY IN INTERPERSONAL COMMUNICATION

We now live in the age of 'perpetual contact' thanks to the ubiquity of smartphones and social media. There are three aspects of this which are especially important to this chapter. We can:

- enhance our relationships with others by careful use of social media;
- use these media to gain initial impressions of others;
- check our own public face through these media and try to limit any misleading messages.

The two case studies in Box 1.3 in Chapter 1 demonstrated how two of our colleagues 'reinvented' themselves and started new careers supported by the specific use of social media. If you are at an earlier stage in your career, you can think about how your own use of the technology can support your personal and professional development.

To think about the range of technologies and their different purposes, consider the example in Box 9.3.

### BOX 9.3 TECHNOLOGIES IN SUPPORT OF INTERPERSONAL COMMUNICATION

Our example here is the use of technology to support the mentoring of undergraduates by industry professionals. Preparing undergraduates for industry is becoming an increasingly high priority for universities, and various approaches have been adopted to support this, including the development of 'graduate attributes' and employability skills. Industry placements are a common feature of many university programmes and there is a Year in Industry scheme operated by a charity called the Engineering Development Trust which provides students with an 'industry gap year' either before or during an undergraduate programme, where students are mentored by an industry professional as one of the support methods.

Mentoring by industry professionals is adopted across a range of universities – for instance, the University of Westminster Business School provides MBA students with a module option of being mentored by a business person; at the University of Middlesex School of Service Management, students similarly have the option of being mentored by an industry professional. In the latter case, students participate in a series of workshops to develop their appreciation and understanding of the value of mentoring as a development tool and they then experience being mentored. Typically, such mentoring processes focus on (mutually agreed) specific issues, skills or activities, with the mentor supporting the mentee in planning and exploring the issues/skills/activities and helping them to reflect on what they have learnt and how they have developed. The mentor–mentee relationship helps to provide students with increased knowledge of industry as well as helping them to contextualise their academic studies.

*continued . . .*

**BOX 9.3** ***Continued***

In schemes such as these, digital technologies are typically used to support the mentoring process. There are a number of options:

- Simple message tools like Twitter can provide regular contact.
- Social media like Facebook may not be seen as appropriate but there are now private peer-to-peer networks like myApollo.
- Web-conferencing (e.g. Skype, Google Hangouts) can replace face-to-face meetings, but also complement them – e.g. to follow up on actions agreed at a face-to-face meeting.
- Digital tools to support personal development planning and recording of learning (journals) include online blogs such as the open source WordPress blogging tool, or dedicated e-portfolios such as PebblePad.

All these tools support the mentor–mentee relationship by providing some form of structured and shared online environment to help in personal development planning, recording of the learning (mentoring) journey and helping the mentee to reflect on what they have learnt.

So we can use the technology to support face-to-face conversations. But does it always work? Experience to date with the use of such online tools for personal development planning and recording of learning journeys has shown that there are mixed results with implementing them. Some mentees and mentors perceive them as an 'information dump' and an added burden, while others use them to underpin the mentoring process itself. The key criterion for successful use of e-portfolios/blogs is to 'develop' both mentors and mentees in effective mentoring processes and how digital tools can underpin these processes.

## BECOMING 'MINDWISE' AND PUTTING THE SKILLS TOGETHER

Earlier in this chapter, we argued that social skills depend on social understanding. You need to *understand* how and why people are behaving as they do in order to select the appropriate way to behave. We are very suspicious of communication skills training which does not emphasise the need for social understanding and research to accompany the practice of techniques. We are not alone in this concern – Deborah Cameron surveyed a range of communication skills courses and training materials and found 'consistent disregard for those bodies of knowledge that derive from the empirical investigation of naturally occurring talk' (Cameron, 2000, p. 51).

However, we also need to become 'mindwise' (Epley, 2014) and recognise that the major barriers to understanding other people include our own often misplaced confidence in our abilities to understand the way that we come across to other people and to interpret their behaviours and feelings – what Epley calls the 'illusion of insight' (ibid., p. 11). For example, think of your current partner and/or a close friend and give yourself a percentage rating on the following questions, where 100 per cent means 'completely' and 0 per cent means not at all.

a How high is your partner's sense of self-worth (self-esteem)?
b How confident are you in this judgement?

Following the typical pattern of research on this topic, we would expect you to be reasonably (but *not* perfectly) accurate on question (a) and to be significantly over-confident on question (b). Your degree of confidence in your judgement is likely to be up to twice as strong as your actual accuracy and this does not depend on the length of time you have known the other person. If anything, we seem to become more confident but not more accurate in our judgements over time. And the same pattern of results appears when you ask people to make judgments about others' verbal and non-verbal behaviour.

Epley describes a number of cognitive and social processes which explain these results. Particularly important for this book is his analysis of how we interpret others' behaviour and three important traps we can fall into.

### Projecting from our own mind

We tend to be too self-centred in our social judgements and that can include overestimating our own contributions to a group effort and feeling more self-conscious about our own behaviour than is actually warranted (often called the spotlight effect). We assume that other people interpret the world in much the same way as we do, so we can seriously underestimate the degree of ambiguity in certain messages.

### Basing our judgements on stereotypes

If we rely on a stereotype when making a judgement about others (e.g. age, gender), then we can be misled. For example, Epley refers to the common stereotype that 'women are more emotional than men' (ibid., p. 125). Physiological studies of reactions to emotional scenes demonstrate that men and women have much the same emotional reaction, but social and cultural factors come into play when we look at how men and women express (or do not express) their reactions. So we will be misled if we rely on a stereotype which does not distinguish between feeling (the invisible internal reaction) and expressing feeling (the outward behaviour which is influenced by a range of social and cultural factors).

### Inferring someone's intentions just from the way they act

Attribution theory tells us that we are likely to be more sensitive to contextual influences when we try to explain our own behaviour than when we try to explain that of others – e.g. 'I failed the test because the environment was so hot and uncomfortable; he failed it because he is not very bright'.

### So we cannot just rely on skills

As a result, Epley suggests that we cannot and should not expect to fully understand others by relying just on our own 'skills'. Our observations and interpretations of others' body language may be limited or misleading and we may have real problems in trying to put ourselves in their position (what he calls perspective-taking, which has been a key component of many self-help books on communication since the classic text by Dale Carnegie – Principle 8 of *How to Win Friends and Influence People*).

Epley describes several studies where conscious attempts at perspective-taking – e.g. in negotiation, made things worse as it led to people acting on inaccurate conclusions. Being 'mindwise' is about 'Knowing the shortcomings of your social sense', which will then 'push you to be more open in sharing what's in your own mind with others, but also more open to listening to others' (ibid., p. 187).

One practical way of thinking about this is to approach face-to-face communication as a process with a series of stages in a way that allows a genuine exchange of perspectives, as in Table 9.1.

This table emphasises the planning and preparation which you can undertake before an important face-to-face communication. At first sight this might seem a very deliberate or perhaps even a manipulative approach to human relationships. However, we are not advocating that you lose all spontaneity and plan *every* encounter in minute detail. We agree with some points made by Peter Honey:

- 'on many occasions we need consciously to *organise* our behaviour';
- 'one of the hallmarks of an interactively skilled person is that they frequently declare their objectives openly and explicitly';
- 'if you have got objectives, your behaviour should be in step with them'.

(Honey, 1988, pp. 18ff.)

Honey is very critical of people whose behaviour is 'out of step' with their declared objectives, such as the manager who invites staff to contribute ideas and suggestions and then seems to relish pointing out the defects of every idea but his own. He also comments that planning is not just something we do before an event or activity: 'On-going planning requires us to size up the situation as we are in it' (Honey, 1988, p. 22).

This point highlights a potential criticism of our approach, which implies that we walk into a situation with a single predetermined plan and then simply try to achieve it. Taking the situation described in Table 9.1, what would you do if you received a very negative reaction from X when you asked for help/advice? Suppose X's response was 'I'm surprised you don't know that. Aren't you properly qualified for this job?' You need to respond to this not very subtle attack before you can proceed toward your objective. What do you say?

You could respond in a way which allows X to reinforce their negative image of you. For example, if you responded by asserting how well qualified you are, this could allow X to say 'Well, you're so well qualified that you obviously don't need my help.' You have just made the relationship worse – X is even more convinced that you are the 'know-it-all' who is just trying to show off your superiority.

So the key to effective interpersonal communication is the flexibility to respond to the other person in order to maintain the original objective. Perhaps asking X for advice is too indirect an approach. Should you adopt a more direct approach and explain how you see the problem to X? – 'I feel that we've not managed to sort out how we work together and I'd like to talk about it.' Would this achieve the first step?

**Table 9.1** *Interpersonal communication as a staged process*

| *Stage* | *Content* | *Points to watch* | *Example* |
|---|---|---|---|
| Decide the general goal | What do you want to achieve overall? | | You are a new member of the organisation and have been sent to join a new project team. One of the older members of the team seems to be deliberately unco-operative with you. You want to develop a better relationship with this colleague |
| Consider the context | What has happened in the past?<br>Who are the participants?<br>What is the setting? | Are there any hidden agendas because of the history?<br>What do your audience need or expect to happen? | What do you know about the history of this group and about X? Suppose you find out from other members that X is generally suspicious of 'new, young, know-it-alls' who want to come in and take over.' So this is the pattern of behaviour which X is expecting of you |
| Plan | Decide on the objectives<br>Decide on the structure | Make your objectives realistic and achievable<br>Make sure your structure leads up to your objective | Your objective is to show X that you value and respect his opinion<br>You find something which X is very familiar with and you are not: some aspect of the history of the project or some complex company procedure which is new to you. You plan to ask their help by asking them to explain it |
| Act | Use the relevant skills | What are the most important skills in this situation – e.g. listening, questioning etc.? | You need to choose the right moment so that X feels that the request is genuine and you need to make sure that you listen carefully and don't say anything which X could interpret as criticism |
| Follow-up | What can ensure that the communication has been effective? | What can you do to reinforce what you have done? | Some time in the near future you should take the opportunity to thank X for the help and show that you have taken the information seriously |

We cannot provide a definitive answer to this example because so much depends on the context. What if X feels that all is well and you have misinterpreted his NVC? In this case, a very direct approach might make X feel defensive. And this reflects one of the most important points in this chapter – communicating effectively with other people is *not* just applying special techniques or behaviours which 'always work'. A fundamental issue is how we perceive the other person and recognise their needs. This is an important theme of the next chapter.

## SUMMARY

- The process of interpersonal communication can be complex. Unless you understand some basic features of this process, you can easily behave in ways which the other person does not accept or appreciate.
- You can analyse social interaction as skilled behaviour. It has many of the characteristics of other skills, including the importance of goals and feedback. However, it is also important to emphasise that social skills are not the same as motor skills. There are important differences, including the fact that other people may have different goals and the importance of personal feelings.
- There are a number of important interpersonal skills, including non-verbal communication (NVC), listening, self-disclosure and assertiveness.
- Many authors stress the advantages of assertiveness without highlighting potential problems. For example, assertive behaviour may be seen as aggressive; there are issues of gender roles; and there are important cultural differences to consider.
- There are several 'popular' models of effective communication which are virtually ignored by social science researchers but which are often used in business and management training. We commented briefly on Neurolinguistic Programming. It does offer some interesting ideas, but we also raise some important concerns. For example, it has been over-simplified and applied too 'mechanically', and often seems to ignore cultural differences.
- Major barriers to understanding other people include our own often misplaced confidence in our abilities to understand the way we come across to other people and interpret their behaviours and feelings. We need to engage with others in ways that allow a genuine exchange of perspectives.
- You can approach face-to-face communication as a process with a series of stages, from deciding the goal through planning and on to action. However, this must be seen flexibly – effective communication must be based on flexible behaviour which is appropriate to the specific context.

## FURTHER READING

Cameron, D. (2000) *Good to Talk*. London: Sage.

This is an essential read for anyone who is interested in exploring some of the values and critical issues associated with attempts to improve people's communication skills.

Epley, N. (2014) *Mindwise: How we understand what others think, believe, feel and want*. London: Allen Lane.

An essential read if you seriously want to reflect on the ways we understand ourselves and others.

Hargie, O. (2011) *Skilled Interpersonal Communication* (5th edn). Routledge: London.

This has rightly become one of the standard texts on the nature of social skills.

Hartley, P. (1999) *Interpersonal Communication* (2nd edn). London: Routledge.

This book is now rather dated as it was written in the pre-digital era, but it still has some useful discussion of many of the issues explored here and relates social skills to the model of interpersonal communication used in this chapter.

Chapter 10

# How do interpersonal skills work in practice?

## INTRODUCTION

The previous chapter emphasised that effective communication depends on personal awareness, interpersonal skills and the context in which people operate. We also argued that these factors may not be sufficient. If we have an inaccurate perception of ourselves or of the other person, then we may apply the wrong approach or techniques. We need to establish a dialogue which allows the participants to understand each other.

This chapter applies these ideas to common face-to-face situations of two very different types:

- The more casual, unscheduled or informal interactions and exchanges of information which go on all the time – the conversations and discussions in the office, shop floor or service area.
- The more formal interactions which are often subject to company rules, regulations and procedures, such as interviews.

In all these situations, we can look at how the participants are working together (or not!) to achieve some understanding which will have an impact on the effectiveness of the organisation. As well as highlighting specific skills which we described in the last chapter, we need to examine the way that participants understand or make sense of the events which unfold, and this is a major theme of the case study which starts the chapter.

### OBJECTIVES

*This chapter will*:

- show how the principles developed in Chapter 9 can be applied to common face-to-face situations in organisations;
- analyse a case study which shows how misunderstanding and 'miscommunication' can develop through conversations and discussion in the organisation;
- summarise general principles of selection and appraisal interviews, and show how communication influences their outcomes.

## CONVERSATIONS IN THE OFFICE – THE CASE OF THE MISSING SERVICE ENGINEER

Jo Brown is General Manager of ABC Computer Services. Jo receives an urgent call from XYZ, an important customer in Durban who has a 'major fault in his computer system' and demands a service engineer immediately as his whole operation has ground to a halt. Jo tries to contact Edward Smith, the Service Manager, at once but finds he is out visiting PRQ Engineering, another important customer. As Jo considers that the Durban problem is urgent, she goes to the Service Department and finds service engineer, Helen Jones, working at her desk. They have the following conversation:

JS: Have you any really urgent work on hand?
HJ: Well, I'm sorting out a few patches for the new system we've sent to PRQ. Mr Smith is expecting me to have them done by tomorrow.
JS: But is it really urgent?
HJ: Well, I don't know . . . I don't suppose so.
JS: Good – you can sort out the Durban problem first.

Jo then decides that Helen should fly to Durban on an afternoon flight so she can start work at XYZ first thing in the morning. Jo suggests that she leave the office immediately to pack and get to the airport. As she is about to leave Helen says, 'I had better leave a message for Edward Smith'. Jo says, 'Don't worry, I will let Edward know what is happening so he can reschedule your work for the next few days.'

Jo returns to her office and phones XYZ to confirm that Helen Jones will be there first thing in the morning. She then calls Ann Botham, her personal assistant, leaves a number of messages and instructions, and answers some queries. At the end of the call, she says, 'Oh, by the way, let Edward Smith know that Helen Jones will probably be in Durban for a few days working on XYZ's computer problems.'

When Edward Smith returns just after 2pm, he finds that Helen Jones is not at her desk. So he leaves a note instructing her to drop everything and go to clear up an urgent problem at PRQ engineering first thing in the morning. He then leaves the office at 3.30pm to meet another customer and does not return that day.

After working through the other jobs from Jo by around 3.45pm, Ann Botham sends an email to Edward Smith, saying that Helen Jones will probably be in Durban for a few days on the XYZ job.

Next morning, Edward Smith arrives, notes that Helen Jones is not there and assumes that she has gone to PRQ Engineering. He has an urgent report to finish so does not check his email as he usually does first thing. About 9.30am, he receives an irate phone call from PRQ Engineering saying that the promised service engineer has not arrived and threatening to cancel the lucrative service contract. At first no one else in the office knows anything about Helen Jones's whereabouts. As a last resort he checks his email to find the message from Ann Botham: 'Jo has asked me to let you know that Ms Jones will probably be in Durban at XYZ for a few days.' He is both puzzled and annoyed by the brief message.

About five minutes later, Smith storms into Brown's office and says, 'How the hell do you expect me to run an efficient Service Department, when you send my staff round the country without letting me know? We will probably lose the PRQ Engineering contract because Helen Jones did not report there this morning as I promised.'

## What do you think of communication at ABC?

Before reading on, you might like to consider the following questions:

- What are the most important problems of interpersonal communication illustrated in this case study?
- What are the key factors (both process and meaning) which have created these problems?
- Who was responsible for the problems?
- How could the participants have behaved differently to avoid these problems (both short-term and long-term)?
- Does this case study simply illustrate poor interpersonal communication, or do you recognise any broader issues?

## Our analysis

There are many ways to analyse this incident and we focus on the interpersonal issues. However, perhaps there are broader problems in the organisation and this conflict is simply a symptom. For example, we have not mentioned the physical surroundings and researchers have suggested that this can have important influences, as we suggest in Box 10.1. Moving back to the interpersonal difficulties, we have picked out the following problems. Each one suggests that the participants are not paying much attention to the impact of their communication – they could do with some urgent training in listening, NVC, etc. For each problem, we also suggest an important practical principle which has been ignored.

### *The request from Jo Brown*

Consider the way Jo communicates her own agenda to Helen Jones. If your boss asks you, 'Have you any really urgent work on hand?', this implies that a request is about to follow which *is* really urgent. How is Helen Jones supposed to respond? What does 'really urgent' actually mean? Why did Jo not start on a more neutral note and ask what jobs Helen was undertaking?

*And the principle:* other people will always try to interpret the *intention* behind what you are saying. This can be a particular problem when status differences are involved.

### *Jo's reassuring message to Helen*

When Helen says she 'had better leave a message for Edward Smith', Jo says, 'Don't worry, I will let Edward know what is happening.' Jo does not do this – she leaves a message for Edward but makes no real attempt to ensure either that Edward has received it, or that the full urgency of the situation is explained.

*And the principle:* if you give a commitment and a reassuring message, you should make sure that you act on it in the way that you have implied.

### *Jo's message to Edward*

Jo does not contact Edward directly but leaves it to Ann Botham. But note the way Jo does this: 'Oh, by the way, let Edward Smith know that Helen Jones will probably be in Durban for a few days working on XYZ's computer problems.' There are several hints in this sentence that the message is not very important – 'by the way' and 'probably'. Ann gives it low priority by leaving it until later.

*And the principle:* if you delegate a job then you need to *explicitly* communicate its urgency or priority. Otherwise, the other person will assume the priority from the way you pass it on. In this case, the casual way the message was expressed signalled 'low priority'.

### *Edward's attempt to contact Helen*

When he finds that Helen is not in her office, he leaves a note instructing her to 'drop everything' – if the demand is so urgent, is a note sufficient to explain what needs to happen? Surely not. Edward makes no further attempt to check that the message has been received and understood.

*And the principle:* always try to receive feedback on messages you send, especially if they are important or urgent.

### *Edward's confrontation with Jo*

How would you respond as Jay to Edward's opening comment: 'How the hell do you expect me to run an efficient Service Department, when you send my staff round the country without letting me know?' This immediately puts Jo on the defensive, both in the tone and the specific accusation – it is aggressive rather than assertive. Jo will almost certainly respond to the accusation and the conversation will turn to arguing over who told what to whom, rather than resolving the immediate crisis.

*And the principle*: the opening to a conversation will establish the tone and the agenda. If you 'say' you want a fight, do not be surprised if you get one.

## Resolving the issues

As with so many problems in organisational communication, this crisis could have been avoided if the participants had communicated more carefully – and everyone contributed to the crisis. Even Ann who simply passed on the message can be criticised – she did not check whether the message was important or urgent which she *could* have done.

The most significant outcome in our case study is the conflict which has now emerged between Jo and Edward. Of course, we have not explored their history – this may be one symptom of a long-standing personal dispute. Jo does not seem to make much attempt to consult Edward. Or it may be a symptom of confused or sloppy management style. If we assume that there is no personal animosity between them, what could Edward have said? He could have presented the *problem* to Jo: 'We have a crisis as we have both assigned Helen Jones to urgent jobs with different customers. We may lose an important customer if we do not respond promptly.' This form of expression sets out the problem, assumes joint responsibility, does not assign blame, and suggests what needs to happen – it is *assertive* rather than aggressive. Deciding what went wrong and how it should be resolved long term is best left until the crisis is over.

### BOX 10.1 HOW IMPORTANT ARE THE PHYSICAL SURROUNDINGS IN THE WAYS WE COMMUNICATE?

The idea that our physical surroundings influence how we communicate persuaded many organisations to move to open-plan offices. However, the outcomes can be more complex. Moving to open plan does give more opportunities for conversations and can lead to *perceptions* of improved communication. However, studies report consistent difficulties in having confidential conversations, and this is a longstanding finding. For example, Sundstrom concluded that 'visual accessibility of work spaces is *not consistently associated with communication'* (our italics) but does tend to increase 'discretionary, work-related conversations or formal contacts that the initiator considered desirable but not necessary' (Sundstrom, 1986, pp. 266ff.).

As we have discovered many times, communication cannot be determined by a simple change. What have been called 'gathering places' may be more significant than the individual's workspace. These places are where staff typically congregate or meet during their daily routines, by vending machines, photocopiers, in canteens, etc. Organisations should ensure that these places are conveniently situated to encourage communication.

Another aspect of physical space which is relevant to this chapter is the way that staff can manipulate office layouts. For example, Sundstrom quotes the executive who arranged his office so visitors had to sit opposite him and directly in the light, so it was easier to study their faces.

One common issue which runs through all these conversations is the way that the participants build up ideas about what an incident means and then translate this into action which may be counterproductive in the long term. One very useful way of analysing this process is described by Linda Ellinor and Glenna Gerrard, building on work by Chris Argyris and Peter Senge (Ellinor and Gerrard, 1998, pp. 82ff.). They talk about the way we interpret data, make assumptions, draw conclusions and then act on the basis of those conclusions. Other people use a different 'ladder of inference' and arrive at different conclusions from the same event. Table 10.1 below shows the steps in the left-hand column. If you start from the bottom and work up, you can see how two people (A and B) can arrive at very different conclusions and actions from the same starting point. The logic of person A is taken from Ellinor and Gerrard.

***Table 10.1*** *The ladder of inference*

| | *Person A* | *Person B* |
|---|---|---|
| Take action | I won't give Sally any key tasks | I must see Sally for a counselling interview |
| Adopt beliefs | Good team players follow the rules and attend meetings on time | Staff who are on top of their job are able to explain problems to the team |
| Draw conclusions | Sally is not a good team player | Sally is under pressure at the moment |
| Make assumptions | Sally does not think this meeting is important | Sally must be worried about something if she didn't explain |
| Add meaning (personal and cultural) | Being late is not acceptable | People should explain if they cannot attend on time |
| Select data (personal and cultural) | Sally came to the meeting late. She didn't say why | Sally came to the meeting late. She didn't say why |

## SUPPORTIVE COMMUNICATION

Another way of looking at conversations is to ask whether they are supportive or defensive. Several of the conversations in the case study put the other person 'on the spot', as in Jo's initial request to Helen. This was manipulative and did not encourage Helen to respond openly.

Andrews and Herschel (1996) summarise the way that ideas of supportive communication developed. They suggest five important characteristics: (pp. 103–106).

1 It focuses on the problem, not on the person. Contrast what Edward said to Jo in the case study above with our suggestion.
2 It is based on 'congruence' where what we communicate is really based on what we think and feel. In other words, we are not trying to mask what we say – the critical comment delivered with a smile is an example of incongruent behaviour, which puts the other person on the defensive.
3 It is descriptive rather than evaluative. Again, compare what Edward said to Jo with what we recommend.
4 It is 'conjunctive' – in other words, it flows from what has already been discussed and does not interrupt or cut across others.
5 It 'validates' individuals – in other words, it gives the impression that 'whatever the difference in official organisational rank, she or he considers the other individual of equal worth as a person' (pp. 105–106). Box 10.2 gives an example which shows how brief comments can have a very destructive impact.

Andrews and Herschel also suggest that these principles may be especially important in communications between superiors and subordinates given some of the research which suggests that 'superiors believe they communicate with subordinates more effectively than they actually do' (p. 110).

## MANAGING DIFFICULT CONVERSATIONS

Another related approach which has received positive endorsement is a development of the Harvard Negotiation Project – *Difficult Conversations* by Stone *et al.* (2010). This proposes a common underlying structure to every difficult conversation we have to have, either at work or home. They suggest that: 'no matter what the subject, our thoughts and feelings fall into the same three categories, or "conversations." And in each of these conversations we make predictable errors that distort our thoughts and feelings, and get us into trouble' (p. 7).

The three categories that we have to address and hopefully resolve are:

- *What happened?* We need to agree on what actually happened which led up to the conversation.
- *Feelings*. What do we do with the various feelings (often ones of anger and hurt) which we are experiencing?
- *Identity*. What does this situation mean for us in terms of our self-image and self-esteem?

Managing difficult conversations then 'requires learning to operate effectively in each of the three realms' (p. 8).

### BOX 10.2 HOW TO DESTROY A RELATIONSHIP IN ONE EASY SENTENCE

The dangers of the careless sentence is revealed in the following example which shows how non-supportive communication can have a powerful and lasting impact:

> The meeting had been quite productive but we had got to a point where we seemed to be a bit stuck and no way forward was emerging. I proposed a possible solution. The senior manager in the meeting immediately responded: 'You obviously have not been listening to me. That solution is not appropriate because . . .' I felt quite shocked and humiliated by this retort. I had been listening very carefully indeed – we just didn't agree on the way forward. I never trusted that manager again.

## WHEN ORGANISATIONS PROVIDE THE SCRIPT . . .

Many modern organisations train their employees to follow a 'script' in particular situations – e.g. in sales or telephone conversations with customers, as the following examples illustrate:

- The 'have a nice day' from the restaurant as you leave.
- The 'come again soon' plus 'cheery wave' which restaurant staff were forced to deliver every time.
- The designer clothes shop whose sales staff are forbidden to describe clothes as 'lovely' or 'nice' (among the right words are 'exquisite' and 'glamorous').
- The supermarket whose staff must smile and make eye contact with all customers and are graded on these behaviours as part of performance appraisal.

(Cameron, 2000, p. 57)

The problem with all such scripts is that they assume that the same behaviour means the same thing to all receivers and they assume that everyone can deliver the same script in a completely uniform way. Both these assumptions are suspect. We have argued throughout this book that communication is sensitive to context and is inherently ambiguous. We have also argued that skilled behaviour is flexible. In the long term, organisations which believe that 'good communication' simply equals a 'standard script' may find they have very disgruntled employees.

## COMMUNICATION AND INTERVIEWS

One useful definition of an interview comes from Maureen Guirdham:

> In an interview, two people meet, face to face, to accomplish a known purpose by talking together. An interview is different from either a negotiation or a problem-solving meeting because it is one-sided – as the words 'interviewer' and 'interviewee' suggest.
>
> (1995, p. 180)

This definition ignores the possibility that there might be more than one interviewer in some situations (e.g. the selection panel). However, it does highlight the explicit 'known purpose' which is recognised by both sides and the different roles involved. Guirdham goes on to discuss the obligations that this places on the interviewers. They are in control and must not only take responsibility to achieve the purpose but also to treat the interviewee fairly and honestly. As we shall see in some later examples, interviewers sometimes ignore this last responsibility and 'play games' which cannot be justified.

The purpose of the interview can also be complex. For example, the purpose of a selection interview is to select the right person for the particular job. However, this is not the only goal which the interviewers have to work towards – they must also realise that they are 'representing the organisation' to candidates. Candidates will use the interviewers' behaviour and competence as information about 'what the organisation is really like' and 'what it might be like to work here'. There is the well-known tale of the organisation which decided that the best test for managerial candidates was a series of short, aggressive and stressful interviews. The candidate who performed best in these – staying calm, sticking to his arguments under pressure – was offered the job. He immediately refused it and walked out, commenting that 'if this is how you treat your prospective employees, then I do not want to work for you'.

There are many different types of interview with different purposes, which means that interviewers have to adopt a different approach and use different skills. For example, the typical selection interview will demand good questioning technique; the counselling interview will place more emphasis on reflecting and listening techniques. To illustrate these differences we shall examine two types of interview in more detail: the selection interview and the performance appraisal interview.

## COMMUNICATION IN THE SELECTION INTERVIEW

In theory, the selection process is a process of logical steps:

- *Job description* – where the nature and demands of the job are thoroughly reviewed and analysed.
- *Person specification* – where the job demands are translated into the skills and personal characteristics which the person will need to do the job well.
- *Advertising the vacancy* – so that everyone who might meet the specification has the opportunity to apply.
- *Sorting and short-listing applications* – to select candidates who fully satisfy the person specification.
- *The selection event itself* – which will normally include an interview (see Box 10.3 for data on how this differs across cultures) but which increasingly includes other tests such as psychometric tests or group tasks.

In practice, this process can be both difficult and time-consuming. For example, the job demands may be changing and there may be some argument as to how this should be decided. There may also be argument about which of the characteristics in the person specification are the most important. The choice of selection methods may also be controversial. For example, there is debate about the value of psychometric tests. Unfortunately, some organisations do use selection methods which have very dubious validity, such as graphology – the analysis of a person's handwriting.

We do not have the space to explore these issues fully. Perhaps the most important implication for communication is the possible ambiguity and uncertainty which can creep into the interview room. If the job description and person specification are poorly prepared, then the interviewer might not have a very clear idea of what they are looking for. If there is a panel interview, there might be confusion or even clear disagreement between interviewers. The candidate might also have developed a misleading picture of the job, depending on how the advertising material was prepared.

Despite continuing concerns about the reliability of interviewer judgements, the interview remains one of the most popular selection methods. Research suggests that its reliability can be improved in several ways, notably by training interviewers to avoid the problems we listed above. If interviewers are sufficiently trained, if they know what characteristics they are

## BOX 10.3 SELECTION PRACTICES VARY ACROSS CULTURES

Various studies have shown that there are significant variations between countries in terms of the methods they use to select employees. For example, an early study by Hodgkinson and Payne (1998) reviewed how British, Dutch and French organisations selected university graduates. Among the significant differences were:

- Traditional interviews were always used by nearly all organisations in the UK and Netherlands (89 per cent and 85 per cent respectively). Only 45 per cent of French organisations always used them.
- Criterion-referenced interviews were used much more in France than in the UK. Nearly half the UK organisations never used them.
- Graphology is used much more in France than in the Netherlands – 82 per cent of French organisations sometimes used it.

Research on selection interviews has identified many potential problems and pitfalls in the interview process. For example, Mike Smith (1982) suggests five main sources of unreliability:

- Different interviewers may look for different characteristics in the interviewees.
- The setting of the interview may influence the interviewee in ways which are unrelated to their skills for the job. For example, a candidate recently told us how he had failed his last interview after being 'overwhelmed' by the surroundings. Instead of the expected formal panel interview, he was taken to a lounge with low, comfy chairs.
- Poor structure. The same candidate can give a very different impression, depending on which sequence of questions they receive.
- Interactive problems. Even interviewers with clear plans and objectives may make unreliable decisions unless they recognise that their behaviour in the interview can influence the way it progresses.
- Interviewers may use the information they have gained from candidates in different ways. One bias that may be especially important in interviews is the finding that interviewers can place too much emphasis on negative or unusual information.

looking for and if they follow a clear (but not over-rigid) interview plan, then they can perform well. They must also have the specific social skills we highlighted in the last chapter.

The general issues we have identified are summarised in Table 10.2 which applies the model developed in Chapter 9 to the selection interview. This also shows that the specific skills covered in Chapter 9 are all relevant to interview practice. The example of opening and closing will illustrate this.

## BOX 10.4 FAIR TREATMENT OR INCOMPETENT PRACTICE?

How would you have responded as a candidate to the following three interview situations?

1 'I was straight out of college and this was one of my first interviews, for a copywriting trainee in an advertising agency. I was shown into the manager's room and sat on the low, comfy chair facing his desk. He looked up and leaned back in his chair, looked me straight in the eye and said, "Hello, Tony". I said "Hello" and paused. I was expecting the first question. Nothing happened. He continued to look me straight in the eye. After an awkward pause where I started to panic, I realised he was not going to say something so I started: "I suppose you'd like to hear something about me." He nodded slightly but still did not say anything. So I started to talk about myself. I wasn't prepared for this, so I didn't feel I was giving a very coherent presentation. After about 10 minutes (it seemed a lot longer), I said: "And I'd really like to work for an organisation which has exciting development plans. What are your plans?" He leaned back again and said: "That's a very interesting question – what do you think we should be doing?" After a few more minutes of desperate improvisation I was told the interview was over. I crawled out of the office, feeling completely dispirited, angry and frustrated. I did not get the job. In retrospect, I'm glad I wasn't offered it.'

2 'I was pleased to be offered an interview for this post in local government as it meant more responsibility, better career prospects, and a useful promotion from my present post. I also wanted to move to that part of the country. I was asked to attend for interview at the local college. When I arrived I was asked to wait as apparently the "interviews are running a few minutes late". Eventually, I was escorted to Lecture Room 6. When I walked in, I was shown to a chair in the position where the lecturer would usually be. I looked up and discovered I was in a banked lecture hall and there must have been about 70 people sat looking at me. I was asked six questions by different members of the audience who introduced themselves before their question. None of my answers received any follow-ups or probing questions. If I had known this was going to happen I would have given fuller answers. After my six questions I was thanked and asked to leave. Afterwards, I discovered that these six questions were a standard procedure. The job was controversial because of local politics so the large audience was because all the interested parties had exercised their formal right to see the candidate.'

3 'I walked into the interview room. The interviewer was standing behind the desk, clutching a stopwatch. He didn't say anything so I sat down in what was obviously the interviewee's chair. He leaned over towards me and said, "Right, you've got 10 minutes to sell yourself to me. Go!" He clicked the stopwatch to start the time and sat down with arms folded.'

*continued . . .*

**BOX 10.4 *Continued***

In all three situations, the candidate expected to receive a conventional interview: a series of relevant questions, some probes and follow-ups, the chance to add their own comments and the chance to ask questions.

In all three situations, the organisation ignored these expectations and presented the candidate with a very different challenge (although situation 2 is closest to the expected format, the setting is totally unexpected). In each case, was the organisation behaving legitimately? Does it have a rationale for the specific tactics? How will candidates feel about this 'induction' to the organisation? Why weren't candidates told what to expect?

There is no real evidence to suggest that 'shock tactics' help an interviewer to arrive at a better opinion of the interviewee's competence and potential. The evidence points the other way. All these three organisations are failing to communicate clear expectations to their candidates. If they make bad selection decisions, they should not be surprised.

## Opening and closing

The choice of opening can be very important in formal situations such as an interview where the opening can establish either a positive or negative atmosphere. Which of the following opening techniques would you prefer in a selection interview:

- The interviewer gives you a positive welcome and spends some time in social conversation – breaking the ice – before getting down to business.
- The interviewer starts by describing important features about the company and the job, and then goes straight into critical questions like 'What are the most important attributes you have for this job?'

The first strategy is designed to make you feel relaxed so you can put on the best performance you can. The second is much 'colder' and more official. If it is repeated to every candidate, you can wonder whether this opening is the best use of interview time – why not have a general briefing to all candidates?

A variety of tactics are also available to close or conclude the interview. The good interviewer will make sure that the interviewee has a chance to clear up any points they have not understood and that they know what is going to happen as a result of the interview. We know from our own experience that this does not always happen.

## When cultural differences make the difference

As we argued in the previous chapter, it is not sufficient just to 'know the techniques' to become a skilled interviewer. The skilled communicator must also be looking for the different meanings which might affect different participants. Many advice books on interview performance are written from a perspective which favours candidates from particular cultural

**Table 10.2** *The interview as planned communication*

| *Stage* | *Content* | *Points to watch* | *Example* |
|---|---|---|---|
| Decide the general goal | What do you want to achieve overall? | | You have been asked to carry out the first round of interviews on the candidates for the supervisor position. You have to interview eight candidates, all external, and recommend three for a second interview |
| Consider the context | What has happened in the past?<br>Who are the participants?<br>What is the setting? | Are there any hidden agendas because of the history?<br>What does the other person need or expect to happen? | As all the candidates are external, there should not be any problems because of 'internal politics'. Will the candidates know what this first interview is for? What sort of interview will they expect?<br>What setting will be the best place to interview them to give a professional impression of the organisation (not a corner of a busy office with phones ringing all the time) |
| Plan | Decide on the objectives<br>Decide on the structure | Make your objectives realistic and achievable<br>Make sure your structure leads up to your objective | Your objectives are to:<br>1 Find which three candidates match the job and person spec.<br>2 Give them the best chance to show what they can offer.<br>3 Show them that the organisation is a good place to work.<br>You must make sure that you have done your homework: read all the applications; research the job and person spec.<br>You must have an interview plan which is well-structured (and check your questions before the event) |
| Act | Use the relevant skills | What are the most important skills in this situation e.g. listening, – questioning, etc.? | Give the interview a clear, confident introduction<br>Make sure you listen to each candidate<br>Make sure you probe the answers to uncover 'the evidence'<br>Give the candidate the chance to ask questions |
| Follow-up | | | Complete the documentation<br>Make sure that all candidates are told of the outcome |

backgrounds (often reflecting middle-class white American values). Candidates from different cultural backgrounds may not recognise or adapt to the 'hidden rules', as the following examples illustrate (from Hargie, 1997):

- The question 'Why have you applied for this position?' may be recognised as an opportunity to show how your skills and background fit you for the position. From a different cultural expectation, it may be seen as too obvious to warrant a detailed answer.
- The question 'Do you have any questions to ask us?' offers an opportunity to impress by asking intelligent questions about prospects and development. It may be ignored by candidates who have the cultural norm of showing respect to the person of high status. From this perspective, asking would be disrespectful.

## ORGANISATION AND STRUCTURE IN THE SELECTION INTERVIEW

Another characteristic which is emphasised in interviewer training is the importance of a clear structure in the interview. Structure can be discussed at two levels: the overall structure of the interview, and the way that questions can be organised in a sensible sequence.

### Overall structure

The simplest way of summarising the likely structure of a selection interview is to say that it will have a beginning, middle and end:

***Table 10.3*** *Stages in the selection interview*

| *Section* | *What they might contain* |
|---|---|
| Beginning | Candidate is welcomed |
| | Interviewer(s) introduce themselves and explain how the interview will be conducted |
| | Opening questions are designed to make the candidate feel at ease |
| Middle | Interviewer asks main questions and follow-ups |
| Ending | Interviewer invites candidate to ask any questions |
| | Interviewer explains what will happen next |

There are several models of the selection interview which are more elaborated versions of this. Problems occur when interviewers 'change the rules' without giving a clear idea of what to expect, as Box 10.4 illustrates.

### *Question sequences*

In the last chapter, we introduced the difference between open and closed questions. Open questions invite the candidate to answer in any way they see fit; closed questions ask for a yes/no or specific answer. Hargie *et al.* (1994) suggest that other types of questions are important, including:

- *Leading questions* – which 'lead the respondent towards an expected response' (Hargie *et al.*, 1994, p. 107) and which could give a misleading impression in a selection interview if the candidate felt obliged to give the 'expected answer'.
- *Multiple questions* – where two or more separate questions are bundled together as one. This confuses candidates – which question should I answer first?

Of course, there is no guarantee that a specific type of question will elicit the intended response, as the following examples illustrate:

Q: 'How long did you spend in the Sales Department?' (closed question anticipating short, factual answer).
A: 'Well, I don't think that I really spent long enough as I felt that I should have been able to. . .' (extended answer).
Q: 'What do you think about expanding international links?' (open question anticipating a long answer).
A: 'Very good idea' (restricted answer).

Interviewers may need to ask a series of open or closed questions to get the response they want from candidates, and this is where *sequences* of questions and the use of probes becomes important. Probes are designed to 'probe' the previous answer in order to get a more detailed picture. For example, suppose you were interviewing a young graduate and wanted to check their IT competence. You might start with a general question: 'How much IT did you use at college?' Suppose the candidate simply said 'We used it quite a bit.' This answer could be probed in a number of ways. One sequence could be:

- Which software packages have you used?
- What did you use them for?
- What is the most complex task you've done with IT?

This sequence and further probes should establish both the breadth and depth of the candidate's expertise. Good interviewers will also probe to establish the evidence behind the candidate's answers. For example, does using IT 'quite a bit' mean 'word-processing one essay a month' or 'using the Internet and computerised databases every day'.

Popular sequences of questions include:

- *Funnel sequence* – which starts with open questions and then narrows down, using closed questions and probes.
- *Inverted funnel* – which starts with closed questions and then opens out.

- *Tunnel sequence* – where all the questions are at the same level. They are usually closed.

(Hargie *et al.*, 1994, pp. 102ff.)

## COMMUNICATION AND FEEDBACK IN THE APPRAISAL INTERVIEW

Most modern organisations have an appraisal system with the following characteristics:

- A formal meeting takes place between a boss (appraiser) and subordinate (appraisee) which takes place at least once per annum and which reviews how the appraisee has performed over the previous period.
- The appraiser gives feedback to the appraisee and the meeting discusses this feedback.
- The meeting is based in some documentation which both parties have to consider before the meeting.
- The outcomes of the meeting are a formal assessment (usually written and kept) of how the appraisee has progressed and what this means for future performance (e.g. future targets agreed) and staff development (e.g. agreed training or development plan).
- These procedures are usually established and monitored by the human resources function within the organisation.

You can analyse the appraisal interview in the same way that we analysed the selection interview – as planned communication; as an interaction with expected structures; as an opportunity for interviewers to make systematic errors, etc. (and we do this on the website). In this chapter, we shall focus on the process of feedback, which is a key component of many interactions.

### Do the appraisers have the necessary skills to give productive and supportive feedback?

If the appraiser does not have the necessary social skills, the system can easily collapse. Is there training to make sure that everyone is adopting a consistent approach?

Clive Fletcher summarises research evidence on the factors which determine the effects of feedback. He identifies six factors:

- *The amount of critical feedback.* He quotes one study which found that appraisees received an average of thirteen criticisms per interview and another where managers were spending on average around one quarter of the interview criticising or attacking the apraisee. In these circumstances, it is not surprising if the appraisees adopt a defensive attitude.
- *The balance in the performance review.* The balance between positive and negative feedback is very important.
- *The content of the feedback.* For example, is it clear and unambiguous? Is it relevant to what the person does or does it focus on more personal characterisitics?

- *The use of a range of measures.* If there is a wide range of evidence on how well the person is doing and if this evidence is available before the meeting, this will support the discussion.
- *The way the interview is organised and conducted.* Perhaps the critical factor here is how well and how much the appraisee is able to participate in the discussion.
- *The relationship between the appraiser and appraisee.* If there is already a good relationship, this will make the appraisal much easier.

(Fletcher, 1994, pp. 119ff.)

The problems with many appraisal schemes has led to new variations emerging. For example, some organisations have put much more emphasis on self-appraisal as a device for encouraging staff to reflect on their performance and suggest ways they can improve. Another way is to increase the variety of feedback available, as in 360-degree feedback, which we describe in Box 10.5.

## BOX 10.5 360-DEGREE FEEDBACK

Peter Ward is one consultant who has used this method in a number of British organisations. He defines the method as: 'The systematic collection and feedback of performance data on an individual or group, derived from a number of stakeholders in their performance' (Ward, 1997, p. 4).

For example, suppose you are a junior manager in a retail company. Data on your performance would be collected from relevant stakeholders such as your staff, your boss, other managers you have to deal with and your main customers. The data would be collected systematically using questionnaires or interviews, or perhaps both. You will receive a written report which summarises the results and you will have a chance to reflect on this report before you discuss it with your appraiser. The discussion will cover four areas:

- *Your strengths* – those behaviours where you see yourself as strong and where others also rate you as strong.
- *Your development areas* – those behaviours where you think you need to improve and so do others.
- *Discrepancies* – those behaviours where you see yourself as strong but where others do not. In other words, there is a discrepancy between how you see yourself and how others see you.
- *Hidden strengths* – those behaviours where others see you as strong but where you have not rated yourself highly.

As our brief summary implies, this system is both complex and time-consuming. If it is implemented carefully, it can make a significant impact on the culture of a company over time. If it is treated as a 'quick fix', it will probably do more harm than good. As with all these schemes, the quality of communication is critical to its success.

## THE SKILL OF FEEDBACK?

Feedback is obviously a critical component of the appraisal interview, but there are a number of less formal situations where someone might need to receive feedback on their performance. So is there a 'correct' way of delivering feedback so that the person accepts it without becoming antagonistic or defensive?

A number of guidelines are available, most of which focus on the issues identified by Harry Levinson who offers the following advice, especially when giving negative feedback (quoted in Goleman, 1996, pp. 153–154):

- *Be specific.* Feedback should highlight specific events or examples rather than just general advice. It should also be specific about what the person did.
- *Offer a solution.* Feedback should suggest ways of resolving any problems. There is little or no point in offering negative feedback where there is no way the person can improve.
- *Deliver the feedback face-to-face.*
- *Be sensitive.* This is simply a reminder that feedback, even negative feedback, should be delivered in a positive way rather than simply attacking the other person.

### SUMMARY

- The skills and techniques which were explained in Chapter 9 can be applied in common face-to-face situations in organisations, both the more casual, conversations and discussions, and more formal interactions, such as selection and appraisal interviews.
- One important issue is the way that participants understand or 'make sense' of the events which unfold. We can easily jump to misleading or unwarranted assumptions, and base our communication on these. This can very easily lead to confusion and conflict.
- Supportive communication is important, especially in encounters where there is a status difference.
- Organisations which train employees to use standard, inflexible scripts in certain situations are adopting a very limited view of human communication.
- In formal situations like interviews, the person in control, the interviewer, has special responsibilities to manage the interaction so that communication is open and focused on the specific objectives.
- A range of communication problems can affect formal interviews like the selection interview, and interviewers should be trained to avoid these.
- Feedback is a particularly important and difficult process which needs careful attention.

## FURTHER READING

Cameron, D. (2000) *Good to Talk*. London: Sage.

This offers some very interesting analysis of the formulaic routines which are recommended in some workplaces, e.g. see Chapter 3.

Duck, S. (2007) *Human Relationships* (4th edn). London: Sage.

Many of our examples have important implications for the relationships between the participants. This book offers a very clear and comprehensive introduction to the study of human relationships, inside and outside.

Stone, D., Patton, B. and Heen, S. (2010) *Difficult Conversations: How to discuss what matters most*. London: Penguin.

This book offers analysis and practical techniques to resolve the three components of a difficult conversation.

Chapter 11

# How can we organise effective meetings?

## INTRODUCTION

The problem of ineffective meetings has been described as one of the most important issues facing contemporary organisations. If presentations make us nervous, then meetings seem to make us disappointed and cynical: 'a meeting brings together a group of the unfit, appointed by the unwilling, to do the unnecessary' (quoted in many texts, e.g. Stanton, 1996).

This chapter concentrates on principles and techniques which can overcome these criticisms. We shall mention some of the group dynamic issues which can affect meetings but which are covered more fully in Chapter 13.

We start by looking at important differences between business meetings and then review various ways to improve their effectiveness. Applying the ideas and principles in this chapter should enable you to run the sorts of meetings which John Tropman describes as 'excellent', where:

- decisions are made and agreed;
- the group does not have to revisit or rework 'old' decisions;
- the decisions are good – well worked out and successful;
- members enjoy the meeting and feel that it has been productive.

(Tropman, 2003)

We can also improve meetings by taking advantage of recent developments in computer technology – e.g. using videoconferencing to make sure that everyone can attend, and reviewing discussions and decisions using presentation techniques such as concept mapping.

**OBJECTIVES**

*This chapter will:*

- analyse the main differences between different types of meetings;
- identify principles which have been associated with effective meetings, highlight potential pitfalls and problems, and identify important skills for meeting chairs;
- review different procedures and practical steps which have been proposed to improve meetings;
- show how we can use new technology to make meetings more effective.

## WHAT SORT OF MEETINGS ARE THESE?

Consider the following two extracts (based on real business meetings) and identify what you think are the most important differences.

### Meeting A

SPEAKER 1: OK, well we need to consider John's concerns about the store in Smallville.

SPEAKER 2: It's just not doing enough business for a store that size. You can see from the figures in Table 3 in the report sent out last week.

SPEAKER 3: So how can we bump up business? Any ideas, Paul?' (Everyone looks at the large screen monitor for a contribution from Paul – Speaker 4 – who is joining the meeting through a videoconferencing link.)

SPEAKER 4: The only way is to put up a slow down sign and lay a series of small sharp spikes across the road way just outside the store.

SPEAKER 5: Pardon?

SPEAKER 4: It's obvious. People will slow down, get a puncture and stop. While they're waiting for the breakdown services to arrive, they will have no choice but to go in the store and spend some money.

SPEAKER 5: You're not serious?

SPEAKER 4: Of course not. But can you see my point? (Pause: some other members of the meeting groan at the very tortured pun.) We do need to get more people in that store. Look at the figures in Table 4 which compares different stores across the region. Have you all got the figures? They are in the email I sent you this morning. (Everyone agrees.) You can see from column 5 that the customers who go in to Smallville spend more on average than customers who visit some of our other stores. We just need to get more people through the door.

SPEAKER 1: So are we agreed that the best strategy is to work out how to attract more customers to visit the store? OK, so how can we do that?'

### Meeting B

SPEAKER 1: We are a quorate so we can now move to the first item in the agenda – the proposal that we close the South Street office in Smallville. You will all have received the paper on this, reference 99/8/2, and I will ask the writer, John Smith, to summarise the main points for us.

SPEAKER 2: The critical point here is that if we combined the Smallville offices on our main street site, we could offer a much better service to the local community. Apart from some savings due to greater efficiency, we would be more competitive. We could offer a wider range of services by putting the two offices together. We also have no evidence that the existing customers at South Street would be disadvantaged. In fact, we feel that many of them, if not most of them, would find it more convenient to come to Main Street.

Speaker 1: So the proposal is that we merge the two offices on the main street site. Have we any comments or further proposals?

SPEAKER 3: I have to say that my staff are very concerned about this proposal, in terms of the messages it sends to loyal and hard-working staff. You have glossed over the fact that the South Street office is extremely profitable and has won awards for the quality of its service and management.

SPEAKER 1: John, can you respond to that?

SPEAKER 2: We have considered these points. I can assure you that there will be no redundancies and all of the staff will be accommodated at Main Street.

SPEAKER 1: Any other comments? (Pause.) So if there are no further points, can we move to a vote?

SPEAKER 4: Point of order, please, chair. According to our terms of reference, I do not believe that we can make this decision without further consultation.

SPEAKER 1: Yes, we shall need to check that. Rather than hold up this meeting, I shall ask the Secretary to check that during the coffee break and we shall return to this item of business at the end of the meeting. Moving on to item two on the agenda . . .

So what were the main differences between these two meetings? There are obvious similarities. Both aimed to reach a decision on an important issue. There was an exchange of opinions and the discussion moved towards the final decision.

The differences, however, are more striking. For example:

- More members spoke in meeting A.
- In B, every comment was directed through the chair (Speaker 1).
- The style of conversation was more light-hearted in A (as in the rather feeble joke from Speaker 4).
- There were several references to formal rules and regulations in B (the debate over the terms of reference, and the check on whether the meeting was a quorate).
- The behaviour of the chair was very different (Speaker 1 in both cases).

- The procedures were different (e.g. the automatic move to a vote to close the decision in B).
- The use of videoconferencing technology in A.

These examples illustrate two of the main dimensions along which meetings can vary:

- The use of formal rules and regulations.
- The degree of formal structure in the meeting.

You can represent these dimensions as follows (see Figure 11.1) and you can imagine meetings which fall in different sections of the diagram. At position A, a meeting is very tightly structured and follows formal rules and regulations. An example here would be the annual general meeting of a company or the monthly meeting of a local government committee. At position B, the meeting is tightly structured but not subject to very formal rules. An example here might be a project or management team meeting.

One obvious implication is that each meeting should be at the appropriate spot on the diagram. For example, suppose you wished to run a meeting to introduce new people to one another and to generate some fresh ideas for new projects. Organising in style A would be counterproductive, and you would probably use style C. On the other hand, the meeting of a very large official committee might have to follow format A to satisfy legal requirements.

We have not identified the use of technology as a separate dimension as it can be used in any of the four main types. One obvious use is to set up the meeting so that some or all participants can attend online – e.g. using a Skype connection or Google Hangouts. In both situations, you need to have working practices which enable the virtual participant to contribute when they need to. In a meeting where everyone is online you need a skilled chair to ensure that everyone is engaged. In a totally online meeting, you also have the advantage of a text chat box so that participants can post comments and suggest links without interrupting the discussion.

There is also the problem that individuals may be coming to the meeting with specific hidden agendas – see Box 11.1.

| B | Tight structure | A |
|---|---|---|
| | | |
| Few rules of procedure | | Many rules of procedure |
| | | |
| | | |
| C | Loose structure | D |

***Figure 11.1*** *Dimensions of meetings*

### BOX 11.1 WHEN MACHIAVELLI COMES TO THE MEETING

Political issues and hidden agendas may influence meetings even when the majority of participants are trying to arrive at the most 'rational' decisions. Buchanan and Badham (1999) highlight some of the consequences of 'power games' which can affect events such as meetings: 'Agendas are restricted to "safe" issues; controversial issues are excluded from informal conversations and from formal decision-making processes' (p. 55).

Martin (2000) describes bargaining tactics which can be used in meetings to gain an advantage, such as describing a worse situation than actually exists and then backtracking to the position which you wanted in the first place. For example, 'We have to increase prices by 10 per cent' after discussion becomes 'We agree to increase prices by 5 per cent' where 5 per cent was the original hidden objective. The problem with all devious tactics like this is that they can rebound on you if they are discovered. And you may *never* achieve trust if others suspect you of these tactics.

## What makes meetings effective?

Every textbook on business communication includes some advice on how to run effective meetings, but much of this advice seems to be based on the author's personal experience rather than on more comprehensive research. Research studies comparing meetings in different organisations and contexts are relatively thin on the ground. One notable exception is the work by John Tropman, reporting the conclusions of the Meeting Masters Research Project (Tropman, 2003). This American project aimed to identify individuals who ran excellent meetings and decide how they did it. The research suggested that 'Meeting Masters' followed seven main principles, described below.

### *The orchestra*

This emphasises the strong co-operation necessary to complete the task, as in a symphony orchestra. The meeting chair is analogous to the conductor – he or she makes sure that everyone delivers their best performance and that everything fits together.

### *The three characters principle*

Tropman suggests that you can only do three things in a meeting:

- announce something;
- decide something;
- discuss something.

Tropman also suggests that each agenda item can only do one of these three things. The meeting should be organised so that members clearly know which item is which. Items should be dealt with in that order:

- first, all announcements, then . . .
- all items where you need decisions, then . . .
- items which need to be discussed.

### *The role*

The person in the chair should act as a role model to encourage other members of the group to contribute openly and positively.

### *No new business*

The meeting should only cover items which have been placed on the agenda and which the members have had some chance to think about, otherwise members will not be prepared for the discussion.

### *No more reports*

Members are never asked simply to 'report from their department', as individuals may concentrate on topics which show them in the best light and fail to identify important issues.

### *The imperative of proactivity*

Meetings should always include some items which deal with future plans or problems. Early discussion can enable members to have an impact on future events.

### *High-quality decisions*

Not only are decisions made, but those decisions show 'evidence of quality'.

## The rule of six

Tropman suggests rules which can help you apply these principles. Among the most interesting are the following:

- About one-sixth of the items on an agenda should be from the past. These have not been completed or perhaps been deliberately held over.
- About four-sixths of the items should come from the present. These are important issues that need to be dealt with immediately.
- About one-sixth of the items should come from the future. These are issues which are likely to be important in the future and which need discussing before they become urgent.

This way of structuring a meeting also allows Tropman to introduce a subrule: the two-meeting rule. This rule suggests that controversial items should be discussed first at one meeting without any decision being taken. They should then be *decided* at the next meeting. This allows members to discuss the item freely and possibly disagree quite strongly and then leave some time to reflect on the issues so that the final decision is not made in the heat of an argument.

### The role of the chair

Tropman emphasises the importance of pre-meeting preparation and the influence of the chair's behaviour. We agree with this emphasis. There is also British research which complements Tropman's analysis of what effective chairs usually do. For example, based on a series of very detailed meeting observations, Rackham and Morgan (1977) showed that effective chairs behaved very differently from the average member of the meetings – for example, they did much more summarising and testing understanding.

## DEVELOPING AND REPORTING THE AGENDA

One of the most important devices for structuring a meeting is the agenda. Tropman proposes seven categories of agenda items which should be organised as follows in a two-hour meeting (Table 11.1).

This distribution of time gives a bell-curve and so Tropman talks of the 'Agenda Bell' (Tropman, 2014, pp. 40ff.). His argument for placing the 'most difficult' item in the middle of the meeting, starting about one-third of the way through, is to 'take advantage of peak attendance, high energy, and the momentum that usually comes from handling less difficult items successfully' (ibid., p. 43).

Whether meetings follow this exact distribution or not, it is critical that members know the status and priority of each item on the agenda: 'Are we just discussing this or do we have to make a decision?'; 'Do we have to make a decision today?' The agenda should communicate

***Table 11.1*** *Tropman's seven categories of agenda items*

| *Category* | *Item* | *Type* | *Time (minutes)* |
|---|---|---|---|
| 1 | Minutes | | 10 |
| 2 | Announcements | | 15 |
| 3 | Decision | Easy | 15 |
| 4 | Decision | Moderately difficult | 15 |
| 5 | Decision | Hardest item | 25–40 |
| 6 | Discussion | | 15–30 |
| | Discussion | Easiest item | 10 |

Source: Adapted from Tropman, 1996, pp. 24–27.

this information to members. Unfortunately, many agendas do not. This may be just a matter of adding a subheading to the title of the item. For example, consider the difference between these two agenda items:

4 Report from J. Smith on the Eureka Project.

5 Report from G. Smith on the Alumni Project:

- review progress
- allocate resources for the next financial period
- decide whether to extend the project to the central site.

Item 4 gives no indication of what should be discussed or decided; item 5 gives very clear information on what needs to be done.

## Minutes and follow-up

The minutes of a meeting can be very different in style and detail. At one end of the scale, we have decisions or action points recorded as a list with no explanation or elaboration of the discussion. This is appropriate for some meetings – say, a small project group. At the other end, we have a complete record of what everyone said. This verbatim report is far too time-consuming and unnecessary for most, if not all, business meetings. A useful compromise is to prepare what Tropman calls 'content minutes' – for each item on the agenda, a minute is written as two separate paragraphs which

- summarise the main points in the discussion;
- summarise the decision taken or the action agreed, naming whoever has to carry it out, and giving the timescale or deadline.

From this, we can suggest that effective minutes must convey all the following information:

| *Details of the meeting itself* | *Details of the outcomes* |
|---|---|
| Who was present and who did not attend | What was agreed |
| When and where it took place | Who has to take actions as a result and by when |
| When and where the next meeting will take place | |

There is also the problem of deciding the style and layout of minutes. For example, should the minutes identify who said what? Baguley (1994, p. 94) gives an example of minute structure which includes the following item:

4 Joan Harris reported that software development was on target and still had an anticipated beta version completion date of end of March. There were, however, still problems with Ron Stanning's lack of co-operation over graphics programming availability.

*Action agreed:* Valerie Williams to set up meeting with Ron Stanning and Joan Harris to resolve problems.

*Completion by:* 21 Nov 1994.

This example does meet many of the suggestions given above. However, there is one important issue – the minutes record that Ron Stanning *is* being 'unco-operative'. Should this have been recorded? Did the meeting establish this 'fact' or is it simply Joan Harris's opinion? If you were Ron and felt there were good reasons not to supply a graphics programmer, how would you respond to this judgement in the minutes? Should that sentence have read 'Ron Stanning had not supplied a graphics programmer to the project'? Or is a more fundamental change of style required? As minutes remain as a formal record of what has happened, you need to be very careful that they are accurate and that they do not record as 'fact' anything which could be contested later.

Given that minutes are an important issue, it is worth thinking about different ways of producing them. One strategy which we have used is to create the minutes in the meeting itself using a collaborative document format like Google Docs. At the end of each major item the chair reviews the minute on-screen and ensures that everyone agrees before moving on. There are also a number of apps available to make other parts of the meeting process easier to manage – see Box 11.2.

### BOX 11.2 AND THERE'S AN APP FOR IT

A range of apps for tablets, laptops and mobile phones now exists to help with aspects of the meeting process, offering suggestions for structuring different types of discussion, taking notes, taking minutes, and so on. One main advantage of many of these apps is their ability to sync with or send to other software, like your calendar and email. For example, Peak Meetings HD offers structures for seven different types of meeting and offers a searchable catalogue of files including agendas, plans, notes, etc. See the website for further examples. If you have regular meetings with a specific team, it is worth discussing possibilities with the team members as the use of a common app can often be very productive and increase collaboration and sharing.

## PLANNING MORE EFFECTIVE MEETINGS: PROCEDURES AND TECHNIQUES TO CONSIDER

Several techniques have been recommended to improve particular aspects of meetings, either by changing the whole approach to the meeting or by including a specific technique at a certain point within a meeting. If you are planning a meeting you should at the very least consider the following approaches:

- flexible meeting techniques to encourage more dialogue and discussion;
- brainstorming, to produce more creative ideas;
- structured problem-solving;
- Nominal Group Technique, also designed to help problem-solving and decision-making;
- Delphi technique, for a group which cannot physically meet;
- techniques for encouraging group innovation;
- techniques for clarifying decision-making.

### Flexible meeting techniques

If you are organising a meeting which might attract a large attendance, it is worth considering some of the techniques which have been shown to work with large groups, such as Open Space and World Café. These techniques can also be applied with small groups where you can also use approaches with specific supporting toolkits such as Ketso. These approaches share the aim of giving the participants as much opportunity as possible to shape the meeting agenda and outcomes, and encouraging dialogue across all the group members, regardless of their status.

### Open space

This term and approach was originated by Harrison Owen in the 1980s (Owen, 1993; user guide available from: www-new1.heacademy.ac.uk/assets/documents/heinfe/Open-Space-Technology—UsersGuide.pdf) and its key features include the opening session where, after a short introduction to the theme of the meeting, participants propose the key issues which then form the detailed agenda. Participants can then work on these in a flexible way over the course of the meeting and can move around different issues as they see fit, so you will usually find a number of discussions going on at the same time. The role of the meeting facilitator is to support this process and to ensure that the outcomes and proposals are suitably recorded. There is a very useful summary on Wikipedia and you can find details of recent developments at: www.openspaceworld.org.

### World Café

The World Café approach is described on their website as follows: 'Drawing on seven integrated design principles, the World Café methodology is a simple, effective, and flexible format for hosting large group dialogue.' World Café can be modified to meet a wide variety of needs. Specifics of context, numbers, purpose, location and other circumstances are factored into each event's unique invitation, design and question choice, but the following five components comprise the basic model:

1. *Setting*: Create a 'special' environment, most often modelled after a café.
2. *Welcome and introduction*: The host begins with a warm welcome and an introduction to the World Café process, setting the context, sharing the Café Etiquette, and putting participants at ease.
3. *Small group rounds*: The process begins with the first of three or more 20-minute rounds of conversation for the small group seated around a table. At the end of the 20 minutes, each member of the group moves to a different new table.
4. *Questions*: Each round is prefaced with a question designed for the specific context and desired purpose of the session.
5. *Harvest*: After the small groups (and/or in between rounds, as desired) individuals are invited to share insights or other results from their conversations with the rest of the large group.

The website (www.theworldcafe.com/index.html) provides a more detailed discussion of these steps and the design principles, and links to the toolkit and book which gives a full insight to the method.

## Ketso

As their website explains (www.ketso.com):

> Ketso offers a structured way to run a workshop, using re-usable coloured shapes to capture everyone's ideas. Ketso is unique in that each part is designed to act as a prompt for effective engagement. . . . Ketso is not just a re-usable 'workshop in a bag'. It comes with a growing range of *free, open-source support resources*, including workshop plans that you can customise to suit your needs.

The practical kit to support a Ketso workshop includes reusable cards of different types on which participants write their ideas and comments, and large felt sheets on which participants can stick the cards to build a concept map which everyone can view and amend. There is also an Action Planner resource. After the meeting, the maps can be photographed or typed up to inform future actions.

## Which flexible meeting to use?

There is no easy answer to this question and we are not aware of research which directly compares the different formats. Other formats are also available – see our website for further discussion.

We have used/experienced all three of these techniques and found them valuable in terms of generating useful ideas and stimulating more discussion than would have been possible in traditional meeting formats. We think that they are especially useful in encouraging open discussion in situations where the team or group is relatively new and/or seem to be a bit 'stuck' and not making the progress they would like. However, not everyone feels initially comfortable in these more open-ended formats, and you do need a skilled organiser to set the meeting going and keep everyone involved. For example, the Ketso website does recommend that a meeting organiser should pilot/practise the method before running it 'for real'.

As well as running a complete meeting in one of these formats, you can, of course, also consider using some specific techniques from the different approaches to match your own context.

## Brainstorming

Brainstorming is a technique which has received a good deal of publicity and generates very mixed reactions. There have been some objections to the terminology and some organisations have used 'thought showers' as an alternative term (www.telegraph.co.uk/news/uknews/2162568/Council-bans-brainstorming.html).

Opinions about its value are also divided:

- 'brainstorming provides a free and open environment that encourages everyone to participate. Quirky ideas are welcomed and built upon, and all participants are encouraged to contribute fully, helping them develop a rich array of creative solutions' (from www.mindtools.com/brainstm.html).
- 'there is a problem with brainstorming. It doesn't work' (Lehrer, 2012; see at www.newyorker.com/reporting/2012/01/30/120130fa_fact_lehrer?currentPage=all. This article from the New Yorker also contains a number of links to useful studies).

There are two general principles behind brainstorming: that problem-solving is best done in stages and that each stage should obey certain rules. The first stage is the generating of ideas. *All* the ideas generated during this stage are recorded for later consideration. Brainstorming sessions usually have someone to lead the session who can enforce the rules and act as scribe. This first stage should also have a definite time limit – say, 10 minutes. During this time, everyone in the group must obey the following rules:

- no evaluation, no one is allowed to criticise or evaluate any of the ideas being expressed;
- no censorship, so all ideas are accepted and recorded;
- you are encouraged to produce as many ideas as possible in the given time;
- you are encouraged to hitchhike – i.e. to build on the ideas that have been suggested by others in the group.

After the time limit is up, each idea is looked at in turn to see if it is worth pursuing.

### *But does brainstorming 'work'?*

This is difficult to answer and demonstrates some of the problems of undertaking social research. Current research and recent summaries usually do not support the original claims of more productive and creative ideas. However, some of the research studies have not been very 'realistic' tests of the method. Our conclusion is that we do not have definitive evidence either way. Perhaps the best conclusion is to argue that brainstorming is worth considering as a technique but should be used carefully:

> I will continue to use brainstorming groups because they can have important social effects – they can act as an 'ice-breaker' to help a group develop more of a co-operative spirit. They can also produce good ideas, especially when a group has tried other ways and is getting 'stuck' on a particular issue. But they are not a magic solution which will guarantee success.
>
> (Hartley, 1997, p. 16)

## STRUCTURED PROBLEM-SOLVING

This is the philosophy on which techniques like brainstorming are based – break down the problem-solving process into discrete stages and then deal with each stage in turn, as in:

- study/discuss/analyse the situation;
- define the problem;
- set your objective;
- generate alternative solutions;
- establish evaluation criteria;
- evaluate alternatives;
- choose among alternatives.

There are many slight variations on this theme. For example, you can argue that deciding the evaluation criteria – on which you judge the possible solutions or decisions – should be done earlier.

### Nominal group technique

Nominal group technique (NGT) also tries to organise decision-making to give everyone in the group equal status. NGT mixes group discussion with an independent generation of ideas and independent judgement. Robbins (1996) describes it as: 'A group decision-making method in which individual members meet face-to-face to pool their judgements in a systematic but independent fashion' (p. 324). It has been used by a wide range of groups in organisations (e.g. Horton, 2007. See online at: http://onlinelibrary.wiley.com/doi/10.1111/j.1365-2044.1980.tb03924.x/abstract).

Usually supported by an external facilitator, the specific steps are:

- the problem is fully explained to the group;
- individuals work independently to write down ideas and possible solutions;
- each individual presents one idea to the group in turn until all the ideas are recorded (on a flipchart or whiteboard, or using Post-it notes on the wall);
- each idea is discussed, clarified and evaluated by the group;
- individuals privately rank the ideas;
- the group decision is the idea which achieves the highest average ranking.

### Delphi

This does not involve a face-to-face meeting. It uses the same steps as NGT and has been used in many different types of organisations since its early development in the 1950s (Hargie and Tourish, 2000). The group never meets and comments are usually collected electronically. The main stages are:

- enlisting the group of experts;
- distributing the statement of the problem to the group members and inviting them to respond;
- compiling the responses;
- sending out the compiled responses for further comment.

These last two phases are then repeated until a consensus is reached. We have used this technique successfully on research projects which demanded that we convene a panel of experts who were unable to physically meet.

## ENCOURAGING GROUP INNOVATION

Michael West and colleagues have carried out a number of studies which suggest that four factors encourage team innovation:

- vision;
- participative safety;
- climate for excellence;
- support for innovation.

Research suggests that these factors accurately predict whether a team will be able to produce innovative ideas and solutions (West, 2012).

## CHANGING DECISION-MAKING

A group or committee should consider its present strategy for making decisions – what are its advantages and disadvantages? There are numerous alternatives. Table 11.2 below lists many of these and identifies one major advantage and disadvantage of each:

***Table 11.2*** *Decision-making methods*

| *Method* | *Advantage* | *Disadvantage* |
|---|---|---|
| Decision by authority without discussion | Speed | Does not use members' expertise |
| Decision by authority after discussion | Allows everyone to express opinion | Members may not be committed to the decision |
| Decision by expert member | Good decision if really expert | May be difficult to identify the most exert member |
| Average members' opinions | Speed | Members may not be committed to the decision |
| Majority control | Speed | Minority can be alienated |
| Minority control | Can be useful if not everyone can attend | Members may not be committed to the decision |
| Consensus | Members will be committed to the decision | Can take a great deal of time, skill and energy |

Source: Hartley, 1997.

There are, of course, additional advantages and disadvantages to each, and we cannot decide on the 'best' unless we know the context and the demands of the situation.

## COMPARING GROUP METHODS

It is difficult to offer a definitive opinion on which of these methods to use as there is insufficient research on their everyday applications. The research to date does suggest a number of general conclusions:

- Groups using systematic procedures probably do make better decisions.
- Members of groups using these procedures seem both more satisfied and more committed.
- Groups which regularly review their own procedures are usually more effective than those who do not. So we should also apply this to committees and working groups in terms of their meetings.

This analysis of meetings has assumed that the members are co-operating and are genuinely interested in problem-solving. We must not forget that many real meetings are constrained or influenced by political factors.

## VIRTUAL MEETINGS

Technology has given us several options to improve the process of face-to-face discussion as we have already suggested – e.g. the use of online documents, the use of mind or concept mapping to suggest and record ideas etc. As we implied earlier in this chapter, new technology has also given us two major possibilities to improve the process for:

- *Enabling one or two remote participants to join a face-to-face meeting*. There is no excuse nowadays for excluding a remote member from participating in a face-to-face meeting. The combination of a meeting room equipped with PC/laptop and projector, Wi-Fi connectivity, appropriate audio-visual hardware, and software like Skype can enable a remote participant both to attend and participate. The meeting chair needs to conduct the meeting so that they can bring in the remote attender at the right time.
- *Running a complete meeting online*. With a small group you can use software like Skype or Google Hangouts. For a larger group you may want to use software which has a wider range of facilities, as we suggest in Box 11.3.

**BOX 11.3 SOFTWARE FOR VIRTUAL MEETINGS**

A wide range of software is now available to support a virtual meeting. Depending on the budget and networking facilities available, you can choose software which has the particular functions you need. From our experience, we suggest that you think particularly about:

- *Support for presentations*. You should be able to display PowerPoint and other types of presentation but certain features may not be supported (e.g. animations on the slides) and check for compatibility. We recently (in 2014) had the experience of a PowerPoint prepared on a Mac which would not load in the conferencing software.
- *Application sharing*. You may want to show a screenshot or some other software during the meeting and you need to be confident that you can share this application through the meeting software.
- *Chat box*. Having a space for text enables anyone without a mic on their set-up to participate as well as encouraging additional comments from everyone.
- *Polling and feedback*. You can ask for reactions from members of the meeting and most software will have icons which allow participants to 'show a smiley face' or other signal of agreement or disagreement. Some software offers more sophisticated polling options, which can be especially useful in large meetings.
- *Use of webcams*. It can be really useful to be able to see other participants as you can pick up on communications clues from, e.g. facial expressions, although video signals require good quality telecommunications and this is not always available.

## How different are virtual meetings?

We are often asked how different online or virtual meetings are from their face-to-face counterpart. This is a difficult question to answer as we suggest that you should use face-to-face and virtual meetings in different ways. Table 11.3 below summarises some of the key issues. See the website for more extended discussion and examples.

If you are using software which allows both audio and video links, you need to think about how you present yourself on screen. We say more on this in the next chapter. You need to consider such issues as how you 'respond to silence' given that you normally receive little or no immediate feedback from the audience for your presentation (Koegel, 2010).

***Table 11.3*** *Comparing face-to-face and virtual meetings*

| *Issue* | *Face-to face meetings* | *Virtual meetings* |
|---|---|---|
| Especially good for? | Establishing relationships<br>Extended open discussion | Saving time and expenses when team is distributed<br>Keeping everyone up to date |
| Not so good for? | Keeping everyone updated under time pressure given the time to arrange/organise | Establishing relationships<br>Extended open discussion |
| Ideal timing? | Probably no more than 2 hours | 1–1.5 hours as maximum |
| Role of chair? | Should be very clear on purpose of the meeting to avoid the meeting going off on tangents | Needs to be very good at enabling participation and summarising progress |
| Need for training? | People are generally accustomed to meetings, though many would benefit from training in how to maximise their effectiveness | Participants should be provided with technical training, particularly to use the more advanced systems and features |

## SUMMARY

- Business meetings differ in terms of the level of formality (rules and regulations) and the structure. We need to ensure effective organisation and communication in all the different types.
- The American Meeting Masters Research Project identified individuals who ran excellent meetings and summarised what they did in seven key principles.
- Agendas and minutes are important documents which can support effective meetings. Both need careful attention to style and approach.
- Various innovative meeting formats and techniques have been suggested to improve different aspects of meetings – e.g. Open Space, brainstorming, Nominal Group Technique, etc. However, we have limited evidence on actual business practice to offer solid recommendations on which are the most effective. Meetings should regularly review their own approaches and procedures and find the most appropriate solutions.
- There are now various ways of using technology to support and enhance your meetings, ranging from the use of desktop videoconferencing (to allow everyone to contribute regardless of where they are) to new methods of transcribing and summarising meeting discussions.

## FURTHER READING

Koegel, T.J. (2010) *The Exceptional Presenter Goes Virtual*. Austin, TX: Greenleaf Book Group Press.

This contains useful practical advice on techniques for virtual presentation.

Martin, D. (2000) *Manipulating Meetings: How to get what you want, when you want it*. London: Prentice Hall.

This book is not based on any systematic research programme but does offer a wide range of case studies and examples to illustrate how participants and chairs can try to manipulate meetings to their advantage.

Tropman, J.E. (2014) *Effective Meetings: Improving group decision making* (3rd edn). London: Sage.

Tropman, J.E. (2003) *Making Meetings Work: Achieving high quality group decisions* (2nd edn). Thousand Oaks, CA: Sage.

Tropman's 2014 text offers updated advice. His 2003 book summarises the results of the Meeting Masters Research Project and explains the principles which emerged from the research.

Chapter 12

# How can we plan and deliver effective presentations?

## INTRODUCTION

Most people are anxious about standing in front of an audience to deliver a talk. A survey by the Aziz Corporation in the UK found that 76 per cent of people in business believe that public presentations are 'the most daunting task they have to do in the world of commerce' (Aziz, 2000, p. 49).

Concerns about presentation skills seem universal. For example, Kakepoto *et al.* (2012) identified 'poor oral communication skill' as an important barrier for engineers in Pakistan. These engineers were not fully prepared by their previous technical education for the demands for oral presentation in the workplace.

As with meetings that we discussed in the last chapter, presentations are often criticised for being poorly organised or badly planned. This chapter concentrates on principles and techniques which can overcome these criticisms, and also introduces some of the possibilities which are offered by new technology to make a presentation part of a systematic communications campaign or process rather than a 'one-off' event.

New technology also gives us the chance to both present to a remote audience relatively easily and also to review online a very broad range of speakers and compare techniques and approaches. As with all other forms of communication, you need to find a personal style which plays to your strengths and we suggest some alternative approaches and strategies.

New technology has also delivered a wealth of examples and guidance which we can use to reflect on and improve our personal style.

**OBJECTIVES**

*This chapter will:*

- explain why oral presentations are still important in modern organisations;
- summarise the main techniques which speakers can use to improve their performance and decrease anxiety;
- offer alternative approaches to 'the presentation' which will apply in specific situations;
- review developments in technology which you can consider for your future presentations.

## WHY ARE ORAL PRESENTATIONS IMPORTANT?

One answer is that they are now very common and possibly becoming more important. Some organisations now use presentations in meetings where previously they might have received lengthy written reports. This can speed up the decision-making. However, a poor presentation might not do justice to the ideas presented, so organisations want staff who can present convincingly and will not confuse or irritate an audience.

Presentations are also widely used in recruitment, especially for managerial and supervisory positions. Organisations will select staff who deliver convincing presentations. This does not necessarily mean people who can 'perform' in a theatrical sense, although this sort of skill can come in handy if you are addressing large audiences. In keeping with the general theme of this book, we are looking for 'effective' speakers.

Effective speakers make sure the presentation 'flows' and is clearly organised. They deliver confidently. A speaker lacking in confidence may well distract an audience from the main topic. One of our most painful memories was the anxious conference speaker who tried to conquer his nerves by preparing far too many slides for his 20 minutes (in the days when presenters used acetate slides on an overhead projector). As the time went on, he went faster and faster in a desperate attempt to fit all the slides in. The audience's attention turned to whether he would finish the race in time (and he failed, which gave the presentation a fumbling and embarrassing ending). We have since met several people who attended that conference – they all remembered the 'battle with the slides' but so far none have actually remembered what the talk was about.

Having said that, there are certain critical features, you also need to develop your own style which suits your personality. Guidebooks and training texts offer different approaches, as we illustrate in Box 12.1.

### Why are people so worried about giving presentations?

The previous paragraphs provide part of the answer to this question. One reason is the 'fear of disaster'. We have probably all attended at least one disastrous presentation, and we remember how embarrassing and uncomfortable these experiences were. So, we mentally anticipate the possibility that we could be responsible for a similar disaster.

There are two ways to resolve these anxieties:

1 To make yourself *feel* less nervous both before and during the presentation, accepting that it is perfectly normal to feel nervous to some extent.
2 To *behave* in ways which are likely to conceal your nerves. In other words, you behave confidently and this creates confidence in the audience.

There are several techniques which can help you to achieve (1), including:

- being really well-prepared;
- relaxation exercises such as deep breathing.

Techniques which can help to achieve (2) include:

- Entering the presentation in a very deliberate way. Remember that you are being observed by the audience from the moment you enter the room (or switch on the webcam connection in a virtual presentation). Try not to 'leak' (see p. 65) any non-verbal cues of anxiety.
- Rehearse not just the presentation itself but also how you will set out your notes, slides, etc. This obviously means that you need to check the venue in advance. We can remember the stress of a colleague who was delayed and turned up at the conference room just in time to find that there was no space on the lectern for both his laptop and notes. From our seats at the back of the room, we could only empathise with his increasing anxiety level.
- Deliver the talk in a way which does not attract attention to your level of anxiety. For example, if you know that your hand will shake, do not use cue cards which you have to hold in front of you. Or hold cue cards but use the other hand to keep your arm steady.

**BOX 12.1 WHY DON'T THE TRAINERS AGREE?**

We have already discussed the fact that advice on 'effective written communication' is often confused or even contradictory. The same is true for oral presentations. For example, how much rehearsal is appropriate?

- Michael Klepper argues that you should 'Practice. Practice. Practice.' until you 'are so bored with the speech you couldn't possibly be afraid of it' (Klepper, 1994, p. 120).

*continued . . .*

**BOX 12.1** ***Continued***

- Khalid Aziz recommends 'at least two full rehearsals', while warning of the dangers of over-rehearsal (Aziz, 2000, p. 54).
- Lee Bowman suggests that it is 'unwise to do more than one rehearsal' if you are using notes (Bowman with Crofts, 1991, p. 61).
- 'Rehearsal is essential and you cannot over-rehearse' (Provan, 2009, p. 57).

Given all the evidence that communication depends on context, it is unwise to rely on 'golden rules'. You need to find a process that suits you, after you have considered all the alternatives. And this is an area where you might be able to make some 'small experiments' and receive feedback on your performance. You should be able to find opportunities to deliver presentations which will not matter too much in terms of your career development or reputation and where you can try out new approaches.

## PLANNING THE PRESENTATION

The most popular advice to would-be or developing presenters is to plan what you are doing in terms of key stages or key areas. For example, Rasberry and Lemoine (1986) suggested a four-step process: organisation, construction, practice and delivery. Gallagher *et al.* (1998) suggest a similar eight-step approach, starting by setting the objective. They suggest that a simple, one-sentence objective is a good way of clarifying your purpose, as in their example: 'As a result of my presentation, my audience will understand and be impressed by the new Customer Services system in Central Branch' (p. 130).

There is considerable overlap and common ground between these and other common recipes. Table 12.1 uses the diagram structure we introduced in Chapter 11 to identify main stages and important issues.

Before we try to highlight the most fundamental issues that presenters must deal with, it is worth emphasising a few notes of caution:

- The danger with any series of stages is that it can be interpreted too rigidly. As we said earlier in this book when we reviewed strategies for preparing written documents, you need to be flexible and constantly revisit your objectives.
- As we suggested in Table 12.1, you need to find a system for preparation and delivery that suits you rather than follow a rigid recipe from one of the guide books. For example, we tend to use concept maps or mind maps to work out structures – see the website for examples – but some people find this an unnatural way of organising notes. Some prefer a more structured or hierarchical method like the pyramid principle we introduced in Chapter 5. The important thing is to find a method you can work with, then make sure that it delivers a plan which ensures clear structure in your talk.

**Table 12.1** *Planning a presentation*

| *Stage* | *Content* | *Points to watch* | *Example* |
|---|---|---|---|
| Decide the general goal | What do you want to achieve overall? | What amount of research are you expected to do?<br>How far can you offer your personal opinion? | You have been working for the last six months in a sales team, promoting a new product which has only been distributed in your region. You achieved the most sales. You have been asked to deliver a 10-minute presentation to the regional sales management team on the likely prospects if they promote and distribute the product nationally |
| Consider the context | What's happened in the past?<br>Who are the participants?<br>What is the setting? | Are there any hidden agendas because of the history?<br>What do your audience need or expect to happen? | What do you know about the history of the sales management team in terms of their reaction to proposals? Is it usual to ask someone at your level to make a presentation of this type? You need to check whether you might be 'being tested'<br>You need to find out what criteria have been used to decide on a product's future after test marketing. And you need to know what level of detail the managers expect |
| Plan | Decide on the objectives<br>Decide on the structure | Make your objectives realistic and achievable<br>Make sure your structure leads up to your objective | Your objectives are to deliver a presentation which:<br>– argues that the product should (or should not) be developed more widely on the basis of sensible evidence<br>– shows that you can present effectively to a given brief<br>– your structure should reflect the criteria which the managers will use to judge the product |
| Act | Use the relevant skills | What are the most important skills in this situation – e.g. listening, questioning, etc.? | Explaining and presenting are obviously critical. You will also need to respond to questions and show evidence of research and preparation<br>And you *must* keep to time |
| Follow-up | What can make sure the communication has been effective? | What can you do to reinforce what you have done? | Ask for feedback on the quality of the presentation as soon as possible after the event. This could give useful tips for next time as well as showing you are willing to learn |

## PRESENTATION AS PROCESS OR EVENT?

There is a further complication that we think you should consider which seems to be neglected in many handbooks and guidelines. Most of the advice on presentations treats a presentation as a single 'event'. For example, Harvard Business School suggests that you need to 'tailor your presentation to these factors:

- size of the audience;
- formality of the situation;
- regularity of the meeting (one-time, occasional, frequent);
- time of day and other particulars of the occasion.

(Morgan, 2007, p. 5)

Morgan also talks about taking questions and the implication is that these are face-to-face. He suggests caution if you allow questions during a presentation 'because it may cause you to lose control of your talk' (ibid., p. 55).

This is sensible advice although we have some slightly different views and comments on 'control', to which we return later. However, the main assumption is that the presentation is an 'event' which you need to prepare for. This is true but could also be misleading if it forces you to think *only* on what happens in the presentation itself. It is worth stepping back and considering where your presentation fits into the broader history and context of your organisation. For example, what opportunity do you have to make contact with the audience beforehand and perhaps discover some of their issues and concerns? What opportunity do you have for dialogue with your audience before, during and after the presentation? Various forms of new technology can give us options to extend our communication beyond the traditional boundaries. We shall discuss some of these options later in this chapter, including:

- surveying your audience beforehand to uncover their existing positions and expectations;
- making some content available online beforehand;
- offering the chance to communicate while the presentation is ongoing, using the 'backchannel';
- setting up some online discussion either before or after the event.

All of these options can now be realised with simple and accessible software. For example:

- A short survey (up to 10 questions) can be constructed at no cost using SurveyMonkey or Google Forms.
- Part or all of a presentation can be made available through SlideShare or a folder in Dropbox.
- Twitter can be used to provide a backchannel.

## THE IMPORTANCE OF STRUCTURE IN PRESENTATIONS

As we say many times in this book, structure is critical. It must be clear to you and to the audiences with written documents there are various patterns you can use. Which one is most effective will depend on the audience and context. For example, suppose you have to deliver a presentation which advocates that the company adopts a new procedure for handling customer enquiries. Would the following outline be appropriate?

- *Give the vision statement* – e.g. 'We are leaders in customer care'.
- *State the goal and objective* – e.g. 'We need to handle customer enquiries more effectively than our competitors'.
- *Summarise today's situation* – e.g. 'We deal with X enquiries at the moment/we have seen increasing complaints from customers that we do not provide very good support'.
- *Explain how we got to this position* – e.g. 'We have not reviewed the staffing or the methods since the year X'.
- *Summarise available options* – e.g. 'There are new answering systems and techniques on the market and our competitors are doing this'.
- *Make a recommendation* – e.g. 'We need to move to a new system and ensure that our staff are properly trained'.

The above list is based on an outline which is offered as one of the templates within Microsoft Powerpoint. It is similar to an outline suggested by Wilder and Fine, 1996:

- Present situation
- Situation problems
- Possible solutions
- Recommendations
- Requirements
- Overcoming obstacles
- Next steps.

This second outline goes further into the implementation of the recommended solution – overcoming obstacles and so on. The exact outline is probably not as important as making sure the audience knows where you are heading. There are various ways of achieving this and this highlights the importance of the first few minutes of any talk. Consider the strategies for opening and closing listed in Box 12.2.

### Alternative structures and styles

Perhaps in part as a reaction to the misery of 'Death by PowerPoint' (which we discuss later), a number of recent guides have suggested moving away from conventional presentation styles in an attempt to make presentations feel less like a 'performance' and more like a conversation. Typical advice along these lines comes from Gary Reynolds:

> Naturalness in delivery, then, should not be a formal, one-way didactic lecture. Rather, imagine the delivery of your presentation as a conversation between friends or coworkers, teacher and student, a master and apprentice, or scientist to scientist. They all involve personal connection by way of natural expression.
>
> (Reynolds, 2011, p. 13)

This does not mean that you just 'let the presentation happen' but that you reflect very carefully on your style and approach. And you can use a combination of techniques to create your own style. For example, one of us (PC) has successfully used voting/polling to ask the audience what areas they would like to explore further, using a pyramid-style mind map for the overall structure.

One important ingredient of many modern guides is the use of 'story-telling'. To quote again from Reynolds:

> we tend to forget lists and bullet points, but stories come naturally to us. Stores are how we've always attempted to understand and remember the bits and pieces of our experiences . . . you should not fight your natural inclination to frame experiences into a story. You should, instead, embrace this and tell the story of your experience/topic to your audience.
>
> (p. 46)

### BOX 12.2 STRATEGIES FOR OPENING AND CLOSING

Lewis (1996) suggests six 'classic openings':

1. Provide a 'startling fact' which relates to your main theme.
2. Tell a 'strong and relevant anecdote'.
3. Give a 'striking example' which illustrates one of your themes.
4. Pay your audience a compliment.
5. Raise a 'challenging question'.
6. Tell a joke.

(pp. 133–138)

For all these openings, his advice is that they should clearly relate to the main topic that you are presenting. This can be a particular problem for opening 6. The presenter who starts with an irrelevant joke will be seen by the audience as patronising or unprofessional.

Lewis also suggests six 'classic closes':

- The 'surprise ending', where you make a comment which offers an original twist on your main argument.
- The summary.
- A joke.

*continued . . .*

**BOX 12.2 *Continued***

- An 'upbeat or uplifting exhortation'.
- A 'call to action'.
- A final compliment to the audience.

(pp. 139–152)

Of course, there are other alternatives, but don't forget the following important principles when you choose your opening and closing.

The opening comments establish the tone of what you are going to say and also establish your credibility. It can be very difficult to rescue a presentation from a poor or indecisive opening.

In most business presentations, the opening few minutes should provide clear signposts so the audience know where you are going and what you are trying to cover. Otherwise, the audience will place their own interpretation on what you are trying to do.

The closing remarks will leave your audience with a particular impression. You need to make sure that this confirms and reinforces the main argument you have offered.

Psychological research suggests that we often remember the opening and closing parts of a presentation and tend to forget the details in the middle.

## CRITICAL ISSUES AND SKILLS IN PRESENTATIONS

Emphasising the common points in the approaches listed above, we suggest that the most critical questions to raise are as follows:

- Do you have clear objectives?
- Do you know your audience? (What are they expecting? What views do they already have on the topic?)
- Do you have a clear structure?
- Is your style of expression right?
- Can you operate effectively in the setting? (What technology are you using? How confident are you with it?)

### Critical skills

Baguley suggests five 'core' skills:

- Clarity
- Emphasis
- Using examples
- Organisation
- Feedback.

(Baguley, 1994, p. 107)

We have already stressed the importance of organisation, so it is worth making comments on the other four skills. As a cautionary tale, we offer an embarrassing example of how not to do it in Box 12.3.

### *Clarity*

As the size of the audience increases, so your chances decrease of simply defining what your audience will understand. You need to be especially careful with technical terms and jargon. Consider the jargon surrounding many descriptions of computer systems and see which of the following speakers you would prefer to explain a new package to you. This example illustrates the point that you can explain in a way that most levels of user will follow if you use everyday analogies.

### *Emphasis*

Good presenters usually give you a very clear sense of their main points. In other words, they emphasise what they think are the most important parts of what they say. There are various ways of doing this, including:

- Using NVC to emphasise the verbal message, such as gestures.
- Pausing before key points.
- Stressing key parts of the sentence.
- Using rhetorical devices to emphasise: as in the recent British political party slogan 'We have three priorities: education, education and education', or by saying 'And if there is one thing I would like you to remember from this talk, it is . . .'
- Signposting that a main point is coming: 'and this highlights one of the most important things I have to say'; 'and so my three main concerns are . . .'

Of course, visual aids can be a major vehicle to convey the emphasis. One final point is the value of a brief handout to summarise main points.

**Table 12.2** *Different speaker styles*

| *Speaker A* | *Speaker B* |
|---|---|
| 'I want to explicate and demonstrate the additional functionality' | 'This package can do things we can't do on the present system. I want to explain what the package can do and show you how it does it' |
| 'We've redesigned the user environment for improved ease-of-use' | 'We've redesigned how it looks on the screen to make it easier to use' |

### *Using examples*

Baguley suggests that examples on their own are 'not sufficient' (p. 108). He draws on the work of Brown and Armstrong who suggest that examples should be used to illustrate general rules in a particular sequence, depending on the audience, as follows:

- If the audience is familiar with the topic but need to review or be reminded of the rule, you can use either the rule – example or the example – rule sequence.
- If the audience is not familiar with the topic, you should use the rule – example – rule sequence. In other words, you tell them the rule, give them an example, and then remind them of the rule.

Another important point about examples is that they must clearly highlight the rule and not be open to very different interpretations or contain too much irrelevant detail.

### BOX 12.3 HOW TO SHOOT YOUR PRESENTATION IN THE FOOT IN THE FIRST FEW MINUTES

I (PH) recently attended a seminar where an experienced speaker from industry opened the afternoon session (using PowerPoint). He included all the following statements in his opening few minutes:

- 'This is the graveyard slot, just after lunch.'
- 'The previous speakers have said much of what I'm going to say. . .'
- 'Some of you will have seen these slides before.'
- 'You can go to sleep now.'
- 'This is not the most exciting theme of the day.'

No prizes for guessing how much interest and enthusiasm this presentation generated in the audience!

## PRESENTATION TECHNOLOGY

Only a few years ago, the *only* presentation technology mentioned in many guidebooks was Microsoft PowerPoint (e.g. Levin and Topping, 2006). PowerPoint is now the 'conventional method' and it has been criticised for the restricted way it is often used. For example, one senior manager advises us to 'constantly question to get beneath the platitudes of PowerPoint presentations' (Woodford, 2012, p. 31).

The reliance on standard techniques such as bulleted lists and stock visual aids does not guarantee interest or enthusiasm and has generated the phrase 'Death by Powerpoint' – searching for this phrase online will take you to this subheading on the Wikipedia PowerPoint page and will point to multiple sources of advice on how to avoid this misery.

More importantly, the unthinking use of PowerPoint has been blamed for some serious misrepresentations and distorted arguments. One of the most serious examples is the work by Edward Tufte on the engineering presentations used by NASA where the standard method was PowerPoint (www.edwardtufte.com/bboard/q-and-a-fetch-msg?msg_id=0001yB&topic_id=1). Tufte analyses the PowerPoint slides used in 2003/2005 and it is well worth looking at his detailed analysis of particular slides to see how technical data should *not* be reported. His analysis reinforces the conclusions of the Columbia Accident Investigation Board that 'distinctive cognitive style of PowerPoint reinforced the hierarchical filtering and biases of the NASA bureaucracy'. Important technical issues were effectively buried in the detailed bulleted lists of PowerPoint presentations such that the important safety messages were not revealed or highlighted. He concludes that 'for nearly all engineering and scientific communication, instead of PowerPoint, *the presentation software should be a word-processing program*, capable of capturing, editing, and publishing text, data, tables, data, graphics, images, and scientific notation'.

As a result, you need to consider very carefully the nature of the information and messages you wish to present. Looking at the examples in Tufte's article above, we would say that the problem lay not just in the default structures of Powerpoint but in the way it was used by the NASA scientists and engineers. They could have used the software in a much more flexible way and they could have supplemented the presentations with detailed technical notes in different formats. However, they did not and this led to tragic and avoidable accidents.

Whatever the type of information you are presenting, we suggest that you need to avoid the 'mindless' application of PowerPoint and develop a broader range of skills. You should consider a range of alternatives, such as the following.

*Using PowerPoint in a more flexible and varied style, especially if that is the standard organisational system.*

- One of our colleagues is a very enthusiastic user of PowerPoint on the grounds that it offers a lot of control over the space on the screen. However, he never uses any of the standard templates and designs his own from scratch. You may not be able to do this if you have to conform to an institutional template but you can use the variety of slide styles to ensure that you are not burying or obscuring important information.

*Using other software such as Keynote from Apple to take advantage of different styles and templates.*

- There are now other presentation packages such as Apple's Keynote which offer a similar broad range of facilities to PowerPoint.
- There is an increasing range of presentation packages which enable quick construction of simple messages with libraries of images and icons to help you. Examples include Haiku Deck and Adobe Voice – see the website for further details and discussion.

*Using software with a very different style of navigation such as Prezi.*

- Prezi treats your presentation as a giant canvas and zooms in and out on the particular slides which you move to. We think this should be used very carefully as the 'roller-coaster' transition between slides can be disorienting.

*Using embedded presentation tools*

- An example of a presentation tool is the presentation builder in our preferred concept mapping software (Cmap – http://cmap.ihmc.us) or alternatives available in many mind map applications.

Whatever software you choose you should make sure that you are thoroughly familiar with:

- The navigation controls and options.
- The computer set-up in the location. Screen resolution on the data projector can be a particular problem if you are using your own laptop or tablet.

## Alternative presentation strategies

There are also some important alternatives to the conventional presentation strategy of 'delivery plus questions/comments'.

### *Using pre-presentation surveys*

The availability of free or inexpensive survey tools like Survey Monkey or Google Forms means that we can all prepare simple surveys to test opinions.

### *Polling the audience during the presentation*

There are various ways of doing this, including a number of ways of integrating polls into standard Powerpoint presentations.

### *Incorporating the back-channel for discussion and comment*

### *Flipping the presentation*

The idea of the flipped classroom has received considerable publicity over the last few years although the method has a longer history than some current accounts give credit for. In its simplest form the method reverses the conventional lecture and seminar structure that has been a main feature of further and higher education. The presentation which was the traditional lecture is made available online in advance so that students come to the face-to-face class session having worked through the basic content and ready to engage in workshop and/or discussion activity. This has a number of advantages, including the fact that students can work through the content at their own pace and at a time which suits their own lifestyle.

## USING VISUAL SLIDES WHICH ENGAGE THE AUDIENCE

An important aspect of any presentation is to use visual images and style to support the argument you are making. Robin Williams (2010) suggests that we apply four general principles of 'conceptual presentation design' as we develop and plan the presentation:

- *Clarity* – making sure that your presentation is 'clear and understandable and that viewers can easily assimilate your information'.
- *Relevance* – eliminating all irrelevant material and making everything relevant to the specific audience.
- *Animation* – using animations to clarify your argument.
- *Plot* – making sure that you 'tell the story'.

You can then apply a further four principles of 'visual presentation design' to deliver a professional impression through your slides:

- *Contrast* – using contrast, help organize information on your slides.
- *Repetition* – keeping some constant elements on the slides to give a coherent impression.
- *Alignment* – keeping items aligned.
- *Proximity* – using spacing to show the audience which information goes together.

## CAN YOU HANDLE A VIRTUAL PRESENTATION?

Increasing pressures on time and resources have led to the increasing use of virtual presentations – webinars – using desktop conferencing software, in both the commercial and educational worlds. The software is easy to use and will run effectively on any modern desktop or laptop PC and more recently tablets. This form of presentation will continue to grow and you should be prepared and able to use it. These presentations are often recorded so you have an additional incentive to make a good impression.

All of the suggestions made earlier in this chapter about face-to-face presentations (the importance of objectives, structure, etc.) also apply to virtual presentations. There are some additional things to worry about and prepare for.

### Your on-screen presence

You are presenting to an audience you probably cannot see. Even the best large-screen systems can only give you a partial view of the audience and you will not be able to focus on individuals in the same way that you can in a face-to-face presentation.

## Back-channel

Webinar software typically allows the audience to interact with you in different ways – voting on a question, asking questions by signalling for access to the microphone, and the ongoing chat box which allows anyone to type a comment or message. How do you manage all these?

Some experts argue that this complexity means that you should adopt a team approach to avoid the overload of multitasking. In a team approach, the presenter focuses on his/her arguments and engaging the audience and recruits a colleague or colleagues to manage the technical process and channel the questions/comments (e.g. Koegel, 2010). We have used this process effectively in large conference sessions which brought together an audience in the room and virtual delegates from across the world. For smaller session and audiences, we think that an experienced presenter can effectively manage the whole process. For more suggestions on this, see the guide produced by Peter Chatterton for JISC – Designing for Participant Engagement: www.jisc.ac.uk/whatwedo/programmes/elearning/collaborate guidance.aspx.

### SUMMARY

- Presentations are increasingly common in organisations. You should be prepared to confidently deliver presentations where the presentation flows and is clearly organised.
- There are two main ways to resolve anxieties about presentations. First, you can make yourself feel less nervous by using relaxation techniques and being well prepared. Second, you can behave in ways which conceal your nerves.
- Characteristics of effective presentations include a clear structure which is communicated to the audience. Other important issues are clear objectives, how far you know your audience, your style of expression, and whether you can operate effectively in the setting. All depend on the audience and context.
- Microsoft Powerpoint is the industry-standard presentation software so you need to be able to use it. However, you also need to decide when and where to use different software or a different approach.
- There are some important alternatives to the conventional presentation strategy of 'delivery plus questions/comments'. Alternatives worth considering include: the use of pre-presentation surveys; incorporating the back-channel; flipping the presentation.
- Increasing pressures on time and resources have led to the increasing use of virtual presentations – webinars – using desktop conferencing software and you should be prepared and able to use this form of delivery.

## FURTHER READING

Aziz, K. (2000) *Presenting to Win: A guide for finance and business professionals.* Dublin: Oak Tree Press.

Bowman, L. with Crofts, A. (1991) *High Impact Business Presentations: How to speak like an expert and sound like a statesman.* London: Business Books.

Provan, D. (2009) *Giving Great Presentations.* Southam: Easy Steps.

This trio of books offer interesting comparisons on effective techniques and approaches. Aziz summarises the techniques which his company teaches to business professionals. Bowman argues that many of the 'standard guides' are wrong and offers his company's training system. The main principle is that you do not learn a range of 'new techniques' – you simply need to develop your normal style of conversation. Provan is an example of a typical current practical guide.

Koegel, T.J. (2010) *The Exceptional Presenter Goes Virtual.* Austin, TX: Greenleaf Book Group Press.

This contains useful practical advice on techniques for virtual presentation.

Reynolds, G. (2011) *The Naked Presenter: Delivering powerful presentations with or without slides.* Berkeley, CA: New Riders.

Reynolds is one of the best known American advocates of a 'natural' approach to presentations – see his blog at: www.presentationzen.com.

Tufte, E.R. (2006) *Beautiful Evidence.* Cheshire, CT: Graphics Press.

You can find further details of the range of Tufte's work at: www.edwardtufte.com/tufte/

Williams, R. (2010) *The Non-Designer's Presentation Book: Principles for effective presentation design.* Berkeley, CA: Peachpit Press.

This book offers further details on the principles for slide design we used in this chapter with many examples and illustrations.

## Chapter 13

# How can we build effective teams?

## INTRODUCTION

Many organisational analysts relate the success of an organisation to the levels of teamwork it employs. Some writers have even suggested that teams will be the 'primary building blocks of company performance in the organization of the future' (Katzenbach and Smith, 1998, p. 173). Certainly, many companies worldwide have invested in team training for staff. For example, it is claimed that the majority of 'top trainers' in the UK use the model of team roles explained in this chapter (according to Belbin, 2000).

We need to know the essential characteristics of a successful team, define the most important processes which contribute to effective teamwork and work out what can go wrong when we try to develop teams. This chapter confronts all these questions and emphasises that the quality of communication, allied to the quality of the team members, makes the real difference. And we now have a range of new technologies which can either help or impede this communication.

This chapter also highlights another important issue. Organisations can consider the more fundamental challenge of moving to a team-based structure. This is a radical reorganisation of the way work is designed and allocated. We identify some of the main issues.

### OBJECTIVES

*This chapter will:*

- define an 'effective team';
- show how important effective teams are to modern organisations and comment on moves to 'empower' work teams;
- analyse important processes which can influence group and team working, including team roles, leadership and problem-solving;
- suggest ways in which new technologies can support and enhance teamworking;
- discuss how we can develop teams in organisations.

## WE NEED A TEAM!

Consider the following extract from a management meeting and decide whether their plan of action is likely to be successful. Jim is the senior manager:

HUGO: We've been contacted by ABC who are offering us an upgrade on the network software for a special price.
MO: We'd better check this out carefully before we commit ourselves.
JAN: Then we'd better ask a team to investigate it and report back quickly.
MO: You'll need Harry and Fran from my department – they've got the right technical expertise.
HUGO: We can't forget the finance – Michael and Mika should be involved.
SASHA: Don't forget the users – I would involve Helen from head office and Joe to represent the other sites.
PAT: That team will never work together – they are all too concerned with their own issues. Who is going to co-ordinate them?
JIM: They'll be all right. All they need is a clear deadline. It won't take them more than a couple of meetings.

What chance would you give this working group of working effectively as a team? What confidence would you have in their recommendations after a couple of meetings?

## WHAT MAKES A TEAM?

Jim, our senior manager in the conversation above, has no time for this question. As far as he is concerned, all you need to do is put together a group of people with the necessary technical expertise, give them a deadline and you can expect a clear result. However, that result may be disastrous. There are numerous examples of working groups, composed of intelligent people who also had the necessary technical skills, which made terrible decisions.

But what are the most important differences between 'teams' and 'groups'? Leading American experts, Katzenbach and Smith, distinguish different types of team/group and argue that high-performance teams are much more effective than working groups. Working groups are formed when staff meet together to share information and to co-ordinate and make decisions. This is very different from what they call a 'real team': 'a small number of people with complementary skills who are committed to a common purpose, performance goals, and a working approach for which they hold themselves mutually accountable' (Katzenbach and Smith, 1998). The critical differences they see between teams and working groups are the levels of commitment and the strong sense of mutual support and accountability. Think of a working group that you have been involved in. What happened when something went wrong? Did *everyone* feel *equally* accountable and did they *all* pull together to put it right? Or did the group search out and perhaps 'punish' the member who had made the mistake? According to Katzenback and Smith, a real team will always do the former – they will always take collective decisions and they will always hold themselves mutually responsible.

They suggest six basic elements of a team. High-performance teams score highly on *all* these elements:

- *Size*: is it large enough to do the job but small enough for easy communication?
- *Skills*: does the team have all the necessary skills?
- *Purpose*: is this 'truly meaningful' – do all members understand it and see it as important?
- *Goals*: are they clear, realistic, specific, shared and measurable?
- *Working approach*: is this also clear, shared, fair and well understood?
- *Mutual accountability*: is everyone clear on their individual and joint responsibilities? Do they feel mutually responsible?

Katzenback and Smith accept that working groups can be effective and make sensible decisions. However, they also argue that 'real teams' will be much more effective. They also define other varieties of group/team, described below.

## The pseudo-team

A working group may call itself a team when actually there is no real shared responsibility – the members act as individuals and are really only interested in the progress of their own department or area. This is the pseudo-team. Their failure to share and co-ordinate may make them perform worse than a working group which has fewer pretensions.

## The potential team

The potential team is the group which is trying to move to full teamwork but which is probably still not clear on its goals and priorities, and which is still struggling with the problem of individual responsibilities and loyalties. Whether it makes the transition will depend on the quality of the leadership/management and the commitment of the members. Box 13.1 gives an example of how *not* to manage this transition.

### BOX 13.1 HOW NOT TO MOVE TO TEAMS

The workers in the British factory of a large American corporation were called to a mass meeting on Friday afternoon. They received a presentation which talked about the advantages of 'self-managing teams' whereby the work team was responsible for setting targets and monitoring quality, and was left to get on with the job, without continual supervision from management. They were then told that the factory was moving to this system the following Monday morning and that all the existing supervisors had been reallocated to other work within the company. The presentation finished, the workers were thanked for their attention, and everyone went home for the weekend.

*continued . . .*

**BOX 13.1 *Continued***

What do you think happened on Monday morning? An immediate upturn in productivity and morale? Or confusion, chaos and anxiety? And why were an intelligent management group surprised when it was the latter?

The other major issue in this discussion about the nature of teams is the amount of control and power which the team has over its operations and progress. Many organisations have not just been training workers to work together more co-operatively, but also giving the teams more responsibility. These 'empowered' or 'self-managing' teams have discretion over how the work is completed and the assignment of tasks; they are also likely to be rewarded as a group (Hackman, 1990; Stewart *et al.*, 1999).

## GROUP AND TEAM PROCESSES

Turning groups into teams is not easy. It takes time and it depends on an understanding of fundamental group dynamics, issues such as:

- group development;
- team roles;
- leadership;
- problem-solving and decision-making;
- intergroup relationships (relationships *between* groups).

Looking at a few of these will highlight major issues.

## GROUP DEVELOPMENT

Many business texts paint a very definite picture of how groups change over time, as in: 'After a team has formed, normed and stormed then, and only then, can it move on to the most successful stage of team behaviour' (Nickson and Siddons, 1996, pp. 100–101). This account – four stages in a definite sequence – is based on the work of Tuckman (1965) who surveyed all the studies of small group development he could find and suggested this was the common pattern. Groups start with a period of uncertainty. They then move into a phase of conflict where members argue about the task and on a more personal basis. Roles and relationships then get established, but it takes some time before the group is really ready to get on with the job in hand.

However, is this the 'natural' or typical sequence for *all* small groups? Tuckman himself was not so certain, pointing out some limitations in the studies he surveyed. Nonetheless, his account has become the dominant model, as summarised in Table 13.1 in terms of the content – how members approach the task – and the process – how members relate to one another.

**Table 13.1** *Tuckman's four-stage model of group development*

| *Stage* | *Content* | *Process* |
|---|---|---|
| Forming | Members try to identify the task and how they should tackle it<br>The group decide what information they need and how they are going to get it<br>Members try to work out the 'ground-rules' | Members try to work out what interpersonal behaviours are acceptable<br>Members will be very dependent on the leader and the reactions of other members |
| Storming | Disagreement and argument over the task | Members are hostile to the leader and to other members |
| Norming | The group agrees on the task and how it should be done | Group members start to accept each other and group norms will develop |
| Performing | The group concentrates on completing the task | Group members take on roles which enable them to complete the task |

In 1977, Tuckman decided that this model could still account for all the studies he could identify, provided you added a final fifth stage – adjourning. In this final stage, group members know that the group is about to part or split up. They make efforts to complete the task and say farewells to the other members.

We have certainly experienced these phases in *some* project groups and teams we have been involved in. However, is this life cycle inevitable? In fact, several stage theories offer variations on the themes set out by Tuckman, and many of these suggest that stages can occur in various different sequences (e.g. Hartley, 1997, Chapter 4). For example, Susan Wheelan (1996) proposed five stages which usually occur in the order summarised in Box 13.2. She also pointed out exceptions: groups can get 'stuck' or 'regress' to a previous stage. For example, some groups remain dependent for long periods of time and cannot function without the leader present. Another example is the group which gets stuck in a conflict phase and self-destructs.

The important principle here is that members of groups should try to work out what stage of development they are in and act sensitively to 'move the group along' (see Box 13.2 for an example). The problem is that real work groups are not likely to follow the 'textbook' sequence of stages in such an orderly and predictable way. There are several good reasons why we can expect more complex and more fluid development:

- Membership may change, forcing the group to re-form in some way.
- The task facing the group may change.
- Deadlines may change.

## BOX 13.2 GROUPS CAN DEVELOP DIFFERENTLY

Susan Wheelan (1996) proposes five stages of group development, usually in the order shown in Table 13.2.

**Table 13.2** *Wheelan's model of group development*

| *Stage* | *What happens* |
|---|---|
| Dependency and inclusion | Members are very reliant on the leader |
| | Communication is very tentative and polite |
| | Members are anxious and fearful |
| | Members shy away from the task |
| Counterdependency and flight | Conflict occurs either between the leader and member(s) or between members |
| | Members continue to shy away from the task |
| | Individuals try to work out their roles |
| Trust and structure | Conflict is successfully resolved |
| | Norms and rules can now be decided |
| | Communication is more open |
| | There are fewer power struggles |
| | Members feel more secure |
| Work | The group works effectively |
| Termination | The group disbands having completed the task |

Wheelan also offers practical advice to members and leaders. Table 13.3 summarises critical advice for leaders and members of work groups at each stage. It is not just the leader who is responsible for helping the group develop.

**Table 13.3** *Working through Wheelan's stages of group development*

| *Stage* | *What leaders need to do* | *What members need to do* |
|---|---|---|
| Dependency and inclusion | Enable open discussion of values, goals, tasks and leadership | Request information about goals<br>Raise their personal concerns |
| Counter-dependency and flight | Make sure that the conflicting issues are dealt with constructively | Work to resolve conflicts constructively |
| Trust and structure | Organise in ways that make the group productive | Organise in ways that make the group productive |
| Work | Periodically assess how the group is going to ensure that it can adjust to any changes | Periodically assess how the group is going to ensure that it can adjust to any changes |

## UNDERSTANDING LEADERSHIP

An enormous range of books claim to unravel the mysteries of leadership: from social science research, through the literature from management and business studies, and on to the various leading personalities who want to tell us how to 'do it right'. You can also find interesting mixtures of fact and fiction, as we illustrate in Box 13.3. Although very diverse, many texts agree on a few fundamental points:

- leaders have special qualities which we can identify;
- leaders have an important effect on their organisations;
- we need leaders, and only one leader in each situation.

However, all of these views can be (and have been) disputed, at least in some contexts. Many researchers do not believe that we really understand enough about leadership and that we have ignored cultural factors.

### BOX 13.3 DIVERSE VIEWS OF LEADERSHIP

Many management texts on leadership have wandered into fantasy and parable to make their points more entertaining. For example, Wess Roberts's *Make it So* (1995) is a series of leadership lessons supposedly written by Captain Jean-Luc Picard – well known to film and TV audiences across the world as a previous captain of the starship *Enterprise*. Picard summarises some of his adventures and highlights the characteristics of the competent leader, including communication, initiative, focus and urgency. However, can we transplant the qualities required by a group of intrepid space travellers confronting the unknown on a regular weekly basis to the office or factory? You can ask the same question about Roberts's previous bestseller *The Leadership Secrets of Attila the Hun*.

To illustrate this diversity further, sample an article in the 1992 *Harvard Business Review*. This contained five parables based on lessons from the temples of the Kyung Nan province in Korea. These were intended to show:

> the essential qualities of leadership and the acts that define a leader: the ability to hear what is left unspoken, humility, commitment, the value of looking at reality from many vantage points, the ability to create an organization that draws out the unique strengths of every member.

Dominant views on leadership have changed over the years and some views have slipped out of favour. For example, the search for personality traits and characteristics to underpin leadership was very popular in the early twentieth century. However, researchers found that different traits were important in different situations. Studies failed to show strong relationships between the leader's character and team performance. More recently, this line of research has been revived and some modern theorists emphasise the importance of the personality of the leader and how this is perceived by followers.

One recent example of this interest is the study of so-called charismatic leadership, who 'is regarded by his or her followers with a mixture of reverence, unflinching dedication and awe' (Bryman, 1992, p. 41). Rather than see this form of leadership as just emerging from the leader's personality, this style of leadership is often conceptualised as a particular form of relationship between leader and followers.

Recommendations about leadership often have strong moral or ethical overtones as illustrated by this quote from Simon Sinek: 'Leadership is about integrity, honesty and accountability. . . . To be a true leader, to engender deep trust and loyalty, starts with telling the truth' (Sinek, 2014, p. 150).

The difficulty with many of these recipes for success and the underlying studies is that they often focus on the 'movers and shapers' of corporations or on people who have responded heroically in emergencies. Do the same considerations apply when we think of more modest attempts to lead?

## The search for leadership functions and style

Looking at what leaders do has taken a number of directions, one of which was to try to define the functions of leadership. For example, a series of American studies suggested that effective leaders should score highly on both the following dimensions:

- initiating structure – i.e. organising to complete the task;
- consideration – i.e. developing good relations with the members.

In the UK, the work of John Adair has been used for leadership training in a wide variety of organisations. He suggests that leaders fulfil three functions:

- achieving the task;
- building the team, maintaining good working relationships throughout the team;
- developing the individuals in the team, dealing with the members' needs as individuals.

(Adair, 1986)

If we know what leaders do, perhaps we can also define an ideal leader style. Many texts still quote the classic study from 1939 by Lewin *et al.* in a way which suggests that democratic leadership was unequivocally the 'best'. This is not a very full picture of the results. The democratic groups did report the highest morale and satisfaction, kept working even when the leader was absent, and produced the highest quality models. The autocratic groups produced the most models but only when the leader was present. When the autocratic leader was absent, their groups quickly turned to misbehaviour as their preferred activity. Later studies produced mixed results, especially when comparing groups from different cultural backgrounds. Despite mixed research findings, the notion of an ideal style of leadership which blends concern for the task and support for the members is still popular.

### Contingency approaches

Given that research on style and functions did not always deliver consistent results, some researchers turned to more complex models, suggesting that effective leadership depends on (is contingent upon) a number of factors. This view can be illustrated by looking at the work of Fred Fiedler (who developed probably the most famous and still the most controversial of these models).

#### *Fiedler's contingency theory*

In the 1960s, Fiedler started from the idea that there were two types of leader – task and socio-emotional – and that these were taken on by different types of people. He developed a measure of these leadership styles and tried to investigate which style was effective in which situation. He concluded that the effective style depended on the amount of control which the leader was able to exert over the group. This control varied from situation to situation as it depended on three factors:

- relations between the leader and the members – how they liked each other;
- how structured the task was;
- the position power of the leader – the amount of authority which the leader can use legitimately in the situation.

Fiedler's results suggested that:

- task leadership is most effective where situational control is extremely high or extremely low;
- socio-emotional leadership is most effective where situational control is intermediate.

#### *Evaluating Fiedler*

Although Fiedler cites an impressive range of studies which support his conclusions, there have been important criticisms of his approach. In particular, critics have questioned whether leadership style is as fixed as he maintains. Other contingency theories have been developed which incorporate the level of maturity of the group members and the cultural context. Unfortunately, the message from this and other research summaries is that any simple model of leadership behaviour is almost certainly mistaken.

## LEADERSHIP AND MANAGEMENT

Another important issue is the difference between leadership and management, which are often discriminated in the way summarised in Table 13.4. The general distinction is between the notions of 'direction' and 'vision' associated with leadership and notions of 'competence' and 'efficient operations' associated with management. This is often summarised in the catchphrase 'leaders are people who do the right things and managers are people who do things right'.

***Table 13.4*** *Comparing leadership and management*

| *The leader* | *The manager* |
|---|---|
| Creates and communicates the vision | Controls |
| Develops power base | Is appointed |
| Initiate and lead change | Maintains status quo |
| Sets objectives | Concentrates on results |

Another way of dealing with this distinction is to say that leadership is simply *one* of the many roles which managers may play. One influential example of this approach is the work of Henry Mintzberg (1973). He suggests that managers can occupy ten roles: three interpersonal roles, including leader; three informational roles, including monitor and disseminator of information, and four decisional roles, including negotiator and entrepreneur. This concern with the roles associated with leadership is just one of the important recent trends in leadership research to which we now turn t.

## Recent developments in leadership research

We are still searching for a definitive account of leadership. Barbara Kellerman has spent a good deal of her professional life 'making a living from leadership' through writing, teaching and research. Yet her recent book castigates what she calls the 'leadership industry' (all the training, books, courses, etc.) for failing to deliver: 'while the leadership industry has been thriving . . . leaders by and large are performing poorly, worse in many ways than before' (Kellerman, 2012, p. xiii).

She argues that times have changed but our leadership practices have not responded and cites multiple examples of failure, including the finding that (in the USA) 'only a dismally low 7percent of employees trust their employer' (ibid., p. 170). Given this level of scepticism with the conventional wisdom, how can we respond?

If you are preparing for a leadership position, our recommendation is that you should look at proposals for leadership style which aim to respond to the world of digital connections such as the concept of the network leader which can be represented as three overlapping areas (Hall and Janman, 2010, pp. 91ff.):

- *Cognitive flexibility* – being able to face new and unanticipated challenges.
- *Strategic resilience* – with strong perseverance and focus on outcomes.
- *Network excellence* – the quality of our connection to others.

The importance of networking is paramount – 'everything that leaders think, do or aspire to is mediated through the thoughts and actions of others with whom they interact' (ibid., p. 109).

Another approach which ties in with much of the thinking is this book is the work by Clampitt and DeKoch based on the idea that effective leadership leads to progress and 'Leaders who are willing to embrace certain strategies and tactics can become progress makers' (Clampitt and DeKoch, 2011, p. 6)

We also suggest that you keep a watchful eye on other important themes which have emerged from recent research, including:

- *Vision, communication and networking* – emphasising the leader's need to communicate a clear vision for the group or organisation.
- *Culture and values* – emphasising the leader's role in building and maintaining an appropriate culture for the group to work in and for the leader to be concerned with values and goals.
- *Leadership as 'situated action'* – trying to provide a more sophisticated analysis of the situations that leaders find themselves in than you find in earlier contingency theories.
- *Leadership as skilled behaviour* – making a more detailed analysis of the skills and behaviour which 'good' leaders use.
- *Cultural differences* – recognising that there may be some common qualities required of leaders in many cultures but that these will be expressed differently.
- *Power and authority structures* – looking at the different forms of power which leaders may use and how followers see their power and authority.

**BOX 13.4 THE LEADER AS COMMUNICATOR**

Georgiades and Macdonell suggest that leaders must carry out four 'explicit imperatives':

- Scrutinise the external environment.
- Develop a vision and communicate its strategic implications.
- Develop the organisation culture so that it can deliver this vision and its strategy.
- Specify what management has to do to 'drive the desired culture'.

(1998, p. 21)

## THE SEARCH FOR GROUP ROLES

Until recently, the typical description of roles in small groups borrowed the three-way distinction originally set out by Benne and Sheats (1948):

- *group task roles* – such as initiating ideas, requesting or giving information;
- *group maintenance roles* – such as supporting or encouraging others, or resolving tension;
- *individual roles* – such as blocker or recognition-seeker.

But this is purely descriptive – it does not tell you which combination of roles is most effective. An important example of work which tries to answer this question comes from Meredith Belbin (Belbin 2010a and b).

## Belbin's team roles

Over a period of around ten years, Belbin and colleagues observed several hundred teams of managers on management games and exercises (Belbin, 2010a). He found that:

- the behaviours of team members were organised in a limited number of team roles;
- these team roles were independent of the members' technical expertise or formal status;
- managers tended to consistently adopt one or two of these team roles;
- these preferred team roles were linked to personality characteristics;
- the effectiveness of the team depended on the combination of team roles adopted by the team members.

Originally, Belbin identified eight team roles, as described below. He later added the role of 'specialist' who brings specialist expertise to the group. Their main contribution to the group is summarised in Table 13.5. Belbin's recipe for success is described in Box 13.5. You can find the latest development in his thinking at the website: www.belbin.com/rte.asp.

***Table 13.5*** *Belbin's team roles*

| *Role* | *Main contribution to the group* |
|---|---|
| Chair | Organises and co-ordinates |
| | Keeps team focused on main objectives |
| | Keeps other members involved |
| Team leader (shaper)* | Initiates and leads from the front |
| | Challenges complacency or ineffectiveness |
| | Pushes and drives towards the goal |
| Innovator (plant) | Provides new and creative ideas |
| Monitor-evaluator | Provides dispassionate criticism |
| Team worker | Promotes good team spirit |
| Completer | Checks things are completed |
| | Monitors progress against deadlines |
| Implementer (company worker) | Is practical and hard-working |
| | Focuses on the practical nitty-gritty |
| Resource investigator | Makes contacts outside the group |

* The titles in brackets are the original labels used in Belbin's earlier book, 1981.

## BOX 13.5 BELBIN'S RECIPE FOR SUCCESS

Once you know which roles are strongly represented in the group, you can check whether your group has all the recommended ingredients.

*The right person in the chair*
Make sure that the person who is carrying out the functions of chairing the group meetings has the appropriate personality and skills.

*One strong plant in the group*
Do you have at least one person who is both creative and clever in terms of the job at hand?

*Fair spread in mental abilities*
What is needed is a spread of abilities, including the clever plant and competent chair.

*Wide team-role coverage*
As many of the roles should be there as possible.

*Good match between attributes and responsibilities*
This is where members are given roles and jobs which fit their abilities and personal characteristics.

*Adjustment to imbalance*
If the group can recognise any gaps in its make-up, can it adopt strategies to make good these problems?

## SOME IMPLICATIONS OF BELBIN'S WORK

There are at least three very important implications of Belin's approach:

- All the roles are needed and valuable, unlike other approaches which suggest that some roles are destructive or negative.
- Groups *can* develop strategies to adjust any perceived imbalance.
- The third implication is best expressed as a question. Using Belbin's role descriptions, who is the leader? Is it the chair or the shaper? Belbin says it depends on the situation.

We still do not have enough research evidence to assume that Belbin offers the definitive account of group roles. There are both critical and supportive studies, especially concerning his self-report questionnaire. Belbin now uses Interplace, a computer-based system which integrates self-reports and observations. This system is only available on a commercial basis.

You can find early copies of his questionnaire in the *Management Teams* book from 1981, but you should also consider his recommendations that people should seek feedback from others (his system uses observer ratings as well as the questionnaire data) before accepting any classification. We are not necessarily accurate judges of our own behaviour.

Other systems of classifying roles are available which have some similarities to Belbin, including the Team Management Wheel from Margerison McCann at: www.tmsdi.com. You can also find free inventories on the Web often based on the Myers Briggs model of personality – e.g. at: www.teamtechnology.co.uk With any/all of these self-test systems, remember Belbin's warning that you should supplement any results with reliable feedback from others.

## PROBLEM-SOLVING AND DECISION-MAKING

There have been many studies which show that groups can fail to solve problems or make ineffective decisions if they ignore some of the following:

- *Determining the type of task* – for example: Can the task be divided into subtasks (divisible) or not (unitary)? Does the group need to produce as much as possible (maximising) or are they trying to achieve some predetermined standard (optimising)?
- *Problem-solving barriers, biases and traps* – for example: We may perceive selectively. We may have subconscious biases. We are very sensitive to contextual influences. We sometimes use inappropriate heuristics (a heuristic is a general rule of thumb). We use misleading frames of reference. We can fall into problem traps, such as overconfidence, which is usually inversely related to accuracy. The more confident people are, the more likely they are wrong.

## COMMUNICATION AND DECISION-MAKING

On the positive side, we can suggest that the quality of communication is critical on both simple and complex tasks. What is still not clear are some of the relationships between communication, interaction and other components of the decision-making-process.

We can say that group goals are important – e.g. groups working towards specific, difficult goals perform better than those groups without specific goals. Research in this area suggests the following practical strategies:

- setting goals which cover all aspects of the performance;
- providing regular feedback on progress;
- encouraging communication between members;
- encouraging and supporting planning activities;
- helping group members manage failure.

Another problem is where groups fail to recognise that they are not considering all the alternative information or courses of action which they need to arrive at a balanced decision. For example, in 1961, work by James Stoner suggested that groups would tend to move towards more risky decisions than those initially expressed by the individuals involved. He called this the risky shift. Later work by Serge Moscovici and Zavalloni concluded that the actual group process was what they called group polarisation – the group response will be more extreme than the average of the individuals but in the same direction as the individual tendencies. So, if the individual average is on the cautious side, then the group decision will be more cautious than the average of the individual opinions. If the individual average is on the risky side, the group decision will be more risky than the average of the individual opinions.

## Will this group make effective decisions?

How much trust would you place in decisions from a group which had the following characteristics?:

- they are very cohesive;
- they seem to be insulated from information from outside sources;
- as decision-makers, they rarely make a systematic search through alternative decision possibilities;
- they feel under stress to make quick decisions;
- they are dominated by a directive leader.

This describes a group which suffers from 'groupthink'. This concept comes from the work of Janis, who looked at historical accounts of poor group decisions. He decided that the particular group processes listed above lead to 'concurrence seeking tendencies' which then lead to faulty decisions. You need a cohesive group with all these processes at work to fall victim to groupthink, but the good news is that groups can work out strategies to avoid these problems. For example, Janis cited the Kennedy administration as victims of groupthink after the Bay of Pigs crisis in the 1960s, which nearly escalated into the Third World War. A year later, they successfully managed an even more serious crisis – they had put in place strategies to avoid groupthink. For example, they appointed one member of the group to play 'devil's advocate' at each meeting, making sure this role was rotated round the group so it did not become one person's responsibility. This made sure that every decision was scrutinised with a critical eye.

## How widespread is 'groupthink'?

Other investigators have queried some of Janis's conclusion, questioning whether his historical analysis is so clear-cut and arguing that he might have under-estimated political forces. Other researchers have questioned the role of cohesiveness. Some studies suggest the opposite relationship – low cohesiveness associated with groupthink – or no strong relationship between the two. The style of the leader has come out as very important in many studies.

More recent research looking at the detailed impact of group communication and interaction processes on decision-making has identified five critical functions:

- Is the problem thoroughly discussed?
- Are the criteria for a successful solution thoroughly examined?
- Are *all* realistic alternative solutions proposed?
- Are the positive aspects of each proposal fully assessed?
- Are the negative aspects of each proposal fully assessed?

(Hirokawa and Poole, 1996)

Problem-solving groups which can honestly claim to achieve all these functions in open communication have the best chances of success.

### BOX 13.6 ALTERNATIVE RECIPES FOR GROUP OR TEAM SUCCESS

Michael West (2012) offers one of the most comprehensive reviews of effective teamwork in organisations and suggests five main components, which we have turned into questions listed below:

- Does the team meet its task objectives?
- Do the team members develop in terms of well-being?
- Is the team viable over time?
- Does the team innovate effectively?
- Does the team co-operate effectively with other teams?

Other books offer variants along these lines such as Kohn and O'Connell (2009) with their six secrets.

## INTERGROUP RELATIONSHIPS

QUESTION: When is 'a' group not 'one' group?
ANSWER: When it's an intergroup!
In other words, when we communicate with another person we may choose to communicate with them on the basis of the social categories which we occupy, as in the following examples:

- I am lecturer, you are student.
- I am manager, you are trade union representative.
- I am engineer, you are from sales and marketing.

In each case, we may be more aware of our 'group responsibilities' than our more individual characteristics, and this can have a very powerful influence on our behaviour. The easiest way to illustrate this is to briefly describe a classic study from social psychology and explore its implications for organisational behaviour.

The Sherifs (Muzafer and Carolyn) wanted to understand the process of conflict development and discrimination, and wanted to use a 'natural' situation. They chose an American summer camp and did a series of naturalistic experiments where they manipulated events in the camp without the boys knowing about it. For example, they let boys make friends and then split them into two different groups to see if that would affect subsequent competition; they developed solidarity in groups before they introduced competitive situations; they set up 'frustrations' which affected both groups in camp to see how they would react.

They were surprised how easy it was to create discrimination as opposed to 'healthy competition' and noticed how the groups changed to focus on this conflict. Both groups developed biased perceptions ('We're OK but they are rubbish!'); groups became more cohesive; leadership became task-centred and authoritarian. They were also surprised how difficult it was to resolve the conflict and to restore open communication between the groups: only a *series* of what they called 'superordinate goals' made any real difference. Superordinate goals are goals where both groups need to co-operate on something which is equally important to both of them.

The Sherifs suggested that this conflict and the breakdown in communication was a product of the conflict of interests – the groups attempted to build their self-esteem by winning the conflict. Later research suggested that intergroup conflict could be much more deep-rooted in the way we build our sense of self-identity by comparing ourselves with other groups (see Hartley, 1997, Chapter 9).

We cannot resolve the theoretical issues here but we can highlight important implications for organisational life. An organisational team which contains members from different areas or functions within that organisation may fail because members may have negative stereotypes of the other members and may use the team to foster their own group interests. In other words, the team becomes an arena for intergroup conflict. For example, Putnam and Stohl (1996) describe several studies which show how cross-functional teams can manage and control intergroup differences or can fail to do so. One team was characterised by 'win–lose' negotiation, strong allegiance to the home department and continuing 'power plays'. The members took every opportunity to highlight departmental differences, including a series of sarcastic wisecracks about ordering and paying for lunch. This continuous conflict 'stifled decision making and led to delays in product introduction' (Putnam and Stohl, 1996, p. 160). It is difficult to see how the techniques for improving meetings we suggested in the last chapter would make much difference to this situation until the more deep-rooted conflict had been confronted.

In contrast, groups which were sensitive to these problems managed much better – for example, where the different department representatives worked very hard to create 'win–win' negotiations (in other words, trying to create superordinate goals which everyone could commit to). This highlights the importance of negotiation and communication processes, recognising that there are likely to be different views of reality, as illustrated in Box 13.7.

### BOX 13.7 MULTIPLE VIEWS OF REALITY

One consequence of intergroup difficulties is that there are multiple perceptions of reality. We expect that different groups will have views of reality which reflect their experience and interests, but sometimes this can have very serious consequences. An example is the accident which befell the NASA space shuttle – *Challenger* – which exploded just after take-off after a component failed. Subsequent investigations showed that the potential for this disaster had been recognised and investigated by NASA engineers. So why was the launch given the go-ahead? Could one problem have been the different perceptions held by different groups in the organisation? Yiannis Gabriel contrasts the claims by management that communication was 'open and free' and resolved any technical issues with other testimony that engineers 'agonised over flaws in their equipment' but 'did not feel that they could voice their concerns' (Gabriel, 1999, pp. 2–5). For further comment on *Challenger*, see Hartley, 1997; for a personal account of the commission which investigated the accident, see Feynman, 1988.

## HOW CAN WE DEVELOP MORE EFFECTIVE TEAMS AND WORKING GROUPS?

One approach is simply to identify all the process problems which might be impeding the group progress and try to resolve each one in turn. Robbins and Finley (1997) list 14 major problems, including confused goals, bad leadership, lack of team trust and unresolved roles. For each problem, they identify the main symptom to observe and a possible solution. For example, consider the problem of unresolved roles. The main symptom is that 'team members are uncertain what their job is' and the solution is to 'inform team members what is expected of them' (ibid.,1997, p. 14).

They also suggest that teams must be moved 'through stages towards success' (p. 187). They use Tuckman's four-stage model and again suggest that '*all successful teams* go through all four of these stages' (p. 187, our italics). Their strategy for team development depends on recognising which stage your group has reached and knowing how to move it on to the next stage.

A similar list of problems comes from Joiner Associates (Scholtes, 1988), a leading team of American management consultants. They include clarity in team goals, clearly defined roles, clear communication, beneficial team behaviours (what we described earlier as positive task and social behaviours), well-defined decision procedures, balanced participation, established ground rules and awareness of the group approach. They also add an improvement plan, including a flow chart of the project in hand which defines necessary resources and assistance – and use of the scientific approach – which is the insistence that opinions are supported by data and that the group avoids jumping to conclusions and unwarranted assumptions.

Many of these notions are very similar to Katzenbach and Smith's high-performing teams, which we discussed earlier. Another example based on observation of a real 'world-class' team in action is from Hilarie Owen (1996). Once again, the team is characterised by expectations and striving for outstanding performance. Strategies and skills required to create such teams include open communication, negotiating the success criteria, planning both the goals and the process, and effective leadership. A more recent example with a range of case studies comes from

The context in which the team operates is important. McIntyre (1998) argues that management teams face distinctive challenges – for example, they are composed of individuals who will be leaders in their own departments, but who have to work collectively to make critical decisions.

## DIFFERENT WAYS OF MENDING TEAMWORK

West (2012) suggests the main types of team-building interventions. These have different aims and scope, and will satisfy different needs and different situations.

### *Team start-up*

A newly formed team may need work on clarifying the team objectives, deciding the member's roles and co-ordination, and other forming issues.

### *Regular formal reviews*

This may involve 'away-days' where the team takes a day out of the usual routine and environment to reflect on how things are going and being done.

### *Addressing known task-related problems*

This also involves some time out but perhaps not so much as an away-day to focus on a very specific problem.

### *Identifying problems*

This is where the focus of the team review is on identifying task-related problems, where a team feels that it is not functioning as effectively as it could but is not sure why. This may involve discussion or some questionnaire analysis or use of an external facilitator.

### *Social process interventions*

Here the focus is very much on the social climate and member relationships.

### *Role clarification and negotiation*

West describes a useful exercise for this on p. 100.

## NEW TECHNOLOGIES AND TEAM BEHAVIOUR

David Sibbert suggests and illustrates a number of ways in which teams can now incorporate new technologies into their work and group process (Sibbert, 2011, pp. 219ff.), including:

- Teleconferencing with documents distributed beforehand.
- Web conferencing with documents on-screen plus audio links and Web chat.
- Use of graphics tablets and shared document access to develop collaborative documents.

Perhaps the most important point is that these methods will certainly add value to a team that has already developed effective team dynamics. Planting new technology on an already dysfunctional group is likely to simply speed up or further complicate the mess.

## RETURNING TO SELF-MANAGED TEAMS

Richard Hackman argues that their success depends on three factors:

- The group task is 'well designed' so that members are motivated by a task which is 'meaningful'and receive clear feedback.
- The group is 'well composed' so that members have the necessary range of skills.
- The group's authority and accountability is clearly specified.

(Hackman, 1990)

Ulich and Weber (1996) emphasise that teams must tackle 'whole tasks', where they can set goals, plan what needs to be done, decide how the work should be done, and receive clear feedback on their performance.

These recommendations complement the points we made at the beginning of the chapter when we looked at the differences between groups and teams. The important implication is that organisations cannot just expect these groups to happen overnight: 'the spread of 'self-managing teams' will be a slow process . . . it involves very complex organisational interventions, which must be consistent both with the values of an organization and its technology' (Ulich and Weber, 1996, p. 273).

Research studies reinforce these issues. For example, Stewart *et al.* (1999) provide a number of examples of team interventions in organisations. They highlight some major organisational benefits: for example, Texas Instruments Malaysia (TIM) moved to an organisational design based on self-managing work teams in the 1990s and reported major savings, quality improvements, low absenteeism, etc. They also highlight some of the major lessons which can be drawn from this and other cases:

- team practices must be compatible with overall company philosophy and values, and with a revised organisational structure;
- team practices must be supported by senior management;

- team members will need new social and technical skills to become self-managed;
- effective implementation is a long and careful process.

It took TIM 12 years to benefit from the implementation of team-based practices.

## Not everyone is convinced

Not everyone is convinced that the way forward for large organisations is to move to team-based structures. For example, Elliot Jaques (1994) argues that organisations must employ *individuals* who are accountable for the work of their subordinates, and that groups cannot take on this accountability. He argues that improving leadership is the best way forward.

Kanter (1994) suggests that the practical difficulties of implementing team-based structures may not be worth the effort and some researchers question the nature of any impact. A very detailed case study from Barker (1999) suggests that the move to self-organising groups may replace external control with an even more demanding regime of control based on peer pressure.

### SUMMARY

- Truly effective teams differ from working groups. Research suggests that the critical differences are the level of commitment and the strong sense of mutual support and accountability.
- In order to create effective teams, we must understand the most important processes which can influence group and team working, including group development, team roles, leadership, problem-solving and intergroup behaviour.
- There are several models of group development but none are inevitable if the members make an open attempt to review their processes.
- The role of leader may be critical and modern views of leadership place particular emphasis on aspects of communication.
- Models of team roles (e.g. Belbin) suggests that we all have consistent preferences. The effectiveness of the team depends on the combination of team roles adopted by the team members. The outcome is not predetermined – the effective group adjusts to any imbalance in roles.
- Group communication and interaction processes have an important impact on decision-making.
- Teams which are sensitive to intergroup issues tend to be more effective as they can communicate and negotiate in ways which can minimise these problems.
- We can develop teams through improved communication, either by conscious reflection on their major processes and adopting strategies for effective working or by using specific team-building interventions.
- It is important to choose the right team-building intervention to suit the situation: different types have different aims and scope, and will satisfy different needs.
- Many organisations now use self-managed teams. They are not a 'quick fix' and involve very complex organisational interventions.

## FURTHER READING

Clampitt, P. and DeKoch, R.J. (2011) *Transforming Leaders into Progress Makers: Leadership for the 21st century.* London: Sage.

Also see their website at: www.imetacomm.com/pm.

Hall, T. and Janman, K. (2010) *The Leadership Illusion: The importance of context and connections.* Basingstoke: Palgrave Macmillan.

As well as valuable discussions of social capital and connected leadership, they suggest important trends for organisational structures.

Hartley, P. (1997) *Group Communication.* London: Routledge.

Contains more detailed discussion of the earlier research.

Kellerman, B. (2012) *The End of Leadership.* New York: HarperCollins.

A very detailed and interesting critique of the 'leadership industry'.

Sibbert, D. (2011) *Visual Teams: Graphic tools for commitment, innovation and high performance.* Hoboken, NJ: John Wiley.

Contains many useful suggestions for practical group process with graphic tools.

West, M.A. (2012) *Effective Teamwork: Practical lessons from organisational research* (3rd edn). Oxford: BPS Blackwell.

This book is our recommendation for a comprehensive recent review of the research.

Chapter 14

# Change, communication and future-gazing

## INTRODUCTION

The purpose of this chapter is to discuss how communication relates to organisational change and then suggest trends which may be particularly important in the future for our professional practice in communication at work.

Modern organisations experience different influences and different types of change. This shows the importance of recognising the stage or process which an organisation is experiencing and monitoring their environment. Examples of specific strategies for implementing change show how effective communication is essential – in both the acceptance and implementation of organisational change. This also emphasises the need for management to adopt a strategic and planned approach to communication. Otherwise, even the most imaginative and creative change strategy is likely to misfire.

Writing anything that requires predicting the future, particularly if it involves technology, is fraught with pitfalls. Just look back at predictions made by people supposedly 'in the know': the chairman of IBM predicting 'a world market for maybe five computers' (1943); a senior employee of a US telecommunications company saying 'this "telephone" has too many shortcomings to be seriously considered as a means of communication' (1876) and the head of a large computing company saying 'there is no reason anyone would want a computer in their home' (1977). The final part of this chapter tries to avoid placing feet in mouth and suggests general trends to look out for rather than trying to predict the future in detail. As well as identifying some socioeconomic, cultural and technological trends, we suggest particular implications for the ways we manage our professional development in future.

## OBJECTIVES

*This chapter will:*

- show how communication is involved in different ways in change processes and strategies;
- show how communication is an essential feature in both the acceptance and implementation of organisational change;
- identify key social, cultural, technological and economic trends and scenarios in the ways we work, live, communicate and learn;
- (hopefully) stimulate you to continually reflect on these trends and scenarios and adopt the 'review, plan and improve' philosophy.

## CASE STUDY: HOW DO WE EVALUATE CHANGE?

All organisations have projects of one kind or another and project evaluations typically aim to learn from successes and failures. The reality is sometimes different from the rhetoric, though, with human factors creeping in, bringing in a raft of agendas not necessarily associated with the spirit and intentions of the project. Project evaluations can be exercises that 'are done to' the project team – i.e. external personnel carry out the evaluation often in the spirit of an audit, and often tend to be more backward-looking rather than learning and moving forward. All these points tend to make 'evaluation' a rather daunting and unwelcome exercise for project teams. The exercise can become one of political 'face-saving', losing the opportunity to use the project outcomes to improve organisational practice.

In the UK higher education sector, a different approach has been adopted by institutions carrying out innovation and change projects which use new technologies and media for curriculum transformation. They have developed a more 'self-review' approach to evaluation which starts early on in the project and is more 'facilitated' by an external evaluator, rather than having the external evaluator performing the evaluation at the end of a project. The evaluator sets up a wiki that is used as a framework for the self-review evaluation as a collaborative exercise for the project team and the project stakeholders. Such a framework has three key areas of focus:

1. *Establishing the outcomes*: looking at the relevant and usefulness of project outcomes, both anticipated and unanticipated.
2. *Benchmarking impact*: developing the 'vision' for long-term impact and doing a gap analysis (deciding what still needs to be done).
3. *Planning for sustainability and embedding*: action planning to plug the gap.

The use of a wiki to record all this allows all the project stakeholders to contribute towards the evaluation and to build on each other's ideas. This creates a more collegiate and 'continuous improvement' approach to evaluation that starts early on in a project and means that the focus is always on the long-term impact. It also means that changes to the project can be made as the project progresses if the evaluation process makes recommendations to do so, unlike an end-of-project evaluation, where it is often too late to make changes.

## WHAT ARE THE DIFFERENT TYPES OF CHANGE IN MODERN ORGANISATIONS?

Different definitions of the organisational environment suggest different types and 'triggers' of change.

### The organisational environment

There are several ways of categorising factors which make up the organisation's environment. One popular mnemonic – PEST – identifies four factors:

- *Political/legal* (including government legislation and ideology, employment law, taxation policy, trade regulations, etc.).
- *Economic* (including business cycles, inflation, interest rates, etc.).
- *Sociocultural* (including social mobility, lifestyle changes, attitudes to work and leisure, education levels, consumerism etc).
- *Technological* (including new discoveries, speed of technology transfer, rates of obsolescence, etc.).

These factors combine in particular ways to trigger certain changes.

Barbara Senior and Stephen Swailes (2010) suggest that organisations operate in at least three types of environment:

- *Temporal*: the historical development over time. This can be seen in two ways: in terms of the general cycle of development which affects all organisations, in particular industries or sectors; and in terms of the specific life cycle of the particular organisation.
- *External*: this is the sum total of the factors identified above in PEST.
- *Internal*: this is what Senior calls 'the first-line responses to changes in the external and temporal environments' (Senior and Swailes, 2010, p. 23). Examples could include the appointment of new management following a period of poor economic performance, or the installation of new computer software caused by changes in legal or fiscal requirements.

### Triggers and sense-making

Change can be 'triggered' in a number of ways. This depends on the organisation noticing or anticipating relevant change and responding appropriately. And this depends on communication. The history of commerce is full of examples of organisations which failed to appreciate key changes in their environment. For example, the British motor-cycle industry refused to believe that new, cheaper machines from Japan would affect their sales, reasoning that customers would pay more for 'traditional quality'. By the time they recognised the threat, the British industry was in terminal decline.

Many organisations have placed increasing emphasis on 'sense-making' – i.e. trying to ensure that their managers and staff are continually scanning the environment and their competitors' behaviour to look for signs of impending change. Management may use particular strategies to ensure this is done – e.g. setting up special groups or task forces with members drawn from across the organisation. These strategies will only succeed if the results of such monitoring are quickly and accurately communicated to the decision-makers within the organisation. If these decision-makers do not accept the need for change, the organisation may be in trouble. And this highlights the need for senior management to create an organisational culture which allows information of this sort to surface at high levels.

One issue which might prevent this 'surfacing' is the possible isolation of senior managers. This is a longstanding issue. Chaudry-Lawton and Lawton (1992) reported that senior executives can suffer from 'feedback starvation', where 'subordinates may constantly try to provide their leader with a flow of support and good news' (p. 7). If this happens, executives will not receive the full picture of the organisation's performance. This sort of problem can be exacerbated by poor management (see Box 14.1) or be alleviated by good management and sensible use of technology.

**BOX 14.1 WHO DO YOU CONSULT ABOUT CHANGE?**

Many of the on-screen features we take for granted in our modern PC can be traced back to developments by Xerox – the use of icons to represent the desktop, using the mouse to move objects around, etc. So why did not Xerox become the early market leader? Why was it left to Apple, who came along several years after? One factor was the way that Xerox demonstrated the prototype computer with these features (the Alto). The Alto was presented to the male Xerox executives and their wives. Many of the wives had secretarial or administrative experience and were immediately impressed with the machine and its ease of use. However, the men did not understand the benefits as they 'had no background, really, to grasp the significance of it' (one of the Alto inventors quoted in Shapiro, 1996, p. 127). You may not be surprised to realise who Xerox listened to! It would be nice to think that modern organisations had left behind sexist attitudes, but there is plenty of evidence that such practices are still prevalent.

## Type and rate of change

We also have to consider the rate and scale of the change involved. One useful and typical model here comes from Dunphy and Stace (1993) who suggest four different types of change:

- *Scale type 1*: fine tuning – i.e. change at department level such as new training methods.
- *Scale type 2*: incremental adjustment – i.e. gradual change to working practices, such as certain product lines being phased out over time.
- *Scale type 3*: modular transformation – i.e. radical change to one part of the organisation, such as outsourcing a particular function.
- *Scale type 4*: corporate transformation – i.e. radical change right across the organisation with major changes to the organisation's structures and procedures. This usually means a major overhaul of the organisation's values and priorities.

The drawback with this model is that it assumes that everyone in the organisation shares the same definition or understanding of the change involved. What senior management sees as incremental adjustment might be perceived as a much more fundamental shift by the employees directly involved.

Again, this raises issues of communication. In what terms is the change communicated to staff: how is it described? For example, consider the case of the organisation which wished to put all its salaried staff on a new 'more flexible' contract. Senior management extolled the virtues of the 'new, professional contract' in a series of meetings and in the company newsletter. They saw this as an incremental step towards creating a more flexible organisation. Staff saw the new contract as a fundamental shift in their relationship with senior management and reacted very strongly to the implication that their previous contract (and behaviour) was somehow 'not professional'.

There is also the question of the pace of change. Where the centre of the organisation is very powerful, it can almost literally change overnight.

## The organisational life cycle

Chapter 13 reviewed models of working groups and teams progressing through a series of stages. We can also suggest that organisations grow through at least four main stages:

- *Entrepreneurial*: the new organisation starts from a small number of people with good ideas. If it becomes successful and grows, it will confront a crisis of leadership – it must decide its future strategy.
- *Collective*: the organisation has grown, so the appropriate division of labour is critical. Departments or other subdivisions need to be managed and co-ordinated.
- *Formalisation*: the organisation is now big enough to need more formal systems and procedures. These could easily become over-bureaucratic and there may be a crisis of 'red tape'.
- *Elaboration*: the company has now reached a plateau and its performance may even be declining. Can it change to remain competitive? (Senior and Swailes, 2010, pp. 47ff.).

A further complication is that organisations can be affected at different times by 'waves' of change. Change does not just happen and go away – it continually reappears in various forms. A period of relative calm involving some incremental change may be followed by one or more periods of dramatic and turbulent change.

## STRATEGIES FOR CHANGE

We can also see the importance of communication within the change process if we review various strategies for change. There are various alternatives, involving different approaches to communication, including:

- education
- participation
- intervention/manipulation
- management direction
- coercion.

These vary in terms of the degree of management control and the opportunities for involvement for those who will be directly affected by the changes. Each strategy has potential benefits and problems. For example, using participation can be very time-consuming but increases the chances of acceptance. A very directive strategy may be quick but it may be resented and obstructed by the staff.

A review of organisational change theory and research in the 1990s suggested that an effective change message incorporates five components (Armenakis and Bedeian, 1999):

- this organisation needs to change;
- we can change successfully
- change is in our best interest;
- the people affected support the change
- this change is right for this organisation.

Four examples will illustrate the main issues:

- Lewin's stage models of the change process;
- Les Robinson's 'Changeology';
- dynamics of culture change;
- the 'learning organisation'.

### Lewin's stage modes of the change process

One of the most common models of the change process suggests three main stages:

- unfreezing
- changing
- refreezing.

This three-step model was first proposed by Kurt Lewin (1951) after a series of experiments looking at attitude change. He concluded that people must see a reason to move from their existing attitudes or beliefs. In other words, their existing attitudes must be 'unfrozen' to make way for new ones. After new attitudes have been adopted, there is a period when these new attitudes are tested out to see if they 'work'. The new attitudes will only become embedded if this refreezing process is successful.

A practical example of how this process can be neglected is the effectiveness of management training courses. Suppose such a course is designed to make supervisors more democratic in their leadership style. And suppose the course 'works' if we measure supervisors' attitudes immediately after the course. However, what if we send these supervisors back to an autocratic environment where nothing else has changed? Research into situations like this suggests that, after a few months, supervisors' attitudes will be more autocratic than they had been before the course. The refreezing stage has been ignored.

Johnson and Scholes offer a framework for managing strategic change which expands this three-step model.

#### *Unfreezing – organisational anticipation*

This may be down to management to persuade staff of the need to change, perhaps by highlighting external problems or threats.

#### *Organisational flux*

This is where 'competing views surface about the causes of, and remedies for, the problems' (p. 453).

#### *Information building*

During this stage, managers try to find information which supports their position. A proactive management will try to manage this process rather than leave it to political in-fighting. Johnson and Scholes suggest strategy workshops for management and the use of project groups to make sure that information and options are fully considered (the latest edition of their best selling text on corporate strategy is Johnson *et al.*, 2014).

#### *Experimentation*

Some new ideas are tried out.

#### *Refreezing*

Once new ideas have been adopted, organisations can use various methods to make sure that the new practices are thoroughly embedded and that staff are supported during this transition.

### Changeology

Les Robinson is described by his publishers as 'Australia's most experienced and knowledgable change facilitator'. He has distilled his experience of supporting and implementing change into six essential ingredients of successful change efforts:

- *'Positive buzz'* – when people share optimistic stories about change.
- *An offer of hope* – when people make the connection between a novel action and their own hopes and frustrations.
- *An enabling environment* – when people's environments make new behaviours easy to do and sustain.
- *A sticky solution* – when behaviours are reinvented to better fit people's lives.
- *Expanded comfort zones* – when people are helped to reduce their fears.
- *The right inviter* – when inspiring, trusted peers invite action.'

(Robinson, 2012, p. 49)

Robinson uses examples and case studies to argue that 'successful and sustained change efforts happen when (these) six different ingredients come together' (ibid., p. 12). His book also contains some useful tools and techniques to enable these ingredients.

## The dynamics of culture change

Many organisations have seen culture change as a major way of resolving problems and increasing competitiveness. Williams *et al.* (1993) suggest six main ways that organisations set about this:

- Changing the people in the organisation. This can be painful as many large programmes lead to redundancies or early retirement. Are the management open about this in their communication with the workforce? A less painful way of changing the people is to focus on the selection and recruitment process. Improving this process can ensure that new recruits are fully aware of and accept the company ethos before they join. Again we can highlight potential problems in communication. Will applicants really understand the full implications of the culture before joining? Will they be fully attentive to the company messages at recruitment or induction, or will they be more dismissive of the 'company PR'?
- Changing the people's positions in the organisation.
- Changing beliefs, attitudes and values.
- Changing behaviour. Many conventional psychological models of attitude and behaviour change suggest that you have to change someone's attitudes or beliefs before they will change their behaviour. However, there is also evidence to support the view that you can change behaviour directly and attitude change may 'follow on'. One example is action taken by many police forces to stamp out racism or other discriminatory behaviour. The focus in training and performance review is on making sure that the police officers *behave* in a non-racist way. If this behaviour is continually reinforced and rewarded, it will become the norm. Genuine long-term attitude change may then be the long-term result.
- Changing systems or structures. The systems often changed are reward, appraisal, budgeting and quality control.
- Changing the company image. Trying to increase the employee's commitment to the organisation is a common goal and this often involves internal and external

advertising, usually associated with some new logo or slogan. As with all promotional efforts, this must be tied to 'real' activities which the employees can recognise or the effort may create a more cynical reaction.

The importance of symbolic gestures and clear communication cannot be over-emphasised in relation to all these different strategies.

If communication is critical to successful culture change, it is also worth emphasising that communication must address the right issues. As an example of rapid cultural change in a large organisation, Shapiro (1996) cites General Electric (GE) in the early 1980s. Described around 1980 as 'thoughtful and slow-moving' (Deal and Kennedy, 1982), this same organisation was described by an employee only a few years later as follows: 'At GE, you perform or you die' (Shapiro, 1996, p. 52). This transformation was attributed to the man who became chairman in 1981, Jack Welch. According to Shapiro, Welch had acted directly upon what she calls '"the internal game", the set of implicit, unwritten rules about how to survive and excel within the organisation' (Shapiro, 1996, p. 53).

We have already commented many times in this book that messages can be interpreted at various levels, and that what is 'unsaid' can have a very powerful meaning. The 'hidden' rules which senior managers had recognised at GE in the 1970s was that good performance meant a level of growth on a par with the overall economy and that managers had to meet this performance level no matter what. Having worked as a senior manager himself under these conditions, Welch changed the rules immediately he took office. The new objective for every business within GE was to be number 1 or 2 within their sector with a substantial increase in business *every quarter*. Business units which did not meet these criteria were sold off, and over 100 left in the first 4 years of his reign, along with nearly 20 per cent of the staff.

Was this change successful? It did achieve economic gains in the short term, although you might find it difficult to persuade all the 80,000 or so people who left the company. It is difficult to identify the characteristics of long-term health within a company or organisation.

Welch's ideas and business practices continue to be controversial. At GE he instituted what he called differentiation in the annual performance review where managers had to rate their subordinates in the top 10 per cent, the middle 80 per cent, or the bottom 10 per cent. This meant the end of their GE career for the latter group – 'their manager helps them find their next job with compassion and respect' (Welch, 2013; see online at: http://online.wsj.com/news/articles/SB10001424052702303789604579198281053673534).

## Learning organisations as the answer?

One solution to problems of increasing and ongoing change which was strongly advocated in the 1990s was the notion of the 'learning organisation' – an organisation which actively embraces change as an ongoing and inescapable process, and where all employees commit themselves to continuous learning and self-improvement.

This approach challenges traditional models of organisational structure. For example, the traditional separation of research and development (R&D) into a specific department or section is abandoned on the grounds that everyone is responsible for contributing to development. As a result, the R&D function is merged into the production facilities.

Another important aspect of this form of organisation is the role and communication of the leader. Senge (1994) argued that learning organisations must abandon the traditional view of leaders 'as special people who set the direction, make the key decisions, and energise the troops' (p. 5). Instead, leaders must focus on the 'creative tension' created by the gap between where the organisation is at the moment and where it wants to be in the future. This also highlights the need for a coherent vision of where the organisation wants to be.

Senge then goes on to highlight how leaders can influence people to view reality at three different levels:

- *'Events'*: this is the analysis of current facts, or what he calls 'who did what to whom'.
- *'Patterns of behaviour'*: this is the attempt to identify trends and look for underlying patterns.
- *'Systemic structure'*: this is the 'most powerful' explanation as it looks for what *causes* the patterns of behaviour.

Whereas many organisations seem content to use the first two of these levels, Senge characterises the learning organisation as concerned with all three. An important role for the leader is to enable all staff to contribute to the debate and enquiry which will answer the questions raised at this third level.

## EVOLVING SCENARIOS AND THE IMPLICATIONS FOR COMMUNICATION

### Future working scenarios

We think that there are a number of developing scenarios, many of which we introduced in earlier chapters, which will be particularly significant.

#### *Globalisation*

This means different things to different people. For some, this is interpreted as certain types of jobs being transferred to emerging economies, although a more accurate picture focuses on international integration arising both from a business perspective as well as cultural integration. In business, it is not just about transfer of jobs, but a much broader context of global working and trading.

There are different views of how such trading will evolve: some foresee a 'scattered' world, reflecting a future of monopolistic unregulated competition while others see a more connected world where companies collaborate domestically and internationally with enlightened governments regulating for the global good. Underpinning such integration and potential collaboration is the Internet, energising global trading and driving forward the interdependence of economies, communications and cultures.

Whether the scattered or connected scenario of globalisation emerges, workers across the world will need to develop mutual understanding of each other's cultures, ways of working and communications. The Internet can potentially be a strong force for good in facilitating such understanding, although the attributes of the media present barriers to effective communication – e.g. the difficulty in knowing the cultural background of members of a social network and the lack of body language clues.

### *Portfolio careers and job change – look to the past to see the future*

In many developed economies, there is still the notion of a 'job for life'. This idea has been gradually eroding in the private sector (less so in the public sector) and this is leading to a whole range of different work arrangements – for example, full-time, part-time, contract, self-employment, loose networks of self-employed professionals and job-share, with large companies increasingly outsourcing their staffing and services to companies of all sizes. For the individual worker, this means concepts such as 'portfolio careers', less upward promotion and more horizontal career development, periods of unemployment and underemployment, and increasing part-time employment. All this is exacerbated by an ageing population, some of whom wish to continue working after official retirement, and economic crises which make it difficult for young people to gain their first experience of employment.

The key impact of the fragmentation of the jobs market is the need for individuals to take more control of their careers as early as possible, and recognising that careers may well include several major career changes.

### *Flexible and virtual working*

Flexible and virtual working is a concept that has been growing gradually and is often seen by employees as very desirable, although there are a range of challenges associated with it. The term 'flexibility' also means different things to different people: some see it purely in terms of flexible working hours while others see it as encapsulating ideas such as home-based working, mobile working, job-share, part-time working. The degree of flexibility is often inextricably aligned with the degree of job autonomy that employers allow – for instance, large management and IT consultancies often allow their employees a relatively high degree of autonomy, particularly if they are managed through 'results' rather than 'attendance'; in such cases, professional staff typically vary their working location to suit company and project needs – it may be at home, in the office, at client premises or even in more mobile scenarios such as hotels, rented meeting rooms, airports and restaurants/cafés.

The key to making such flexible and mobile working practical and efficient are ICT systems that, ideally, need to provide staff with the same access to communications, information and company resources that they would have if they were located in their offices. This presents many challenges to IT departments mostly based around security as well as compliance with a range of internal protocols and government regulations – e.g. data protection.

The challenges are not just technical. Some staff who move to home-based working can find the lack of social engagement and face-to-face communications with colleagues problematic. However, the concept of home/mobile working is maturing with a recognition of the need to address the lack of social communications. With increasing numbers of such workers, local networks of such home/mobile workers are developing and many staff, particularly those with children, recognise the benefits of flexible working in enabling them to blend everyday domestic activities (such as taking children to school) with their professional working activities. Technology is playing a key role too, in linking home/mobile workers together – e.g. the concept of the 'digital water-cooler' based on the 'water-cooler' moment, where staff in offices gather around a water-cooler to engage in social chat. Such digital water-cooler concepts are based around the use of social networks, instant messaging and Web-conferencing tools such as Skype and Google Hangouts, and while they cannot replicate a face-to-face experience, they can help staff to feel part of groups or communities, and to build bonds and bridges to a certain extent.

### *Blurring of professional and private lives*

The changes described above will lead to increasing blurring of professional and private lives, and the emergence of the 'prosumer' concept (individuals who are both consumers and producers in the digital world). For many staff, such blurring of professional and private lives creeps up on them until they suddenly realise that their online social interactions include both business colleagues and friends, and sometimes their physical networks have a similar blend. However, some people deliberately set out to maintain separation between their private and professional lives – e.g. by having separate identities on social media sites, although there is perhaps a rather large irony in embracing the concept of a 'private' life with social media.

### *Work–life balance*

It is extremely difficult to predict how future generations will cope with the concept of work–life balance. It is probably true that many in the current generation face challenges in achieving an acceptable work–life balance, due to pressures such as both parents working, high costs of housing and insecurities in the jobs market. Such pressures are likely to increase and may result in issues of isolation, inequality, rising cynicism, distrust of institutions, decline of happiness, gender identity issues, families being 'rearranged' and a mismatch between 'dream jobs' and reality.

### *Offices as meeting places*

Increases in flexible and mobile working beg the question 'What will offices be for?' There is likely to be a shift from offices housing all an organisation's staff to one of flexible working and meeting places. Such ways of working can already be seen in companies such as the large management consulting companies where the concept of 'hot-desks' is already established practice – staff bring their laptops to the office, find a spare desk to work at and then plug their laptop into the network. They can also typically book meeting rooms for meetings with colleagues and clients.

### *Collaboration, collaboration, collaboration*

How ever business and sector models emerge in the upcoming years, a core capability for all professional staff will be the capability to collaborate effectively – not just with local colleagues, but with business partners, suppliers, associates and clients – locally, nationally and internationally, and in different business models – e.g. supply networks, outsourcing. Some view collaboration in a rather minimalistic way – a sort of variation on working together, while others perceive true collaboration to be a core capability with many advantages – for instance, collaboration can result in more credibility, influence and ability to achieve objectives and can create sustained change.

### *Digital literacy is critical*

The thread running through all the above scenarios is the absolute dependence of organisations and individuals on IT systems to support the more flexible and mobile modes of working, and providing access to different communications channels, networks, systems, data and information. The concept of digital literacy will therefore become ever more important. As Chapter 2 described, this will not just be about skills in using IT systems; rather, it will require a more sophisticated capability for individuals and groups to be able to become more proactive in identifying, choosing and implementing technology in the pursuit of business goals.

### *Open innovation and new product development*

The open innovation idea emerged in the 1960s and has taken hold with the emergence of the Internet. It covers a broad range of concepts related, for example, to companies extending creative dialogue about new product development to outsiders or companies partnering with other companies to share risk and development costs. Open innovation also occurs in a much less organised way. In a TED talk in 2007, Charles Leadbeater described how the mountain bike evolved – initially the brainwave of a group of Californian kids who were frustrated by normal bikes for riding over rough terrain. Between them, they managed to cobble together parts (e.g. from motorcycles) to construct the first 'mountain bike' – an idea totally driven by consumer need – which made it easier to ride up and down mountains.

The Internet now makes open innovation practices much more likely:

- Companies can use social media to create communities of interest and interact with customers (and potential customers) to help them to identify new needs, new markets and new ideas for product developments.
- Open source products offer another model. Here, disparate individuals (and sometimes companies) collaborate to develop products that are 'open for use' – i.e. there is no fee for their use. Examples that come to mind include open source content management systems such as Joomla, Drupal and Wordpress.

All these open approaches require a more 'social' and co-operative approach to innovation which does chime with the original underlying ethos of the Internet.

## FUTURE SCENARIOS FOR LEARNING

Taking responsibility for your own learning is one overarching principle to follow in the future – whether you or your employer are funding your learning programmes. The uncertainty of the jobs market, the emergence of 'portfolio' careers and the likelihood of step-changes in careers means that employers are less likely to fund on-going professional development, leaving individuals to pick up the tab for their 'lifelong learning'. Alongside this will be the increasing adoption of the 'learn while you earn' approach with individuals undertaking part-time courses, distance-learning courses or participating in work-based learning programmes, sponsored by employers. Smart universities and colleges will work more closely with employers and design learning programmes that serve the dual purpose of developing employees as well as helping the employer organisation to improve – e.g. through designing learning programmes around the organisation's development projects and aligning with its strategic goals. The even smarter universities and colleges will help the organisation to measure the impact of these improvements.

More and more online services will likely become available to support individuals in progressing and managing their ongoing learning, and not just from traditional providers. The growing movement for 'open' approaches to education and training is illustrated by the availability of OERs (open educational resources), available from a range of OER directories. Such OERs may comprise small chunks of digital learning materials which course developers are allowed to incorporate into their course while other types of OERs can be entire modules or courses. There are also developments of the OER concept such as the MOOC (massive open online course), which are online courses that are underpinned by OERs, but are typically facilitated to greater or lesser degrees by trainers and tutors. In time, more of these courses will be accredited.

Other learning concepts likely to increase in use include the following.

### Personalisation of learning

In the last decade, higher education in the UK has absorbed increasing numbers of students as deliberate government policy to meet the demands of the 'knowledge society'. However, this often led to the 'depersonalisation' of learning due to the numbers involved. Worldwide student numbers will continue to increase in higher education (especially from developing countries), and educators generally acknowledge the need to focus on 'personalisation' of learning, helping learners to plan their learning to align with their own needs and goals, and to help them monitor and assess their development. Core to making this all work will be the efficient and effective use of communications technologies and online learning techniques.

### Social, informal, peer and work-based learning and assessment

Increasing recognition of the importance of learning that occurs in social and work-based environments and not just in the classroom leads to more collaborative programmes, increasing accreditation of experiential learning – Accreditation of Prior Experiential Learning (APEL) – as well as designing learning programmes that are based around individual employees' working practices and activities. Communications technologies will be crucial to making such social and informal learning work cost-effectively.

### Increasing coaching/mentoring

The increasing availability of information, educational resources and learning tools on the Internet raises questions for the future role of universities, colleges and training providers. Of course, one crucial role is that of accreditation and 'brands' are, of course, extremely important in the education sector. However, there is more to education than just downloading on-demand chunks of knowledge/learning. There are issues of broadening horizons, raising aspirations and motivation, stimulating creative and critical thinking and, overall, instilling a passion for learning. Coaching and mentoring can be very effective techniques here, both face to face and remotely using Web-conferencing technologies.

## KEY TECHNOLOGY TRENDS

It is always a good idea to start off a section focusing on technology futures with a few statistics, which invariably involve staggeringly large numbers. For instance, the US National Science Foundation predicts that there will be 5 billion people using the Internet by 2020; Eric Schmidt from Google predicts that *everyone* will be online by then.

Our trawl of Internet data in May 2014 came up with the following statistics – you may wish to find the statistics which apply when you are reading this to see the rate of change:

- China is the world Internet leader in terms of number of users – 604 million users in September 2013, mostly accessing the Internet through mobile phone (from internetstatstoday.com).
- The UK has over 80 per cent of the population who have used the Internet in the last 12 months; the USA has 81 per cent; Sweden has 94 per cent; Algeria has 15 per cent; India has 12 per cent (from maps.google.com).
- Some 90 per cent of American adults have a mobile phone with 58 per cent owning a smartphone. Among mobile phone owners, 29 per cent say it is 'something they can't imagine living without' (from pewinteret.org).

See the website for more statistics and discussion.

Of particular interest is the rise of mobile communications in developing countries, where the desktop PC seems to have been 'bypassed' in favour of mobile devices. Also of interest is the uptake of the Internet by children (92 per cent of American children have some type of online presence by the time they are 2 years old).

### Disruption

The word 'disruption' is often associated with the emergence of technologies that create major and sudden changes in how we work, learn and live, and are typically linked to low technology costs. Digital photography and video is just such an example. Technologies now commonplace on a variety of devices (e.g. mobile phones) had a disruptive influence on many businesses, such as Kodak, which did not adapt its business quickly enough to embrace the digital technologies.

Crowdfunding is an example of one of the more truly disruptive examples of the use of social media. This includes peer-to-peer funding, based on collaboration/community membership, shared knowledge and transparency, to support the development of new innovations and ventures, including those focused on socially good projects such as micro-loans in developing countries and charity-donation communities. More recently, online companies have started up to support new ventures in different markets such as the creative industries (e.g. music, film and publishing) and the health sector, which could begin to shape investments in these sectors – and bring with it a 'power of the people' – e.g. ethical perspectives. While some of these crowd-funding examples are based more on donations or loans (hence the motivation of funders is probably more for social good), there are increasingly more examples based on the investment form of contribution, where the form of return is proportional to the business doing well (and sometimes includes rewards based on intangible benefits). In early 2013, the UK FSA (Financial Services Authority) approved an online venture that allows the public to take direct equity stakes in small unlisted businesses, thus providing a degree of confidence and reassurance to investors, who can potentially claim compensation from the FSA if things go wrong.

### *Divergence, convergence and divergence*

The number of options for online communications is growing – e.g. email, discussion groups, social networks, blogs, wikis – combined with the growing availability of low-cost media devices such as digital still/video cameras, mp3 recorders/players and mobile phones, and the ability to manipulate and store multimedia information online. The rapidity of change is also remarkable. For example, Twitter was created in 2006 and by 2012 had over 500 million active users, creating over 340 million tweets each day with over 1.6 billion daily search queries; the latest statistics we could find in May 2014 suggest that there are now over a billion users with 100 million active each day (from expandedramblings.com). In 2014, Facebook took over the WhatsApp messaging app, founded in 2009, now with 500 million monthly users and 350 million of these using it every day. The average number of new users each day is now one million (also from expandedramblings.com).

This trend is likely to continue, presenting users with rich but complex environments in which to communicate where for some, there are just too many choices to cope with. Such trends can be described within the concept of 'divergence', where innovative technologies introduce new ways of doing things. Alongside this, we also see technology convergence happening – the trend towards technologies merging into new forms that bring together different types of media and applications. Convergence can be seen in computers, mobile phones, tablets and TVs. The mobile phone, for instance, has evolved into the smart phone, where making phone calls is just one function among many, including the ability to records digital pictures and video, accessing the Internet and even watching TV. TVs are growing in similar ways and it is becoming increasingly common practice for TVs to include network connections for Internet access. Converging technologies bring both positives and negatives.

For some, devices such as smartphones enable just one device to be carried allowing users to email, text, use social networks, listen to music, use ebooks, watch videos and make phone calls. Others find that a single device is rarely able to be fully effective for all these different uses – for example, a smartphone has a small screen and keyboard which can make it difficult to use as a computer. There is another downside to convergence: it can begin to stifle innovation and lead to a lack of variety, and in some instances can encourage monopolistic practices. The future trend is therefore likely to be one of periods of divergence, convergence and then more divergence alternating in a cyclic fashion.

### *Anytime, anywhere communications*

Consider the following news report from late February 2014: 'Americans used smartphone and tablet apps more than PCs to access the Internet last month – the first time that has ever happened' (James O'Toole at: http://money.cnn.com/2014/02/28/technology/mobile/mobile-apps-internet/).

This has come about due to a number of technology trends. First, is the growth in both mobile phone data networks and in wireless networks – these technologies are improving all the time, providing a broadband wireless infrastructure that can be accessed via wide ranges of devices, such as phones, tablets, computers. Having said that, there are a number of problems associated with mobile phone data networks from reliability in access (using data networks on trains remains a less than satisfactory experience) to issues associated with international roaming and billing (we still hear of mobile phone customers unwittingly running up bills in the thousands of pounds when on an overseas trip). Also contributing to the 'anytime, anywhere communications' trend is the availability of low-cost consumer devices (e.g. smartphones, tablets, laptop computers) that take advantage of the mobile and wireless networks, and even businesses are embracing such consumer devices. Another factor is the trend towards cloud computing, where data and software applications are stored and used in the cloud – best illustrated through systems such as GoogleDocs which provides word-processing facilities, accessed through a Web browser. One of the great advantages of such cloud computing is the collaboration capability where many users (those given 'permission' by the document creator) can edit such documents. While this type of cloud application is an increasing trend, it will not always provide a single approach to computing – there will be times where people do not have access to a broadband connection and will need to use their offline computer to work. To this end the concept of synching is often adopted, where resources stored in the cloud can be synched to local computers. The need for such synching capability is likely to persist for some while until telecommunications companies can provide comprehensive coverage with the same reliability as a data connection through a landline and at sensible costs for international travellers.

### *Computing as ubiquitous utility*

The concept of computing as a ubiquitous and reliable utility will drive demand for connectivity, especially for those in remote rural areas and those on the move (both nationally and internationally). It will also reduce the 'digital divide' in respect of access.

The utility concept also implies the integration of computer processors into a whole range of devices, many of which will be small and inexpensive, and focused on commonplace functions and potentially linked into the Internet. Home automation systems are an example, which provide facilities to remotely control different devices in the home, such as heating, lighting, home alarms, security devices and curtain pulling.

### *The intelligent Web and devices*

Increasingly, devices connected to the Internet will be designed to be smarter and to support humans in decision-making, and some will include sensors to help input local data. Potential technologies will include nanotech, cybernetics immersive virtual environments and cognitive computing. There is insufficient room to explore these ideas in more detail, but suffice it to say that everyday devices will get 'smarter'.

Another concept that will develop more is the idea of 'intelligent agents'. These are designed to make computing easier – for instance, they can monitor how people use the Web and what they search for, and then make suggestions for future searchers that are more personalised to your history of use of the Web and analysis of how other people use it. There are, of course, issues associated with such technologies – for instance, users do not know what 'decisions' the intelligent agent is making on their behalf. However, there are some very useful examples of 'smart' devices – e.g. low-cost car satellite navigation systems, which can be used not just to help drivers navigate, but will also take data from a range of sources, such as traffic density and flow, and recommend optimum routes that will meet driver preferences – e.g. the fastest and easiest route. Overall, this leads to a future where people are more connected to devices which are aware of contexts and locations.

### *Big data – Big Brother*

IBM have a statistic on their website: 'every day we create 2.5 quintillion bytes of data – so much that 90% of the data in the world today has been created in the last two years alone' and they remark 'this data is **big data**'. Few would argue!

Such data comes from a wide range of sources – not just from computers, but also from devices, sensors, audio, video, and so on – and from a vast array of source. From all of this come both opportunities and threats in respect of analysing the data and making use of it. For companies, it can mean that they can use data analysis tools to build up pictures and trends of their customers and how their customers use products, and this can all be fed back into product development. Credit card companies can use such software tools to build very detailed pictures of customer buying habits and telecommunications companies can keep track of how individuals use the Internet. From the individual perspective, all this can be both good and bad. Systems can be designed to help individuals make choices from huge ranges of possibilities, drawing on patterns of behaviour of both the individual and others. However, not everyone will be happy with this and the collection of such data can be used for purposes that individuals may not welcome, such as junk mail.

However, the more worrying area of concern is when different systems are joined together enabling the joining up of 'big data' – e.g. linking surveillance camera networks with facial recognition systems, tracking of devices (such as mobile phones) and purchasing/travel data, allowing those with access to these different systems to comprehensively intrude into an individual's working and social life. There are positives, of course – e.g. the ability for government health departments to spot and predict health trends and generally for government departments to target services more towards community needs. However, there have been numerous examples of where both companies and government departments' rhetoric about data privacy and security are not matched by practice or adequate procedures, and thus rekindles the concept of Big Brother watching over us.

Probably the best introduction to this area is the recent book by Victor Mayer-Schonberger and Kenneth Cukier (2013). They suggest that big data 'represents three shifts in the way we analyse information that transform how we understand and organise society' (p. 12). The first shift is the fact that we can now analyse and integrate much more data than ever before. The availability of these enormous datasets means that we do not have to be as precise or as exact with specific details as we did when we were only using small datasets – and this is the second shift. The final shift is what they call 'a move away from the age old search for causality' (p. 14). Using big data allows us to reveal previously hidden patterns and correlations which we can then investigate to discover what they mean. Of course, we need to be very careful in interpreting the meaning of any correlation. We need to beware of spurious correlation where a direct link or strong association does not mean that we can easily work out what causes what. How would you explain the very strong relationship between the per capita consumption of cheese in the USA and the number of people who died by becoming tangled in their bedsheets? See the 'spurious correlations' website for this and other examples at: www.tylervigen.com.

### *Openness*

Openness is a growing movement in the area of technology and education which has certain characteristics associated with it, such as those described by Educause:

- The use of open standards and interoperability of systems.
- Open and community source software development.
- Open access to research data.
- Open scholarly communications.
- Open access to, and open derivative use of, content (often referred to as open educational resources (OERs).

Examples of such open approaches include:

- Drupal community-developed Web content management software.
- Moodle, the open-source virtual learning environment (VLE).

MOOCs (massive open online courses) were mentioned in Chapter 2 as a useful tool and these are based on open approaches. There is insufficient space in this book to explore the pros and cons of open approaches, particularly in relation to how such approaches will evolve over time. However, at the very least, it is an important aspect of being a good communicator that developments in open approaches are monitored to identify how effectively such approaches can be exploited in communications and education.

### *Green computing*

The green, or sustainability movement will be well known to everyone and is of prime importance when it comes to technology. The Electronic TakeBack Coalition in the US published some interesting statistics in 2010: 29.9 million desktops, 31.9 million monitors and 12 million laptops discarded in 2007 in the US and in 2008, 3.16 million tons of e-waste was generated in the US, with only 13.6 per cent recycled. It also reports that the manufacturing of one computer takes 530 pounds of fossil fuels, 48 pounds of chemicals and 1.5 tons of water – apparently 81 per cent of a desktop computer's energy use is in making it, not using it, although energy costs for running computers are equally staggering.

The report from the McKinsey management consultancy, 'Revolutionizing Data Center Efficiency', predicted that the total energy bill for US data centers in 2010 would be £11.5 billion. Green computing must therefore encompass processes that begin with design and manufacture, and go on to use, disposal, recycling and biodegradability. There will be increasing environmental and economic pressures for the IT industry and governments to introduce greener approaches. We are concerned that many manufacturers (and consumers) still don't generally seem to have an appetite for such green approaches. Some of the most popular electronic devices – e.g. tablets and smartphones – are manufactured with obsolescence in mind – e.g. through the use of sealed cases and batteries and components that cannot be replaced.

### *Social resistance to technology*

While all the trends in technology are driving greater social interaction across the world – and this can be very positive for communications – it is not set in stone that such interactions will continue. The question to ask is 'Is such digital social interaction a fad/fashion or is it the beginning of a trend?' There is no shortage of evidence of problems in digital social interactions – cyber-bullying, criminal activity, non-stop SPAM, cyber-terrorism, etc. So all the positive moves towards sharing and interaction could be disrupted by unforeseen events – for instance, any increase in crime against children on the Web could start to affect the culture of sharing and openness. Social resistance could develop as quickly as social interaction has developed.

## HOW CAN WE COPE WITH ALL THIS UNCERTAINTY AND CHANGE?

This brief speculation about the future paints a world of change, uncertainty and unpredictability as the pace of technological innovation increases and disrupts the way we work, learn and live. As well as considering evidence on the key developments (such as the work by Lynda Gratton we highlighted in Chapter 1), we advocate an approach based on two of the key tenets of this book.

## Adapt basic principles of effective communication to your context

Chapter 2 described our basic principles of communication and we hope that these will stand the test of time and apply equally to the world many years down the line from when this book was written. Use and adapt these principles to guide you in how you (and your organisation) communicate irrespective of which media/technologies you adopt in the future.

## Adopt a review, plan and improve approach to your learning, communication and personal development

Chapter 1 introduced the 'review, plan and improve' approach to learning and personal development, based on Kaizen philosophy. You can use this approach to underpin how you cope with emerging technologies and new media. It will, of course, require effort to spend time horizon-scanning and getting to grips with emerging technologies and working out how best you and your organisation can use them. We strongly advocate that you do this and not rely on IT departments to guide you. Unfortunately, IT departments do not have a good track record of coming up with creative and innovative uses of technology.

At the beginning of this book, we suggested that you decide which areas of communication to focus on. Figure 14.1 gives an overview of our major areas which you can use as a starting point (see more discussion on the website).

## Focus on the future

There is perhaps one final message about dealing with the unpredictability of emerging technologies: rather than focusing on predicting the future, focus instead on 'inventing the future'. We can't all be digital entrepreneurs, but we can all influence and shape the way we adopt and use new technologies for communications purposes and it is important to believe that we can 'invent' (or at least influence) the future – this is, after all, one of our basic principles of communication – 'The ability to influence has become a key communication skill in modern organisations'.

## Engage with our worldwide community of practice

We are complementing this written text with an online site with a view to developing an online community of practice and enabling us to update the written text with commentary on emerging technologies and new media, and how these are changing and influencing how we communicate. We welcome contributions to the site, such as the following examples:

- *Good or bad communications* or organisational approaches to communications that you have experienced.
- *Challenges* arising in the digital world. We already know some of these – e.g. information overload, but we would like to hear what challenges you come across.
- *Opportunities* that arise to enhance communications – e.g. using digital technologies and good practice tips.

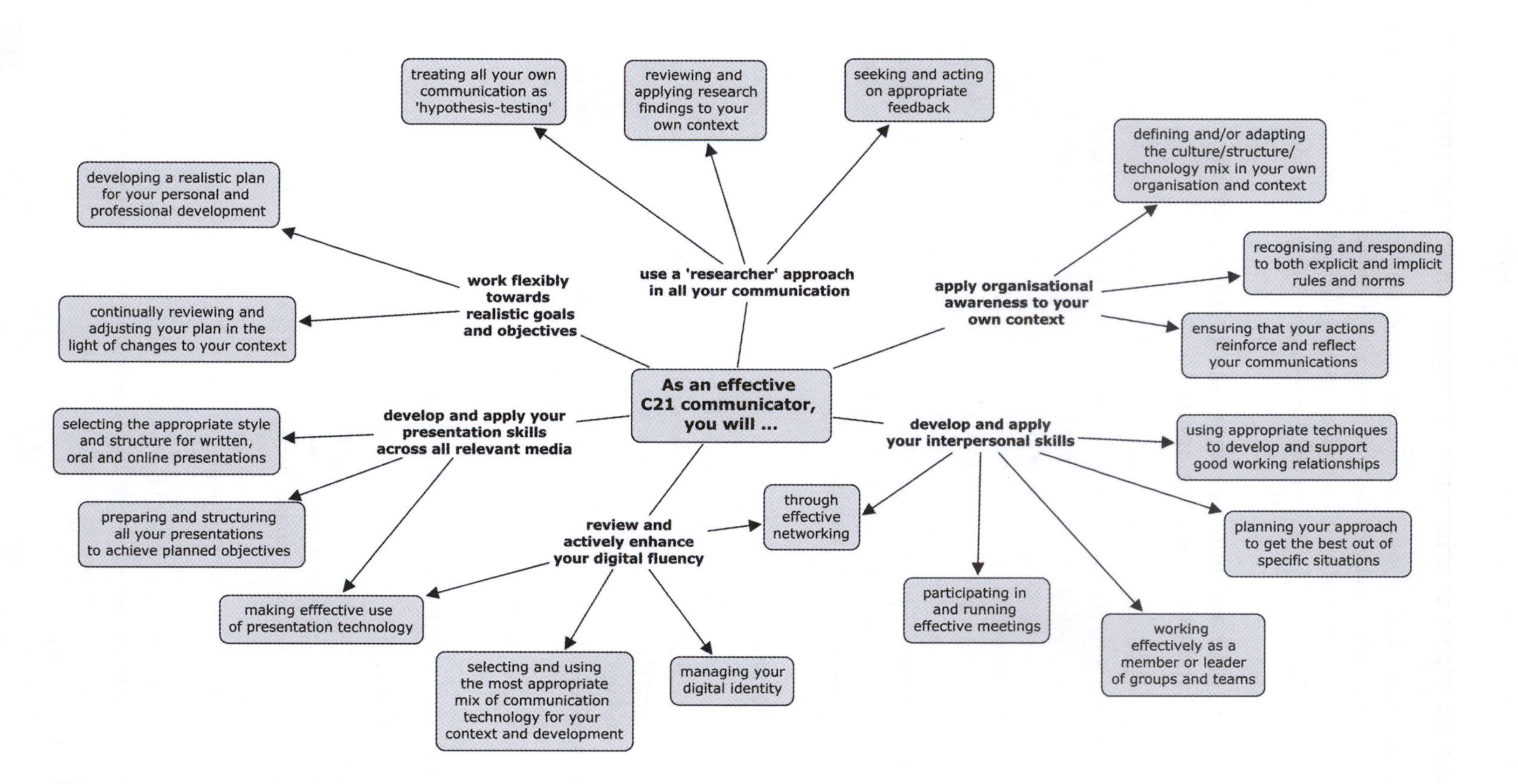


***Figure 14.1*** *The twenty-first century communicator*

We hope you will be able to share these on our site,which is located at: www.rethinkbuscomm.net. We look forward to meeting you there.

## SUMMARY

- Modern organisations experience different types of change, influenced by factors in the environment. Organisations operate in at least three types of environment: temporal (the historical development over time), external (the PEST factors) and the internal environment.
- As a result, many organisations have placed increasing emphasis on 'sense-making'– i.e. trying to ensure that their managers and staff are continually scanning the environment and their competitors' behaviour to look for signs of impending change.
- We must also consider the rate and the scale of the change involved. This can range from small adjustments at department or division level ('fine tuning') up to 'corporate transformation', which involves radical change right across the organisation.
- Examples of change strategies and approaches demonstrate that effective communication is an essential feature in both the acceptance and implementation of organisational change.
- We need to consider the implications of future scenarios on working practices, learning and technology. Practical steps to cope with this uncertainty include using the principles and strategy of continuous review that we set out earlier in this book. You can join our community of practice through the website.

## FURTHER READING

Quirke, B. (1995) *Communicating Change*. London: McGraw-Hill.

An interesting example of advice to company management from an experienced consultant.

Robinson, L. (2012) *Changeology: How to enable groups, communities and societies to do things they've never done before*. Totnes: Green Books.

A very readable synthesis of practical approaches and theory/examples.

Senior, B. and Swailes, S. (2010) *Organisational Change* (4th edn). London: Prentice Hall.

This is a very readable introduction (with companion website) to major theories and change practices.

Stacey, R.D. (2000) *Strategic Management and Organisational Dynamics* (3rd edn). Harlow: FT/Prentice Hall.

This offers a more radical approach to strategy than some other texts, emphasising 'unpredictability and the limitations of control'. It incorporates psychodynamic approaches and management narratives, as well as some very interesting case studies.

# References


Adair, J. (1986) *Effective Leadership: A modern guide to developing leadership skills*. London: Pan Books.

Adler, H. (1996) *NLP for Managers: How to achieve excellence at work. London: Piatkus.*

Adler, H. and Heather, N. (1999) *NLP in 21 Days: A complete introduction and training programme*. London: Piatkus.

Ahmed, C. and Hartley, P. (1999) Weapons of the weak: Stories from Malaysia. Paper at the 17th Standing Conference On Organisational Symbolism, Napier University.

Albrow, M. (1997) *Do Organisations Have Feelings?* London: Routledge.

Ames, D.R. (2009). Pushing up to a point: Assertiveness and effectiveness in leadership and interpersonal dynamics. In Brief, A. and Staw, B. (eds), *Research in Organizational Behaviour*, 29, 111–133.

Andrews, P.H. and Herschel, R.T. (1996) *Organisational Communication: Empowerment in a technological society*. Boston, MA: Houghton Mifflin.

Argyle, M. (1994) *The Psychology of Interpersonal Behaviour* (5th edn). Harmondsworth: Penguin.

Armenakis, A.A. and Bedeian, A.G. (1999) Organisational change: A review of theory and research in the 1990s. *Journal of Management*, 25(3): 293–315.

Aziz, K. (2000) *Presenting to Win: A guide for finance and business professionals*. Dublin: Oak Tree Press.

Back, K. and Back, K. (2005) *Assertiveness at Work: A practical guide to handling awkward situations*. London: McGraw-Hill.

Baguley, P. (1994) *Effective Communication for Modern Business*. London: McGraw-Hill.

Bandler, R. and Grinder, J. (1990) *Frogs into Princes: Neuro linguistic programming* (revised edn). Garden Grove, CA: Eden Grove.

Barker, A. (1999) *Writing at Work: How to create successful business documents*. London: Industrial Society.

Baron, N.S. (1999) *Alphabet to Email: How written English evolved and where it's heading*. London: Routledge.

Baron, N.S. (2008) *Always On: Language in an online and mobile world*. New York: Oxford University Press.

Bates, L. (2014) *Everyday Sexism*. London: Simon & Schuster.

Baym, N.K. (2010) *Personal Connections in the Digital Age*. Cambridge: Polity Press.

Beattie, G. (2011) *Get the Edge: How simple changes will transform your life*. London: Headline.

Belbin, R.M. (1981) *Management Teams: Why they succeed or fail*. Oxford: Heinemann.

Belbin, R.M. (2010a) *Team Roles at Work*. Oxford: Butterworth-Heinemann.

Belbin, R.M. (2010b) *Management Teams: Why they succeed or fail* (3rd edn). Oxford: Heinemann.

Benne, K.D. and Sheats, P. (1948) Functional roles of group members. *Journal of Social Issues*, 4(2): 41–49.

Bhatia, V. and Bremner, S. (2014) *The Routledge Handbook of Language and Professional Communication*. London: Routledge.

Bhatt, I. (2012) Digital literacy practices and their layered multiplicity. *Educational Media International*, 49:4, 289–301.

Bolton, R. (1986) *People Skills: How to assert yourself, liten to others, and resolve conflicts*. Sydney: Prentice Hall.

Bovee, C. and Thill, J. (2013) *Business Communication Essentials*. London: Pearson.

Bovee, C. and Thill, J. (2014) *Business Communication Today*. London: Pearson.

Bowman, L. with Crofts, A. (1991) *High Impact Business Presentations: How to speak like an expert and sound like a statesman*. London: Business Books.

Brown, G.A. and Armstrong, S. (1984) Explaining and explanations. In Wragg, E.C. (ed.) *Classroom Teaching Skills*. London: Croom Helm, pp. 121–148.

Browne, J. (2014) *The Glass Closet: The risks and rewards of coming out in business*. London: Harper Business.

Browning, L.D. (1992) Lists and stories as organisational communication. *Communication Theory*, 2: 281–302.

Bryman, A. (1992) *Charisma and Leadership in Organisations*. London: Sage.

Bryson, B. (1990) *Mother Tongue: The English language*. London: Penguin.

Bryson, J.M., Ackermann, F., Eden, C. and Finn, C.B. (2004) *Visible Thinking: Unlocking causal mapping for practical business results*. Chichester: John Wiley.

Buchanan, D. and Badham, R. (1999) *Power, Politics and Organisational Change: Winning the turf game*. London: Sage.

Buchanan, D.A. and Badham, R.J. (2008) *Power, Politics and Organizational Change: Winning the turf game* (2nd edn). London: Sage.

Burkeman, O. (2011) *Help! How to become slightly happier and get a bit more done*. Edinburgh: Canongate.

Buzan, T. with Buzan, B. (1995) *The Mind Map Book* (revised edn). London: BBC Books.

Cain, S. (2012) *Quiet: The power of introverts in a world that can't stop talking*. London: Penguin.

Cameron, D. (1995) *Verbal Hygiene*. London: Routledge.

Cameron, D. (2000) *Good to Talk*. London: Sage.

Cameron, K.S. and Quinn, R. E. (2011) *Diagnosing and Changing Organizational Culture: Based on the competing values framework*. San Francisco, CA: Jossey Bass.

Carnegie, D. (2006) *How to Win Friends and Influence People* (new edn). London: Vermillion.

Chabris, C. and Simons. D. (2011) *The Invisible Gorilla: And other ways our intuition deceives us*. London: HarperCollins.

Chapanis, A. (1988) 'Words, words, words' revised. *International Review of Ergonomics*, 2: 1–30.

Chaudry-Lawton, R. and Lawton, R. (1992) *Ignition: Sparking organisational change*. London: Book Club Associates.

Chesher, M. and Kaura, R. (1998) *Electronic Commerce and Business Communication*. London: Springer-Verlag.

Cialdini, R.B. (2007) *Influence: The psychology of persuasion* (revised edn). London: Harper Business.

Clampitt, P.G. (2010) *Communicating for Managerial Effectiveness* (4th edn). Thousand Oaks, CA: Sage.

Clampitt, P.G. and DeKoch, R.J. (2011) *Transforming Leaders into Progress Makers: Leadership for the 21st century*. London: Sage.

Clark, T. (1998) Encouraging critical thinking in business memos. *Business Communication*, 61(3): 71–74.

Clyne, M. (1994) *Intercultural Communication at Work: Cultural values in discourse*. Cambridge: Cambridge University Press.

Collinson, D., Kirkup, G., Kyd, R. and Slocombe, L. (1992) *Plain English* (2nd edn). Buckingham: Open University Press.

Cooke, C. (1999) Not so much 'what' you say but 'how' you say it. *Journal of Communication Management*, 3(2): 180–196.

Crystal, D. (2009) *Txtng: The Gr8 Db8*. Oxford: Oxford University Press.

Crystal, D. (2013) *Spell it Out: The singular story of English spelling*. London: Profile Books.

Cutts, M. (2013) *Oxford Guide to Plain English* (4th edn). Oxford: Oxford University Press.

Czerniawska, F. (1997) *Corporate Speak*. London: Palgrave.

Daniels, T.D. and Spiker, B.K. (1994) *Perspectives on Organisational Communication* (3rd edn). Madison, WI: W.C.B. Brown & Benchmark.

Danziger, K. (1976) *Interpersonal Communication*. Oxford: Pergamon.

David, W. (1995) *Managing Company-Wide Communication*. London: Chapman & Hall.

Deal, T. and Kennedy, A. (1982) *Corporate Cultures: The rites and rituals of corporate life*. Reading, MA: Addison Wesley.

Deal, T. and Kennedy, A. (1999) *The New Corporate Cultures: Revitalising the workplace after downsizing, mergers and re-engineering*. London: Ryan.

Dean, J. (2013) *Making Habits, Breaking Habits*. London: Oneworld.

Delbridge, R. (1998) *Life on the Line in Contemporary Manufacturing*. Oxford: Oxford University Press.

Denning, S. (2011) *The Leader's Guide to Storytelling: Mastering the art and discipline of business narrative* (2nd edn). San Francisco, CA: Jossey Bass.

Duck, S. (2007) *Human Relationships* (4th edn). London: Sage.

Dunphy, D. and Stace, D. (1993) The strategic management of corporate change. *Human Relations*, 45(8): 917–918.

Dutton, K. (2011) *Flipnosis: The art of split-second persuasion*. Croydon: Arrow.

Dweck, C.S. (2006) *Mindset: The new psychology of success*. New York: Ballantine.

Eden, C. and Ackermann, F. (2013) Problem structuring: On the nature of, and reaching agreement about, goals. *EURO Journal on Decision Processes*. Springer-Verlag Berlin Heidelberg and EURO – The Association of European Operational Research Societies. Available at: http://link.springer.com/article/10.1007%2Fs40070-013-0005-6/fulltext.html (accessed 31 May 2014).

Ehrenberg, A.S.C. (1977) Rudiments of numeracy. *Journal of the Royal Statistical Society A*. 140: 227–297.

Ellinor, L. and Gerrard, G. (1998) *Dialogue: Rediscover the transforming power of conversation*. New York: John Wiley.

Ellis, A. and Beattie, G. (1986) *The Psychology of Language and Communication*. London: Weidenfeld & Nicolson.

Epley, N. (2014) *Mindwise: How we understand what others think, believe, feel and want*. London: Allen Lane.

Finan, A. (1998) *Corporate Christ: The world-changing at changing secrets of management and marketing genius*. Chalford: Management Books.

Finn, T.A. (1999) A case of telecommunications (mis)management. *Management Communication Quarterly*, 12(4): 575–579.

Fisman, R. and Sullivan, T. (2014) *The Org: How the office really works*. London: John Murray.

Flowers, S. (1996) *Software Failure: Management failure: amazing stories and cautionary tales*. Chichester: John Wiley & Sons.

Foley, M.J. (2013) CEO Ballmer's reorg mail to the troops: 'One Microsoft all the time'. Available at: www.zdnet.com/ceo-ballmers-reorg-mail-to-the-troops-one-microsoft-all-the-time-7000017943/ (accessed 31 May 2014).

Foley, M.J. (2014) How the 'One Microsoft' mission is changing Microsoft Research. Available at: www.zdnet.com/how-the-one-microsoft-mission-is-changing-microsoft-research-7000029144/#ftag=RSSc6e0c33 (accessed 31 May 2014).

Gabriel, Y. (1999) *Organizations in Depth: The psychoanalysis of organizations*. London: Sage.

Gallagher, K., McLelland, B. and Swales, C. (1998) *Business Skills: An active learning approach*. Oxford: Blackwell.

Geisler, C. (2014) *Designing for User Engagement on the Web: 10 basic principles*. Abingdon: Routledge.

Georgiades, M. and McDonnell, R. (1998) *Leadership in Competitive Advantage*. Chichester: Wiley.

Glass, M.C. and Noonan, J.L. (2012) The hard truth about telecommuting. *Monthly Labour Review*. June: 38–45.

Goleman, D. (1996) *Emotional Intelligence*. London: Bloomsbury.

Gowers, E. (1987) *The Complete Plain Words* (3rd edn). Harmondsworth: Penguin.

Gratton, L. (2014) *The Shift: The future of work is already here.* London: Williams Collins.

Guirdham, M. (1995) *Interpersonal Skills at Work* (2nd edn). Hemel Hempstead: Prentice Hall.

Gwynne, N.M. (2013) *Gwynne's Grammar: The ultimate introduction to grammar and the writing of good English. Incorporating also Strunk's guide to style.* London: Ebury Press.

Hackman, J.R. (1990) *Groups that Work (and those that don't): Creating conditions for effective teamwork.* San Francisco, CA: Jossey Bass.

Hall, E.T. (1959) *The Silent Language.* New York: Doubleday.

Hall, T. and Janman, K. (2010) *The Leadership Illusion: The importance of context and connections.* Basingstoke: Palgrave Macmillan.

Hammer, M. and Champy, J. (1993) *Rengineering the Corporation: A manifesto for business revolution.* London: Nicolas Brealey.

Hargie, O.D.W. (1997) *The Handbook of Communication Skills* (2nd edn). London: Routledge.

Hargie, O.D.W. (2011) *Skilled Interpersonal Communication* (5th edn). Routledge: London.

Hargie, O.D.W. and Tourish, D. (eds) (2000) *Handbook of Communication Audits for Organisations.* London. Routledge.

Hargie, O.D.W. and Tourish, D. (eds) (2009) *Auditing Organizational Communication: A handbook of research, theory and practice.* London: Routledge.

Hargie, O.D.W., Saunders, C. and Dickson, D. (1994) *Social Skills in Interpersonal Communication* (3rd edn). London: Routledge.

Hargie, O.D.W., Dickson, D. and Tourish, D. (1999) *Communication in Management.* Aldershot: Gower.

Harper, R.H.R. (2010) *Texture: Human expression in the age of communications overload.* Massachusetts, MA: MIT Press.

Harris, M. (1998) Rethinking the virtual organization. In Jackson, P.J. and Van Dale Wieland, J.M. (eds) *Teleworking: International perspectives.* London: Routledge, pp. 74–92.

Hartley, P. (1984) Principles for effective documents. Paper given at Scottish Communication Annual Conference. Edinburgh: Napier University.

Hartley, J. (1994) *Designing Instructional Text* (3rd edn). London: Kogan Page.

Hartley, P. (1997) *Group Communication.* London: Routledge.

Hartley, P. (1999) *Interpersonal Communication* (2nd edn). London: Routledge.

Hayes, J. (1991) *Interpersonal Skills: Goal-directed behaviour at work.* London: Routledge.

Heen, S. and Stone, D. (2014) *Thanks for the Feedback: The science and art of receiving feedback well.* London: Portfolio Penguin/Viking.

Henning, K. (1998) *The Digital Enterprise: How digitization is redefining business.* London: Century.

Hirokawa, R.Y. and Poole, M.S. (1996) *Communication and Group Decision Making.* Thousand Oaks, CA: Sage.

Hirschberg, J. (1998) *The Creative Priority: Driving innovative business in the real world.* Harmondsworth: Penguin.

Hodgkinson, G. and Pain, R.L. (1998) Graduate selection in three European countries. *Journal of Occupational and Organizational Psychology,* 71(4): 359–365.

Honey, P. (1988) *Face to Face: A practical guide to interactive skills* (2nd edn). Aldershot: Ashgate.

Horton, W. (1997) *Secrets of User Seductive Documents: Wooing and winning the reluctant reader*. Arlington, VA: Society for Technical Communication.

Hott, R. and Leeds, S. (2014) *NLP: A Changing Perspective*. CreateSpace. Available at: www.createspace.com/diygb?ref=1231856&cp=70170000000bqtJ&ls=Paid_Search&utm_id=6041&sls=Google_DIY (accessed 31 May 2014).

Howard, G. (1993) *The Good English Guide: English usage in the 1990s*. London: Macmillan.

Hutchens, D. (2009) Applications of narrative and storytelling as an organizational discipline. Available at: www.davidhutchens.com/Biz%20Writing/articles/organizationalst.html (accessed 31 May 2014).

Jack, R.E., Garrod, O.G.B. and Schyns, P.G. (2014) Dynamic facial expressions of emotion transmit an evolving hierarchy of symbols over time. *Current Biology*, 24(2): 187.

Jackson, J. (ed.) (2012) *Introducing Language and Intercultural Communication*. London: Routledge.

James, J. (1995) *Body Talk: The skills of positive image*. London: Industrial Society.

Jaques, D. (1994) Managerial leadership: The key to good organization. In Mabey, C. and Isles, P. (eds) *Managing Learning*. London: Routledge.

Jay, R. (1995) *How to Write Proposals and Reports that Get Results*. London: Pitman.

Jenkins, S. and Hinds. J. (1987) Business letter writing: English, French and Japanese. *TESOL Quarterly*, 121(2): 327–354.

Johnson, G., Whittington, R., Scholes, K., Regnér, P. and Angwin, D. (2014) *Fundamentals of Strategy* (3rd edn). London: Pearson.

Joseph, A. (1998) *Put it in Writing!: Learn how to write clearly, quickly, persuasively*. New York: McGraw-Hill.

Jourard, S.M. (1971) *The Transparent Self* (revised edn). New York: Van Nostrand Reinhold.

Kahneman, D. (2011) *Thinking, Fast and Slow*. London: Penguin.

Kakepoto, I., Said, H., Buriro, G.S. and Habil, H. (2012) Beyond the technical barriers: Oral communication barriers of engineering students of Pakistan for workplace environment: preliminary results. *Research on Humanities and Social Sciences*, 3:10 (2013).

Katz, S. (1998) Part 1: Learning to write in organizations: What newcomers learn about writing on the job. *IEEE Transactions on Professional Communication*, 42(2): 105–115.

Katzenbach, J.R. and Smith, D.K. (1993) The discipline of teams. *Harvard Business Review*, 71, March–April, 111–146.

Katzenbach, J.R. and Smith, D.K. (1998) *The Wisdom of Teams: Creating a high-performance organisation*. London: McGraw-Hill.

Kay, J. (2011) *Obliquity: Why our goals are best achieved indirectly*. London: Profile Books.

Kellerman, B. (2012) *The End of Leadership*. New York: HarperCollins.

Kimble, J. (2012) *Writing for Dollars, Writing to Please: The case for plain language in business, government, and law*. Durham, NC: Carolina Academic Press.

Kirkman, J. 1992) *Good Style: Writing for science and technology*. London: E. & F.N. Spon.

Klepper, M.M. with Gunther, R. (1994) *I'd Rather Die than Give a Speech.* New York: Irwin.

Knapp, M.L. and Hall, J.A. (2010) *Non-verbal Behaviour in Human Interaction* (9th edn). Fort Worth, TX: Harcourt Brace.

Koegel, T.J. (2010) *The Exceptional Presenter Goes Virtual.* Austin, TX: Greenleaf Book Group Press.

Kohn, S. and O'Connel, V. (2009) *6 Habits of Highly Effective Teams.* London: Crimson.

Krum, R. (2013) *Cool Infographics: Effective Communication with Data Visualization* and *Design.* Indianapolis, IN: Wiley.

Levin, P. and Topping, G. (2006) *Perfect Presentations.* London: McGraw-Hill.

Lewin, K. (1951) *Field Theory in Social Science.* New York: Harper.

Lewin, K., Lippitt, R. and White, R.K. (1939) Patterns of aggressive behavior in experimentally created social climates. *Journal of Social Psychology.* 10: 271–301.

Lewis, D. (1996) *How to Get Your Message Across: A practical guide to power communication.* London: Souvenir Press.

Lichty, T. (1989) *Design Principles for Desktop Publishers.* Glenview, IL: Scott, Foresman.

Linehan, M. and Egan, K. (1983) *Asserting Yourself.* London: Century.

Littlejohn, S.W. (1983) *Theories of Human Communication* (2nd edn). Belmont, CA: Wadsworth.

Luntz, F.I. (2007) *Words that Work: It's not what you say, it's what people hear.* New York: Hyperion.

McBride, P. (1993) *Excel at Interviews: Tactics for job and college applicants.* Cambridge: Hobsons.

McDaniel. E.R. (1994) Non-verbal communication: a reflection of cultural themes. In Samovar, L.A. and Porter, R.E. (eds) *Intercultual Communication: A reader* (8th edn). Belmont, CA: Wandsworth.

McIntyre, M.G. (1998) *The Management Team Handbook: Five key strategies for maximising group performance.* San Francisco, CA: Jossey-Bass.

McLean, R. (1980) *The Thames and Hudson Manual of Typography.* London: Thames & Hudson.

Marquis, K.H. and Cannell, C.F. (1971) *Effect of Some Experimental Interviewing Techniques of Reporting in the Health Interview Study.* Washington, DC: US Department of Health Education and Welfare.

Marsh, D.R. and Dodson, A. (2010) *Guardian Style* (3rd edn). London: Guardian Books.

Martin, D. (2000) *Manipulating Meetings: How to get what you want, when you want it.* London: Prentice Hall.

Mattelart, A. and Mattelart, M. (1998) *Theories of Communication: A short introduction.* London: Sage.

Mayer-Schonberger, V. and Cukier, K. (2013) *Big Data: A revolution that will transform how we live, work and think.* London: John Murray.

Meyer, E.K. (1997) *Designing Infographics.* Indianapolis, IN: Hayden.

Miller, J., Wroblewski, M. and Villafuerte, J. (2013) *Creating a Kaizen Culture: Align the organization, achieve breakthrough results, and sustain the gains.* New York: McGraw-Hill.

Minto, B. (2002) *The Pyramid Principle: Logic in writing and thinking* (3rd edn). London: Pearson.

Mintzberg, H. (1973) *The Nature of Managerial Work*. New York: Harper & Row.

Morgan, G. (1997) *Images of Organisation* (new edn). London: Sage.

Morgan, N. (2007) *Giving Presentations*. Boston, MA: Harvard Business.

Morris, D. (1994) *Bodytalk: A world guide to gestures*. London: Jonathan Cape.

Moscovici, S. and Zavalloni, M. (1969) The group as a polarizer of attitudes. *Journal of Personality and Social Psychology*. 12(2): 125–135.

Mulholland, J. (1999) E-mail: uses, issues and problems in an institutional setting. In Bargiella-Chiappini, F. and Nickerson, C. (eds) *Writing Business: Genres, media and discourses*. London: Longman.

Murray, D.E. (1995) *Knowledge Machines: Language and information in a technological society*. London: Longman.

Naughton, J. (1999) *A Brief History of the Future: The origins of the internet*. London: Weidenfeld & Nicolson.

Nickson, D. and Siddons, S. (1996) *Business Communications*. Oxford: Butterworth-Heinemann.

Novak, J.D. (2010) *Learning, Creating, and Using Knowledge: Concept maps as facilitative tools in schools and corporations*. London: Routledge.

Owen, H. (1996) *Creating Top-Flight Teams*. London: BCA.

Penman, R. (1993) Unspeakable acts and other deeds: A critique of plain legal language. *Information Design Journal*, 7(2): 121–131.

Perloff, R.M. (2013) *The Dynamics of Persuasion: Communication and attitudes in the 21st century* (5th edn). London: Routledge.

Peters, T.J. and Waterman, R.H. (1982) *In Search of Excellence: Lessons from America's best run companies*. New York: Harper & Row.

Plous, S. (1993) *The Psychology of Judgment and Decision Making*. New York: McGraw-Hill.

Poole, S. (2007) *Unspeak: Words are weapons* (2nd edn). London: Abacus. See also the blog at: www.unspeak.net (accessed 31 May 2014).

Provan, D. (2009) *Giving Great Presentations*. Southam: Easy Steps.

Quirke, B. (1995) *Communicating Change*. London: McGraw-Hill.

Qvortrup, L. (1998) From teleworking to networking: Definitions and trends. In Jackson, P.J. and Van Der Wielen, J.M. (eds) *Teleworking: International Perspectives*. London: Routledge, pp. 21–39.

Rasberry, R.W. and Lemoine, L.F. (1986) *Effective Managerial Communication*. Boston, MA: Kent.

Reed, J. and Stolz, P.G. (2011) *Put Your Mindset to Work: The one asset you really need to win and keep the job you love*. London: Portfolio Penguin.

Reynolds, G. (2011) *The Naked Presenter: Delivering powerful presentations with or without slides*. Berkeley, CA: New Riders.

Ritzer, G. (1996) *The McDonaldization of Society* (revised edn). Thousand Oaks, CA: Pine Press.

Ritzer, G. (2013) *The McDonaldization of Society: 20th anniversary edition* (7th edn). Thousand Oaks, CA: Sage.

Robbins, S.P. (1996) *Organisational Behaviour: Concepts, controversies, applications* (7th edn) Englewood Cliffs, NJ: Prentice Hall.

Robbins, S.P. (1998) *Organisational Behaviour: Concepts, controversies, applications* (8th edn). Englewood Cliffs, NJ: Prentice Hall.

Robbins, H. and Finley, M. (1997) *Why Teams Don't Work: What went wrong and how to make it right*. London: Orion.

Robinson, L. (2012) *Changeology: How to enable groups, communities and societies to* do *things they've never done before*. Totnes: Green Books.

Rogers, P.S., Taylor, J.R. and Finn, T.A. (1999) A case of telecommunications (mis)management case analyses. *Management Communication Quarterly*, 12(4): 580–599.

Sandberg, S. (2013) *Lean In: Women, work, and the will to lead*. London: W.H. Allen.

Sandberg, S. (2014) *Lean In: The graduate edition*. London: W.H. Allen.

Schein, E.H. (2009) *The Corporate Culture Survival Guide* (revised edn). New York: John Wiley.

Schein, E.H. (2010) *Organizational Culture and Leadership* (4th edn). San Francisco, CA: Jossey-Bass.

Schmidt, E. and Cohen, J. (2014) *The New Digital Age: Reshaping the future of people, nations and business*. London: John Murray.

Sellen. A.J. and Harper, R.H.R. (2003) *The Myth of the Paperless Office*. Cambridge, MA: MIT Press.

Senge, P.M. (1994) The leaders new work: Building learning organisations. In Mabey, C. and Iles, P. (eds) *Managing Learning*. Routledge: London, pp. 5–21.

Senior, B. (1997) *Organisational Change*. London: Pitman.

Senior, B. and Swailes, S. (2010) *Organisational Change* (4th edn). London: Prentice Hall.

Shapiro, E.C. (1996) *Fad Surfing in the Boardroom: Reclaiming the courage to manage in the age of instant answers*. Oxford: Capstone.

Sharples, M. (1999) *How We Write: Writing as creative design*. London: Routledge.

Shimko, B.W. (1990) New breed workers need new yardsticks. *Business Horizons*, November/December: 34–36.

Sibbert, D. (2011) *Visual Teams: Graphic tools for commitment, innovation and high performance*. Hoboken, NJ: John Wiley.

Sinek, S. (2014) *Leaders Eat Last: Why some teams pull together and others don't*. New York: Portfolio Penguin.

Sless, D. (1999) The mass production of unique letters. In Bargiela-Chiappini, F.and Nickerson, C. (eds) *Writing Business: Genres, media and discourses*. Harlow: Longman, pp. 85–99.

Smith, M. (1982) Selection interviewing: A four-step approach. In Breakwell, G.M., Foot, H. and Gilmour, R. (eds) *Social Psychology: A practical manual*. London: Macmillan, pp. 19–37.

Smith, R.C. and Eisenberg, E.M. (1987) Conflict at Disneyland: A root-metaphor analysis. *Communication Monographs*, 54: 367–380.

Solomon, D. and Theiss, J. (2013) *Interpersonal Communication: Putting theory into practice*. London: Routledge.

Sparks, S.D. (1999) *The Manager's Guide to Business Writing*. New York: McGraw-Hill.

Spiekermann, E. and Ginger, E.M. (1993) *Stop Stealing Sheep and Find Out How Type Works*. Mountain View, CA: Adobe Press.

Stacey, R.D. (2000) *Strategic Management and Organisational Dynamics* (3rd edn). Harlow, Essex: FT/Prentice Hall.

Stanton, N. (1996) *Mastering Communication* (3rd edn). Basingstoke: Macmillan.

Stewart, R. (1991) *Managing Today and Tomorrow*. London: Macmillan.

Stewart, R. (ed.) (1999) *Gower Handbook of Teamworking*. Aldershot: Gower.

Stoner, J.A.F. (1961) *A Comparison of Individual and Group Decisions Involving Risk*. Cambridge, MA: MIT Press.

Suchan, J. (1998) The effect of high impact rating on decision-making within a public sector bureaucracy. *Journal of Business Communication*, 35(3): 299 –327.

Sundstrom, E. (1986) *Work Place: The psychology of the physical environment in offices and factories*. Cambridge: Cambridge University Press.

Swisher, K. (2013) 'Physically together': Here's the internal Yahoo no-work-from-home memo for remote workers and maybe more. Available at: http://allthingsd.com/20130222/physically-together-heres-the-internal-yahoo-no-work-from-home-memo-which-extends-beyond-remote-workers/ (accessed 31 May 2014).

Taggart, C. (2011) *Pushing the Envelope: Making sense out of business jargon*. London: Michael O'Mara Books.

Tannenbaum, R.S. (1998) *Knowledge Machines: Language and information in a technological society*. London: Longman.

Thompson, P. and Warhurst, C. (eds) (1998) *Workplaces of the Future*. London: Macmillan.

Tibballs, G. (1999) *Business Blunders*. London: Robinson.

Timm, T. and Bienvenu, P.R. (2011) *Straight Talk*. London: Routledge.

Tourish, D. (1997) Transforming internal corporate communications: The power of symbolic gestures and barriers to change. *Corporate Communications: An International Journal* 2(3): 109–116.

Tropman, J.E. (2003) *Making Meetings Work: Achieving high quality group decisions*. (2nd edn). Thousand Oaks, CA: Sage.

Tropman, J.E. (2014) *Effective Meetings: Improving group decision making* (3rd edn). London: Sage.

Truss, L. (2003) *Eats, Shoots and Leaves: The zero tolerance approach to punctuation*. London: Profile Books.

Tuckman, B.W. (1965) Developmental sequences in small groups. *Psychological Bulletin*, 63: 384–389.

Tufte, E.R. (1983) *The Visual Display of Quantitative Information*, Cheshire, CT: Graphics Press.

Tufte, E.R. (2006) *Beautiful Evidence*. Cheshire, CT: Graphics Press.

Turk, C. and Kirkman, J. (1989) *Effective Rating: Improving scientific, technical and business communication* (2nd edn). London: E. & F.N. Spon.

Turk, C. and Kirkman, J. (1994) *Effective Writing: Improving scientific, technical and business communication* (2nd edn). London: E. & F.N. Spon.

Ulich, E. and Weber, W.G. (1996) Dimensions, criteria and evaluation of work group autonomy. In West, M.A. (ed.) *Handbook of Work Group Psychology*. Chichester: John Wiley, pp. 247–282.

Vermeulen, F. (2010) *Business Exposed: The naked truth about what really goes on in the world of business.* Harlow: Pearson.

Waller, D.S and Polonsky, M.J. (1998) Multiple senders and receivers: A business communication model. *Corporate Communications,* 3(3): 83–91.

Wansink, B. (2010) *Mindless Eating: Why we eat more than we think.* London: Bantam.

Ward, P. (1997) *360-degree Feedback.* London: Independent Publishers' Distribution.

West, M.A. (2012) *Effective Teamwork: Practical lessons from organisational research* (3rd edn). Oxford: BPS Blackwell.

Wheelan, S.A. (1996) *Group Processes: A developmental perspective.* Boston, MA: Allyn & Bacon.

Wilcocks, G. and Morris, S. (1996) *Putting Assertiveness to Work: A programme for management excellence.* London: Pitman.

Wilder, C. and Fine, D. (1996) *Point, Click and Wow: A quick guide to brilliant laptop presentations.* San Diego, CA: Pfeiffer.

Williams, R. (2010) *The Non-Designer's Presentation Book: Principles for effective presentation design.* Berkeley, CA: Peachpit Press.

Wilson, T.D. (2011) *Redirect: The surprising new science of psychological change.* London: Allen Lane.

Winston, B. (1998) *Media Technology and Society: A history: From the telegraph to the internet.* London: Routledge.

Wiseman, R. (2012) *Rip it Up: The radically new approach to changing your life.* London: Macmillan.

Woodford, M. (2012) *Exposure: From president to whistleblower at Olympus.* London: Penguin.

Wright, P. and Reid, F. (1974) Written information: Some alternatives to prose for expressing the outcome of complex contingencies. *Journal of Applied Psychology,* 57: 160–166.

Zuboff, S. (1988) *In the Age of the Smart Machine: The future of work and power.* New York: Basic Books.

# Index